THE COUNSELOR EDUCATOR'S SURVIVAL GUIDE

THE COUNSELOR EDUCATOR'S SURVIVAL GUIDE

Designing and Teaching Outstanding Courses in Community Mental Health Counseling and School Counseling

Dilani M. Perera-Diltz

Kathryn C. MacCluskie

EDITORS

Routledge
Taylor & Francis Group
New York London

Routledge
Taylor & Francis Group
711 Third Avenue
New York, NY 10017

Routledge
Taylor & Francis Group
27 Church Road
Hove, East Sussex BN3 2FA

Routledge is an imprint of Taylor & Francis Group, an Informa business

Printed in the United States of America on acid-free paper
Version Date: 2011928

International Standard Book Number: 978-1-4398-2556-3 (Hardback)

Library of Congress Cataloging-in-Publication Data

The counselor educator's survival guide : designing and teaching outstanding courses in community mental health counseling and school counseling / [edited by] Dilani M. Perera-Diltz, Kathryn C. MacCluskie.
p. ; cm.
Includes bibliographical references and index.
ISBN 978-0-415-87589-9 (hardcover : alk. paper)
1. Community mental health services. 2. Mental health counseling--Study and teaching. 3. Mental health counselors--Education. I. Perera-Diltz, Dilani M. II. MacCluskie, Kathryn C.
[DNLM: 1. Community Mental Health Services--organization & administration. 2. Counseling--education. 3. Curriculum. 4. Education, Graduate. 5. Health Educators--education. WM 18]

RA790.C6827 2011
362.2'2--dc23 2011015456

Visit the Taylor & Francis Web site at
http://www.taylorandfrancis.com

and the Routledge Web site at
http://www.routledgementalhealth.com

Contents

Preface

Faculty members in institutions of higher learning have job descriptions comprised of multiple types of scholarly activity. Some institutions categorize these responsibilities into three realms: research, teaching, and service. A traditional route to meeting such responsibilities is to integrate one's research interests and activities with the courses which one is assigned to teach. An alternative approach is to conceptualize teaching itself as a focus of scholarly inquiry, with the aim of maximizing the educational impact and maximizing the integration of learning models with counseling content.

We compiled this edited book in the hope of offering readers resources for course development or enhancement. Readers with a wide range of teaching experience, from doctoral students in a counselor education program, to seasoned faculty teaching a course for the first time, or someone looking to enrich a course he or she has taught numerous times, are very likely to find some useful material in these pages.

The first authors of each chapter are all senior faculty at their respective institutions. Many of them chose to coauthor, and in all cases the coauthors are individuals with a wonderful range and breadth of experiences related to either teaching or the content area or both. We specifically sought senior authors who are established and recognized as experts in their content areas, and so they speak with authority about the material related to that course content. We chose to include those courses that are often required in two counselor education tracks: clinical mental health counseling and school counseling.

There are two chapters of this book, chapters 1 and 16, that deviate from the format of the other chapters. Both chapters 1 and 16 deal exclusively with pedagogical issues that can be overlaid across any course. The first chapter provides a discussion of learning theory, a rationale for the importance of active learning techniques in counselor education, and an overview of the standards and objectives established by the Council for the Accreditation of Counseling and Related Educational Programs (CACREP). The final chapter provides a discussion about how to adapt a course for an on-line format, offering specific suggestions about how to structure and sequence learning in an on-line environment.

We will provide readers here with a brief overview of the chapter features among the chapters that correspond to specific courses. Each chapter begins with an overview of the course, offering a bit of background information about the nature of that particular content area and dilemmas that instructors commonly face in the context of that content. We asked each author to write about the main things they intend students to acquire or master in that course, and the dilemmas and decision points as they relate to that course content. Some chapters provide a discussion on how to choose topics for the course (e.g., chapter 13) and others provide a dialogue among the chapter authors (e.g., chapter 5) or other experts in the field (e.g., chapter 8). The purpose of each overview section is to provide readers with a context for that content and to allow the authors to express, in their own voices, the most pertinent information necessary for establishing the conceptual foundation of the content.

The Council for Accreditation of Counseling and Related Educational Programs (CACREP) outlines both general and program-specific guidelines relevant to the knowledge, skills, and practices associated with counselor education (CACREP, 2009). The CACREP standards appear in the Appendix of this text. Each chapter author has provided objectives for their course and the CACREP standards met by those objectives. Course objectives related to specific CACREP standards are referenced in a standardized fashion across the chapters. We consulted with CACREP on proper notation for those objectives and followed their recommendation, using one of two stipulated styles. Each chapter also delineates recommended criteria for evaluating a text in that content area and some suggested texts. In addition, each chapter provides many suggestions for supplemental course resources.

The chapters are organized in the following sequence:

- An introduction by the relevant chapter author(s)
- Objectives and CACREP standards
- Criteria for evaluating a text
- Most popular texts
- Supplemental reading
- Web sites
- Learning activities
- Counseling vignettes (if available)
- Audiovisual material (if available)
- Assignments
- A tentative course schedule
- Concluding comments, including one or two "pearls of wisdom." Authors were asked to identify what they love most about teaching that course and also the one or two most important pieces of wisdom they would offer someone teaching that course for the first time.
- References
- Grading rubrics (if available)

CONSTRUCTING A SYLLABUS

The following information may be especially helpful to new instructors developing their initial syllabus. In addition to what each chapter offers, that might be included in a syllabus, there are numerous other pieces of information that should be included in an effective course syllabus (Woolcock, 2006). An effective, thorough syllabus will have all of the following information:

- Course prefix, number, title, with each as they appear in the institution's course catalog
- The number of credit hours
- The academic term and year
- Location and time of class meetings
- Instructor name, title, contact information
- Office hours
- Catalog course description
- Course objectives and CACREP standards to which those objectives pertain
- Required text(s)
- Method of instruction
- Course requirements
- Grading scale
- Institutional policy on academic misconduct and accommodations for students with disabilities
- Communication and electronic device policy (if instructor has one)
- Reference list of additional sources for information

REFERENCES

Council for the Accreditation of Counseling and Related Educational Programs. (2009). *2009 CACREP Standards*. Retrieved from http://www.cacrep.org

Woolcock, M. J. (2006). *Contructing a syllabus: A handbook for faculty, teaching assistants, and teaching fellows* (3rd ed.). Providence, RI: Harriet W. Sheridan Center for Teaching and Learning, Brown University. Retrieved from http://www.brown.edu/Administration/Sheridan_Center/docs/syllabus.pdf

About the Editors

Dilani M. Perera-Diltz is a counselor educator at Cleveland State University, Ohio. She is licensed in Ohio as a professional clinical counselor (PCC-S), licensed independent chemical dependency counselor (LICDC), and school counselor (provisional). She has worked in a variety of settings as a chemical dependency and mental health counselor. Her research interests include addictions, trauma, and school counselor issues. Dilani enjoys spending time with her daughter, watching her cats do cat things, and gardening.

Kathryn C. MacCluskie is a professor of counselor education at Cleveland State University, where she has been teaching since 1994. She was among the first faculty at CSU with tenure granted on the basis of "Excellence in Teaching." Her professional interests are broad, ranging from counseling student development to mentoring junior faculty and studying the variables that contribute to global sustainability. Her avocational activities include spending time with her family, skiing, gardening, and biking.

About the Contributors

Kerry A. Bartlett, MEd, NCC, is a part-time instructor at the University of Nevada–Las Vegas in the Department of Counselor Education. She has taught several courses, including Introduction to Human Services, Drugs and Behavior, and Prevention Strategies and Developmental Theories in Addiction. Additionally, Ms. Bartlett was the Chi Sigma Iota International Fellow serving on the Chapter Analysis Subcommittee of the Community Engagement Committee. She has published several journal articles, conducted research, served as a peer reviewer, and presented at state, regional, and national conferences. She is very passionate about creating access to mental health services for students within the school setting. She is credentialed in both school counseling and mental health. She is a native of Massachusetts and an avid Red Sox fan.

M. Cecile Brennan is the coordinator of the school counseling program at John Carroll University. She brings to John Carroll a wealth of teaching and counseling experience. She has taught and counseled at the middle school, high school, and undergraduate and graduate levels of college. Also licensed as a professional clinical counselor, she has worked in a variety of agency and private practice settings. Her interest in the educational process has resulted in her own research being centered on the counselor education curriculum, with a particular focus on how ethics is taught. When not teaching or counseling, she enjoys long road trips chauffeured by her husband and accompanied by plenty of reading material.

Sherlon Pack-Brown is a licensed professional clinical counselor with supervisory status and professor of mental health and school counseling at Bowling Green State University. Sherlon is a past president of the Association for Multicultural Counseling and Development and a Fellow of the American Counseling Association. Dr. Pack-Brown teaches graduate courses in the theory and practice of counseling, group counseling, and counseling the culturally diverse. Her research interests are broadly defined under the diversity, multicultural, and social justice competence umbrella. Sherlon loves to travel and spend time with her family.

Paula J. Britton is currently a professor in the community counseling program at John Carroll University, where she coordinates the practicum/internship programs. She has taught practicum and internship for over 15 years and is also responsible for managing the sites and placement. She is a licensed psychologist and a professional clinical counselor with the supervision endorsement in the State of Ohio. She has over 20 years of diverse clinical experience including as an administrator and supervisor in a family service agency and a project director of a large research grant, and currently maintains a small private practice. She has given over 100 local, state, and national professional presentations and workshops in the areas of supervision and ethics and authored numerous publications. Additionally, she is a supervisor of master's level therapists in private practice and doctoral interns for the community counseling program. As a mother of two adolescents, she considers herself an excellent cab driver.

Stephanie A. Calmes is a doctoral student in the Department of Counselor Education and School Psychology at the University of Toledo. She is a licensed supervising professional clinical counselor (PCC-S) in the state of Ohio, a licensed chemical dependency counselor–III (LCDC-III), and a national certified counselor (NCC). Stephanie has taught undergraduate courses on counseling skills and techniques, marriage and family issues, and cultural influences in mental health and has also assisted in several master's-level practicum courses. Her research interests include chemical dependency counseling and supervision, dual diagnosis, multiple relationships, and stigma. Stephanie has experience working in community mental health settings, as well as in both outpatient and residential chemical dependency treatment programs. Stephanie is also the current (2010–2011) secretary for the Ohio Association for Counselor Education and Supervision (OACES).

Debra Cobia currently directs a doctoral program in counseling at the University of West Georgia. Prior teaching experiences include 19 years as the school counseling program coordinator at Auburn University. Scholarly interests include the assessment of student learning, program evaluation, professional and ethical issues, and school counseling. Outside academia, Dr. Cobia has been developing skill in the design and fabrication of jewelry. She added silversmithing to her teaching resume in 2010.

Sarah Coulter is a master's student in the mental health counseling program at Bowling Green State University (BGSU), Bowling Green, Ohio. Ms. Coulter facilitates prejudice reduction and diversity training workshops at BGSU. Her research interests include investigating motivation to engage in cross-cultural interactions; dealing with racism in counseling relationships; attachment styles and grief among lesbian, gay, and bisexual clients; and coping skills and help-seeking behavior of couples in mixed orientation marriages. Ms. Coulter loves to read, sing, and travel.

Paula R. Danzinger holds a PhD in urban education counseling from Cleveland State University. She is an associate professor of counselor education and director of the professional counseling program at William Paterson University, New Jersey. She has been teaching since 1998 and has a special affection for teaching research. Her research interests include older adults, ethical issues, and most recently the use of actors to teach psychopathology. Her favorite pastimes are theatre and pottery.

Jill D. Duba, PhD, LPCC, NCC, CTRTC, is a graduate of Kent State University. She is an associate professor and the coordinator of the mental health counseling program in the Department of Counseling and Student Affairs at Western Kentucky University. She has been a long-standing board member of the International Association of Marriage and Family Counselors. She presently serves as an editorial board member for *The Family Journal* and the *Journal of Counseling & Development*. She is engaged in research projects related to long-term marital satisfaction, religious training in counselor education, and reality therapy. Dr. Duba has a small private practice in Bowling Green, Kentucky.

Christopher M. Faiver is a summa cum laude graduate of Hiram College. He is a member of Phi Beta Kappa. He received his master's and doctorate from Case Western Reserve University. Licensed in counseling and psychology in Ohio, he is certified by NBCC and as a clinical consultant in hypnosis by the American Society of Clinical Hypnosis. He is listed in the National Register of Health Service Providers in Psychology. He has extensive clinical experience in a variety of settings and maintains research interests in the interface of counseling and spirituality. He has made numerous presentations and is the author of many journal articles and two books, one of which is in its third edition. With over 30 years of university teaching, Dr. Faiver is professor in the community counseling master's program at John Carroll University in Cleveland, Ohio. He was presented the University's Distinguished Faculty Award in 2006. He enjoys traveling, the theater, and spending time with family and friends.

LaShonda Fuller holds a PhD in Counselor Education from Western Michigan University (WMU) and is an assistant professor at Central Michigan University. She has cotaught counseling techniques, multicultural counseling, and practicum for 2 years while at WMU, and has worked as a school counselor in Muskegon Heights Public School. She has facilitated state and national workshops and presentations on diversity, school counselor preparation, and multiculturalism. Her research interests include group counseling with African American females; personal counseling for counselors in training; multiculturalism: race, oppression, and social justice; and supervision and preparation for school counselors. LaShonda enjoys water and winter sports, traveling, and fellowshipping with family and friends.

Samuel T. Gladding is the chair of and a professor in the Department of Counseling at Wake Forest University in Winston–Salem, North Carolina. He is a past president of and a fellow in the Association for Specialists in Group Work, past editor of the *Journal for Specialists in Group Work*, and the author of *Groups: A Counseling Specialty*, which is now in its fifth edition. Samuel's research interests are in group development, creativity, and family counseling. When not teaching, researching, or writing, Samuel enjoys swimming, tennis, reading humor and history, and interacting with his wife, Claire, and their three young adult sons.

Mary Amanda Graham is an assistant professor at Seattle University in the counseling and school psychology program. She has worked in community counseling settings as well as schools. She is a certified school counselor for the State of Washington and has worked in elementary, middle, and high schools. She has recently completed training through the Glasser Institute as a Glasser Scholar. Her research interests include creativity in counseling, counseling supervision, school counseling advocacy, and social justice advocacy. Mary is the mother of two wonderful children and an avid runner.

Holly L. Harper is a contributing faculty member for Walden University in the PhD counselor education and supervision program. She was an assistant professor at the University of Toledo and has 5 years of teaching experience and clinical experience working in medical, private, community, and school settings with various populations. Some of the courses she has taught include Advanced Theories, Counseling Theories, Consultation, Counseling Supervision, Ethics, Diagnosis and Treatment, and School Counseling. She is a licensed professional counselor (Ohio) and a national certified counselor. Dr. Harper's research interests include assessment, collaborative health care, cognitive complexity, and eating disorders. She has published articles in peer-reviewed journals. She presents at the national, regional, and state levels; has been president of the Ohio Association for Counselor Education and Supervision (OACES); and has been involved in various leadership roles in the counseling profession. In her spare time, Dr. Harper enjoys reading, running, and time with family and friends.

Nicholas (Nick) Heck, MA, is a doctoral candidate in clinical psychology at the University of Montana. He has taught a variety of undergraduate courses and has provided supervision for graduate students enrolled in Dr. Sommers-Flanagan's introductory interviewing course. Nick's research involves identifying and evaluating potential protective factors that offset risks for developing substance use disorders and other forms of psychopathology among sexual minority populations. In his spare time, Nick enjoys playing volleyball and tennis and eating waffles.

Nathaniel Ivers is an assistant professor in the Department of Counseling at the University of Texas at San Antonio. He has taught undergraduate- and graduate-level counseling courses at Wake Forest University and at the University of North Carolina at Greensboro. Nathaniel's research interests include group counseling with Latinas/Latinos, wellness, terror management theory, and multicultural counseling competence. In his free time, Nathaniel enjoys spending time with his family and playing sports.

John Laux received his PhD in counseling psychology from the University of Akron. John is a PCC-S, an LICDC, and a psychologist. His areas of clinical and research interest include dual diagnosis, personality disorders, and personality assessment. He has clinical experience in a variety of treatment settings including the Cincinnati VAMC, a community mental health center, a campus counseling center, and an inpatient chemical dependence treatment center.

Bill McHenry, PhD, is an associate professor at Texas A&M Texarkana. Over the course of his 8-year career, he has taught many different counseling courses, such as Lifespan/Human Development, Assessment, Theories, Prepracticum, Couples and Family, Group, Multicultural, Practicum, Field, Play Therapy, and Grief/Loss. His writing and research interests include counseling techniques, the role of professional school counselors in today's educational world, grief and loss counseling and the relationship across mental health issues, and incarcerated individuals and rehabilitation. Bill's leisure activities include spending time with his wife Melissa; children Meghan, Billy, Katie, and Shane; fishing; woodworking; and playing golf.

Jim McHenry, PhD, is Professor Emeritus at Edinboro University of Pennsylvania. Over the course of his 32-year career as a counselor educator, he taught nearly every course offered in a counseling master's degree program. Additionally, he helped the counseling program at Edinboro to receive both CORE and CACREP accreditations. His writing and research interests include effective therapeutic approaches and school counselor identity. Jim's retirement activities include spending time with his wife Paula; children Lisa, Linda, and Bill; and grandchildren Nick, Jake, Alexa, Ryan, Ian, Meghan, Billy, Katie, and Shane.

Nancy L. Murdock, PhD, is professor and chair of the Division of Counseling and Educational Psychology at the University of Missouri–Kansas City. She has served as the Vice President for Education and Training of the Society of Counseling Psychology and is a past chair of the Council of Counseling Psychology Training Programs. Her research interests include professional issues, counseling/supervision process, and

family systems theory. She is the author of *Theories of Counseling and Psychotherapy: A Case Approach, Second Edition* (Prentice Hall, 2009). Dr. Murdock teaches advanced theories of counseling, theories and techniques of family systems theory, and couples and family practicum. She is an artist, an avid tap dancer, and lives on a lake with her German Shepherd, Jezebel.

Donald R. Nims, EdD, LMFT, LPCC, RPT/S, is a graduate of Vanderbilt University. He is a professor and the coordinator of the marriage and family therapy program in the Department of Counseling and Student Affairs at Western Kentucky University. He has 30 years of clinical experience in a variety of settings. His expertise is working with the families of children and adolescents with severe emotional disability He has published in the area of family systems counseling and, more recently, solution-focused play therapy. He also has presented nationally and internationally in the area of play therapy.

Daniel P. O'Donnell is a counselor in practice with the Cleveland Clinic Health System. He completed his master's degree in community agency counseling at Cleveland State University where he is also pursuing a PhD in urban education: counseling psychology. His clinical experience includes intervention and psychological assessment of college students, clinical assessment and intervention in adult and older adult psychiatric populations, and chemical dependency assessment. In addition to ethics, his research and practice interests include the development of effective cross-cultural training of mental health professionals. He has presented and taught on ethics, group work, and counseling theories. As a lover of the outdoors, he's always looking for the next rock wall to climb or mountain bike trail to ride.

Dr. Dale-Elizabeth Pehrsson is professor for Counselor Education and associate dean for the College of Education at the University of Nevada Las Vegas. Dale has been a private practice, school, and mental health counselor. Prior to becoming a counselor she worked as a registered nurse. Dale's teaching and research interests include diversity, mentorship, and biblio- and play therapy. Dale is a nationally certified counselor, approved clinical supervisor, distance credentialed counselor, registered play therapist–supervisor, licensed clinical professional counselor–supervisor, and trained disaster mental health counselor. She has developed 29 new course preps in the last 12 years of teaching and really wishes a book like this was written much earlier! In her spare time she hikes, reads, gardens, swims, bikes, and makes art.

Carl F. Rak is a Professor Emeritus at Cleveland State University in the Department of Counseling, Administration, Supervision and Adult Learning. He served as director of Doctoral Studies in the College of Education for 7 years. During his tenure in the college, Dr. Rak was chair, methodologist, or member on 61 doctoral dissertation committees. His favorite courses were theories of personality and qualitative research. Dr. Rak was awarded the Charles "Chuck" Weaver Award for Long Distinguished Service to the Counseling Profession in 2004 by the Ohio Counseling Association. Among his many published articles, his favorite is "Heroes in the Nursery. . . ." This piece is in contrast to the great psychoanalyst Selma Fraiberg's paper "Ghosts in the Nursery." Dr. Rak was trained as an adult psychoanalyst at the Cleveland Psychoanalytic Center and graduated in 2005. He has four grown daughters and two granddaughters. He lives with his wife Georgine and they share travel, film, bird watching, and New York City together. He is a frustrated poet and yoga participant.

John Sommers-Flanagan is an associate professor of counselor education at the University of Montana. He has been teaching and writing about helping skills since 1986. His primary research interests include (a) strategies and techniques for enhancing positive therapeutic relationships; (b) the (in)effectiveness of antidepressant medications for treating depression in youth; and (c) brief consulting strategies with parents. John's favorite holiday is April Fool's Day, his favorite book is *The Brother's K*, one of his favorite films is *Billy Elliot*, and currently his least favorite political organization is the Tea Party.

Asti Sproul, MEd, has her professional school counseling license in the state of Nevada. She is a part-time instructor at the University of Nevada–Las Vegas and is currently teaching interpersonal skills in human relationships. Along with this, Ms. Sproul is the director of School Based Counseling Services for the nonprofit organization Communities in Schools. She has also presented at state and national conferences. These presentations have included creative therapies such as poetry and sandtray therapy, along with representing UNLV's Omega Alpha chapter of Chi Sigma Iota. Beyond counseling, she has a passion for the art of dance, spends her spare time with loved ones, and enjoys her two fun-loving Yorkshire terriers.

Sarah Toman is an associate professor at Cleveland State University. She obtained her master's and doctorate degrees from Kent State University and is also a graduate of the Gestalt Training Program, Gestalt Institute of Cleveland. She has formerly served as chairperson of the National Career Development's Research Committee and as secretary of the Association for the Advancement of Gestalt Therapy (AAGT). Sarah has several career development publications that highlight interest inventory assessment, including articles in the *Career Planning and Adult Development Journal*, which merge her two areas of interest: career development and Gestalt therapy. She contributed chapters about use of the Kuder Career Search in *Using Test Data in Clinical Practice* (SAGE, 2002) and is coeditor of the 2005 text, *Gestalt Therapy: History, Theory and Practice* (SAGE, 2005). Sarah maintains a psychotherapy practice with offices in Medina and Beachwood, Ohio. (http://www.gestaltcleveland.org/faculty.php)

Carrie A. VanMeter, MA, is a doctoral candidate and graduate assistant in the Department of Counselor Education and School Psychology at the University of Toledo. She is licensed as a professional counselor (PC) and as a professional school counselor in the state of Ohio. Carrie has taught undergraduate courses on pathology in mental health, case management, and essentials of helping relationships and has also assisted in several master's-level courses. Her research interests include domestic violence, ethics, and play therapy.

Chia-Chih D. C. Wang, PhD, is an associate professor in the Division of Counseling and Educational Psychology at the University of Missouri–Kansas City. He teaches theories of counseling, methods of counseling, and assessment methods of professional counseling. His research focuses on examination of cross-cultural validity of adult attachment constructs and psychosocial adjustment of immigrant and minority individuals. Dr. Wang is a bilingual person who enjoys jogging, watching movies, and traveling.

Elizabeth Reynolds Welfel is a professor at Cleveland State University where she has been teaching graduate students in counseling for 20 years. Prior to her appointment at Cleveland State, she was on the counseling faculty at Boston College. She earned her doctorate in counseling and student personnel psychology at the University of Minnesota. She has authored numerous articles on the ethics of professional practice and her book *Ethics in Counseling and Psychotherapy: Standards, Research and Emerging Issues* (Brooks Cole, 2009) is in its fourth edition. Her current research projects focus on ethical issues in the use of technology in professional practice and psychologists' understanding of their legal responsibilities with violent clients. Along with Dr. Elliott Ingersoll, she has coedited the *Mental Health Desk Reference* (Wiley, 2004). Her third book, *The Counseling Process* (Brooks Cole, 2006), coauthored with Lewis Patterson, is in its sixth edition. She has conducted numerous continuing education programs on professional ethics across the nation. She has also presented numerous continuing education programs to mental health professionals in the nation. She loves teaching even more than she loves traveling and vacationing in Hawaii.

1 Introduction
Foundations of Instructional Strategies for Counselor Educators

Kathryn C. MacCluskie

This chapter establishes the conceptual foundations and rationale for including particular chapter features in the remainder of this book. A logical beginning point is to explore relevant theories and their pertinence to counselor training. There are multiple lines of thought, and corresponding empirical studies, that offer compelling justification for inclusion of active learning strategies in any course. Furthermore, there are salient aspects of training counselors that are unique in comparison to graduate training in other disciplines, which raise to a critical level the importance of self-awareness and active learning.

An educational milieu, by definition, involves at least two individuals: an instructor and a learner. Each of those individuals has expectations about what constitutes fulfillment of his or her role. Each holds expectations for the other person's behavior, too. As in any relationship, explicit communication about expectations for oneself and for the other can serve to increase the likelihood that expectations will be met.

Two of the first questions an instructor must ask is, "In what way do I want the learners to be transformed as a result of my effort? How will students' engagement in my instructional environment impact them?" It is quite helpful, and important, to ponder these questions carefully in order to become explicitly clear on one's intentions for the class; to have a map of the beginning point, the journey, and the final destination. This map thus becomes the context that allows the instructor to identify and implement teaching strategies that will actualize those intentions. Even if the course we are teaching is one that has been given to us with a prescribed syllabus and format for course delivery, it nevertheless helps to have an image of how we hope our students will be changed upon conclusion of the course.

Making those expectations objects of our awareness is the first step. The first section of this chapter explores three components of pedagogy (i.e., self-awareness, Bloom's taxonomy, and the conscious competence learning model) including the principles of "active learning" and how each lends itself to a counselor education curriculum. Following that, readers will be presented with the overall structure of the Council for the Accreditation of Counseling and Related Educational Programs (CACREP), a brief history of how CACREP developed and has evolved, and the relationship of CACREP standards to pedagogy.

THREE ESSENTIAL CONCEPTS: SELF-AWARENESS, BLOOM'S TAXONOMY, AND THE CONSCIOUS COMPETENCE MODEL

The field of educational psychology has much to offer anyone who desires to become the most effective instructor possible. There is an extensive body of knowledge about the psychology of learning and optimal conditions under which people acquire and assimilate new material. Three constructs in particular lend themselves to our focus: self-awareness, Bloom's taxonomy, and conscious competence. Armed with the knowledge and theoretical grounding from these constructs, instructors can mindfully craft learning experiences for their students that can maximize the potential impact on their learners' growth over the duration of a course. One of the critical assumptions is that self-awareness, Bloom's taxonomy, and conscious competence can be applied and implemented through the use of active learning strategies. Thus, a preliminary definition of *active learning* is in order before examining the subsequent constructs and their operationalization.

A Definition of Active Learning

"Active learning" refers to educational strategies that require students to energetically collaborate as partners in their own learning. Some instructional models may define the student role as sitting attentively, passively receiving education. In contrast, the active learning stance recognizes tha the learner's attitude and participation constitute a full 50% of the educational process. Active learning involves students in the process throughout a class meeting, and although there may be less content covered in comparison to a class that consists only of lecture, there actually is a higher degree of content retention after the active learning class (Allen, 1995; Jacobson & Mark, 1995; Keyser, 2000; Ridgeway, 1989; Sheridan, 1990).

Self-Awareness and Hills' Personal Meaning

Counselor educators prepare learners to be human service professionals. Regardless of the particular specialty area, graduates of a counselor education program will have learned basic helping skills, case conceptualization, and many other aspects of service delivery. Most will have had coursework in lifespan development, career development, group counseling skills, and legal and ethical issues.

Throughout all of the coursework, there is a breadth and range of specific knowledge that students need to master if they are to earn their respective credentials (certification or licenses). However, obtaining and maintaining one's credentials as a school counselor or a clinical mental health counselor is not just a matter of mastering content in key areas. It also requires the ability to integrate and synthesize content to problem-solve novel situations, accurately assess issues and choose an appropriate course of action in a variety of ambiguous situations, and be capable of maintaining emotional stability in the face of multiple stressors and role demands, some of which may, at times, be excessive.

Development of emotional stability and the ability to maintain appropriate professional boundaries between oneself and one's students or clients requires self-awareness and insight. This author posits that the process of acquiring insight and self-awareness in the context of other counseling topics is a critically necessary component of counselor education. Readers may be familiar with "medical student syndrome" (Hunter, Lohrenz, & Schwartzman, 1964), in which medical students imagine themselves to have the symptoms of whatever disease they are studying at the moment. Counseling students may also have an inclination to become highly vigilant of whatever symptoms or problems are being studied and question whether they have themselves had that problem. Additionally, the necessity of clearly defined boundaries in codes of ethics (American Counseling Association [ACA], 2005; American School Counselor Association [ASCA], 2004) and state law makes obvious the need to teach students how to become aware of their own boundaries and how to maintain professional boundaries on the job.

One potential difficulty for counselor trainees is to accurately differentiate between a client's problems and issues, and the trainee's values, beliefs, and worldviews. A trainee's life experiences, cultural templates, and temperamental preferences can all exert influence over how he or she perceives a client's concerns. For this reason, it is extremely important for counselor education students to become fully aware, cognitively and emotionally, of what they bring to their training and future work. The ability to differentiate between personal history, personal preferences, and ethical and professional duties and responsibilities, falls in the realm of "professional boundaries".

Paradoxically, one way to teach students about professional boundaries is to push them to examine their own personal preferences, learning histories, and family and cultural learning histories and how those characteristics interplay with their ideas about appropriate professional behavior. One means of accomplishing this task is to provide class activities that intentionally maneuver learners' natural tendencies to apply personal meaning. Some authors (Hills, 1987; Hills & Knowles, 1987) have identified the construct of personal meaning as playing a central role in knowledge and skill acquisition among learners.

The meaning we attach to any stimulus arises from our schemas, values, and unique personal learning histories. Though our meanings change and evolve over time, the process of attaching meaning remains constant. Combs (1982) noted that:

> According to perceptual theory, the behavior of a person at any moment is the product of his or her perceptual field at that instant. What is meant by the "perceptual field" is all those perceptions or personal meanings existing for the person at the moment of acting. (p. 39)

Personal meaning refers to the tendency of a learner to take new material or concepts and integrate it with her or his existing memory network. In other words, any learner has a natural inclination to take memories that are internal representations of past events and apply them to the concept or construct that is being studied (Hills, 1987). Thus, with a career development theory, or a theory of life span development, students are very likely learning about that theory while simultaneously applying it to their own lives and their own awareness of themselves. There is a natural tendency to do this, perhaps especially among counseling students, who as a rule seem to be quite introspective and motivated to understand themselves. Hills further suggested conceptualizing three phases through which the stages of personal meaning are optimized.

Phase 1: Conducive Classroom Environment

The first phase is to create a classroom environment that is conducive to personal exploration. The instructor must communicate respect and empathy for the learners, encourage candor, and model nondefensiveness; these environmental characteristics provide fertile ground for creating a learning milieu in which students thrive.

Phase 2: Presentation of Content

The second phase is provision of learning or content with which we want the learners to interact. This is the phase where active learning happens through classroom activities that require students to use the new material and apply it to structured situations.

Phase 3: Guided Integration

The third phase is to explore how the new material or learning experiences relate to or interact with what students previously knew or thought. This is where exploration of personal meaning, or identification of the meaning that each individual attaches to the new content, is actually *critical*, to ensure consolidation and integration with the learner's existing cognitive structures. There are probably individual differences in the extent and style of learners' integration. However, if an instructor intentionally creates these opportunities for consolidation and integration, it becomes a controlled process rather than an uncontrolled process varying randomly across students.

Self-awareness and personal meaning complement one another; the process of associating personal meaning to new content is one that occurs naturally in learners, and self-awareness is simply helping the learners become cognizant of their internal process. Self-awareness in the context of counseling courses takes on another meaning as well, which is to become aware of one's own values, issues, and unfinished business, in order to differentiate between one's own issues and the issues of one's clients or students. Though the concept of exploring personal values and beliefs has been advocated in learning about diversity and multiculturalism (e.g., Sue, Arrendondo, & McDavis, 1992), this author (along with many others in the discipline) advocates such exploration of values and beliefs in virtually every learning experience throughout a counseling curriculum. Neglecting to do so increases the likelihood of a student inadvertently causing damage to a client at some future time.

Bloom's Taxonomy

Anyone who has taught a new skill to someone else, whether it was skiing, playing a musical instrument, or interpreting test data, has likely observed developmental stages through which learners progress as they move toward mastery of content. There have been numerous models developed in the field of educational psychology that offer descriptions and definitions of those stages. One model that defines those stages of learning in straightforward terms is Bloom's taxonomy, a system of classification that is sometimes applied to curriculum development. Bloom's taxonomy is a model for understanding increasing complexity of information acquisition, and is a useful tool for organizing both a course curriculum and also a rubric, or rationale, for evaluating student performance. It is being presented here because it offers a concise, concrete model for conceptualizing levels of content acquisition in learners.

Bloom's (1956) method of classifying educational objectives is hierarchical—each step of this progression requires mastery of the previous step, and is as follows:

1. Knowledge—the lowest level of processing, which is memory and recall of previously learned material. Rote memorization, terminology and word definition, and knowledge of theories and structures fall in the realm of knowledge.
2. Comprehension—requires the ability to manipulate data and facts for the purpose of organizing, comparing, translating, and the ability to summarize main ideas.
3. Application—using acquired knowledge to solve novel problems in a new way.
4. Analysis—using acquired knowledge to dismantle components in a new way, understanding elements, analyzing relationships, and analyzing the principles that organize the components in identifiable relationships/contexts.
5. Synthesis—pulling together several broad ideas/concepts into a completely novel approach for understanding and analyzing a phenomena. Also can be development of a new theory or model.
6. Evaluation—analyzing a model and identifying strengths and weaknesses of a model, or a response, based on an informed opinion about competing models of explanation.

If one examines the general education courses required in a typical undergraduate curriculum, many of those are likely survey courses, intended to give students a broad overview of the field in general (for example, Introductory Anthropology or Fundamentals of Algebra). Such basic courses are intended to move students through the first couple stages of Bloom's taxonomy: knowledge and comprehension.

In contrast, by the time students complete any master's degree, the associated skills have become much more sophisticated and specialized. Graduates need to be capable of performing at Bloom's upper levels, in several discipline-specific content areas. Though a class might begin with some basic knowledge (e.g., standard statistical terms and operations in an assessment course), by the end of the course, graduate students should be demonstrating capability that reflects mid-range to upper phases of Bloom's taxonomy (application, analysis, synthesis, evaluation). Additionally, the instructors' expectations of students' demonstrated sophistication and precision in their artifacts should be correspondingly higher than they would be at the undergraduate level. These stage definitions can offer instructors a rationale for creating classroom activities in a particular sequence, intended to move learners into these advanced phases of mastery in knowledge and ability.

This author has been teaching an introductory counseling skills course for many years. New counseling students with aspirations to be of service to others commonly seem to begin the basic helping skills course highly confident (perhaps overly) that they already know how to help people. Invariably, by the end of the course, students often marvel at their new awareness of what they did not know about effective helping at the beginning of the course. The very first assignment is specifically intended to catalyze their dawning awareness. Students are instructed to record a baseline tape—a conversation with someone in which the students try to be as helpful as possible. The baseline recordings are collected and stored by the instructor without being reviewed or evaluated, other than simply to verify that the students did complete the task. In the final weeks of the course, the students are then required to listen to their baseline recordings and critique which aspects of their helping behaviors have remained constant and which aspects have shifted significantly. Use of self-evaluative techniques such as the baseline recording exercise is an excellent introduction to the process of structured introspection.

Broadening the scope to look at professional counselor preparation in general, requisite behaviors and skills across numerous content areas have been outlined and described in great detail by many different organizations and constituencies (CACREP, ACA, state licensure laws).

Developing ability in those realms can be conceptualized as skill acquisition no different from any other skill, ranging from an athletic activity to a cognitive, problem-solving activity. Research has been conducted to describe the process of movement from lack of skill and lack of awareness through mastery of skill and ability to perform a skill without conscious awareness of the skill-related behaviors being exhibited. That process has been referred to as *automaticity* (Bargh, 1992; Brown, 1989; Patterson, Rak, Chermonte, & Roper, 1992; Phillips & Hughes, 1988; Rak, MacCluskie, Toman, Patterson, & Culotta, 2003).

As a course progresses and students are given additional knowledge and information, the active learning should evolve, commensurate with learner development. Classroom activities *application* and *synthesis* of that new knowledge. By the time students are completing their academic training, at the conclusion of their counseling internship, they should have moved into the realm of unconscious competence. Counselor educators who have taught several courses may have observed a similar developmental sequence watching students progress through their programs, beginning with an entry helping skills course and concluding with their final counseling sessions as they conclude their internships.

One other aspect of skill integration worthy of mention is a brief exploration of the dynamic interplay between learner stages, learner behavior, and the role of feedback and mentoring across learners' successive approximations toward skill mastery. Chapman (2006) posited the following progression of stages:

- Stage 1—Unconscious Incompetence

  This stage is very similar to Prochaska's (1999) readiness stage of precontemplation. The learner is not cognizant that there is any need for learning and therefore may be somewhat less motivated and/or receptive to instruction. At this stage, it is necessary to establish the learner's awareness of the need for change (learning). This stage of unconscious incompetence is the presumed stage when the baseline recording assignment is given in the introductory helping skills course, described in the section above.
- Stage 2—Conscious Incompetence

  In this stage of learning, the learner becomes much more aware of the need for specific skills and may also be aware of feeling acutely underprepared and incompetent with regard to that particular skill set.
- Stage 3—Conscious Competence

  At this stage, a learner can perform a skill without assistance but needs to consciously think about it in order to demonstrate the skill.
- Stage 4—Unconscious Competence

  By this point, the skill has become so integrated that it can be performed without the learner even being aware that he or she is performing it. This is *automaticity* and is the desired end stage for counselor education students.

In a further refinement and articulation of the learner's internal process throughout the manifestation of the conscious competence model, Taylor (2007) stated,

> We revisit conscious incompetence, making discoveries in the holes in our knowledge and skills, becoming discouraged, which fuels incentive to proceed (when it does not defeat). We perpetually learn, inviting ongoing tutelage, mentoring and self-study (ongoing conscious competence). We continually challenge our "unconscious competence" in the face of complacency, areas of ignorance, unconscious errors, and the changing world and knowledge base: We challenge our unconscious competence when we recognize that a return to unconscious incompetence would be inevitable. We do this in part by self-study and use of peer review—such that mature practice encompasses the entire "conscious competence" model, rather than supersedes it as the hierarchical model might suggest. (p. 7)

This author believes that use of this model as a cognitive frame is immensely useful when designing the active learning components of a counseling course. Intentional, mindful use of the conscious competence model may create a platform from which students can use their active learning experiences for further growth and skill refinement.

We shift focus now, away from theoretical models of learning and toward the content standards and the professional organization that established and maintains them.

CACREP: HISTORY AND STANDARDS

Program accountability is surely an ongoing consideration for any graduate program in an institution of higher education. University administrations require programmatic assessments in every discipline on a regular basis in order to ensure quality instruction as well as efficiency and effectiveness of the curricula. Beyond the university administration, there are additional constituencies to whom counselor education programs are accountable: the student body, state licensure boards, and the general public.

A historical context will be helpful in establishing how program accreditation has become a consideration. CACREP was established in order to serve three purposes:

1. To provide review guidelines that reflected the profession's expectations.
2. To promote professional quality.
3. To strengthen the profession's credibility (Accredited Counselor Education Programs, 1982; Bobby, 1992; Bobby & Kandor, 1992).

Two of the largest national professional bodies that maintain educational standards in counselor education are the National Board for Counselor Certification (NBCC) and CACREP. Faculty among programs who are already CACREP accredited are fully aware of the role CACREP standards play in course construction and delivery. Faculty whose programs are *not* CACREP accredited may not be aware of CACREP standards as they apply to course content.

Pros and Cons of CACREP Accreditation

Though this text is not intended to necessarily advocate that programs should acquire CACREP accreditation, there are numerous advantages to accreditation. In order to present a balanced view, the advantages and disadvantages of program accreditation will be briefly examined.

Advantages of CACREP Accreditation

- Public preference and prestige

  A number of studies have suggested that the general public favors accredited programs as being an indication of prestige (Fretz & Mills, 1980; Haight, 1992; Kassebaum, Cutler, & Eaglan, 1998; Peer, 1980).

- State licensure exam passage rates among students
  Analysis of a national sample of counseling program graduates has strongly suggested that graduates from accredited programs have a higher frequency of passing the National Counselor Exam, which is the exam required for licensure in many states (Adams, 2006).
- Reinforcement of the movement for professional identity
  Consistent with licensure laws governing scope of practice, maintaining a curriculum aligned with standards that have been established by a learned society reinforces and promotes the case for professional identity. Professional identity has been a topic that engenders much concern among professional counselors.

Disadvantages of CACREP Accreditation

- Necessity of institutional support
  There are aspects of program accreditation requirements that necessitate a strong overall institutional commitment to meeting CACREP standards. For example, there are program requirements regarding the ratio of faculty to full-time students, the number of full-time faculty assigned to teach counseling courses, and the credentials of the faculty teaching the clinical counseling courses. If the university administration does not support, or agree with, the importance and value of counselor education, it could be difficult at best to gain approval and funding for program faculty. Fiscal commitment is necessary to meet the various requirements, such as hiring properly credentialed full-time faculty, who may command higher salaries than non-credentialed adjunct instructors, or retaining enough tenure track faculty positions to maintain the faculty/advisee load ratio prescribed by CACREP.
- Cost
  Being able to meet these criteria requires not only that a program chairperson be observant of those requirements but that the upper level administrators in the educational institution grant approval and authorize funds to be spent meeting these requirements. Given the economic hardships among colleges and universities as a result of the national economy, gaining administrative support for a voluntary, optional accreditation could be challenging.

  There are initial and ongoing fees for the accreditation itself. Secondarily, hiring and maintaining a sufficient number of full-time faculty may be prohibitively expensive, especially for institutions that are experiencing a decline in enrollment.
- Loss of autonomy and creativity
  Beyond the pragmatic aspects of cost and needing permission of one's administrative superiors lies the more esoteric consideration of succumbing to being "in the box" as opposed to "out of the box" with regard to philosophy and curriculum construction. Programs that heavily emphasize a particular philosophical approach, or that encourage student autonomy and individuality in designing one's curriculum, might experience accreditation as stifling.

> The very process of uniformity of content and quality control, which is in many ways an important movement in service provision to the greater community, is also a process of curtailing individuality and potential creativity. Accredited programs have less latitude than nonaccredited programs in the composition of their curricula and in the content of each required course.

Thus, as with many things in life, program accreditation is a double-edged sword; it has multiple, compelling advantages but is not without cost. The following chapters each include a section that identifies the specific CACREP objectives that are covered by that course, to make the chapters maximally useful to faculty, regardless of their program's accreditation status.

The suggested syllabi and corresponding topics for each of the courses as presented in this text are designed to be in compliance with CACREP standards. The intention of developing the text in this manner is to accommodate the needs of faculty in CACREP-accredited programs. However, even among those programs that are not CACREP accredited, inclusion of the recommended topics may enhance the comprehensiveness of students' preparation for their state licensure exams.

CONCLUSION

This introduction has provided readers with an overview of the theoretical rationales that guided the editors' thinking about how to direct contributing authors in crafting their chapters. The models presented have empirical grounding, and the face validity with regard to applicability to counselor education is readily apparent. The review of CACREP history and standards was similarly intended to provide readers with an ideological context from which to consider course objectives and outcomes for each of the respective courses in their counselor education curriculum.

REFERENCES

Accredited Counseling Programs. (1982). *Personnel and Guidance Journal, 60*, 560–561.

Adams, S. A. (2000). Relationship between national accreditation standards and graduate knowledge as measured by the National Counselor Examination for Licensure and Certification (NCE). *Dissertation Abstracts International, 61*(04), 1305.

Allen, E. E. (1995). Active learning and teaching: Improving postsecondary library instruction. *Reference Librarian, 51–52*, 89–103.

American School Counselor Association. (2004). Ethical standards for school counselors. Retrieved from http://www.schoolcounselor.org/content.asp?contentid=173

American Counseling Association. (2005). *ACA Code of Ethics*. Washington, DC: Author.

Bargh, J. A. (1992). The ecology of automaticity: Toward establishing the conditions needed to produce automatic processing effects. *American Journal of Psychology, 105*, 181–199.

Bloom, B. S. (1956). *Taxonomy of educational objectives*. Boston: Allyn & Bacon.

Bobby, C. L. (1992). *CACREP Accreditation: Setting the standard for counselor preparation*. (ED 347 470). Greensboro, NC: ERIC/CASS.

Bobby, C. L., & Kandor, J. R. (1992). Assessment of selected CACREP standards by accredited and non-accredited programs. *Journal of Counseling and Development, 70*, 677–684.

Brown, T. L. (1989). Automaticity in skill acquisition: Mechanisms for reducing interference in concurrent performance. *Journal of Experimental Psychology: Human Perception and Performance, 15*, 686–700.

Chapman, A. (2006). Retrieved from http://www.businessballs.com/bloomstaxonomyoflearning domains.htm

Combs, A. (1982). *A personal approach to teaching: Beliefs that make a difference*. Boston: Allyn & Bacon.

Fretz, B. R., & Mills, D. H. (1980). *Licensing and certification of psychologists and counselors: A guide to current policies, procedures, and legislation*. San Francisco, CA: Jossey-Bass.

Haight, D. A. (1992). The pursuit of quality: A look into the future of CACREP. *Journal of Counseling and Development, 70*, 688–694.

Hills, M. D. (1987). The discovery of personal meaning: A goal for counselor training. *Counselor Education and Supervision, 27*, 37–43.

Hills, M. D., & Knowles, D. W. (1987). Providing for personal meaning in parent education programs. *Family Relations, 36*, 158–162. doi:10.2307/583946

Hunter, R. C., Lohrenz, J. G., & Schwartzman, A. E. (1964). Nosophobia and hypocondriasis in medical students. *Journal of Nervous and Mental Disorders, 139*, 147–152.

Jacobon, T. E., & Mark, B. L. (1995). Teaching in the information age: Active learning techniques to empower students. *Reference Librarian, 51–52*, 105–120.

Kassebaum, D. G., Cutler, E. R., & Eaglan, R. H. (1998). On the importance and validity of medical accreditation standards. *Journal of the Association of American Medical Colleges, 73*, 549–564.

Keyser, M. W. (2000). Active learning and cooperative learning: Understanding the difference and using both styles effectively. *Research Strategies, 17*, 35–44.

Patterson, L. E., Rak, C. F., Chermonte, J., & Roper, W. (1992). Automaticity as a factor in counseling skills acquisition. *Canadian Journal of Counselling, 26*, 189–200.

Peer, G. G. (1980). Professional identity: A classic case of avoidance. *Counselor Education and Supervision, 19*, 223–227.

Phillips, J. G., & Hughes, B. G. (1988). Internal consistency of the concept of automaticity. In A. M. Colley & J. R. Beech (Eds.), *Cognition and action in skilled behavior* (pp. 317–331). Oxford, England: North-Holland.

Prochaska, J. O. (1999). How do people change, and how can we change to help many more people? In M. A. Hubble, B. L. Duncan, & S. D. Miller (Eds.), *The heart and soul of change: What works in therapy* (pp. 227–255). Washington, DC: American Psychological Association.

Rak, C. R., MacCluskie, K. C., Toman, S. M., Patterson, L. E., & Culotta, S. (2003). The process of development among counselor interns: Qualitative and quantitative perspectives. *Canadian Journal of Counselling, 37*, 135–150.

Ridgeway, T. (1989). Integrating active learning techniques into the one-hour bibliographing instruction lecture. In G. E. Menshing, Jr., & T. B. Mensching (Eds.), *Coping with information illiteracy: Bibliographic instruction for the information age* (pp. 33–42). Ann Arbor, MI: Pierian Press.

Sheridan, J. (1990). The reflective librarian: Some observations on bibliographic instruction in the academic library. *Journal of the Academy of Librarianship, 16*, 22–26.

Sue, D. W., Arredondo, P., & McDavis, R. J. (1992). Multicultural counseling competencies and standards: A call to the profession. *Journal of Counseling & Development, 70*, 477–486.

Taylor, W. (2007). Department of Homeopathic Medicine, National College of Natural Medicine, Portland, OR. Retrieved from http://www.businessballs.com/consciouscompetencelearning model.htm

2 Foundations of Clinical Mental Health Counseling

The Nuts and Bolts of the Profession

Jill D. Duba and Donald Nims

This course provides the foundation or survey of salient topics that all novice counseling students should be privy to from the early stages of their academic careers. We address the most critical topics that we believe should be included in this course. Due to the nature of this course, however, there must be a balance between the quantity (course topics) and quality (depth of conversation, discussion, attention) of information being presented. Although one goal of the course is to increase one's knowledge base, opportunities for conceptualization and application must be provided. We hope that the learning activities we suggest will aid counselor educators in this process. In addition, in such a course, it is important to schedule time at the end of each class for an open discussion about the topic addressed during that class period while asking students what they need in order to proceed into another new topic area. That is, appropriate closure on each topic may prevent students from feeling overwhelmed with the quantity of information being presented.

Finally, some topics may be more significant than others. For example, consider the topic on supervision in counseling. Before professional counselors are eligible to supervise, they must have completed a certain degree of clinical experience. So it may be more appropriate to address what students can *expect* from supervision. Also, consider the topic of consultation. In some programs, this is a separate course, whereas in others consultation is expected to be covered as a learning objective in one particular course (such as the foundations or internship course). Counselor educators must decide how much time should be allotted for any of the subtopics of this course.

Our chapter provides an outline—or a survey—of ideas. Our hope is that counselor educators might take the ideas and tweak them in order to best match their personal styles, as well as the dynamics of the classroom and program. We have organized the resources provided from the Supplemental Reading section onwards under the following topic areas:

- Mental Health Counseling in America or in the 21st Century
- Introduction to Ethics and Legal Issues in the Counseling Profession
- Counseling in a Multicultural Society
- Ethical, Legal, and Professional Behavior and Practice (Competence and Malpractice, Confidentiality, Records, and Technology)
- Professional Counselor as Scholar Practitioner: Yesterday and Today
- Introduction to Counseling Theories
- The Counseling Process: Skills, Assessment, Diagnosis and Treatment
- Counseling Children, Vulnerable Adults (Older Persons, Persons With Disabilities)
- Couples and Family Counseling
- Group Counseling
- School Counseling
- Counselor Supervision
- Career Counseling
- Consultation

OBJECTIVES AND CACREP STANDARDS

The objectives of this course are fitting for an introduction course, as well as for expectations set forth by the Council for the Accreditation of Counseling and Related Educational Programs (CACREP, 2009) Standards. As in any introduction course, a common dilemma is how in depth any particular topic should be covered. Consider the topic of consultation. Some programs may have one course dedicated entirely to consultation. In other programs, this topic is covered in internship. However, some programs meet the relevant CACREP standard by addressing consultation in the introduction course. In the latter case, counselor educators must carefully assess whether or not students have been given appropriate opportunities to master the relevant course objectives. That is, how can any given introduction topic be taught in such a way that a student has developed a proper knowledge or skill base? In what ways will students be encouraged to examine how their dispositions and values will impact any given counseling setting? We hope that this chapter will provide counselor educators with some ideas about meeting the following suggested course objectives.

Knowledge

1. Demonstrate knowledge of the history and philosophy of the counseling profession, including significant factors and events specifically related to marriage and family counseling. (Section II.G.1.a.)
2. Demonstrate knowledge of the professional roles, functions, and relationships with other human service providers. (Section II.G.1.b.)
3. Demonstrate knowledge of professional organizations, primarily ACA, its divisions, branches, and affiliates, including membership benefits, activities, services to members, and current emphases. (Section II.G.1.f.)
4. Demonstrate knowledge of professional credentialing, including certification, licensure, and accreditation practices and standards, and the effects of public policy on these issues. (Section II.G.1.g.; Section II.G.1.j.)
5. Demonstrate knowledge of public and private policy processes, including the role of the professional counselor in advocating on behalf of the profession. (Section II.G.1.h.; Section II.G.1.i.)
6. Demonstrate knowledge of advocacy processes needed to address institutional and social barriers that impede access, equity, and success of clients. (Section II.G.1.g.; Section II.G.2.e.; Section II.G.2.f.)
7. Demonstrate knowledge of ethical standards of the American Counseling Association (ACA) and related entities and applications of ethical and legal considerations in professional counseling specifically related to marriage and family. (Section II.G.1.j.)
8. Demonstrate knowledge regarding general framework for understanding the stages and major models of consultation. (Section II.G.5.f.)
9. Demonstrate knowledge of counselor and consultant characteristics and behaviors that influence helping processes. (Section II.G.5.b.; Section II.G.5.f.)

Skills

1. Demonstrate the ability to recognize counseling issues in clients through effective listening and attending skills and through theoretical models. (Section II.G.5.b.)
2. Demonstrate the ability to recognize multiple factors related to social concerns affecting clients in diverse settings. (Section II.G.2.a.)
3. Demonstrate application of consultative models to cases. (Section II.G.5.f.)

Dispositions

1. Become aware of one's attitudes toward social concerns. (Section II.G.2.e.)
2. Undertake self-analysis. (Section II.G.1.d.)

Values

1. Respect the diverse cultural and social backgrounds of individuals and groups. (Section II.G.2.)
2. Articulate the worth of counseling as a profession to clients and students. (Section II.G.1.a.; Section II.G.1.c.)

CRITERIA FOR EVALUATING A TEXT

There are many ways by which to locate the most appropriate textbook and supplemental course materials. Certainly conducting Internet searches, consulting with publishing representatives, and conversing with colleagues is a way to start. Generally speaking, an appropriate textbook is one that meets the following:

1. Is based in a professional counseling context
2. Is written by practicing and/or knowledgeable professional counselors or counselor educators
3. Includes supplemental materials and resources for the instructor
4. Includes the ACA code of ethics
5. Addresses as many of the course objectives as possible
6. Is current

However, most of us want a book that fits our counseling identity and values. We want materials that we feel connected to, materials that convey what we believe are important about any given topic. So, for example, instead of getting acquainted with a potential textbook, it might be relevant to become acquainted with the authors or editor. Do these individuals have the same professional values? Are they professional counselors? Are they involved in the profession?

MOST POPULAR TEXTS

In any case, the following textbooks appear to be the most popular for an introduction course.

Corey, G., Corey, M. S., & Callanan, P. (2007). *Issues and ethics in the helping professions* (7th ed.). Belmont, CA: Brooks/Cole.

Gladding, S. T. (2008). *Counseling: A comprehensive profession* (6th ed.). Upper Saddle River, NJ: Merrill Prentice Hall.

Kottler, J., & Shepard, D. S. (2007). *Introduction to counseling: Voices from the field* (6th ed.). Belmont, CA: Brooks/Cole.

Nystul, M. S. (2010). *Introduction to counseling: An art and science perspective* (4th ed.). Upper Saddle River, NJ: Merrill Prentice Hall.

Remley, T. P., & Herlihy, B. (2010). *Ethical, legal, and professional issues in counseling* (3rd ed.). Upper Saddle River, NJ: Merrill Prentice Hall.

TOPIC: MENTAL HEALTH COUNSELING IN AMERICA OR IN THE 21ST CENTURY

Supplemental Reading

Beam, A. (2001). *Gracefully insane: Life and death in America's premier mental hospital*. New York: Public Affairs Books.

Buckley-Walker, K., Crowe, T., & Caputi, P. (2010). Exploring identity within the recovery process of people with serious mental illnesses. *Psychiatric Rehabilitation Journal, 33*, 219–227.

Chaiken, S. B. (2010). Creating wellness through collaborative mental health interventions. In C. L. Scott (Ed.), *Handbook of correctional mental health* (pp. 345–376). Arlington, VA: American Psychiatric Association.

Clarke, S. P., Oades, L. G., Crowe, T. P., Caputi, P., & Deane, F. P. (2009). The role of symptom distress and goal attainment in promoting aspects of psychological recovery for consumers with enduring mental illness. *Journal of Mental Health, 18*, 389–397.

Compton, M. T. (2010). *Clinical manual of prevention in mental health*. Arlington, VA: American Psychiatric Association.

Kartalova-O'Doherty, Y. (2010). Recovering from recurrent mental health problems: Giving up and fighting to get better. *International Journal of Mental Health Nursing, 19*, 3–15.

Kelly, T. A. (2009). *Healing the broken mind: Transforming America's failed mental health system*. New York: New York University.

Marshall, S. L., Oades, L. G., & Crowe, T. P. (2009). Mental health consumers' perceptions of receiving recovery-focused services. *Journal of Evaluation in Clinical Practice, 15*, 654–659.

Mears, S. L., Yaffe, J. & Harris, N. J. (2009). Evaluation of wraparound services for severely emotionally disturbed youths. *Research on Social Work Practice, 19*, 678–685.

Merikangas, K. R., He, J. P., Brody, D., Fisher, P., Bourdon, K., & Koretz, D. S. (2010). Prevalence and treatment of mental health disorders among US children in the 2001–2004 NHANES. *Pediatrics, 125*, 75–81.

Newnham, E. A., & Page, A. C. (2010). Bridging the gap between best evidence and best practice in mental health. *Clinical Psychology Review, 30*, 127–142.

Perlick, D. A., Hofstein, Y., & Michael, L. A. (2010). *Barriers to mental health service use in young adulthood.* New York: Oxford University.

Torrey, E. F. (2001). *Surviving schizophrenia* (4th ed.). New York: Harper Collins Books.

Torrey, E. F. (2008). *The insanity offense: How America's failure to treat the seriously mentally ill endangers its citizens.* New York: W.W. Norton.

Vuckovich, P. K. (2010). Compliance versus adherence in serious and persistent mental illness. *Nursing Ethics, 17*, 77–85.

Wells, R., & Punekar, R. S. (2009). Why do some health centers provide more enabling services than others? *Journal of Health Care for the Poor and Underserved, 20*, 507–523.

Websites

- National Institute of Mental Health
  http://www.nimh.org
  This website provides extensive information regarding the status of mental health research and treatment in the United States. Definitions and criteria for mental health diagnosis are also provided. There are also links to other sites with application to mental health treatment.

- National Alliance for the Mentally Ill
  http://www.nami.org
  This website provides information similar to the NIMH but with a perspective from the consumer. Links are provided to state chapters with information regarding meetings.

Learning Activity

During this particular course lecture, the instructor might consider visiting one or two local mental health treatment programs in the area.

Vignette

An individual comes to your clinic wanting to see someone because he or she is depressed. How do you determine the level of severity? How does the availability of payment impact the delivery of service? How does your opinion of potential compliance with treatment influence whether you decide to treat this individual?

TOPIC: INTRODUCTION TO ETHICS AND LEGAL ISSUES IN THE COUNSELING PROFESSION

Supplemental Reading

Jennings, L., Sovereign, A., Bottorff, N., Mussell, M. P., & Vye, C. (2005). Nine ethical values of master therapists. *Journal of Mental Health Counseling, 27*, 32–47.

Kaplan, D. M., Kocet, M. M., Cottone, R. R., Glosoff, H. L., Miranti, J. G., Moll, E. C., . . . Tarvydas, V. M. (2009). New mandates and imperatives in the revised ACA code of ethics. *The Journal of Counseling and Development, 87*, 241–255.

Ponton, R., & Duba, J. D. (2009). The ACA code of ethics: Articulating counseling's professional covenant. *Journal of Counseling and Development, 87*, 117–121.

Werth, J. L., Burke, C., & Bardash, R. J. (2002). Confidentiality in end-of-life and after death situations. *Ethics & Behavior, 12*, 205–222.

Websites

- ACA Code of Ethics
  http://www.counseling.org/Resources/CodeOfEthics/TP/Home/CT2.aspx
  Every student should know how to locate the ACA ethical codes, as well as have them handy for a quick reference throughout the course.

- *A Practitioner's Guide to Ethical Decision Making* by Holly Forester-Miller & Thomas Davis
  http://www.counseling.org/Counselors/PractitionersGuide.aspx
  This on-line article reviews the moral principles, as well as an ethical decision-making model.

Learning Activity

Typically there are activities in the textbooks. However, students may be encouraged to compare and contrast various informed consent and personal disclosure statements. Such example forms and statements can be easily accessed through an Internet search. Students also might write an informed consent document and/or personal disclosure document. Instructors are encouraged to locate any related state statutes and share them with students. A classroom discussion might follow or the state statutes can be compared to the ACA ethical codes.

TOPIC: COUNSELING IN A MULTICULTURAL SOCIETY

Supplemental Reading

Arredondo, P., Toporek, R., Brown, S. P., Sanchez, J., Locke, D., C., Sanchez, J., & Stadler, H. (1996). Operationalization of the multicultural counseling competencies. *Journal of Multicultural Counseling & Development, 24*, 42–78.

Hays, D. G. (2008). Assessing multicultural competence in counselor trainees: A review of instrumentation and future directions. *Journal of Counseling & Development, 86*, 95–101.

Jencius, M., & Duba, J. D. (2002). Creating a multicultural family practice. *The Family Journal, 10*, 410–414.

Johnson, A. G. (2005). *Privilege, power and difference* (2nd ed.). Columbus, OH: McGraw-Hill.

Neville, H. A., & Carter, R. T. (2005). Race and racism in counseling psychology research, training, and practice: A critical review, current trends, and future directions. *The Counseling Psychologist, 33*, 413–418.

Ponterotto, J. G. (1988). Racial consciousness development among White counselor trainees: A stage model. *Journal of Multicultural Counseling and Development, 16*, 146–156.

Tatum, B. D. (2003). *Why are all the Black kids sitting together in the cafeteria? A psychologist explains the development of racial identity*. New York: Basic Books.

Villalba, J. A. (2009). Addressing immigrant and refugee issues in multicultural counselor education. *Journal of Professional Counseling: Practice, Theory & Research, 37*, 1–12.

Websites

- The Online Teacher Resource
  http://www.teach-nology.com/litined/multicultural_education/
  There are various ERIC documents that include topics related to multicultural counselor education and supervision. There are other documents related to multicultural education with youth and children that may benefit some of the school counseling students.

- Do You Speak American?
  http://www.pbs.org/speak/education/
  This website contains various curricular units and addresses how language is patterned and how it can vary among various ethnic groups. For example, Spanish and Chicano, as well as African American, English are reviewed. Free resources, instructional tools, discussion questions, as well as student activities are provided.

- University of Maryland Diversity Database
  http://www.inform.umd.edu/EdRes/Topic/Diversity/Specific/Religion/Bibliographies/

This University of Maryland diversity database provides an exceptional bibliography of various religious texts and resources.

Learning Activities

The following activities are taken from Burke, M. (2010). *Cultural foundations in-class activities: Social categorization, social perception and stereotyping.* Unpublished manuscript.

- Categorinary. This activity allows students an opportunity to discuss identification (including statused identities), the social construction of differences, and categorization and how these concepts relate to stereotypes, stereotype threat, and identity development. The class is divided into teams and each selects a card with a word on it. Each team must draw a picture that *suggests* the word printed on the card. The pictures cannot contain any numbers or letters. Once drawings are complete, the other teams try to guess the word the drawing is intended to represent. Examples of the words on the cards include any of the following: *superintendent of a school district*; *teacher*; *CEO*; *secretary*; *a Native American/American Indian*; *a chef*; and/or *scientist.*

  In a follow-up discussion, each team discusses how they came to a decision regarding what to include in each picture. This activity illustrates how humans are reflexive in that we can categorize, classify, or name concepts/people in particular ways in relation to other social categories or classifications. Furthermore, there is a discussion about how people categorize themselves, others, and groups using concepts and language to make sense of their social environment and how this can invoke meanings in the form of expectations with regard to others' and one's own behavior.

- Who are your friends? Among the people that we trust and to whom we are closest, we each gather opinions about others and ourselves and filter these ideas through a perceptual framework. In this activity, students list the names of 10 people with whom they have engaged socially over the past year. The worksheet contains codes that represent categories such as (a) friends (P), family (F), other (O), such as colleagues; (b) different race/ethnicity (E), socioeconomic group/social class ($), political party identification/affiliation (PP) and religion from me (R); (c) more than a 5 years older than I am (A); and (d) lives more than 10 miles away from my home (L).

  Next to each name, the student must list each category that is applicable to each person listed. Once this is complete, the student inventories the total number for each category. Afterward, the student derives a code, which is the three highest categories. Upon completion, each student conveys his or her code by placing a mark/dot on the board (in which a column represents each category). Subsequently, the class discusses the results (which typically indicate that we associate ourselves/have group membership with people who are very similar to us) and how we tend to interact with others who provide information about which to make judgments and reinforce perceptions (including social identity theory).

TOPIC: ETHICAL, LEGAL AND PROFESSIONAL BEHAVIOR AND PRACTICE (COMPETENCE AND MALPRACTICE, CONFIDENTIALITY, RECORDS, AND TECHNOLOGY)

Supplemental Reading

Daniels, J. A. (2001). Managed care, ethics, and counseling. *Journal of Counseling & Development, 79*, 119–122.

Granello, P. F., & Witmer, J. M. (1998). Standards of care: Potential implications for the counseling profession. *Journal of Counseling & Development, 76*, 371–380.

Kaplan, D. M., Kocet, M. M., Cottone, R. R., Glosoff, H. L., Miranti, J. G., Moll, E. C., … Tarvydas, V. M. (2009). New mandates and imperatives in the revised ACA code of ethics. *Journal of Counseling & Development, 87*, 241–256.

Peluso, P. R. (2003). The ethical genogram: A tool for helping therapists understand their ethical decision-making styles. *The Family Journal, 11*, 286–291.

Remley, T. P., Herlihy, B., & Herlihy, S. B. (1997). The U.S. supreme court decision in Jaffee v. Redmond: Implications for counselors. *Journal of Counseling & Development, 75*, 213–218.

Schlossberger, E., & Hecker, L. (1996). HIV and family therapists' duty to warn: A legal and ethical analysis. *Journal of Marital and Family Therapy, 22*, 27–40.

Shaw, H. E., & Shaw, S. F. (2006). Critical ethical issues in online counseling: Assessing current practices with an ethical intent checklist. *Journal of Counseling & Development, 84*, 41–53.

Welfel, E. R., Danzinger, P. R., & Santoro, S. (2000). Mandated reporting of elder abuse/maltreatment of older adults: A primer for counselors. *Journal of Counseling and Development, 78*, 284–292.

Websites

- The Layperson's Guide to Counselor Ethics
  http://www.counseling.org/Resources/CodeOfEthics/TP/Home/CT2.aspx.

  Although this brief PDF file is written for clients, it captures the responsibilities and rights of both clients and counselors. The document provides a backdrop for what information all counselors should be communicating to their clients during the first counseling session.

- Private Practice Pointers for ACA Members
http://www.counseling.org/Counselors/TP/PrivatePracticePointersMembers/CT2.aspx
Robert Walsh and Norman Dasenbrook provide information about a list of private practice topics including but not limited to informed consent, the Health Insurance Portability and Accountability Act (HIPAA) requirements, managed care and insurance companies, and starting a private practice. ACA membership is required to access this site.

- Professional Ethics in Counseling
http://www.joburbank.com/Professional_Ethics_in_Counseling_Notes.htm
This website is a compilation of notes in outline form related to the following topic areas: central concepts, ethical governance and enforcement, moral principles, legal concerns in various phases of counseling practice, recommended business practices, and ethical climate. The outline captures the most salient legal, ethical, and professional issues in counseling. For visual learners especially, the outline provides order and organization.

- "Transporting Confidential Clinical Records in Laptops: Heads up to Psychotherapists & Counselors" by Ofer Zur & Jeffrey Barnett
http://www.zurinstitute.com/laptoptheftandconfidentiality.html
This article is part of an online course on confidentiality for continuing education. It is a brief selection that outlines, in bullet form, general practice guidelines related to handling electronic documents, as well as the related ethical codes. The information is clear, concise, and specific.

- "Duty to Warn and Protect Against Self-Destructive Behaviors and Interpersonal Violence" by Danica G. Hays, Laurie M. Craigen, Jasmine Knight, Amanda Healey, & April Sikes
http://www.jsc.montana.edu/articles/v7n11.pdf
This article is most fitting for school counseling students. The first section of the article is a review of self-destructive behaviors, as well as interpersonal concerns typically found among children and adolescents. The second section of the article moves the reader to consider when reporting is necessary. Self-reflective questions are provided, along with tables organizing the continuum of danger related to self-destructive behaviors and interpersonal violence.

- *Tarasoff v. The Regents of the University of California Supreme Court of California*, 1976
http://www.adoctorm.com/docs/tarasoff.htm
Though students may read summaries about the *Tarasoff* case in their textbooks, this brief article gets right to the point in describing the facts of the case, as well as the court reasoning and decision.

- Online Therapy Institute: Bringing Together Technology and Mental Health
  http://www.onlinetherapyinstitute.com
  DeeAnna Madfes and Kate Elize Larnia have constructed one of the best sources for online counseling and supervision ethics and practice. This is a must-see for all counseling students.

- SecondLife®
  http://www.counselortech.net, http://SL.CounselorEducation.org
  Dr. Marty Jencius, former chair of the American Counseling Association Cybertechnology Committee, provides information, as well as communication for counselor educators who are using or interested in using SecondLife® for pedagogical use in classes and training.

Learning Activities

Discuss the relationship among ethical codes (American School Counselors Association [ASCA], ACA), moral principles, and personal ethics.

- Upon presenting the relevant materials, review the following: (a) your state's statute related to the duty of a mental health professional to warn intended victims of potential threat or violence; (b) the *Tarasoff* case; The Regents of the University of California Supreme Court of California, 1976; and (d) the Kaplan et al. article noted in Supplemental Reading.
- Based upon the ACA ethical codes, the following discussion questions may be posed: (a) How do you understand privileged communication? Provide an example. (b) What will you do to assure the protection of clients and others? What will you include in your informed consent document to be sure that clients understand this from the beginning of the counseling relationship?

Vignettes

- *Ethics in bartering.* Sam and Candy sought marital counseling about one year ago after their 13-year-old son, Jimmy, was killed in a tractor accident on their family farm. He was Sam and Candy's only child. Sam and Candy were apprehensive about seeking marital counseling for several reasons. They live in a small, rural community and did not want the "secret to be known." Also, they have struggled financially and were afraid that they could not afford the sessions or the gas to drive to and from town to the therapist's office. The couple's health insurance plan did not cover mental health benefits. However, Sam's younger sister encouraged him and Candy to seek help. Sam and Candy were both overwhelmed with grief and decided that it could not hurt to try. After a helpful first session with their therapist, Marilyn, both Sam and Candy decided that they wanted to continue therapy until they thought that they could carry on with their grief on their own. Around the 4-month mark, Marilyn, Sam, and Candy discussed how therapy was progressing thus far. The couple agreed that they were making progress; however, Candy's grief was still affecting her mood daily, which consequently was impacting how the two partners interacted. Sam told Marilyn that he understood how hard this was on Candy, but he "needed to get back on track with his life and his marriage." He "missed Candy desperately." Marilyn continued to help Candy and Sam process their grief, while also attending to the marital relationship. About 2 months later, Sam and Candy mentioned that they were really struggling financially. Candy lost her part-time job at the local grocery store due to its closing. They told Marilyn that therapy had been "unbelievably helpful." They were not ready to terminate and were hoping that Marilyn "could make arrangements." Sam, a well-respected "handyman" in his small community, could fix any household item or automobile. He told Marilyn that he would be willing to contract work if she would like. The couple also offered to pay Marilyn with any vegetables that were in season.

- *Ethics in boundaries.* Kevin began seeing Rich and Patricia about 2 months ago. Rich and Patricia came to Kevin because, as Patricia put it, "they were on the verge of divorce." Over the 2 months Kevin has been aware of his growing attraction to Patricia. He also believes that she has similar feelings toward him due to her constant eye contact, physical closeness when walking to and from the chairs in the office, and the tone of voice that she uses with Kevin. When scheduling appointments with Kevin over the phone, Patricia has mentioned several times that she "wishes Rich was like you." Because of Kevin's desire to become involved intimately with Patricia, he finds himself losing concentration during therapy sessions.
- *Ethics in documentation.* Mrs. Jones brought her eight-year-old son Matt to counseling because she was worried about how quiet he had become since her divorce to Mr. Jones. Mr. Jones recently got married again. He was living with his new wife and her 3 teenage sons. Matt felt very intimidated every time he visited his father. Matt was the identified client on record. Mrs. Jones would usually come to counseling with Matt. On some occasions she allowed Mr. Jones to take Matt to his regularly scheduled counseling appointments when she was called into work. Often the counselor met with Mrs. or Mr. Jones and Matt briefly before spending the rest of the session individually with Matt. On rare occasions, the counselor would meet with Mrs. or Mr. Jones alone to briefly discuss Matt's progress privately. About 3 months into the counseling relationship, Mrs. Jones began talking about how her own psychological condition was affecting Matt's behavior. She spoke about how she felt very hurt and betrayed by Mr. Jones. She also expressed her concerns about his ability to console Matt. She asked for this information to be kept confidential from Mr. Jones. The counselor had made brief notes about these conversations in Matt's progress notes; and was considering opening up a new and separate file on Mrs. Jones. However, before the counselor did so, Mr. Jones came to the next appointment with Matt and asked to see his records.

TOPIC: PROFESSIONAL COUNSELOR AS SCHOLAR PRACTITIONER: YESTERDAY AND TODAY

Supplemental Reading

Aubrey, R. F. (1977). Historical development of guidance and counseling and implications for the future. *Personnel & Guidance Journal, 55*, 288–294.

Jencius, M., & Finnerty, P. (2009). Counselors and social networking. *Counseling Today, 52*, 26–27.

Magnuson, S., Wilcoxon, S.A., & Norem, K. (2003). Career paths of professional leaders in counseling: Plans, opportunities, and happenstance. *Journal of Humanistic Counseling, Education, & Development, 42*, 42–52.

Myers, J. (1992). Wellness, prevention, development: The cornerstone of the professional. *Journal of Counseling & Development, 71*, 136–139.

Myers, J. E., Sweeney, T. J., & White, V. E. (2002). Advocacy for counseling and counselor: A professional imperative. *Journal of Counseling & Development, 80*, 394–402.

West, J. D., Osborn, C. J., & Bubenzer, D. L. (2003). *Leaders and legacies: Contributions to the counseling profession*. New York: Brunner-Routledge.

West, J. D., Osborn, C.J., Bubenzer, D. L., Paez, S. B., & Desmond, K. J. (2006). Leadership and the profession of counseling: Beliefs and practices. *Counselor Education and Supervision, 46*, 2–16.

Websites

- Role in ACA
  http://www.counseling.org/Students/RoleInACA/TP/Home/CT2.aspx
  This website provides a list and accompanying information about the various ways in which students can become involved in the counseling profession, particularly in the American Counseling Association.

- ACA-Related Organizations
  http://www.counseling.org/Students/RelatedOrgs/TP/Home/CT2.aspx.
  This website provides a list of ACA's related organizations, including direct links to each.

- Current Issues
  http://www.counseling.org/PublicPolicy/PositionPapers.aspx.
  The most current and high-priority federal policy issues related to the counseling profession are described here, along with links for advocating for any given issue. Students can practice advocating at the legislative level by visiting and engaging in this site.

- Journals
  http://www.counseling.org/Publications/Journals.aspx.
  All of the American Counseling Association–related journals are listed on this website. Counselor educators who require students to pull from counseling-related literature might refer students to this site.

- Conducting a Literature Review
  http://fcpe.adelphi.edu/library/

- Conducting a Literature Review in Education and the Behavioral Sciences
  http://www.kumc.edu/SAH/OTEd/jradel/effective.html

- Effective Presentations
  http://www.research.ucla.edu/era/present/
  These websites provide information, as well as helpful tips about how to construct literature reviews, write formal papers, as well as conduct presentations. Students who struggle with writing and presenting will benefit from these resources.

Learning Activities

The first author constructed the following assessments and rubrics located as appendixes at the end of the chapter "Professional Counselor as Scholar Practitioner Self-Assessment and Conducting Formal Presentations: Criteria and Guidelines" (see Appendices A and B for complete assessments). Students may compare self-assessments conducted at the beginning and end of the course.

TOPIC: INTRODUCTION TO COUNSELING THEORIES

Supplemental Reading

Dryden, W. (1994). Reason and emotion in psychotherapy: Thirty years on. *Journal of Rational-Emotive and Cognitive–Behavior Therapy, 12*, 83–99.

Ellis, A. (1997). Extending the goals of behavior therapy and of cognitive behavior therapy. *Behavior Therapy, 28*, 333–339.

Ford, J. G. (1991). Rogers's theory of personality: Review and perspectives. *Journal of Social Behavior and Personality, 6*, 19–44.

Joyce, D. P. (1995). The roles of the intervenor: A client-centered approach. *Mediation Quarterly, 12*, 301–312.

Kelly, E. W., Jr. (1997). Relationship-centered counseling: A humanistic model of integration. *Journal of Counseling & Development, 75*, 337–344.

Laungani, P. (1997). Replacing client-centered counseling with culture-centered counseling. *Counseling Psychology Quarterly, 10*, 343–351.

Stolorow, R. D. (1992). Closing the gap between theory and practice with better psychoanalytic theory. *Psychotherapy, 29*, 159–166.

Tobin, S. A. (1991). A comparison of psychoanalytic self psychology and Carl Rogers's personality centered therapy. *Journal of Humanistic Psychology, 31*, 9–33.

Websites

- North American Society of Adlerian Psychology
  http://www.alfredadler.org/
- National Association of Cognitive–Behavioral Therapists
  http://www.nacbt.org/
- Beck Institute for Cognitive Therapy and Research
  http://www.beckinstitute.org
- Association for the Advancement of Gestalt Therapy
  http://www.aagt.org/
- American Psychoanalytic Association
  http://www.apsa.org/
- The William Glasser Institute
  http://www.wglasser.com/
- Solution-Focused Brief Therapy Association
  http://www.sfbta.org/

Learning Activity

Students are divided into groups of three and assigned a particular theory. The groups will role-play a client (see vignette below) and counselor using a particular theoretical orientation. The third person in the group acts as a moderator during the exercise to introduce the approach and comment during the exercise regarding what theoretical principles and techniques are being used.

Vignette

Larry is a 50-year-old Caucasian male. He used to work at a factory as a floor manager monitoring 400 other employees. He is currently doing some side jobs while looking for a full-time job. Larry is recently divorced after being married for 14 years. Larry describes himself as being shy. He also reported to you that while growing up, he was called "fatso" by his parents and four siblings. Larry says that he continues to hear this message even to this day. Since his divorce, the client has found out that his wife was cheating on him. He reported to you that he always knew that she lied to him about finances and her whereabouts; however, he never thought it went to this extent. He described his ex-wife as manipulative and emotionally abusive to him. Despite his continuous efforts to forgive her for her lies, she persisted in doing so. In addition, Larry told you that his wife would always say to him, "You are good for nothing and will never amount to anything." Larry continues to hear this message. Larry also uses Bible verses and scripture to defend why he should be remorseful of this failed relationship. Larry sought counseling because he feels depressed and anxious all of the time. For example, he feels sad, alone, and "good for nothing." He reported to you that when he even thinks about taking a position that requires some degree of independence, he begins breathing heavily and shaking. He told you that he does not feel he will ever "amount to anything." Despite his depressed feelings and anxiety, Larry wants to move on with his life. He told you that he wants to find a full-time position in the machine industry, while also increasing his social life. Based on any given theoretical orientation, consider the following: (a) your initial thoughts about the client; (b) the client's concerns; and (c) possible treatment goals.

TOPIC: THE COUNSELING PROCESS: SKILLS, ASSESSMENT, DIAGNOSIS, AND TREATMENT

Supplemental Reading

Brown, L. S. (2007). Empathy, genuineness and the dynamics of power: A feminist responds to Rogers. *Psychotherapy: Theory, Research, Practice, Training*, 44, 257–259. Retrieved from http://www.choixdecarriere.com/pdf/5671/59-2010.pdf.

Dennin, M. K., & Ellis, M. V. (2003). Effects of a method of self-supervision for counselor trainees. *Journal of Counseling Psychology, 50*, 69–83.

Myers, J. E., Sweeney, T. J., & Witmer, J. M. (2000). The wheel of wellness counseling for wellness: A holistic model for treatment planning. *Journal of Counseling & Development, 78*, 251–263.

Myers, J. E., & Sweeney, T. J. (2008). Wellness counseling: The evidence base for practice. *Journal of Counseling & Development, 86*, 482–493.

Skovholt, T. M. (2005). The cycle of caring: A model of expertise in the helping professions. *Journal of Mental Health Counseling, 27*, 82–93.

Sullivan, M. F., Skovholt, T. M., & Jennings, L. (2005). Masters therapists' construction of the therapy relationship. *Journal of Mental Health Counseling, 27*, 48–70.

Websites

- Internet Mental Health
  http://www.mentalhealth.com
  This website provides extensive information about mental health disorders and diagnosis.

- PsyWeb.com
  http://www.psyweb.com/Diagnosis
  This website provides advanced diagnostic criteria with a descriptive flowchart used in making a mental health diagnosis.

- WebMd: Better information. Better health
  http://www.webmd.com
  This website provides additional information on mental health diagnosis. Information is provided regarding the use of psychiatric medications.

Learning Activities

Discuss the differences and similarities between and among the following: schizoid personality disorder and schizotypal personality disorder; Asperger's and autism; compulsions and obsessions; delirium and dementia; and/or hypochondria, somatoform disorder, and factitious disorder.

Visit the following website http://www.drugpolicy.org/reducingharm/saferinjecti/ ("Safe Injection Rooms"). Although this practice is not permitted in the United States, it offers a backdrop for a discussion about the role that mental health workers can play in the midst of client drug use.

Vignettes

- *George and Kay.* A couple just came into your counseling practice. George has narcissistic personality disorder and is married to Kay, who has developed a generalized anxiety disorder. They dated for 6 months and have been married for 2 years. George lost his job unexpectedly about 2 weeks ago. Based on your knowledge of these diagnoses, suggest (a) reasons why the couple may have sought counseling and (b) what your interventions will be.
- *Hilary's treatment plan.* Hilary presents with symptoms that meet the criteria for a diagnosis of panic disorder with agoraphobia. She reported that her first panic attack occurred after her boyfriend broke up with her. After that, she began to attend to bodily sensations and worried constantly about having another panic attack. Develop one treatment goal with two objectives based on cognitive–behavioral and reality therapy.

TOPIC: CHILDREN AND VULNERABLE ADULTS (OLDER PERSONS, PERSONS WITH DISABILITIES)

Topics related to counseling specialty areas can be weaved throughout the curriculum and schedule of the course. However, counselor educators might find the following source a helpful resource when formulating an introduction to this broad topic:

LoPresit, R. L., & Zuckerman, E. L. (2004). *Rewarding specialties for mental health clinicians: Developing your practice niche*. New York: Guilford Press.

Supplemental Reading

Duba, J. D., & Magenta, M. (2008, October). End-of-life decision-making: A preliminary outline for preparing counselors to work with terminally-ill individuals. *The Family Journal, 16*, 384–390.

Kenel, M. E. (2005). Personal strengths and the aging process. *Human Development, 26*, 5–11.

Oaklander, V. (2001). Gestalt play therapy. *International Journal of Play Therapy, 10*, 45–55.

Schwiebert, V. L., Myers, J. E., & Dice, C. (2000). Ethical guidelines for counselors working with older adults. *Journal of Counseling & Development, 78*, 123–129.

Watts, R. E., & Broaddus, J. L. (2002). Improving parent–child relationships through filial therapy: An interview with Garry Landreth. *Journal of Counseling and Development, 80*, 372–379.

Welfel, E. R., Danzinger, P. R., & Santoro, S. (2000). Mandated reporting of elder abuse/maltreatment of older adults: A primer for counselors. *Journal of Counseling and Development, 78*(2), 284–292.

Werth, J. L., & Crow, L. (2009). End-of-life care: An overview for professional counselors. *Journal of Counseling and Development, 87*, 194–202.

White, J., Flynt, M., & Jones, N. P. (1999). Kinder therapy: An Adlerian approach for training teachers to be therapeutic agents through play. *Journal of Individual Psychology, 55*, 365–382.

Websites

- American School Counselor Association
  http://www.schoolcounselor.org/
  This website is the main site for the American School Counselor Association and provides extensive information on working with children and adolescents in a school setting.

- The Association for Adult Development and Aging
  http://www.aadaweb.org/

- U.S. Department of Justice Americans With Disabilities Act
  http://www.ada.gov/
  This website discusses the impact of federal law upon providing appropriate services to children and adolescents with disabilities or any condition that affects the learning environment. This directly applies to certain mental health disorders that apply to children and adolescents in the public school arena.

Learning Activities

Discuss and provide an example of an ethical dilemma when working with clients or students (or parents) who are disabled.

Vignette

- *Ethics in end-of-life care.* Taken from: Duba, J. D., & Magenta, M. (2008). End-of-life decision-making: A preliminary outline for preparing counselors to work with terminally-ill individuals. *The Family Journal, 16*(4), 384–390. Jamie came to you because he could "not take the pain any longer." Jamie explained that he was trying to deal with the loss of his mother to cancer a month ago. He reported having nightmares about his mother. In his dreams, he saw her hunched over, without hair, and looking "monstrous." He was frightened of the dreams and they made him feel guilty. In addition to the grief that Jamie was experiencing, he was struggling with his sexual identity. He mentioned that his mother was the only one who understood what he went through as a homosexual male in a rather intolerant community. He thought that she had provided him with enough support and insight so that he could live out his life successfully without her. Without her, he felt as if he could no longer be who he wanted to be. Over the course of about 7 months, with weekly sessions, you had helped Jamie grieve the loss of his mother, while also encouraging Jamie to get involved in "safe" organizations again. Two weeks before therapy was terminated, Jamie told you that he just started dating again. Two years later, Jamie sought therapy again. This time he came with symptoms of depression and thoughts of killing himself. He informed you that he has AIDS and that his doctors have informed him that he only has between 6 and 8 months to live. You continued to see Jamie for an additional 4 months until Jamie began canceling appointments. It was obvious from his appearance when he did make his appointments that he was losing his energy and zest for life. He looked fatigued, feverish, and flushed each time you met with him. Jamie was going to the doctor twice a week for pain shots and checkups, which affected his ability to maintain sessions with you. Appointments were difficult to schedule and he was consistently sedated. A week ago Jamie came in to see you. He told you that he was "ready to go" and his partner supported him. He wanted to use therapy to reflect on his life and how he will say goodbye to his father, his partner, and his friends. He is particularly interested in discussing how he might go about informing his family and friends of his decision to kill himself.

TOPIC: COUPLE AND FAMILY COUNSELING

Supplemental Reading

Adams, S. (2010). Who is my client? Maintaining paperwork when the client changes. *The Family Journal, 18*, 70–72.

Bass, B. A., & Quimby, J. L. (2006). Addressing secrets in couples counseling: An alternative approach to informed consent. *The Family Journal, 14*, 77–80.

Brock, G. W., & Barnard, C. P. (1999). *Procedures in marriage and family therapy* (3rd ed.). Needham Heights, MA: Allyn & Bacon.

Duba, J. D., & Watts, R. E. (2009). Therapy with religious couples. *Journal of Clinical Psychology, 65*, 210–223.

Duba Onedera, J. (Ed.). (2008). *The role of religion in marriage and family counseling*. New York: Taylor & Francis.

Glasser, W., & Glasser, C. (1995). *Getting together and staying together*. New York: HarperCollins.

Long, J., & Andrews, B. V. (2007). Fostering strength and resiliency in same-sex couples: An overview. *Journal of Couple & Relationship Therapy, 6*, 153–165.

Love, P. (2001). *The truth about love*. New York: Fireside.

Patterson, J., Williams, L., Grauf-Grounds, C., & Chamow, L. (1998). *Essential skills in family therapy: From the first interview to termination*. New York: Guilford Press.

Peluso, P. R. (2007). *Infidelity: A practitioner's guide to working with couples in crisis*. New York: Taylor & Francis.

Thomas, G. (2000). *Sacred marriage*. Grand Rapids, MI: Zondervan.

Watkins, K., & Baldo, T. D. (2004). The infertility experience: Biopsychosocial effects and suggestions for counselors. *Journal of Counseling & Development, 82*, 394–402.

Websites

- International Association of Marriage and Family Counselors
  http://www.iamfconline.com/
  Students should be introduced to the related ACA division by visiting this website. Various resources and information about membership are provided.

- Association for Lesbian, Gay, & Transgender Issues (LGT) in Counseling
  http://www.algbtic.org/
  Students wishing to specialize in LGT issues will find the resources and information about membership provided on this website helpful. In addition, a link to join the organization's listserv is provided.

- The American Association of Sexuality Educators, Counselors and Therapists http://www.aasect.org/
  Students interested in specializing in sex therapy might find the following website helpful. Further, students might benefit from understanding what course requirements are necessary for AASECT certification prior to graduating.

- The John Gottman Institute http://www.gottman.com/
  Dr. John M. Gottman is one of the most prolific researchers/authors in marriage, couples, and family therapy. Information about the Gottman Institute, his research, as well as training opportunities are provided. In addition, Gottman's published research abstracts and articles are located on the website.

Learning Activity

Construct a three-generational genogram. Synthesize the information based on any given counseling theory.

Vignettes

- *Ethics in dual relationships.* Taken from: Greenwalt, B. C., & Duba, J. D. (2005). Paper presented at the Kentucky Association of Marriage and Family Therapist Ethics Workshop. Emily Andrews is an active member of the small rural community that she has lived in over the last 30 years with her husband and children. In fact, she has belonged to her church's social committee for the last 10 years. She has been on this committee longer than anyone else. Her work in organizing the church's social engagements is well known even in the community at large. Emily also maintains a full-time private practice as a licensed marriage and family therapist on the outskirts of town. During her last 5 years of full-time practice, she has typically seen persons who were not involved in her church. If a member from her church sought her services, she referred them to three other helping professionals in town. This process has so far worked well for her. Emily began seeing Anna and Ted Smith regularly for marriage therapy about one year ago when they moved her from a larger city to be with Anna's dying mother. The stressors of care-giving, moving to a foreign area, and trying to find new jobs were taking a toll on Anna and Ted's marriage. Due to Emily's encouraging the couple to become active in extracurricular activities, Anna and Ted found a church in town and started attending it regularly. Emily was not aware that Anna and Ted were attending the same church because they attended different services. Per Emily's request for extra help on the social committee, as well as a lack of volunteerism, the pastor of the church agreed to appoint members prior to the next social committee meeting. He promised Emily that she could be assured that the newly appointed members would be at the next scheduled meeting. In the meantime, Anna and Ted were appointed by the pastor and enthusiastically agreed to be active on the committee. While Emily was in the middle of assigning tasks to social committee members, Anna and Ted arrived late.

- *Ethics in couples counseling documentation.* You are seeing Mr. and Mrs. Smith as a couple. You like to be flexible in your approach to working with couples. Sometimes you like to see them together and then see them individually and then back together. There are other times where you see the couple together through the entire therapy process. In this case, you see them as a couple and individually. One of the issues in therapy was differing styles of parenting in addition to the issues related to their relationship. While therapy is still ongoing, Mr. Jones files for divorce. Mr. Jones wants custody of the children. His attorney contacts you wanting records of all of the sessions, both individual and conjoint. How would you frame informed consent to cover both conjoint and individual sessions? Is seeing couples both together and individually a potential minefield that outweighs any therapeutic benefit?
- *Risk of harm?* You have been seeing a couple for a year. The husband, in private, without the wife present, told you he was HIV positive and was not going to tell his wife. A few months later they separated. The wife requested their records in regards to obtaining custody of their children. The husband did not give his permission for her to gain access. What do you do?
- *Case of consent.* A man in counseling frequently brings his wife to therapy and asks the therapist to see his wife alone or insists that his wife should be in therapy with him. Neither signed an informed consent for treatment. Does either the husband's or the wife's behavior constitute consent?
- *To report or not report.* A female client whom you are seeing in couples therapy states in front of her husband that she has been having thoughts of killing him since his extramarital affair. How do you proceed with this revelation? What questions do you ask her about her thoughts? How do you assess the seriousness of her thoughts? Is this reportable? To whom would you make the report? How would you document this?

TOPIC: GROUP COUNSELING

Supplemental Reading

Debiak, D. (2007). Attending to diversity in group psychotherapy: An ethical imperative. *International Journal of Group Psychotherapy, 57*, 1–12.

Fieldsteel, N. D. (2005). When the therapist says goodbye. *International Journal of Group Psychotherapy, 55*, 245–279.

Flahive, M. W., & Ray, D. (2007). Effect of group sandtray therapy with preadolescents, *Journal for Specialists in Group Work, 32*, 362–382.
Gerrity, D. A., & DeLucia-Waack, J. L. (2007). Effectiveness of groups in the schools. *Journal for Specialists in Group Work, 32*, 97–106.
MacNair-Semands, R. R. (2007). Attending to the spirit of social justice as an ethical approach in group therapy. *International Journal of Group Psychotherapy, 57*, 61–66.
McKenna, K. Y. A., & Green, A. S. (2002). Virtual group dynamics. *Group Dynamics: Theory, Research, and Practice, 6*, 116–127.
Page, B. J. (2003). Introduction to using technology in group work. *Journal for Specialists in Group Work, 28*, 7–8.
Shapiro, E. L., & Ginzberg, R. (2002). Parting gifts: Termination rituals in group therapy. *International Journal of Group Psychotherapy, 52*, 319–336.
Smokowski, P. R., Rose, S. D., & Bacallao, M. L. (2001). Damaging experiences in therapeutic groups: How vulnerable consumers become group casualties. *Small Group Research, 32*, 223–251.
Veach, L. J., & Gladding, S. T. (2007). Using creative group techniques in high schools. *Journal for Specialists in Group Work, 32*, 71–81.
Ward, D. E. (2006). Classification of groups. *Journal for Specialists in Group Work, 31*, 93–97.

Website

- Association for Specialists in Group Work
  http://www.asgw.org.

  This website provides information regarding group counseling within the context of the American Counseling Association. The *Journal for Specialists in Group Work* is the official publication of this organization.

Learning Activity

As a group leader, how would you respond in each of the situations? (a) A member discloses how excited she is over a current affair and wonders if she should stay with her current partner. (b) A chronically depressed man talks about suicide as his way out of a hopeless situation. (c) A member from a different culture says he is having difficulty in the group because he is not used to speaking so openly about family problems. (d) Imagine that you are leading a group that does not seem to want to get beyond the stage of "playing it safe." Members' disclosures are superficial, their risk-taking is minimal, and they display a variety of resistances. What might you do in such a situation? How do you imagine you'd feel if you were leading such a group? There are important differences between effective and ineffective confrontation. How would you explain this difference to group members? Think about how you might respond to a person who had been in your group for some time and who said: "I don't see why we focus on negative things so much. All we do is talk about problems. Sometimes I just don't feel like even saying anything because I'm sick of talking about bad things."

Vignette

- *Charles.* A counselor is facilitating a group of juveniles who are referred by the court. Group counseling is part of their treatment following release from detention. In a particular session, Charles reveals that he went to visit his child over the weekend. Charles is not married to the child's mother. The parents of the mother have a restraining order keeping Charles away from their daughter and the child. Charles really wants to have a relationship with the baby and hopes to one day actively participate as a father. Charles has been doing well in his aftercare. As the group counselor, what are your responsibilities both to Charles and to the group when information is revealed in group that has potential legal consequences?

TOPIC: SCHOOL COUNSELING

Supplemental Reading

American School Counselor Association (2005). *The ASCA National Model: A framework for school counseling programs* (2nd ed.). Alexandria, VA: Author. http://asca2.timberlakepublishing.com//files/EthicalStandards2010.pdf.

American School Counselor Association. (2004). The role of the professional school counselor. Retrieved from http://www.schoolcounselor.org/content.asp?contentid=240.

Birdsall, B. A., & Miller, I. D. (2002). Brief counseling in the schools: A solution-focused approach for school counselors. *Counseling and Human Development, 35*, 1–10.

Rowell, L. L. (2006). Action research and school counseling: Closing the gap between research and practice. *Professional School Counseling, 9*, 376–384.

Simcox, A. G., Nuijens, K. L., & Lee, C. C. (2006). School counselors and school psychologists: Collaborative partners in promoting culturally competent schools. *Professional School Counseling, 9*, 272–277.

Studer, J. R., Oberman, A. H., & Womack, R. H. (2006). Producing evidence to show counseling effectiveness in the schools. *Professional School Counseling, 9*, 385–391.

Walsh, M. E., Barrett, J. G., & DePaul, J. (2007). Day-to-day activities of school counselors: Alignment with new directions in the field and the ASCA national model. *Professional School Counseling, 10*, 370–378.

Websites

- American School Counselor Association
  http://schoolcounselor.org

  This website is the source of information regarding school counseling in K–12 schools in the United States. There are links to state organizations. Links are provided to various supplemental activities and sources that provide information for school counselors. The site describes the ASCA National Model and information for implementing the model in schools.

- Educational Trust
  http://edtrust.org
  This is the website for the Educational Trust, which is a nonprofit national organization recognized by colleges of teacher education as the paramount organization for tracking teacher education in the United States. The Educational Trust also is actively engaged in transforming counselor education for school counselors. This site describes this effort and identifies the principles of school counselor education in the 21st century.

Learning Activities

- Students are asked to survey a sample of school teachers, students, and parents in order to identify their needs, both academic and social/emotional. Then students determine counseling goals and plans for achieving those goals using individual and small group counseling as well as classroom guidance activities.
- Students interview school counselors with questions regarding theoretical orientation, student issues, professional needs, and various counseling techniques used in a school setting.

Vignettes

- *High school.* A high school student comes to see the counselor. The student reveals that her uncle touched her inappropriately. She does not want you to tell because it was only one time and she respects her uncle. What are the limits of confidentiality? Discuss why students have a need to tell the counselor personal items that will require a report to social services or law enforcement only to then ask the counselor not to break confidentiality.
- *Elementary school.* An elementary student tells you that he is receiving threatening messages on his Facebook page. How do you address the issue of cyberbullying? What is the responsibility of school officials regarding Internet activities that might not happen during school but involve students?

TOPIC: COUNSELING SUPERVISION

Supplemental Reading

Bilot, J., & Peluso, P. R. (2009). The use of the ethical genogram in supervision. *The Family Journal, 17*, 175–179.

Lampropoulos, G. K. (2003). A common factors view of counseling supervision process. *The Clinical Supervisor, 21*, 77–95.

Milliren, A., Clemmer, F., & Wingett, W. (2006). Supervision: In the style of Alfred Adler. *Journal of Individual Psychology, 62*, 89–105.

Montgomery, M. J., Hendricks, C. B., & Bradley, L. J. (2001). Using systems perspectives in supervision. *The Family Journal, 9*, 305–313.

Parker, S. (2009). Faith development theory as a context for supervision of spiritual and religious issues. *Counselor Education & Supervision, 49*, 39–53.

Pearson, Q. M. (2001). A case in clinical supervision: A framework for putting theory into practice. *Journal of Mental Health Counseling, 23*, 174–183.

Pearson, Q. M. (2006). Psychotherapy-driven supervision: Integrating counseling theories into role-based supervision. *Journal of Mental Health Counseling, 28*, 241–252.

Websites

- Association for Counselor Education and Supervision
  http://www.acesonline.net/ethical_guidelines.asp
  Students should be introduced to the related ACA division by visiting this website. Various resources and information about membership and opportunities for student involvement are provided.

- Supervision Models
  http://www.cyc-net.org/cyc-online/cycol-0101-supervision%20models.html
  This web-based article provides a brief review of the developmental, integrated, and orientation-specific models of counseling supervision.

- Clinical Supervision (PowerPoint)
  http://www.neiu.edu/~jkedward/ppt/800/
  This online PowerPoint presentation was written by Dr. Jeffrey Edwards from Northeastern Illinois University. It might be used as a supplemental reading source for students.

- A Sample Contract for Supervision
  http://www.theaca.net.au/docs/Supervision_Sample_Contract.pdf
  This sample supervision contract provides a review of the essential responsibilities and expectations of both counseling supervisors and supervisees.

Learning Activity

Develop a supervision contract or compare and contrast supervision models.

TOPIC: CAREER COUNSELING

Supplemental Reading

Aueback, A. J., & Gale, W. G. (2009). The economic crisis and the fiscal crisis: 2009 and beyond. Retrieved from http://www.brookings.edu/~/media/Files/rc/papers/2009/0219_fiscal_future_gale/0219_fiscal_future_gale.pdf

DeVaney, S. B., & Hughey, A. W. (2000). Career development of ethnic minority students. In D. A. Luzzo (Ed.), *Career counseling of college students: An empirical guide to strategies that work* (pp. 233–252). Washington, DC: American Psychological Association.

Florida, R. (2002, May). The rise of the creative class. *Washington Monthly*. http://www.washingtonmonthly.com/features/2001/0205.florida.html.

Toffler Associates. (2008). *Creating adaptive organizations*. Manchester, MA: Author. Retrieved from http://www.toffler.com/images/ta-create-adaptive-orgs-0810.pdf

Websites

- National Career Development Association
  http://associationdatabase.com/aws/NCDA/pt/sp/Home_Page
  This website provides many resources and information about an extended list of topics including but not limited to career development, occupational and employment trends, job search instructions, current salaries, trade and professional associations, the military, education (e.g., College Navigator), distance education, financial aid, and job search instructions. In addition, various self-assessments are provided free of charge. Finally, the website includes information about NCDA membership, the upcoming conference, and opportunities for student involvement.

- Congressional Budget Office: Employment and Labor Markets
  http://www.cbo.gov/publications/collections/collections.cfm?collect=16
  This website offers a thorough review of various congressional policies that may impact the job market and employment. Counselors who will do any career counseling should be aware of this website and the information it provides.

Learning Activities

- Watch *Shift Happens* http://www.youtube.com/watch?v=pMcfrLYDm2U. Conduct a group discussion regarding the implications of technological advancement as related to matters of work, job training, labor market, etc. Also discuss occupational opportunities and the economy locally, statewide, nationwide, and globally in the context of solutions and implications for

your role as a counselor/educator. You are encouraged to use outside reading (cited) to support your responses.
- Search and review the university's career services center website. Then compare and contrast with a career services center at another university of your choice.
- Complete a self-assessment from the NCDA website; share experiences with class.

Vignette

- *A career genogram.* Based on the following vignette, students should construct a career genogram for client "Jane." *Family Background*: Jane is the oldest of three siblings. She is 21 years old. Her younger sister is 19, and her brother is 16. Jane's mother and father have been married for 27 years. Her father has been a machinist for the last 28 years. Mrs. Doe works part-time as a massage therapist. She did not work outside of the home when the three children were in elementary school. Jane describes herself and her siblings as very good, motivated, and involved students. She does not believe that there is any competition among her siblings; but perhaps each one of them keeps the other one going. That is, there is a message to "always try your very best" and "never give up." Jane appreciates these messages. She feels good about herself when she is achieving. However, Jane describes her father as "not very understanding." She recalls numerous times when her father had become frustrated with her because of her struggles with friends, boyfriends, or school-related issues, especially throughout high school. The message that she receives from her father whenever she is upset is that she "is too sensitive." She agrees with him; however, she wishes he was more supportive. There is not much emotional support among her siblings, although Jane believes this is because of how they were raised. Jane feels very supported by her extended family, particularly by her grandmothers. *Extended Family:* Mrs. Doe's mother worked at a business firm and worked full-time throughout Mrs. Doe's childhood. Mrs. Doe's deceased father worked as a furniture upholsterer. She is the middle daughter of five siblings. The oldest four children are each one year apart. The oldest child, Evan, completed high school and has been working for the city's transportation division ever since. The next child, Amy, holds a master's degree and is a fourth-grade school teacher. The fourth daughter, Caroline, also graduated from college and is a registered nurse. The fifth child, Justin, 10 years younger than Caroline, went into the military, graduated from college, and is now an engineer on a military base. Jane is "somewhat close" to her mother's family of origin. She is especially close to her two aunts. Jane is the second oldest cousin. Her oldest cousin is pursuing a college degree at a state school. Jane's maternal grandmother shows excitement about her grandchildren's academic pursuits. Mr. Doe's parents both worked full-time until they retired. His father was a printer and worked until he was in his mid-70s. His mother was a grammar school teacher. Mr. Doe is the youngest of three children. The oldest child,

Sarah, is five years older than him. She received a master's degree and is an administrator at a private all boys' high school. Keith, 2 years older than Mr. Doe, is a "staff engineer" at an elementary school. He is in charge of the janitorial department. He never went to college. All three of Jane's older cousins are going to or have completed college. Her oldest cousin recently graduated from Stanford and one of her other cousins is attending a reputable university. Jane's paternal grandmother has played a large role as supporter in all of the grandchildren's educations. That is, she has attended every grandchild's graduation, recitals, and award ceremonies since preschool. *Presenting Problem and Related Background:* Jane is in her last semester of undergraduate school. She will have completed a degree in business in 3½ years. Lately she feels "hopeless," "confused," and "depressed." Her parents seemed to be becoming very frustrated with her depressed mood. She has become estranged and distant from her parents because of this, which seems to make the relationship dynamics even worse. After struggling for many months, Jane told her parents that she wanted to seek professional counseling. By saying that she wanted counseling, she felt as if she was sending the message that was confirming what her family already thought of her. However, she believed that counseling could help. Mrs. Doe told Jane that Mr. Doe was very concerned about what messages he would send to his employer with Jane receiving mental health services. Jane internalized this and felt even more depressed. Jane was very excited about coming to counseling. Although she never received counseling before, she knew that she would be supported. Jane and her mother arrived at the office early to complete paperwork. When the counselor asked Jane to join him, Mrs. Doe waited suspiciously. The counselor asked Jane what brought her in. Jane told the counselor that she was depressed and confused about where to go after she graduated from college. She thought about applying to law school. In fact, she had recently attended orientations at two different institutions. She told the counselor that another option was to pursue a master's in business, while taking some classes in art. Jane thought that she might even consider teaching in high school. She expressed excitement in her voice and said, "This is what I would really like to do." Jane was apprehensive about the potentially low salary, compared to one as a lawyer. She was also concerned about how her father might react.

TOPIC: CONSULTATION

Supplemental Reading

Caplan, G. (1995). Types of mental health consultation. *Journal of Educational & Psychological Consultation, 6*, 7–21.

Dinkmeyer, D., Jr., & Carlson, J. (2005). *Consultation: Creating school-based interventions* (3rd ed.). Philadelphia, PA: Brunner-Routledge.
Doerries, D. B., & Foster, C. A. (2001). Family counselors as school consultants: Where are the solutions? *The Family Journal, 9*, 391–397.
Keys, S. G., Bemak, F., Carpenter, S. L., & King-Sears, M. E. (1998). Collaborative consultant: A new role for counselors serving at-risk youths. *Journal of Counseling & Development, 76*, 123–133.
Kurpius, D. J., & Fuqua, D. R. (1993). Fundamental issues in defining consultation. *Journal of Counseling & Development, 71*, 598–600.
Mendoza, D. W. (1993). A review of Gerald Caplan's theory and practice of mental health consultation. *Journal of Counseling & Development, 71*, 629–635.
Moe, J. J., & Perera-Diltz, M. (2009). An overview of systemic-organizational consultation for professional counseling. *Practice, Theory, & Research, 37*, 27–37.
Parker, R. J. (1991). What is really the problem? A simulation to train beginning consultants. *Counselor Education & Supervision, 31*, 81–89.

Website

- Mental Health Consultation
  http://www.strengtheningfamilies.net/images/uploads/program_tools/04_Mental_Health_REV4.pdf.
  This 10-page pdf document describes how mental health consultation fits as a component of early childhood education. Roles of mental health consultants, program examples, and challenges are addressed.

Learning Activity

Construct a consultation outline/guide to any given scenario based on the following lead: Pretend that you were asked to consult with teachers at a nearby school. The teachers were having difficulty with a particular issue concerning their students. Develop an outline based upon the following: (a) the issue or concern; why the consultees need your help; three specific, measurable goals for the consultation project; (b) the roles of everyone involved, including who the consultant, consultee, client/s; and stakeholders; and (c) how the relationship with the consultee will be developed and maintained, including how confidentiality will be maintained; how the roles of the participants will be agreed upon; and how closure will be attained.

Vignette

- *Consultation in the schools.* You have been asked by Mrs. Evans, a school principal at a local elementary school, to help design a parent education program. This program would include weekly parent group discussions that would allow parents to discuss and understand the affective and cognitive aspects of dealing with their children. Mrs. Evans is consulting with you regarding important factors, issues, and points important to the parent group structure.

- If you are the consultant, who or what group will be identified as the consultee, client(s), and stakeholders? Provide support for your answers.
- Consider interprofessional collaborations or relationships that will need to be formed to make this possible. Who and what relationships will be needed?
- As a mental health consultant working in this capacity, what basic counseling skills and portions of particular counseling theories will it be important for you to incorporate into interactions with others?

COURSE ASSIGNMENTS

Literature Research Project (50 Points)

Students should choose a topic to research that is related to the field of professional counseling. To prepare for this project, the following guidelines should be followed: (a) locate, study, and incorporate at least seven professional and peer-reviewed journal articles published no more than 5 years ago and (b) conduct interviews with two different mental health professionals who have at least 5 years of licensed experience in the field, as well as in the given topic area. Interviews can take place face-to-face or via e-mail. Proof of interviews must be included and reference to interviewees should be incorporated appropriately within the outline. The project will be graded on the following:

1. Topic Chosen (12 points)
   a. Clarity of topic
   b. Timeliness and relevance to current counseling and mental health practices
   c. Degree to which topic will contribute to the knowledge base of readers
   d. Innovativeness and novelty
2. One- to Two-Page Comprehensive Outline (20 points)
   a. Information and subtopics are organized through a thorough synthesis of the resources available
   b. Each topic and related subtopics are supported with multiple, relevant, and current references (any given subtopic should not be a summary of one source)
   c. Material matches title (clear and focused)
   d. Interview references are relevant to the topic and are incorporated appropriately to support any given subtopic
   e. Applicability of outline as a guide from which to write the manuscript with ease, efficiency, and clarity
3. Reference Page (8 points)
   a. Includes at least 15 references (7 of which are professional and peer-reviewed journal articles published no more than 5 years ago)

   b. Correct APA format and spelling
4. Class Presentation of Research (10 points)
   a. Ability to summarize the research in a thoughtful, reflective, and knowledgeable manner
   b. Evidence of thought and conceptualization of topic provided through reflection question
   c. Ability to answer one final question from the audience about the topic in a thoughtful, reflective, and knowledgeable manner

Publication Manuscript for Counseling-Related Newsletter (100 Points)

The following criteria should be adhered to when writing the article: (a) formatting of document, including *Publication Manual of the American Psychologic Association* (6th edition) format, writing form, and six-page limit; (b) throughout the paper, the topic remains consistently directed at the given audience population mentioned in the beginning of the document (i.e., marriage and family counselors); (c) the relevance or the importance of the topic to potential readers is clearly spelled out (i.e., in the introduction, the importance of the topic is clear); (d) the focus of the topic is clear and easily comprehended (i.e., the body of the article is focused and addresses objectives); and (e) subject matter is innovative and up to date. The paper must include at least six references, all of which are dated within the last 5 years. Three references must be peer-reviewed journal articles.

Poster Presentation (or Final Exam) (45 Points)

The final exam will be a contribution to a mini-conference. The mini-conference will be made up of a series of poster sessions on professional issues and practice in the field of marriage and family and/or mental health. (Topics should be related to the profession and field rather than to client issues.) Members of the counseling program (i.e., faculty, peers) will be invited. Each student will prepare a poster on a particular topic of interest and professional relevance. The topic addressed in the publication manuscript can be used pending approval of the instructor. Poster sessions may feature a demonstration or information. The posters should be mounted on 36 × 48-inch, free-standing presentation board; standard-size boards are available at places such as Staples, Office Max, or Office Depot. Possible topics might include but are not limited to any of the following: confidentiality/informed consent, dual relationships, ethical concerns facing professional counselors, marketing counseling services, managed care, counselor licensure, legislative issues, ethics in group work, technology. Evaluation will be based on the following:

1. Poster presentation proposal that adheres to the following criteria:
   a. Two paragraphs that each address the following; the entire document should be at least 300 words typed in the APA's *Publication Manual* format: (15 points)

   b. Summary of the topic, specifically related to its relevance and application to the counseling profession
   c. Summary of how the topic and related information will be disseminated and illustrated on the poster. For example, how will all of the elements noted in (b) be shown on the poster?
2. Poster presentation will be graded on the following: (10 points each)
   a. Topic's relevance to the field of professional counseling
   b. Applicability of information presented
   c. Quality of poster (visual display; creativity)

TENTATIVE COURSE OUTLINE

WEEK	*TOPIC*
Week 1	Mental health counseling in America or in the 21st century
Week 2	Introduction to ethics and legal issues in the counseling profession
Week 3	Counseling in a multicultural society
Week 4	Ethical, legal, and professional behavior and practice (competence and malpractice, confidentiality, records, and technology)
Week 5	Professional counselor as scholar practitioner: Yesterday and today
Week 6	Introduction to counseling theories
Week 7	The counseling process: Skills, assessment, diagnosis, and treatment
Week 8	Counseling children, vulnerable adults (older persons, persons with disabilities)
Week 9	Couples and family counseling
Week 10	Group counseling
Week 11	School counseling
Week 12	Counselor supervision
Week 13	Career counseling
Week 14	Consultation
Week 15	
Week 16	

CONCLUSION

What a pleasure this course is to teach! First, it is typical that students who take this course are rather new to the counseling program. Thus, they are particularly excited and motivated to learn about the course material, as well as the counseling profession in general. In addition, the dreaded doldrums of mid-semester are easily combated with the swift pace and constant shifting of topics throughout this course. Secondly, the variety of course topics provides the instructor with an assortment of delivery opportunities. For example, whereas one topic may be best presented through a classroom activity, another might be best introduced by a guest presenter. This is a fabulous course for counselor educators who value creativity, resourcefulness, and originality.

Indeed, this is a course packed with information and potential. Consequently, such a course can also be quite overwhelming for the novice counselor educator. We suggest reminding students at the beginning of the course that much of the information will be addressed in further detail along their course of study. On the other hand, it is in the best interest of the instructor to go into each class period with just a few objectives while also saving time for discussion. In addition, it is helpful to schedule periodic check-ins with the class regarding any questions students may have about anything covered up until that point. Finally, instructors are urged to be patient with themselves, enjoy the process (while relishing the "ah hah" moments), and, above all, join the students on a journey of personal and professional discovery!

APPENDIX A

Professional Counselor as Scholar Practitioner Self-Assessment

Instructions: In the last month, how often has the following been true for you? (0) Never, (2) Sometimes, (3) Often, (4) Always. For each question, choose the best response and write the affiliated number besides the statement.

Consumer

____I apply and adhere to appropriate ethical codes and moral principles when consuming and using information.

____I illustrate interpersonal competence and relationship skills when I am consuming information from others (i.e., interacting with experts in the field, using proper etiquette when networking). These persons would also say that I have competent interpersonal skills.

____I conduct self-checks or self-evaluations about how my own subjectivity impacts my conceptualization of information (i.e., personal values, culture, experiences).

____I am consistently open to self-examination and feedback from others about how one is processing and conceptualizing information. That is, I do not take offense to constructive feedback.

____I am adaptable and will consume current information even if it is not terribly interesting to me.

____I regularly consume new and up-to-date information, as well as current research and developments in the field.
____I properly summarize, evaluate, and synthesize information that will help inform practice (as a clinician, academic, or consultant/administrator).
____I can locate evidenced-based and scholarly information.

Disseminator

____I apply and adhere to appropriate ethical codes and moral principles when disseminating information through any medium.
____I am sensitive to diversity (i.e., ethnicity, cultural, religion, gender, socioeconomic status, sexual orientation, disability) when disseminating and sharing information.
____I illustrate interpersonal competence and relationship skills when sharing information with others (i.e., genuineness, empathy, making eye contact with participants). These persons would also say that I have competent interpersonal skills.
____I am aware and accepting of possible areas of growth when disseminating information through any given medium (i.e., presenting information that is culturally sensitive, maintaining a comfortable disposition when presenting in front of an audience, patience with journal editors, ability to avoid distractions).
____I disseminate information that is appropriate for the given venue (i.e., school counseling conference, counselor education, and supervision-related journal).
____I am open to self-examination and feedback from others (e.g., presentation participants) throughout the process of preparing to disseminate (writing a manuscript) and during the actual dissemination (presentation). That is, I do not take offense to constructive feedback.
____I apply feedback related to how I am disseminating information.
____I conduct self-checks or self-evaluations about how my own personal subjectivity (i.e., personal values, culture, experiences) impacts my goal or purpose for disseminating any given type or topic of information.
____I am adaptable and will disseminate information needed by the profession even if I am not terribly interested in it.
____I reference authors and the creators of information appropriately when disseminating information that I have adopted or adapted from secondary sources.
____I contribute to the field through the dissemination of information in various contexts (i.e., presentation, publication).
____I publish in scholarly venues.
____I write presentation proposals.
____I conduct professional presentations.

Advocate

____I apply and adhere to appropriate ethical codes and moral principles when advocating for clients, the counseling field, or related issues.

___I am sensitive to diversity (i.e., ethnicity, cultural, religion, gender, socioeconomic status, sexual orientation, disability) when advocating for any given cause or persons.
___I illustrate interpersonal competence and relationship skills when advocating for any given cause or persons. These persons would also say that I have competent interpersonal skills.
___When advocating for any given cause, I follow an advocacy theory or process supported by research.
___I adhere to the mission of the professional counseling field when advocating for any given cause or persons (i.e., following code of ethics, working from a wellness perspective).
___I conduct self-checks or self-evaluations about how my own personal subjectivity impacts my goal or purpose for advocating for any given cause or persons.
___I show professional responsibility by staying abreast of current legislative efforts related to the field.
___I show professional responsibility by participating in advocacy activities (e.g., writing legislators) related to current legislative efforts.
___TOTAL SCORE

0–29: A score in this range indicates that your ability to incorporate an appropriate level of awareness, knowledge base, and skill when consuming or disseminating information and advocating for any given cause is poor. You could benefit from reviewing the criteria and standards associated with these tasks as well as seeking mentorship and one-on-one supervision.
30–59: A score in this range indicates that your ability to incorporate an appropriate level of awareness, knowledge base, and skill when consuming or disseminating information and advocating for any given cause is poor to average. You could benefit from reviewing the objectives of these tasks, as well as continuing to practice ways of strengthening your knowledge and skill base and increasing your awareness.
60–89: A score in this range indicates that your ability to incorporate an appropriate level of awareness, knowledge base, and skill when consuming or disseminating information and advocating for any given cause is moderate at best. You could benefit from consulting with a supervisor or peer about ways in which to strengthen your abilities to consume and disseminate information, as well as participating in advocacy activities.
90–120: A score in this range indicates that your ability to incorporate an appropriate level of awareness, knowledge base, and skill when consuming or disseminating information and advocating for any given cause is strong. There is always room to grow. You could benefit from continued practice and continued openness to the process.

Note. Reprinted with permission from Duba (2009).

APPENDIX B

Conducting Formal Presentations: Criteria and Guidelines

- Oral Presentation
    - Evidence of a thorough conceptualization of the material being presented
        - Ability to translate the information into practical applications
    - Illustration of genuineness and honesty
        - Ability to be sincere when unable to answer questions from audience
        - Proper citing of original resources and references
    - Evidence of creativity in presenting (i.e., media, role-plays, participation from audience)
    - Ability to promote audience involvement
        - Leads and maintains discussions during any presentation activities
        - Use of provocative questions, media, questionnaires, handouts
    - Illustration of quality presentation mechanics
        - Presence with audience
        - Maintenance of eye contact
        - Efficient use of time allotted
        - Program title or abstract matches content of presentation
- Resources and Materials
    - Information is applicable to audience
    - Information matches current trends and is relevant to present-day concerns and interests within the field of counseling and mental health
        - Topic fits with today's societal, cultural, and legislative trends
    - Information can be supported by current research studies or literature reviews
    - Resources and references are relevant and match presentation content
- Relationship with Copresenters
    - Maintained consistent communication with copresenters throughout preparation process
    - Shared jointly in the division of presentation preparation labor
    - Contributed a fair share to preparation and in actual presentation
    - Exhibited a sense of professionalism with copresenters
    - Offered creative ideas and suggestions during presentation preparation

Note. Reprinted with permission from Duba (2009).

REFERENCES

Burke, M. (2010). *Cultural foundations in-class activities: Social categorization, social perception and stereotyping*. Unpublished manuscript.

Council for the Accreditation of Counseling and Related Educational Programs (CACREP, 2009). *2009 standards*. Retrieved from http://cacrep.org/doc/2009%20Standards%20with%20cover.pdf

Duba, J. D., & Magenta, M. (2008). End-of-life decision-making: A preliminary outline for preparing counselors to work with terminally-ill individuals. *The Family Journal, 16*, 384–390.

Duba, J. (2009). *Professional counselor as scholar practitioner self-assessment*. Unpublished manuscript, Department of Counseling and Student Affairs, Western Kentucky University, Kentucky, USA.

Greenwalt, B., & Duba, J. D. (2005, February). *Treating couples when one has a severe mental illness*. Paper presented at the International Association of Marriage and Family Counselors Conference, New Orleans, LA.

3

Foundations and Techniques of School Counseling

Preparing for Contemporary Roles

Debra C. Cobia

Generally, one or more courses in a master's degree curriculum is intended to develop the knowledge and skills that apply to the school work setting. School counselor preparation programs include instructional experiences that make it possible for future school counselors to develop the knowledge, skills, and practices necessary to promote the development of all students (Council for the Accreditation of Counseling and Related Educational Programs [CACREP], 2009). There are many different titles for such courses, and counselor educators often refer to them informally by the content emphasized in the course(s) they teach (e.g., organization and administration, programs course, orientation). The course being described in this chapter is the Professional School Counselor and begins with an introduction to the school setting, including how the school counseling program fits within that system, and then focuses on how one develops, implements, and evaluates a program that meets both local needs and addresses typical developmental needs of K–12 students. Although the primary focus is on developing an effective and accountable program, other important content is integrated throughout the course (see topics list below). A catalog description of this course might read:

> Students will gain an understanding of school counseling programs and how these programs support the academic, career, and personal social development of K–12 students. Students will acquire the knowledge and skills necessary to plan, implement, and evaluate a comprehensive, data-driven school counseling program.

School counselors-in-training (SCIT) often experience dissonance during the first few weeks of the course. Many of them have not been previously exposed to the idea that counseling in schools occurs within a comprehensive program model that exists to support the educational mission of the school. They learn that in addition to the knowledge and skills necessary to become effective counselors (i.e., provide individual and group counseling), they are also required to be program managers, collaborators, consultants, advocates, change agents, and leaders (Cobia & Henderson, 2007). This approach to school counseling, reflected in the model program developed by the American School Counselor Association (ASCA), is a fairly recent development in the profession and represents a shift away from providing services as needed to some students toward an integrated model for all students (ASCA, 2005). Consequently, SCIT are learning about professional standards and program models that were not in evidence in the school counseling programs where they obtained their own K–12 education. Additionally, many counselors currently practicing in K–12 schools still operate from a "services oriented for some students" model. Therefore, SCIT may be placed for practicum, internship, and other on-site activities in schools where they do not have an opportunity to observe the application of the content of this course. The discrepancies SCIT observe between "real" and "ideal" often result in confusion and, at times, uncertainty about whether the school counseling profession is one they wish to practice. At times, the ideas and beliefs formed about school counseling (e.g., primarily conducting therapy with youth in a school setting) are quite resistant to change.

To address the confusion that SCIT may experience as they learn about the many roles and responsibilities of school counselors, educators must facilitate conceptual change. That is, we introduce new concepts and provide instructional experiences that help SCIT explore these concepts (Alexander, 2006). Specifically, SCIT must expand their views of school counseling as a profession and the roles of school counselors to include a vision of themselves as competent program leaders and managers. Understanding the depth and breadth of a school counseling program allows students to integrate knowledge and skills developed in other courses into an overall scheme that makes sense to them. For example, as they learn about responsive services (ASCA, 2005) as one of the systems by which services are delivered to students, they gain an understanding of where and how skills and knowledge from other instructional experiences (e.g., individual and group counseling, assessment, and consultation) fit with the school counselor's responsibility to promote academic achievement. As well, SCIT learn about the school counselor's unique contribution to the educational setting and how to develop, implement, and evaluate a comprehensive developmental program including the use of local data to inform decision making about program priorities.

Finally, in this course SCIT develop and/or refine the collaborative skills necessary to work effectively with others, both inside and outside of the formal school setting, who have a vested interest in students' welfare. The rest of this chapter will include objectives that might be covered in the course; instructional experiences that might be used to achieve the objectives; sample rubrics that are used as both a teaching strategy and an evaluative tool; suggested textbooks; and other instructional resources to support each topic covered.

OBJECTIVES AND CACREP STANDARDS

Students will:

1. Design and implement a comprehensive school counseling program. (SC F.1.; SC F.2.; SC F.3.; SC H.3.; SC I.4.; SC J.2.; SC J.3.; SC P.1.; SC P.2.; Section II.G.2.e.; Section II.G.8.b.; Section II.G.8.c.; Section II.G.8.e.)
2. Organize, implement, and deliver a guidance curriculum in the context of a school counseling program. (SC C.4.; SC D.2.; SC I.2.; SC K.3.; SC N.3.; Section II.G.4.e.)
3. Facilitate educational and career development, including predictable transitions, of all students. (SC L.1.; SC L.2.; SC N.1.; Section II.G.4.d.)
4. Demonstrate leadership and advocacy for the school counseling profession and within the individual school setting. (SC A.1.; SC B.2.; SC F.2.; SC F.3.; SC I.4.; SC I.5.; SC J.3.; SC O.5.; SC P.1.; SC P.2.)
5. Demonstrate regard for professional development and ethical standards. (SC A.4.; SC B.1.; Section II.G.1.f.; Section II.G.1.g.; Section II.G.1.j.)

CRITERIA FOR EVALUATING A TEXT

Textbook selection is a uniquely individual task that is influenced by course objectives, major content, instructional experiences, at what point in the graduate program sequence the course is offered, and instructor preferences that are informed by teaching philosophy and style. This author's personal style is influenced by social constructivism. That is, from this perspective learning is active and contextualized, builds on previous knowledge and experience, and social interaction with more knowledgeable peers or guides plays a significant role (Alexander, 2006). Consequently, a preferable text is one that presents information in a straightforward, student-centered manner, contextualizes information in cases that represent those that SCIT will experience in their practice settings, and provides opportunities for collaborative learning activities. Additionally, it is helpful to have a text that uses the CACREP (2009) standards for the preparation of school counselors as one of the organizing features and that incorporates instructional experiences and assignments that lead to the demonstration of student learning outcomes. Finally, the incorporation of contemporary program models (i.e., ASCA national model, national standards, school counselor competencies) and professional developments are also important selection criteria. Below are some of the books that may be useful as either primary or supplementary texts for achieving the objectives stated above.

MOST POPULAR TEXTS

Baker, S. B., & Gerler, E. R. (2008). *School counseling for the twenty-first century* (5th ed.). Upper Saddle River, NJ: Pearson.

Cobia, D. C., & Henderson, D. A. (In press). *Developing an effective and accountable school counseling program* (3rd ed.). Upper Saddle River, NJ: Pearson Education.

Cobia, D. C., & Henderson, D. A. (2007). *Developing an effective and accountable school counseling program* (2nd ed.). Upper Saddle River, NJ: Pearson Education.

Erford, B. T. (2007). *Transforming the school counseling profession* (2nd ed.). Upper Saddle River, NJ: Pearson.

Schmidt, J. (2007). *Counseling in schools: Comprehensive programs of responsive services for all students* (5th ed.). Upper Saddle River, NJ: Merrill.

Wittmer, J., & Clark, M. A. (2007). *Managing your school counseling program: K–12 developmental strategies*. Minneapolis, MN: Educational Media.

SUPPLEMENTAL READING

American School Counselor Association. (2004). *The ASCA national model workbook*. Alexandria, VA: Author.

American School Counselor Association. (2005). *The national model: A framework for school counseling programs*. Alexandria, VA: Author.

Daniels, M. H. (2010). Systematic program evaluation. In C. Sheperis, J. S. Young, & M. Daniels (Eds.), *Counseling research: Quantitative, qualitiative, and mixed methods* (pp. 173–186). Upper Saddle River, NJ: Pearson.

Galassi, J., & Akos, P. (2007). *Strengths-based school counseling: Promoting student development and achievement*. New York: Routledge.

Lewis, R. E., & Hatch, T. (2008). Cultivating strengths-based professional identities. *Professional School Counseling, 12*, 115–118.

Loesch, L., & Ritchie, M. (2009). *The accountable school counselor* (2nd ed.). Austin, TX: ProEd.

Metcalf, L. (2008). *Counseling toward solutions: A practical solution-focused program for working with students, teachers, and parents*. San Francisco, CA: Jossey-Bass.

Parsons, R. D. (2006). *Counseling strategies that work*. Boston, MA: Allyn & Bacon.

Pearson, A. (2009). *Guidance with good measure*. Chapin, SC: Youthlight, Inc.

Remley, T., Hermann, M. A., & Huey, W. (2003). *Ethical and legal issues in school counseling* (2nd ed.). Alexandria, VA: American School Counselor Association.

Stone, C., & Dahir, C. (2010). *School counselor accountability: A MEASURE of student success* (3rd ed.). Upper Saddle River, NJ: Pearson.

Thompson, C., & Henderson, D. (2010). *Counseling children: A developmental approach* (7th ed.). Pacific Grove, CA: Brooks Cole.

Trusty, J., Mellin, E., & Herbert, J. (2008). Closing achievement gaps: Roles and tasks of elementary school counselors. *Elementary School Journal, 108*, 407–421.

Wittmer, J., & Thompson, D. (2006). *Large group counseling: A K–12 sourcebook* (2nd ed.). Minneapolis, MN: Educational Media.

WEBSITES

- America's Career Resource Network
  http://www.acrnetwork.org
  ACRN offers tools for those students and professionals who are interested in career development and decision making. The National Career Development Guidelines are highlighted on this site.

- American School Counseling Association
  http://www.schoolcounselor.org/
  ASCA provides professional literature, tools for professional development, and articles and publications that contribute to the field of school counseling. Additionally, the website contains information about the benefits of school counseling programs for the general public. ASCA members have access to periodicals, tools, resources, and opportunities for professional development via the website. Current issues of importance to the profession are followed on the site.

- American Counseling Association
  http://www.counseling.org/
  The ACA website keeps members informed of ACA and counseling-related news. Resources and publications for counselors at all levels of development and up-to-date information about professional development opportunities are featured. Public policy initiatives impacting the counseling profession are highlighted.

- Child Trends Data Bank
  http://www.childtrendsdatabank.org/index.cfm
  The CTDB collects and disseminates data for each state and many local communities relative to key indicators of child well-being. The databank is especially useful for understanding some of the needs of children who may be underserved in local schools.

- College Board
  http://www.collegeboard.com
  The college board is made up of schools, colleges, universities, and other educational organizations and provides students and parents with programs geared toward college preparation, admission, guidance, assessment, financial aid, enrollment, and teaching. Several of the most recognizable college board programs are the standardized college admission tests (i.e., SAT, PSAT) and the advanced placement program. Counseling professionals will find links to tools to assist them in helping a student along the college prep/admission/financing process.

- Council for Accreditation of Counseling and Related Educational Programs
  http://www.cacrep.org
  On the CACREP website one will find information about the types and requirements of counselor programs that hold CACREP accreditation. As well, information about the benefits of accreditation and a listing of accredited programs are available.

- Kids Count
  http://www.aecf.org/MajorInitiatives/KIDSCOUNT.aspx
  The Annie E. Casey Foundation's primary purpose is to track the status of children in the United States. Major initiatives of the foundation, links to data regarding child well-being, and numerous resources may be found on this site.

- National Assessment of Educational Progress
  http://nces.ed.gov/nationsreportcard/
  This site is the national hub for educational statistics, research, and information regarding educational progress and programs. NAEP provides subject-matter reports related to achievement of groups of students and provides a common metric for state-to-state comparisons of what students know and can do.

- National Association of Peer Programs
  http://www.peerprogramprofessionals.org/
  This site supports the work of professionals who establish, train, supervise, maintain, and evaluate peer programs. The website offers tools for networking, training, certification, and program problem solving. With the bulk of members being in education, the NAPPP also provides link resources to different groups and organizations that peer programs may utilize, such as Partners for Substance Abuse Prevention and National Youth Violence Prevention.

- National Association of School Psychologists
  http://www.nasponline.org/resources/crisis_safety/index.aspx
  A website for school psychologists that provides access to knowledge, professional development, professional resources, and relevant data that can ensure professional competency and effectiveness. For students or preprofessionals

there is a news section, opportunities for membership, national certification, periodicals, advocacy opportunities, and a career center.

- National Career Development Association
  http://www.ncda.org
  NCDA, a division of ACA, provides services for those interested in career development, including research, information, professional standards, advocacy, and recognition of service.

- National Center for Educational Statistics
  http://nces.ed.gov/fastfacts/
  Fast facts highlight statistics relative to educational topics of interest. Information may be located in a variety of ways using data tools built into the site.

- National Center for Transforming School Counseling
  http://www.edtrust.org/dc/tsc
  Working to close the gaps in education caused by race, ethnicity, socioeconomic status, and other social constructs, the NCTSC website offers information about programs working toward that goal. There are links to recent relevant press, areas for K–12 and higher education that show how the educational gaps may be addressed, and links to advocacy opportunities for those programs currently working to close educational gaps.

- U.S. Department of Education
  http://www.ed.gov/index.jhtml
  The U.S. Department of Education is the federal governing body of education in the United States. On the website there are grant opportunities for education-related programs, links for student aid (FAFSA), and information on grants available to students. One can also view the allotment of the DoE budget and funds spent, as well as publications related to educational spending. Educational policy and research areas are also highlighted.

LEARNING ACTIVITIES AND ASSIGNMENTS

The assignments that follow are the instructional experiences that may be used to achieve the learning objectives stated above. Following the description of the assignments, scoring rubrics are included that are used as both teaching tools and evaluative strategies. These rubrics help students be more attuned to all of the aspects of an assignment, and students submit qualitatively better products when they have access to the rubrics as they complete the assignments.

1. Program Development Assignment. Students will work together to complete a comprehensive developmental program for students in grades K–12 that clearly articulates the foundation, delivery, management, and accountability elements defined by the ASCA (see Appendix B). Due Week 13. *Course Objectives: 1, 2, 3*
2. Shadowing Experience. Each student will "shadow" a school counselor and complete a structured interview during the second month of the term. The purpose of this assignment is to give the student an opportunity to observe a counseling program, counselor role, facilities, available resources, as well as the counselor's leadership activities in special programs, advocacy, and accountability efforts. The guidelines for this assignment are as follows:
   a. Contact a school counselor and request an opportunity to spend an entire day observing him or her at work. In addition to the reading assignments for class, review the roles and activities of school counselors online at the American School Counselor Association website: http://www.schoolcounselor.org/content.asp?pl=328&sl=336&contentid=336
   b. Through observation and an interview with the counselor, find out about the role, function, and relationship that school counselors have with other human service providers. Collect any forms, list of resources, etc., that may be helpful to any beginning school counselor. Some suggested activities to observe or participate in include large group classroom-wide activities, collaborative meetings, brokering of services, assessment, use of data, and individual and/or small group counseling activities.
   c. Conduct a short interview with the counselor to gather information that will assist you in completing the written portion of this assignment.
   d. Evaluate the experience in a paper (three to five pages). Introduce the paper by summarizing activities observed or in which the student participated. Answer the following questions when completing the paper:
      i. How do the activities observed at the site fit into a comprehensive developmental program?
      ii. How does leadership apply to the school counseling process?
      iii. How was advocacy evidenced in this program?
      iv. What are some of the creative/innovative techniques or programs being implemented?
      v. What are the most important skills one needs for the job?
      vi. How does the school counselor prioritize time and meet all of the demands of the job?
      vii. How is this position different or the same as that of a school social worker, social psychologist, or community mental health counselor?
      viii. What role does technology play in the school counselor's work?
      xi. How does the school counselor know that what he or she is doing with students and others is helping/working? Due Week 9. *Course Objectives: 1, 3–5*

3. Classroom Guidance Units. Students will work together in groups (academic, career, personal/social) to develop sequential lessons to be delivered as part of a guidance curriculum. A unit containing six lessons will be developed for students in each grade level (elementary, middle, high school). Each group will present at least one lesson from those developed for this project for the entire class. Sign up for groups on the CourseDen site for this course.
   a. Each team will be responsible for introducing, preparing, and leading one lesson from each of the three grade levels on the night these units are due. Introduce each of the three lessons by discussing the important developmental issues and student competencies that school counselors need to consider at each of the three grade levels. Further, identify for the class strategies that school counselors might use to involve parents in meeting these competencies. Conduct a 20- to 25-minute guidance activity for the class, including examples of activities and evaluation procedures. Creating interest, involvement, and opportunities for class members' participation is a significant part of the presentation, as well as developmental appropriateness to the grade level and theme.
   b. Copies of lesson plans, activities, and resources should be made available to all students enrolled via CourseDen (see Appendix C). Due Week 11. *Course objectives: 1–3*
4. Professional Identity Project. Students will develop a professional identity section for a professional portfolio. The portfolio section will consist of the following:
   a. A professional disclosure statement that will be used to communicate clearly and concretely to school-aged clients the nature of counseling and the limits of services offered, counselor qualifications, expectations, and boundaries.
   b. A reflection paper that includes a description of the active professional association memberships, professional development activities (e.g., workshops, conferences), and wellness strategies used by the counseling student to develop and maintain a professional identity as a counselor. The student reflects on the identified activities and strategies to describe how effective they have been, what the student has learned, and how the learning has informed the student's professional identity development.
   c. Finally, the student describes the ethical decision-making model that he or she will consistently use to respond to ethical dilemmas. In addition, the student will reflect upon his or her personal ethics to identify those that may conflict with professional ethical standards. For each area identified, the counseling student will describe steps for addressing these conflicts. Due Week 13.

TENTATIVE COURSE OUTLINE

The schedule below is a suggestion for course organization. It begins with the big view of schooling in general and its purposes and goals. This introduction is useful, particularly for SCIT who do not have a background in education. The focus then moves from this general overview of education to the school counselor's role in the educational enterprise. From there, the focus narrows to school counseling programs and their components and the skills counselors need to be effective program managers. In addition to the assigned readings each week, a sampling of books, articles, and websites that have proven useful in expanding students' understanding of the material and its application is included.

WEEK	*TOPICS*	*SAMPLE INSTRUCTIONAL RESOURCES**
Week 1	Course overview; School counselor identity	http://www.schoolcounselor.org/ (ASCA) State SCA website http://www.counseling.org/ (American Counseling Association) http://www.cacrep.org (CACREP) State school board website
Week 2	Academic excellence for all Overview of the profession of school counseling	http://nces.ed.gov/fastfacts/ (National Center for Educational Statistics) http://www.childtrendsdatabank.org/index.cfm (Child Trends Data Bank) http://www.edtrust.org/dc/tsc (National Center for Transforming School Counseling)
Week 3	Systemic change, leadership, advocacy, collaboration, and teaming	Trusty, Mellin, and Herbert (2008) http://www.schoolcounselor.org/ (ASCA) http://www.edtrust.org/dc/tsc (National Center for Transforming School Counseling)
Week 4	Comprehensive school counseling programs	http://www.schoolcounselor.org (ASCA) State Department of Education school counseling website (e.g., Georgia) ASCA (2005)
Week 5	Data-driven school counseling programs	Lewis and Hatch (2008) http://www.aecf.org/MajorInitiatives/KIDSCOUNT.aspx (Kids Count) http://nces.ed.gov/nationsreportcard/ (National Assessment of Educational Progress)
Week 6	Program evaluation	Daniels (2010) Stone and Dahir (2010)
Week 7	Facilitating academic transitions	Galassi and Akos (2007)
Week 8	Midterm exam	

Week 9	Guidance curriculum	Wittmer and Thompson (2006) Pearson (2009)
Week 10	Individual planning	http://www.ed.gov/index.jhtml (U.S. Department of Education) http://www.schoolcounselor.org (ASCA) American School Counselors Association. (2004). *The ASCA national model workbook*. http://www.acrnetwork.org (America's Career Resource Network http://www.ncda.org (National Career Development Association) http://www.collegeboard.com (College Board) Milsom (2006) Peterson (2006)
Week 11	Responsive services	Costin, Drouhard, and Kress (2006) McAdams and Schmidt (2007) Metcalf (2008) Parsons (2006) Thompson and Henderson (2006) http://www.nasponline.org/resources/crisis_safety/index.aspx (National Association of School Psychologists website) http://www.peerprogramprofessionals.org/ (National Association of Peer Programs website)
Week 12	System support	http://www.schoolcounselor.org (ASCA) Loesch and Ritchie (2009) DePaul, Walsh, and Dam (2009) Sabella (2007) Taub (2006)
Week 13	Legal and ethical issues	Remley, Hermann, and Huey (2003)
Week 14	Academic development guidance presentation	
Week 15	Career development guidance presentation	
Week 16	Personal social guidance presentation	

* Full citations for books and articles listed appear in reference list.

CONCLUSION

Although the particulars of a course such as this one will vary, almost every program has at least one content course where school counseling students are oriented to their new profession. The version described here includes instructional experiences designed to help students understand the ways in which school counselors function in the broader context of the school. Ideally, SCIT leave this course equipped to develop, implement, and evaluate accountable programs; adept at using data to drive decisions about program priorities; determined to be leaders who advocate for the underserved in their schools; and aware of legal and ethical issues common to school counseling practice. For me, the opportunity to influence SCIT's acquisition of knowledge, development of skill, and the demonstration of an optimistic attitude about making a difference in the lives of school-aged youth is a privilege. I also enjoy the development throughout the semester of a professional identity that includes a perception of self as leader, advocate, and collaborator as well as counselor. My favorite part of the course is the very end when students present their program plans. They have generally experienced dissonance, confusion, and frustration during the completion of this task. Each time I teach this course, I am pleased to note that the majority of students emerge from that confusion expressing confidence in their abilities to lead programs and certainty in their commitment to the profession.

For those developing or teaching such a course, especially for the first time, the temptation to include too much material is strong. Rather than overload the course, one might look for ways to integrate some of the essential school counseling content or learning objectives into other foundation courses. For example, rather than spend a lot of time focusing on group counseling in schools as part of this course, focus on helping students understand how the skills and knowledge they acquire in a group counseling course are used in the delivery of responsive services (ASCA, 2005) within a school counseling program. Similar to the way counselor educators encourage school counseling students to work with teachers to help deliver parts of the guidance curriculum, school counselor educators might work with non-school faculty to help them contextualize the foundational material they teach to the work of school counselors. Finally, expressing a passion for school counseling and education in general, emphasizing the rewards associated with the work at least as much as the challenges, and demonstrating an open, accepting attitude toward widely varying perspectives helps students develop dispositions that will be helpful to them as they pursue careers in school counseling.

APPENDIX A

SCORING RUBRIC FOR PROGRAM DEVELOPMENT ASSIGNMENT

PROGRAM COMPONENT	*1. UNACCEPTABLE (<60)*	*2. COMPETENT (60–75)*	*3. PROFICIENT (65–75)*	*4. OUTSTANDING (75–75)*
Foundation	Weak statement of philosophy that does not include an agreed-upon belief system about the ability of every student to achieve Weak mission statement that partially reflects the school's needs and does not clearly link to the vision and mission statement and does not clearly reflect students' growth and developmental needs in the areas of academic, career and personal/social development Competencies and indicators are identified for each applicable grade level that poorly link to the counseling program's mission, goals	Satisfactory statement of philosophy that includes an agreed-upon belief system about the ability of every student to achieve Good mission statement reflecting the school's needs, linking to some extent with the vision and mission statement Developmentally appropriate and measurable competencies and indicators are identified for each applicable grade level that partially link to the counseling program's mission, goals	Good statement of philosophy that includes an agreed-upon belief system about the ability of every student to achieve Strong mission statement clearly reflecting the school's needs, linking with the vision and mission statement and reflecting students' growth and development Developmentally appropriate and measurable competencies and indicators are identified for each applicable grade level and directly link to the counseling program's mission, goals	Exemplary statement of philosophy that includes an agreed-upon belief system about the ability of every student to achieve and includes ethical guidelines and standards Exemplary mission statement clearly reflecting the school's needs, linking with the vision and mission statements and reflecting student growth and developmental needs in the areas of academic, career. and personal/social development Developmentally appropriate and measurable competencies and indicators are identified for each applicable grade level and directly link to the counseling program's mission, goals
Delivery system	Poor: classroom guidance unit is not tied to the ASCA national standards	Good: classroom guidance unit linked to the ASCA national standards and to	Strong: classroom guidance unit composed link directly to the ASCA national	Exemplary: classroom guidance unit link directly to the ASCA national

	or linked to ASCA or school competencies or indicators and school counseling program goals	ASCA or school competencies/indicators and school counseling program goals	standards and to ASCA or school competencies/ indicators and school counseling program goals	standards and to ASCA or school competencies/ indicators and school counseling program goals
			The units are comprehensive enough to enable students to master the appropriate standards and competencies and indicators	The units are comprehensive enough to enable students to master the appropriate standards and competencies and indicators and evaluation methods are clear and appropriate
Management	The percentage of time spent in delivery does not reflect the ideal/suggested use of time	The percentage of time spent in delivery reflects the idea/suggested use of time	The percentage of time spent in delivery correlates with the ideal/suggested use of time	The percentage of time spent in delivery highly correlates with the ideal/suggested use of time
	Calendars are not realistic or representative of the appropriate grade-level activities	Calendars reflect these percentages but do not necessarily correspond with program priorities	Calendars are descriptive and reflect the time allocations	Calendars are sufficiently detailed to convey level of activity, congruence with time allocation, developmental appropriateness, and attention to developmental transitions to parents, administrators, and faculty
			Developmental transitions are clearly represented in activities noted	
Program advocacy	Brochures and websites are not descriptive and fail to reflect the work of the counselors and the goals of the program	Brochures and websites are descriptive and generally reflect the work of the counselors and the goals of the program	Brochures and websites are appropriately descriptive and accurately reflect the work of the counselors and the goals of the program	Brochures and websites are appropriately descriptive and accurately reflect the work of the counselors and the goals of the program
Accountability	Means of assessing program effectiveness are unclear or not included	Means of assessing program effectiveness are described	Means of assessing program effectiveness are clear and appropriate	Means of assessing program effectiveness are clear and appropriate

PARTICIPATION RUBRIC FOR ASSIGNMENT TWO (25 POINTS)[a]

Please complete the information below and submit privately on the day your program assignment is due. Please list yourself first next to the *.

GROUP MEMBERS	*NEEDS IMPROVEMENT (0–18)*	*COMPETENT (18–21)*	*OUTSTANDING (22–25)*
(Please list all members of your group, including yourself* below. Based on the criterion to the right, assign the number of points earned by each in your honest estimation)	Member did not attend all planning sessions and did not follow up with group members following absence(s) Member was pessimistic, complaining, or otherwise a negative force in the group Member did not make an equitable contribution to the development of the program	Member actively participated in planning each week. In case of absence, member actively sought information from group about what he or she might do in order to compensate for absence Member contributed ideas, research, and other labor at a rate sufficient to achieve program development goals Member was cooperative, optimistic, and motivated to develop a meaningful program	Member was present at every class session during which the group worked on their plans Member actively engaged in discussions about group project both inside and outside of class Member contributed ideas, research, and other labor beyond what was absolutely necessary in order to develop the program Member was cooperative, optimistic, and motivated to develop a meaningful program
*			

[a] Points awarded to each member of the group will be totaled and divided by the number of group members to derive an average from 1 to 25 for each participant.

SHADOWING PAPER RUBRIC

CRITERIA	*UNACCEPTABLE*	*ACCEPTABLE*	*PROFICIENT*	*EXEMPLARY*
Description of the school and program	(10 points) Did not follow the assignment outline and/or provided inadequate information to demonstrate understanding of program observed	(15 points) Misses one or two of the key descriptors but provides adequate coverage of topic	(18 points) Thorough description of the school, counselor's role, innovative programs, positive and negative aspects of program	(20 points) Thorough description of the school, counselor's role, innovative programs, positive and negative aspects of program Includes personal reflection on the program observed
Identification of skills used	(5 points) Did not follow the assignment outline and/or provided inadequate information to demonstrate understanding of necessary skills.	(10 points) Misses one or two of the key skills sets, but provides adequate information to demonstrate understanding of skills needed	(13 points) Identifies leadership, time management, theoretical, and technological skills used by the counselor	(15 points) Identifies leadership, time management, theoretical, and technological skills used by the counselor. Also identifies additional important skills needed to do the job well
Relationship to course	(5 points) Did not draw any parallels to what he or she is learning in class about school counseling programs	(10 points) Made some reference to course material but not in depth	(13 points) Drew parallels between course objectives and program observed	(15 points) Provided in-depth information, including personal reflection, about differences between course material and program observed

COLLABORATIVE PROJECT: CLASSROOM GUIDANCE UNITS SCORING RUBRIC: CONTENT

GRADE LEVELS	*UNACCEPTABLE (<40)*	*ACCEPTABLE (35–40)*	*PROFICIENT (40–45)*	*EXEMPLARY (45–50)*
	Literature-based rationale is missing or inadequate to justify the need for the unit	Literature-based rationale is included and provides sufficient support for the unit and the lessons are designed to meet group objectives	Literature-based rationale is well developed and provides strong support for the unit and the lessons are designed to meet group objectives	Literature-based rationale is well developed and provides strong support for the unit and the lessons are designed to meet group objectives
	Lesson plans are not consistent with unit objectives and seem unlikely to achieve desired outcomes	Lesson plans are consistent with unit objectives and seem likely to result in desired outcomes	Lesson plans are consistent with unit objectives and seem likely to result in desired outcomes	Synthesis and integration are apparent
	Lessons too old or too young for the intended audience and are not clearly connected to the lessons at the next level	Lessons are developmentally appropriate	Lessons are developmentally appropriate and provide a foundation for the next grade level	Lesson plans are consistent with unit objectives and seem likely to result in desired outcomes
	Expected outcomes are not clearly related to ASCA competencies specified for unit	Expected outcomes are clearly linked to ASCA competencies specified for the unit	Expected outcomes are clearly linked to ASCA competencies specified for the unit	Lessons are developmentally appropriate and provide a foundation for the next grade level
	Outcomes are not measurable	Outcomes are measurable	Outcomes are clear and measurable	Lessons are creative and engaging

	Materials, procedures, and resources are not clearly explained/identified	Materials, procedures, and resources are clearly explained/identified	Materials, procedures, and resources are clearly explained/identified and cited	Expected outcomes are clearly linked to ASCA competencies specified for the unit
	No measures for evaluating success are identified or included	Measures used to evaluate effectiveness are identified but may not be sufficient to assess intended outcomes	Measures used to evaluate effectiveness are included and are clearly related to intended outcomes	Outcomes are clear and measurable and specify the level(s) of attainment necessary to be successful
				Materials, procedures, and resources are clearly explained/identified and cited such that another counselor could easily deliver the lessons
				Measures used to evaluate effectiveness are included, are clearly related to intended outcomes, and include improvements in areas essential to school success (e.g., attendance, behavior, etc.)
Elementary				
Middle				
Secondary				

PARTICIPATION RUBRIC FOR GUIDANCE LESSONS (25 POINTS)[a]

Please complete the information below and submit privately on the date your unit is due.

GROUP MEMBERS	*NEEDS IMPROVEMENT (0–18)*	*COMPETENT (18–21)*	*OUTSTANDING (22–25)*
(Please list all members of your group, including yourself,* in the space below. Based on the criteria to the right, assign the number of points earned by each in your honest estimation)	Member did not attend all planning sessions and did not follow up with group members following absence(s) Member was pessimistic, complaining, or otherwise a negative force in the group Member did not make an equitable contribution to the development, cohesion, or comprehensiveness of the unit	Member actively participated in planning each week. In case of absence, member actively sought information from group about what he or she might do in order to compensate for absence Member contributed ideas, research, and other labor at a rate sufficient to achieve a comprehensive, developmental set of lessons for the unit Member was cooperative, optimistic, and motivated to develop a meaningful unit	Member was present at every class session during which the group worked on their plans Member actively engaged in discussions about group project both inside and outside of class Member contributed ideas, research, and other labor beyond what was absolutely necessary in order to design the unit Member was cooperative, optimistic, and motivated to develop a meaningful unit
*			

[a] Points awarded to each member of the group will be totaled and divided by the number of group members to derive an average from 1 to 25 for each participant.

GUIDANCE LESSON PRESENTATION EVALUATION FORM

Group Members: ______________________________

Evaluator: ____________________ Date: ____________

Presentation Topic: ______________________________

CRITERIA	*PTS.*	*COMMENTS*
Lesson Design and Development (4)		
___ Clear explanation of goals and procedures		
___ Developed in effective sequence		
___ Concludes with review and clear focus		
___ Has needed materials, supplies, and equipment on hand		
Presentation of Information (13)		
___ Begins by capturing and focusing audience attention		
___ Individual differences in learning are accommodated		
___ Reviews adequately but not excessively		
___ Effective; good oral, written, visual presentation skills for this set of students		
___ Students are attentive		
___ Students are responsive		
___ Uses body posture, movement, and gestures to complement, not distract from lesson		
___ Points are logically linked		
___ Examples are used to support points		
___ Humor is used appropriately		
___ Changes tone of voice and facial expression to maintain interest, pace of lesson		
___ Clear logical questions are posed		
___ Multiple instructional methods are used		
Student-Active Learning (3)		
___ Clearly focused; clear instructions		
___ Effective (significant part of lesson)		
___ Assignments/Activities require critical thinking		
Classroom Management (25)		
___ Positive, educational, supportive environment		
___ Respect for students is demonstrated		
___ Student questions are encouraged		
___ Student questions are answered		
___ Student participation is reinforced		
Total Points	25	

Comments:

APPENDIX B

Checklist for Comprehensive School Counseling Program

Title page:
Name of School System
Name of Counselors-in-Training

1. Foundation
   - Philosophy
     - ☐ A statement of philosophy has been written for the school counseling program
     - ☐ Indicates an agreed-upon belief system about the ability of every student to achieve
     - ☐ Addresses every student's right to a school counseling program
     - ☐ Includes a plan of closing-the-gap activities for underserved student populations
     - ☐ Focus is on primary prevention, intervention, and student-developmental needs
     - ☐ Identifies the persons to be involved in the delivery of program activities
     - ☐ Identifies who will plan and who will manage the program
     - ☐ Defines how the program will be evaluated and by whom
     - ☐ Includes ethical guidelines and standards
   - Mission statement
     - ☐ A mission statement has been written for the school counseling program
     - ☐ Written with the student as the primary client
     - ☐ Written for every student
     - ☐ Indicates the content or competencies to be learned
     - ☐ Links with the vision, purpose, and mission of the state, district, and school
     - ☐ Indicates the long-range results desired for all students
   - Domains, competencies, and indicators (ASCA model)
     - ☐ Goals have been written for the school counseling program
     - ☐ Reflect the domains in the ASCA national standards for school counseling programs (academic, personal/social, career)
     - ☐ Identifies the developmental structure for the school counseling program from K through 12 (and beyond) and what will be measured
     - ☐ Student competencies have been written that directly relate to the domains (academic, career, personal/social)

- ☐ Developmentally appropriate student competencies are specified for each grade-level grouping
- ☐ Selected competencies are based on assessment of student needs and are measurable or observable
- ☐ Goals demonstrate the link with the school counseling program mission, the school's mission, and expected student results

- Program priorities (3-year plan)
  - ☐ Priorities for implementing the program have been established based on the needs evident in the school system at each level
  - ☐ Year one: What needs will be addressed and in what way(s)?
  - ☐ Year two: What additional needs will be met and in what way(s)?
  - ☐ Year three: What additional needs will be addressed and in what way(s)?

2. Delivery System
   - Guidance Curriculum
     - ☐ Guidance curriculum for all three domains has been written and adopted based on local site needs
     - ☐ All students receive, in a systemic way, the content to acquire knowledge, attitudes, and skills to enhance their academic, career, and personal/social development
     - ☐ Content is measurable (by pre–post tests, product creation, or other methods)

   - Individual Planning (not required for this project)

     Note: You may have developed classroom guidance materials that are intended to facilitate career and educational planning. If so, they may be placed in this section along with other programs or plans you develop, or developed, in the career class

   - Responsive Services
     - ☐ Description of the group of students identified through review of the Annie E. Casey Kids Count data
     - ☐ Proposed program/intervention to respond to difficulties
     - ☐ References used to identify best practices used with students in need

     Note: If you have already developed small group counseling plans, individual plans, or consultation plans that would fit into this category in other courses, you may want to add samples when you are finished with this class and refining the program for your use

   - System Support
     - ☐ Master calendars are included that reflect counseling program goals
       One annual calendar that provides an overview in a glance at the topics/content covered each month

Once-monthly calendar that provides specific information about counselor's program, including the balance between types of delivery reflected in the time allocations section

- ☐ Time allocations: What percentage of time will be spent in each of the four recommended delivery systems (guidance curriculum, individual planning, responsive services, systems support)? If you deviate from the recommended ratio, provide a rationale for that decision
- ☐ Budget/resources
  Includes an estimate of the financial and human resources necessary to implement the 3-year plan described in the section above
- ☐ Management agreement with administration
  Sample agreement that will be pursued with building- and system-level administrators regarding program and priorities, time allocations, resource allocation

3. Program Advocacy
   - ☐ Program brochure (What do you want others to know about your program in a brief, brochure format? Publisher has a good brochure maker)
   - ☐ School staff presentation (Brief PowerPoint presentation that you might use to communicate with staff at the beginning of the year the highlights of your program; 10-slide limit)
   - ☐ Parent presentation (Slightly revised version of PowerPoint above to convey to parents the basics of the program; 10-slide limit)
   - ☐ Website (Describe what you would include on such a site)

4. Accountability
   - ☐ Assess Program Results (Based on your program priorities, how will you assess whether you have achieved goals?
   - ☐ Manage Student Progress (What performance indicators will be used (GPA, Attendance, Discipline referrals, test scores, enrollment patterns, etc.) to determine whether responsive services needs have been met?)

APPENDIX C

Classroom Guidance Units Cover Page—Title of the unit, Purpose of the unit, Grade level(s), Your names

1. Identify the student competencies being addressed by this unit and provide a literature-based rationale for the unit (Why is such a unit needed? What do these competencies contribute to students' ability to succeed in school?)
2. For each lesson (four to six depending on grade levels and topic), complete an activity lesson plan following the outline below.

- Session Title
- Session Goals (Should be clearly linked to the unit purpose and stated in terms of who will do what and to what extent)
- ASCA Standards (expected student outcomes for lesson)
- Materials
- Procedure
- Data

REFERENCES

Alexander, P. A. (2006). *Psychology in learning and instruction.* Upper Saddle River, NJ: Pearson.

American School Counselor Association (2005). *The ASCA National Model: A framework for school counseling programs* (2nd ed.). Alexandria, VA: Author.

Cobia, D., & Henderson, D. (2007). *Developing an effective and accountable school counseling program* (2nd ed.). Upper Saddle River, NJ: Pearson.

Costin, A., Drouhard, N., & Kress, V. E. W. (2006). Students who self-injure: School counselor ethical and legal considerations. *Professional School Counseling, 10*, 203–209.

Council for the Accreditation of Counseling and Related Educational Programs. (2009). *2009 CACREP Standards.* Retrieved from http://www.cacrep.org

Daniels, M. H. (2010). Systematic program evaluation. In C. Sheperis, J. S. Young, & M. Daniels (Eds.). *Counseling research: Quantitative, qualitative, and mixed methods* (pp. 173–186). Upper Saddle River, NJ: Pearson.

DePaul, J., Walsh, M. E., & Dam, U. C. (2009). The role of school counselors in addressing sexual orientation in schools. *Professional School Counseling, 12*, 300–308.

Galassi, J. P., & Akos, P. (2007). *Strengths-based school counseling: Promoting student development and achievement.* New York: Routledge.

Lewis, R., & Hatch, T. (2008). Cultivating strengths-based professional identities. *Professional School Counselor, 12*, 115–118.

Loesch, L., & Ritchie, M. H. (2009). *The accountable school counselor* (2nd ed.). Austin, TX: Pro-ed.

McAdams, C. R., III, & Schmidt, C. D. (2007). How to help a bully: Recommendations for counseling the proactive aggressor. *Professional School Counseling, 11*, 120–128.

Metcalf, L. (2008). *Counseling toward solutions.* San Francisco, CA: Jossey-Bass.

Milsom, A. (2006). Creating positive school experiences for students with disabilities. *Professional School Counseling, 10*, 66–72.

Parsons, R. (2006). *Counseling strategies that work.* New York: Allyn & Bacon.

Pearson, A. (2009). *Guidance with good measure.* Chapin, SC: Youth Light.

Peterson, J. S. (2006). Addressing counseling needs of gifted students. *Professional School Counseling, 10*, 43–51.

Remley, T. P., Hermann, M. A., & Huey, W. C. (Eds.) (2003). *Ethical and legal issues in school counseling* (2nd ed.). Alexandria, VA: American School Counseling Association.

Sabella, R. A. (2007). School counseling and technology. In J. Wittmer, & M. Clark (Eds.), *Managing your school counseling program: K–12 developmental strategies.* Minneapolis, MN: Educational Media.

Stone, C. B., & Dahir, C. A. (2010). *School counselor accountability: A MEASURE of student success* (3rd ed.). Upper Saddle River, NJ: Merrill Prentice Hall.

Taub, D. J. (2006). Understanding the concerns of parents of student with disabilities: Challenges and roles for school counselors. *Professional School Counselor, 10*, 52–57.

Thompson, C. L., & Henderson, D. A. (2010). *Counseling children* (7th ed.). Belmont, CA: Brooks/Cole.

Trusty, J., Mellin, E. A., & Herbert, J. T. (2008). Closing achievement gaps: Roles and tasks of elementary school counselors. *Elementary School Journal, 108*, 407–421.

Wittmer J., & Thompson, D. (2006). *Large group counseling: A K–12 sourcebook.* Minneapolis, MN: Educational Media.

Human Growth and Development
Merging Life Span Development With the Counseling Process

4

Bill McHenry and Jim McHenry

As with each of the individual courses you have read about in this text, the coursework directly related to theories of human development helps provide students with useful knowledge and skills to better meet the needs of their future clients. Additionally, as with the other courses, the theories and approaches housed within the human development domain are not stand-alone ideologies but can, and should, be infused into other coursework within a comprehensive counselor education program. What we offer in the pages that follow are our suggestions about how to best meet the needs of your students in this course. We believe this is effectively accomplished by merging theory with practice in order to better prepare students to work effectively with the diverse clientele they may serve during their professional careers.

WHAT WE HOPE STUDENTS GET FROM THIS COURSE

Before considering other aspects of a course on human development, note should be made that in many institutions the course is often covered by a department other than counselor education. Many universities, for example, offer a psychology or educational human development course at the master's level that can be utilized to fulfill this course requirement. In our opinion, such courses often fail to fully meet the academic and counselor development needs of our students. Therefore, although we are completely aware of the presses that universities and departments often have bearing upon them regarding allocation of resources, we suggest that it is generally preferable for counselor education programs to assume the major responsibility for teaching this course to insure that counseling students receive the most counselor-related approach to human development possible. We are, incidentally, not alone in this preference; we have seen a number of programs "take back" the course and fold it back into their staffed offerings. Finally, on this matter, in cases where staffing is not possible, for whatever reason, it is incumbent upon the counselor education department to insure that the course presented be as closely related to the needs of matriculating counselor education students as possible.

However delivered, the challenge in delivering this course is to help students successfully meld a broad range of major theories of development into their counseling skill set in a mere 15 weeks. Two key questions to consider when teaching this class: Where is this course placed within the student's plan of work (program of study)? What general background do students typically possess when they reach this particular point in their program?

WHERE IS THE HUMAN DEVELOPMENT COURSE PLACED WITHIN THE CURRICULUM?

Conscious and purposeful decisions must be made in developing counselor education programs that best help students as they develop into practitioners. Charting this development then requires decisions regarding what the best typical course sequence might be for matriculating students. Interestingly enough, the human development course can be found in a number of different places in various counselor training programs. For some, it is regarded as a necessary prerequisite to many courses and is therefore placed within the first few classes. Other programs treat it as an elective and allow students to take it whenever it fits into their schedules. Without making a broad (and possibly indefensible) statement about where programs should place this course, we suggest that counselor educators' considerations here be based largely on the general makeup and needs that their program students present and want to remind you of the importance of considering the overall makeup of the students in your particular course.

Are the students primarily brand new to the program? If so, then it follows that they will not have anchor points such as coursework in overall counseling theories and clinical skills (e.g., practicum). Further, they may also be so new to the program that they are still wed to the undergraduate style of "take notes, memorize notes, pass test on notes." Often, significant encouragement and opportunities for students to become active, reflective thinkers is then warranted.

Is there a mix of students at various stages of their educational experience in the course? In this case questions abound as to how to best craft the class in a fashion that utilizes the skills of the advanced students to engage new students, while simultaneously creating an environment where advanced students in the program are sufficiently challenged to find the work meaningful.

WHAT STUDENTS TYPICALLY ARRIVE WITH

Interestingly, this is one of the courses in a counselor education program where some, if not most, students have completed earlier undergraduate study. In many instances, students have been exposed to many of the primary theories as a part of their general and/or educational psychology coursework or may have actually taken a class in the area of human development or life span. Consequently, we usually begin by determining whether students are at all familiar with theories such as Erikson's (1963) psychosocial stage model, or Piaget's (1978/1985) cognitive development model. Often we, hear something like, "Yeah, I remember that theory . . . well, I remember us talking about it . . . uh oh, now you are going to expect me to know something about it!" Consequently, many students arrive with vague and somewhat limited working relationships with developmental theories. Fortunately, however, through methods such as mini-lectures, we find that many students are soon able to recall and begin to recall aspects of the models and thus move quickly to a position of possessing a considerable amount of useful material.

The other major position students often bring to the course (and this is especially true if they have had an undergraduate course in stage theories) is the notion that knowing stage theories means that you have memorized the stage names and associated tasks/issues. We have found this position to be a quite challenging and yet a critically important hurdle to cross in helping students make the jump from rote acquisition of knowledge to actual skill implementation. Our goals, of course, are to help students gain a true understanding of different developmental models, to help them learn how to recognize developmental aspects in their clients, and to help them develop at least a beginning ability to work successfully with clients within different stage models.

COMMON DILEMMAS AND DECISION POINTS

As with any counselor education course, a number of decisions need to be made to best ensure student success. We have provided a guide to considering how best to craft this course. As discussed previously, the goals of the course, knowledge and skills of the students, and placement within the program are key factors in helping with these decisions. We have created this table in binary format but fully recognize that many dilemmas and decisions are not simply either/or but rather a combination or some sort of the two. Note that items in option 1 may sometimes be less challenging than some of those in option 2.

COMMON DILEMMAS IN TEACHING HUMAN DEVELOPMENT

DILEMMA OR DECISION POINT	*OPTION 1*	*OPTION 2*
Number of theories covered	One theory every couple of classes	Two or more theories each class session
Type of practice	Role-plays	With a real client
Type of instruction	Lecture	Group work
Type of videos	Movies	Counseling tapes
Measurable outcomes	Papers	Tests
Definition of *human development*	Primary theories that cover all people	Primary theories plus identity theories (e.g., minority individual development)

NECESSARY AND CRITICAL COURSE COMPONENTS

By our nature as professors, counselors, and individuals, we struggle to suggest that anything *must* be placed within this course. Having noted our resistance to prescribing delineated content, however, we do believe that there may be several items that are vital, even critical, to the success of the course. The following items appear because we find them to be essential when we teach this class. This list contains items that are both pragmatic and philosophical in nature.

1. A comprehensive review of major theories of development on each of the following aspects of human functioning:
   a. Cognitive
   b. Moral
   c. Psychosexual
   d. Social
2. A review of special topics, with direct implications for development, that have been agreed upon as significant; for example:
   a. Grief/loss
   b. Identity
   c. Addictions
   d. Spirituality
3. Assignments that require students to apply the material to client cases, the counseling process, and client concerns/solutions.
4. A recognition that human development takes shape in individuals in significantly different ways (e.g., what may look like *mistrust* in Erikson's model may actually be a safety issue for a woman who is gay [Cass' Identity Model, 1979]).

OBJECTIVES AND CACREP STANDARDS

1. To understand major tenets of human development (both individual and family) and the associated implications throughout the life span. (Section II.G.3.a.)
2. To integrate several developmental theories as applicable to case and client understanding and clinical work. (Section II.G.3.e.)
3. To understand and apply human development theory in a variety of professional counseling settings. (Section II.G.3.f.)
4. To learn how human development (life span) theory provides counselors tools for client conceptualization, treatment planning, and clinical work (including intrapersonal, interpersonal, and systemic interventions). (Section II.G.3.b.; Section II.G.3.d.)
5. To provide students with learning opportunities that include demonstrating interviewing, case conceptualization, conceiving developmentally appropriate and developmentally designed interventions, and treatment planning. (Section II.G.3.c.; Section II.G.3.f.; Section II.G.3.g.)
6. To help students learn to work together profitably in task groups and to give and receive meaningful, corrective feedback.

CRITERIA FOR EVALUATING A TEXT

A valuable text should be one that not only provides an overview of theories but moves on to present a refined analysis and discussion of the ways in which the counseling process can be enriched with a deeper understanding of human development. One major factor in evaluating texts for this particular course is to look for those that purposefully and thoroughly include clinical case examples and counseling connections to human development, especially those that utilize various perspectives (theories) and case work with different types of clients.

We want to offer one more perspective on the literature available for this course. Part of our style of teaching has included the use of novels as an adjunct to comprehensive textbooks. We have found that novels and stories present richly written characters, thus giving great opportunities to aid students in capturing essence and meaning into life span and developmental issues.

MOST POPULAR TEXTS

Broderick, P. C., & Blewitt, P. (2010). *The life span: Human development for helping professionals* (3rd ed.). Upper Saddle River, NJ: Pearson Prentice Hall.

Crain, W. (2011). *Theories of development: Concept and applications* (6th ed.). Upper Saddle River, NJ: Prentice Hall.

Kail, R. V., & Cavanaugh, J. C. (2004). *Human development: A lifespan view* (3rd ed.). Belmont, CA: Wadsworth.

Kraus, K. (2008). *Lenses: Applying lifespan development theories in counseling*. Belmont, CA: Wadsworth.

Newman, B. E., & Newman, P. R. (2012). *Development through life: A psychosocial approach* (11th ed.). Belmont, CA: Wadsworth.

SUPPLEMENTAL READING

Gilligan, C. (1993). *In a different voice: Psychological theory and women's development* (Reissue ed.). Cambridge, MA: Harvard University Press.

Grealy, L. (2003). *Autobiography of a face*. Eastsound, WA: Turtleback.

Kegan, R. (1982). *The evolving self: Problem and process in human development*. Cambridge, MA: Harvard University Press.

Maclean, N. (1976). *A river runs through it*. Chicago, IL: The University of Chicago Press.

Middleton, H. (1996). *The earth is enough*. Boulder, CO: Pruett Publishing Company.

Pelzer, D. (1995). *A child called it*. Deerfield Beach, FL: Health Communications.

Topics related to life span development are discussed in various journals. Some of the counseling-specific journals that carry articles related to life span development are *Journal of Counseling and Development*, *AdultSpan Journal*, *Journal of Multicultural Counseling and Development*, and *Journal of Humanistic Counseling and Development.*

Topic: Social Constructionist Theory

Roy-Chowdhury, S. (2010). Is there a place for individual subjectivity within a social constructionist epistemology? *Journal of Family Therapy, 32*, 342–357.

Topic: Psychosocial Development

Marcia, J. E. (2002). Identity and psychosocial development in adulthood. *Identity: An International Journal of Theory and Research, 2*, 7–28.

Stevenson, F., & Zimmerman, M. A. (2005). Adolescent resilience: A framework for understanding healthy development in the face of risk. *Annual Review of Public Health, 26*, 399–419.

Topic: Addiction

Bancroft, J., & Vukadinovic, Z. (2004). Sexual addiction, sexual compulsivity, sexual impulsivity, or what? Toward a theoretical model. *The Journal of Sex Research, 41*, 225–234.

Bonebright, C. A., Clay, D. L., & Ankenmann, R. D. (2000). The relationship of workaholism with work–life conflict, life satisfaction, and purpose in life. *Journal of Counseling Psychology, 47*, 469–477.

Shaffer, H. J., & Kidman, R. (2003). Shifting perspectives on gambling and addiction. *Journal of Gambling Studies, 19*, 1–6.

Topic: Gender Identity Development

Boisnier, A. D. (2003). Race and women's identity development: Distinguishing between feminism and womanism among Black and White women. *49*, 211–218.

Lucas, M. (1997). Identity development, career development, and psychological separation from parents: Similarities and differences between men and women. *Journal of Counseling Psychology, 44*, 123–132.

Peterson, S. (2000). Multicultural perspective on middle-class women's identity development. *Journal of Counseling and Development, 78*, 63–71.

Zukanovic, R. (2005). Identity development in men and its relation to psychosocial distress and self-worth. *Canadian Journal of Behavioural Science, 37*, 70–81.

Topic: Sexual identity Development

Elze, D. (2002). Risk factors for internalizing and externalizing problems among gay, lesbian, and bisexual adolescents. *Social Work Research, 26*, 89–99.

Hammack, P. (2005). The life course development of human sexual orientation: An integrative paradigm. *Human Development, 48*, 267–290.

King, L., & Smith, N. (2004). Gay and straight possible selves: Goals, identity, subjective well-being, and ego development. *Journal of Personality, 75*, 967–994.

Konik, J., & Stewart, A. (2004). Sexual identity development in the context of compulsory heterosexuality. *Journal of Personality, 72*, 815–843.

Singh, A., Dew, B., Hays, D., & Gailis, A. (2006). Relationships among internalized homophobia, sexual identity development, and coping resources of lesbian and bisexual women. *Journal of LGBT Issues in Counseling,* 15–32.

Tozer, E., & Hayes, J. (2004). Why do individuals seek conversion therapy? The role of religiosity, internalized homo-negativity, and identity development. *The Counseling Psychologist, 32*, 716–740.

Topic: Racial Identity Development

Castillo, L. G., Conoley, C. W., King, J., Rollins, D., Rivera, S., & Veve, M. (2006). Predictors of racial prejudice in White American counseling students. *Journal of Multicultural Counseling and Development, 34*, 15–26.

Villalba, J. A. Jr. (2007). Culture-specific assets to consider when counseling Latina/o children and adolescents. *Journal of Multicultural Counseling and Development, 35*, 15–25.

Topic: Grief and Loss

Wilson, A. (2009). Counseling children and adolescents through grief and loss. *Journal of Counseling & Development, 87*, 127–128.

NUMBER OF THEORIES COVERED

Other than, perhaps, the counseling theories course, no other course in the typical curriculum requires such attention from week to week on different major theories and associated concepts. For this reason, one decision that must be made is whether to try to cover many theories throughout the semester or handpick a few to focus upon very heavily.

There are pros and cons to both of these options. Picking a few major theories probably improves the likelihood that material will be covered at greater depth than trying to cover many theories. However, because this course is frequently the only one that focuses on theories of human development, failing to at least introduce different theories, especially ones different from those covered in typical undergraduate coursework, may be quite a significant omission. It also may place students at a disadvantage when they take their respective licensing examinations. Therefore, because one of the primary goals of this course is to prepare students to work with different people in different life stages, a good argument can be made for covering a multitude of different theories. To this effort we have found that most human development courses in counselor education programs attempt to cover at least one theory each class session.

TYPE OF PRACTICE

As with many other courses in counselor education, having students practice skills associated with the course material can be invaluable. Giving students the opportunity to hone and shape their counseling skills as they learn to better understand client issues and problems (in this case, in a developmental way) cannot be overvalued. However, as was noted earlier in this chapter, counseling programs sometimes place this course early in the educational process (or do not have a specific point, allowing the student to take it at any point). Therefore, an ethical and professional decision needs to be made by the course instructor regarding how she or he might structure hands-on experience (of course, that is, if this is a part of the course). In this regard, we have found that this class usually lends itself readily to in-class peer-to-peer role-play and mock interviews.

TYPE OF INSTRUCTION

In many counselor education programs, the first thing the students often do when they get to class is check to see whether the chairs are arranged in a circle. This is because our field relies so heavily on constructed meaning through language and discussion in the classroom. Although even statistics and research courses can be taught from a constructivist position, we have found that of the many courses offered in a counselor education program, the human development course typically requires that a significant amount of lecture materials be delivered on theoretical and developmental stage concepts. Although, of course, each instructor will craft his or her course in his or her own style, it is important to realize that there is a substantial volume of standard material that students need to know regarding the different theories and models being presented. Failing to help them acquire this baseline knowledge will be problematic when they are asked to synthesize and extrapolate from the theories in a meaningful way (e.g., when asked to apply multiple theories to a case).

The use of lecture, of course, must be balanced with the needs of the students in the room, especially within the structure of the typical types of courses being taught in the program. If your program relies heavily on lectures, students are apt to become more comfortable with this format; however, if, as with many programs of which we are aware, your program values group discussion, class time allocated to small-group work, and the like, it may be very important to develop this course in a fashion that skillfully utilizes these techniques to augment lecture materials. Actually, we have found that students' interest and enthusiasm for almost any subject usually drops appreciably if lectures extend much past 45 minutes to an hour. Though this might be a critique of our teaching, we see it as more of a commentary on the depth and heaviness of the theories being presented. To keep students truly engaged with topics such as Vygotsky's (1962) theory of cognitive development, we have found great benefit through coupling instructor lecture material with exercises and activities that give students an opportunity to attempt to apply the theory.

MEASURABLE OUTCOMES

In today's academic climate of accountability and measurable learning outcomes, it is imperative to consider the placement of assessment tools within the class (and, of course, how the course fits within the overall programmatic goals for student learning). Having used both tests and written assignments as means of assessing student retention and application of material, we are able to speak of the value of both. Again, though, we recognize and encourage autonomy on the part of the instructor to engage in best practices within their department and university to best measure student performance.

Tests that require minor application but significant amounts of retention aid students in assuring their knowledge of the theories of human development. In instances when we have used tests prior to application papers, we have found that students seemed to have a greater grasp on the different theoretical language. Additionally, mastery of key elements of developmental theories is essential if students are to successfully challenge state and nationally mandated licensure/certification exams (e.g., the National Counselor Examination). However, one drawback we have found in focusing students' attention directly at the language of the theories is that they may then tend to focus on knowing human development at a seemingly superficial level. Terms and phrases get tossed around with little depth or meaning. In essence, the course then becomes simply a more stringent form of an undergraduate course on human development. Remember, facts lead to conceptualizations, which, eventually—and hopefully—result in student self-direction.

In instances where we have relied heavily on the application of theories upon clinical cases in papers we have found that many students can generate meaningful case analyses. Although this seems to be a prevailing way to assess student acquisition of knowledge across our field, there are some limitations with this approach. Simply having students apply theoretical concepts without having them learn the basic underpinnings can leave the case analysis unconnected, lacking in cohesion. In essence, the papers seem to be parts of several theories moderately woven together.

Of course, these are not clearly delineated poles that one must choose between. Rather, we have found a mix of the two can provide students with necessary language and a deeper reflection and understanding of human development.

DEFINITION OF WHAT *HUMAN DEVELOPMENT* MEANS

One bit of advice we give to students in our statistic, research, and assessment courses is to make sure they understand the operational definition of the construct. We try to heed our own advice when it comes to teaching a course on human development. Incredibly important decisions lie in the choice of which theories we choose to highlight and, consequently, what we want students to recognize about human development and its application to the counseling process.

In a recent survey of developmental stage models, we found that there are well over 100 models to pick from within the common literature. This represents quite a bit of material to try to pack into a 15- or 16-week course. Obviously, decisions must be made about what will and will not be introduced regarding human development. For example, is career development theory part of human development? How about addiction/recovery developmental models? Should grief and loss models be introduced in this course as an aspect of human development? Is the construct of human development only covered by our understanding of developmental models?

The clearer the definition of human development is for the instructor, the easier it will be for students to garner the necessary information and skills presented in the course. Because human development, by its very nature, can be so limitless in definition, instructors must be purposeful in how they (and the department) want to define and teach it to students.

LEARNING ACTIVITIES

- *Small-Group Discussion of Video*—Reviewing and then having small-group discussions around a counseling video that demonstrates an individual struggling with a specific life issue related to stage theories being presented. For example, we find that using a counseling video that demonstrates cognitive or cognitive–behavioral therapy is an excellent connection when reviewing the cognitive development chapter.
- *Focus on a Developmental Issue*—Reviewing movie clips and then having students focus on aspects of the "case" presented using multiple theoretical models. An example of this is from the movie *Footloose* during the scene where the lead characters are driving along talking and she tells him that the reason her minister father doesn't like drinking and dancing is related to the untimely death of her brother (a death that was directly related to drinking).
- *Interview*—Pairing students to complete partner interviews anchored to developmentally based questions. This instructor-developed instrument is

used as a pre- and postassessment for students to evaluate how much deeper they have learned to *hear* others from the start of the semester to the end. Students are paired up in the first class to discuss the questions and then again at the end of the semester. The class discussion revolves primarily around the newly formed understandings the students have regarding partner responses in relation to the models.

- *Demonstrations of Counseling Techniques*—Through live demonstrations, the instructor can *show* students how theory comes to practice and how we can recognize developmental concerns within client issues.

AUDIOVISUAL MATERIAL

- *The Iceman*—In this video, students are introduced in interview format to a man who worked as a hit man for the mafia—killing many individuals through his infamous career as a "hired thug." His demeanor, language, stories, and nonverbal communication during the interviews are both chilling and fascinating. Though only one hour in length, the video captivates students by both the presence of the individual and the developmental issues that his story suggests.
- *Right to Die*—The synopsis of this powerful movie is a woman leading what might be considered by many as the picturesque family life until she is diagnosed with Lou Gehrig's disease (atrophic lateral sclerosis; ALS). Initially, she puts up a valiant fight against the disease. However, her condition rapidly turns for the worse, leaving her in a nearly vegetative state. She then pleads with her husband to help her die.
- *Above the Rim*—This movie powerfully captures the struggle a young man has as he is torn between two worlds (basketball and the streets). Capturing cultural and development issues, the movie offers students a chance to discuss and better understand the complex interplay among individual, cultural, and career development issues.

ASSIGNMENT

Paper—The written paper contains several key pieces:

- A section that requires the student to construct a client case that is developmentally based.
- A section that requires the student to demonstrate case analysis skills related to issues across the life span.

- A section that requires students to highlight selected skills and techniques applicable to developmentally based client issues.
- In addition to the above-mentioned sections, we have found several items that we like to stress in our written assignments:
  - Use of multiple theories
  - Inclusion of multiple stages across the life span
  - Specificity regarding the relationship between developmental causation and issues with thoughts, actions, and behaviors
  - Less emphasis on "knowing what stage they are stuck in" and more focus on how a counselor might effectively facilitate optimum human development

TENTATIVE COURSE OUTLINE

WEEK	*CONTENT/TOPIC(S) COVERED*
Week 1	Introduction to the course
Week 2	Psychosocial theory
Week 3	Major theories for understanding human development
Week 4	Prenatal development & infancy
Week 5	Toddlerhood & early school age
Week 6	Middle childhood
Week 7	Early adolescence
Week 8	Late adolescence
Week 9	Early adulthood
Week 10	Middle adulthood
Week 11	Late adulthood
Week 12	Special topic: Death and dying across the life span
Week 13	Special topic: Racial and gender identity development
Week 14	Special topic: Sexual identity and spiritual/moral development

CONCLUSION

We are pleased and honored to offer our thoughts to you on some of the ways to consider developing your course on the subject of human development. Some of the most touching feedback we have received from students has been that our courses offer them the chance to understand how to use these theories and concepts in real-life counseling. Such should be the goal of each of our courses—utility beyond simply knowing theory.

Any course on human development should have the following components: review of the major theories, explanation and perhaps practice in using such theories, and an emphasis on development as a lifelong process.

In sum, our final thoughts are that counseling students need to understand human developmental theory. They need to know the current accepted understandings existing in the field of human developmental. It is also vital that students gain experience in utilizing their knowledge of human development. And, finally, and possibly most significant, effective counselors need to be able to incorporate the client's worldview in the counseling process.

REFERENCES

Boisnier, A. D. (2003). Race and women's identity development: Distinguishing between feminism and womanism among Black and White women. *Sex Roles: A Journal of Research, 49*, 211–218.

Cass, V. C. (1979). Homosexual identity formation: A theoretical model. *Journal of Homosexuality 4*, 219–235.

Erickson, E. (1963). *Childhood and society* (2nd ed.). New York, Norton.

Land, M., Vromen., A., Bleiberg, E., Davidson, B., Dimbort, D., Donnermeyer, N., Jolivette, V., . . . Short, T., (Producers), & Vromen, A. (Director). (2011). *The Iceman* [Motion picture]. USA: Bleiberg Entertainment, Millennium Films, & RabbitBandini Productions.

Ohlmeyer, D., (Producer), & Wendkos, P. (Director). (2007). *The right to die* [Motion picture]. USA: First Run/Icarus Films.

Piaget, J. (1978/1985). *The equilibration of cognitive structures.* Chicago: University of Chicago Press.

Pollack, J., Medina, B., Cooper, B. M., (Producers), & Pollack, J. (Director). (1994). *Above the rim* [Motion picture]. USA: New Line Cinema.

Rachmil, L. J., Melnik, D., Zadan, C. (Producers), & Ross, H. (Director). (1984). *Footloose* [Motion picture]. USA. Paramount Pictures.

Singh, A., Dew, B., Hays, D., & Gailis, A. (2006). Relationships among internalized homophobia, sexual identity development, and coping resources of lesbian and bisexual women. *Journal of LGBT Issues in Counseling, 1*, 15–32.

Vygotsky, L. S. (1962). *Thought and language.* Cambridge, MA: MIT Press.

5

Multicultural Counseling

Training Culturally Intentional, Competent, and Ethical Counselors for the 21st Century

Sherlon Pack-Brown, Sarah Coulter, and LaShonda Fuller

The demographics of North Americans have changed during the beginning of the 21st century. Larger numbers of multicultural and diverse populations are evident. Clinical mental health and school counselors are more than ever called to serve many populations who differ in values, life experiences, and worldviews. The American Counseling Association (ACA) and the American School Counseling Association have begun to address cultural and social realities and the impact of differences on counseling in their codes of ethics. Counselors, for example, are informed in the Preamble to the 2005 *ACA Code of Ethics* that they are to operate in an ethical framework that recognizes diversity and also embraces a cross-cultural counseling approach that supports the worth and dignity of those they serve, within social and cultural contexts.

This chapter provides general suggestions for counselor educators designing an introductory master's-level course to foster the development of culturally and socially intentional and competent counselors for the 21st century. The chapter is written by three authors committed to training ethical counselors who recognize diversity and embrace a cross-cultural approach in support of the worth, dignity, potential, and uniqueness of people within their social and cultural contexts (ACA, 2005).

Editors' Note: The nature of this course content is by definition an integral component of an individual's identity and self-perception, much more so than other course content in the counselor education curriculum, such as assessment or psychopathology. As a result, even among highly accomplished senior faculty whose chosen specialty is multiculturalism and diversity issues, there are varying perspectives and values about what is most important in teaching a multiculturalism course. Due to the unique relationship between the instructor and this particular course material, we chose to present here a dialogue among the three chapter authors, each of whom holds a somewhat different and unique view about responses to the questions of pedagogy in this course.

The authors represent diverse levels of experience and expertise. Sherlon Pack-Brown is a counselor educator with over 19 years of experience teaching an introductory master's-level multicultural counseling course. LaShonda Fuller is a doctoral candidate in a counselor education program and has taken and taught an introductory master's-level multicultural counseling course. Sarah Coulter has completed a master's-level multicultural counseling course and facilitates prejudice reduction and diversity training workshops in a university setting.

A DIALOGUE AMONG THE AUTHORS

Question One: Generally What Do Students Need to Get From This Course?

Sherlon: While there are many needs students bring to the course, I believe a fundamental issue is students' need to enhance their awareness of personal beliefs, attitudes, and assumptions regarding multiculturalism and diversity. In doing so, students need to become comfortable while talking about and working with difference. They also need to build a strong multicultural and social justice counseling foundation.

LaShonda: I agree with Sherlon. My students needed to be challenged with cultural counseling opportunities allowing them to engage in self-exploration pertaining to learned behavior and self-containing biases, prejudices, and stereotypes leading to unjust cultural understandings and discriminatory or racist behavior. Therefore, based on this alone, students need to get from this course more than a general understanding of multicultural counseling.

Sarah: As a student, it was helpful for me to acknowledge that helping theories and techniques generated within one cultural context may not be appropriate for use in other cultural contexts. It was important for me to walk through the process of approaching different cultural contexts with intentionality, identifying ethical considerations that are relevant to counseling clients who are culturally different from myself, and developing increased awareness, knowledge, and skills for counseling members of specific populations.

Question Two: What Are Common Dilemmas and Decisions Instructors Need to Make?

Sherlon: Over the years I have experienced a number of dilemmas that influence my decisions about how best to teach the multicultural course. A tight spot for me is that students seem to reach an impasse when asked to acknowledge that "difference" exists and can be a powerful counseling tool. My challenge as a culturally intentional and ethical instructor is deciding how to theoretically and clinically respond to three questions. (a) How do I help students comfortably recognize difference as a life reality? (b) How do I help students use difference as a healing tool? (c) What can I do to facilitate adoption of an ethical approach to counseling individuals and communities different from students within a cultural and social justice framework?

LaShonda: In my experience as a counselor educator and as a student and coteaching a multicultural counseling course for three consecutive semesters, I have experienced my White students having difficulty with discussing the idea of "system thinking" as it pertains to privilege, racial identity, and culture; therefore, instructors need to incorporate within class discussions, readings, and assignments the concept of system thinking as it relates to privilege (superiority vs. inferiority) and ensure the classroom is a safe place to have controversial discussions relative to current events (the world we live in) and history (the world that molded our thinking and behaviors) to better prepare our students for social justice issues that will confront them as future counselors and advocates.

Sarah: As a student in the class, I observed a tension between covering a broad range of critical topics and the need for in-depth analysis, processing, and application of those topics. In my student role, I especially appreciated opportunities to apply classroom learning in concrete, specific situations. Processing case studies and real-world experiences was particularly helpful, since this gave me the opportunity to walk step-by-step through the process of acknowledging and addressing difference in counseling relationships. However, in-depth processing can take a great deal of time, time that may be needed for covering additional topics.

Question Three: What Topics Are Absolutely Critical for the Course?

Sherlon: First, I help students construct a foundation so they can hear, interpret, and receive course theory and practice in regards to their work as counselors in a diverse and global society. By that I mean I help students discern what they cognitively, affectively, and physically bring to the course and potentially to their work as counselors so they can more accurately hear with multicultural and social justice ears and look through multicultural and social justice lenses as we progress through the semester. Pillars of the foundation include students' awareness of their

- culturally biased assumptions;
- personal biases, prejudices, stereotypes of working with difference;
- individual and cultural values, worldviews, and life experiences;
- knowledge regarding thematic (common) cultural values, worldviews, life experiences of people different from them; and
- fundamental understanding of multiculturalism, social justice, and advocacy competence.

LaShonda: I believe it is critical students first become aware of their accrediting body's stance on multiculturalism to give students a complete understanding of how important multiculturalism is to their profession. With that said, a historical overview on race in the counseling profession and how multiculturalism became a component of counseling is critical for counselors in training to become knowledgeable of and is important for students to be able to speak to and should therefore be an introductory topic of class discussions.

Sarah: One topic that should be addressed is intersectionality (i.e., how clients may experience oppression around multiple identities simultaneously). A discussion of culturally appropriate intervention strategies would be beneficial as well. Cultural appropriation is an especially important topic for students as they seek to identify and implement culturally appropriate interventions without borrowing cultural traditions or material inappropriately.

OBJECTIVES AND CACREP STANDARDS

To address these common needs and dilemmas, the authors have developed a list of objectives that describe what students should accomplish during the course. Each objective is supported by select Council for Accreditation of Counseling and Related Educational Programs (CACREP) standards. The multicultural counseling course should enable students to

1. Demonstrate an understanding of professional orientation and ethical practice as expressed in the history and philosophy of the counseling profession. (Section II.G.1.a.)
2. Identify their emotional, physical, and psychological responses to economically, socially, and culturally diverse populations and the subsequent impact

thereof on their client's/student's empowerment. (Section II.G.2.b.; Section II.G.2.e.; Section II.G.2.f.)

3. Identify helping tools needed to construct a helping foundation that promotes effective counseling behaviors and conduct with diverse and multicultural communities. (Section II.G.2.c.; Section II.G.2.d.)
4. Identify ethical (ACA *Code of Ethics*) and cultural (AMCD competencies and ACA advocacy competencies) characteristics needed by counselors (and related professionals) to sensitively and appropriately serve multicultural and diverse populations. (Section II.G.2.a.; Section II.G.2.e.)
5. Determine when and how to advocate for diverse populations living within diverse social and cultural milieus. (Section II.G.2.d.; Section II.G.2.e.)
6. Expand technological competence and computer literacy via generating and offering a PowerPoint presentation highlighting ethical and social justice counseling and/or multicultural counseling strategies with multicultural and diverse individuals, families, groups, and/or communities. (Section II.G.2.a.; Section II.G.2.d.; Section II.G.3.b.; Section II.G.3.d.; Section II.G.3.f.; Section II.G.3.h.)
7. Explain and demonstrate how racial identity development impacts the counseling (helping) relationship, process, and outcome. (Section II.G.3.h.)
8. Identify and understand multicultural, social, and pluralistic trends between and within diverse groups. (Section II.G.1.i.; Section II.G.2.a.)
9. Generate a state (all Ohio counselors) and/or national (ACA) conference proposal to facilitate the movement of counselors (helping professionals) from awareness to action in appropriately serving diverse and multicultural populations. (Section II.G.1.f.; Section II.G.1.i.; Section II.G.3.f.)

COURSE RESOURCES

A constant challenge for educators is selecting appropriate resources that will facilitate reaching course objectives and promoting sensitivity and competence among students as they attend to cultural and social justice issues, work within the cultural context of those they serve, and advocate for individuals and communities.

CRITERIA FOR EVALUATING A TEXT

The following are the criteria for evaluating a text in multicultural counseling. An adequate text should

- Address multiculturalism, diversity, social justice, advocacy, and ethics within a cultural framework.

- Provide case examples and concrete recommendations for practice with clients from various cultures.
- Provide readings on sensitive topics such as racism, sexism, and systems of oppression that will help instructors prepare students for difficult discussions.

MOST POPULAR TEXTS

Hays, D. G., & Erford, B. T. (2010). *Developing multicultural competence: A systems approach.* Loyola College.
Helms, J. E., & Cook, D. A. (1999). *Using race and culture in counseling and psychotherapy.* Needham Heights, MA: Allyn & Bacon.
Pack-Brown, S. P., & Williams, C. B. (2003). *Ethics in a multicultural context.* Thousand Oaks, CA: Sage.
Sue, D. W. (2003). *Overcoming our racism: The journey to liberation.* San Francisco, CA: Jossey-Bass.
Sue, D. W., & Sue, D. (2008). *Counseling the culturally diverse* (5th ed.). New York: Wiley & Sons.
Wu, F. (2002). *Yellow: Race in America beyond Black and White.* New York: Basic Books.

SUPPLEMENTAL ARTICLES

Topic: Cultural and Social Justice Competence: Enhancing Awareness

American Counseling Association. (2005). *2005 ACA code of ethics.* Alexandria, VA: Author.

Topic: Cultural Intentionality, Multicultural and Advocacy Competence

Arredondo, P., Toporek, R., Brown, S. P., Jones, J., Locke, D. C., Sanchez, J., & Stadler, H. (1996). Operationalization of the multicultural competencies. *Journal of Counseling and Development, 25*, 42–78.
Bell, T. J., & Tracey Terence, J. G. (2006). The relation of cultural mistrust and psychological health. *Journal of Multicultural Counseling and Development, 34*, 2–14.
Caldwell, L. D., Tarver, D. D., Iwamoto, D. K., Herzberg, S. E., Cerda-Lizarraga, P., & Mack, T. (2008). Definitions of multicultural competence: Frontline human service providers' perspective. *Journal of Multicultural Counseling and Development, 36*, 88–100.
Salyers, K. M., & Ritchie, M. H. (2006). Multicultural counseling: An Appalachian perspective. *Journal of Multicultural Counseling and Development, 34*, 130–142.
Sue, D. W., Arredondo, P., & McDavis, R. J. (1992). Multicultural counseling competencies and standards: A call to the profession. *Journal of Counseling and Development, 70*, 477–486.

Sue, S. (1998). In search of cultural competence in psychotherapy and counseling. *American Psychologist, 53*, 440–448.
Villalba, J. A., Jr. (2007). Culture-specific assets to consider when counseling Latina/o children and adolescents. *Journal of Multicultural Counseling and Development, 35*, 15–25.

Topic: Racism, Oppression, Difference (Counseling Different Ethnic Populations)

Castillo, L. G., Conoley, C. W., King, J., Rollins, D., Rivera, S., & Veve, M. (2006). Predictors of racial prejudice in white American counseling students. *Journal of Multicultural Counseling and Development, 34*, 15–26.
Deyhle, D., & LeCompte, M. (1994). Cultural differences in child development: Navajo adolescents in middle schools. *Theory Into Practice, 33*, 156–165.
Dovidio, J. F., Gaertner, S. L., Kawakami, K., & Hodson, G. (2002). Why can't we all just get along? Interpersonal biases and interracial distrust. *Cultural Diversity & Ethnic Minority Psychology, 8*, 88–102.
Hong, G. K. (1993). Contextual factors in psychotherapy with Asian Americans. In J. L. Chin et al. (Eds.), *Transference and empathy in Asian American psychotherapy* (pp. 3–13). Westport, CT: Praeger.
Hwang, W. (2006). Acculturative family distancing: Theory, research, and clinical practice. *Psychotherapy: Theory, Research, Practice, Training, 43*, 397–409.
Martinez-Taboas, A. (2005). Psychogenic seizures in an espiritismo context: The role of culturally sensitive psychotherapy. *Psychotherapy: Theory, Research, Practice, and Training, 42*, 6–13.
McIntosh, P. (1990). White privilege: Unpacking the invisible knapsack. *Independent School, 49*, 31–35.
Miller, K. E., Martell, Z. L., Pazdirek, L., Caruth, M., & Lopez, D. (2005). The role of interpreters in psychotherapy with refugees: An exploratory study. *American Journal of Orthopsychiatry, 75*, 27–39.
Pedersen, P. (1987). Ten frequent assumptions of cultural bias in counseling. *Journal of Multicultural Counseling and Development, 15*, 16–24.
Ponterotto, J. G., Utsey, S. O., & Pedersen, P. B. (2006). Part II. In *Preventing prejudice* (2nd ed., pp. 57–145). Thousand Oaks, CA: Sage.
Willow, R. A. (2008). Lived experience of interracial dialogue on race: Proclivity to participate. *Journal of Multicultural Counseling and Development, 36*, 40–51.

Topic: Racism, Oppression, Difference (Counseling Sexual Minorities)

Cain, R. (1991). Stigma management and gay identity development. *Social Work, 36*, 67–73.
Dworkin, S. H. (2002). Individual therapy with lesbian, gay, and bisexual clients. In R. M. Perez, K. A. DeBord, & K. J. Bieschke (Eds.), *Handbook of counseling and psychotherapy with lesbian, gay, and bisexual clients* (pp. 157–181). Washington, DC: American Psychological Association.
Garnets, L. D. (2002). Sexual orientations in perspective. *Cultural Diversity & Ethnic Minority Psychology, 8*, 115–129.

Topic: Racism, Oppression, Difference (Poverty and Social Class)

Smith, L. (2005). Psychotherapy, classism, and the poor. *American Psychologist, 60*, 687–696.

Topic: Racism, Oppression, Difference (Religious Privilege)

Schlosser, L. Z. (2003). Christian privilege: Breaking a sacred taboo. *Journal of Multicultural Counseling and Development, 31*, 44–51.

Topic: Racism, Oppression, Difference (Counseling the Differently Abled)

Lambie, G. W., & Milsom, A. (2010). A narrative approach to supporting students diagnosed with learning disabilities. *Journal of Counseling & Development, 88*, 196–203.

Olkin, R. (2002). Could you hold the door for me? Including disability in diversity. *Cultural Diversity & Ethnic Minority Psychology, 8*, 130–137.

Topic: Skill Development

Alberta, A. J., & Wood, A. H. (2009). A practical skills model for effectively engaging clients in multicultural settings. *The Counseling Psychologist, 37*, 564–579.

Cartwright, B. Y., Daniels, J., & Zhang, S. (2008). Assessing multicultural competence: Perceived versus demonstrated performance. *Journal of Counseling & Development, 86*, 318–322.

Gone, J. P. (2010). Psychotherapy and traditional healing for American Indians: Exploring the prospects for therapeutic integration. *The Counseling Psychologist, 38*, 166–23.

Leary, K. (2000). Racial enactments in dynamic treatment. *Psychoanalytic Dialogues, 10*, 639–653.

Maxie, A. C., Arnold, D. H., & Stephenson, M. (2006). Do therapists address ethnic and racial differences in cross-cultural psychotherapy? *Psychotherapy: Theory, Research, Practice, Training, 43*, 85–98.

Pope-Davis, D. B., Toporek, R. L., Ortega-Villalobos, L., Ligiero, D. P., Brittan-Powell, C. S., Liu, W. M., . . . Liang, C. T. H. (2002). Client perspectives of multicultural counseling competence. *The Counseling Psychologist, 30*, 355–393.

WEBSITES

Topic: Racism, Oppression, and Difference

- Project Implicit (The Implicit Association Test/IAT)
  https://implicit.harvard.edu/implicit/demo/selectatest.html
  Project Implicit is a hands-on exhibit designed to allow visitors to examine and understand their biases, attitudes, and stereotypes. The IAT measures unconscious roots of thinking and feeling to promote awareness of personal beliefs and preferences. Students completing the IAT examine (a) what they might not be willing to share regarding private attitudes and (b) attitudes that they may be unaware of. Content of the IAT includes, but is not limited to, age, race, and gender.

Topic: Cultural and Social Justice Competence

- Ed Change—Diversity, Multicultural, Cultural Competence, Inclusion, & Social Justice Training
  http://www.edchange.org
  Ed Change is a team of educators dedicated to equity, diversity, multiculturalism, and social justice who collaborate to provide professional development, research, and a site of resources for diversity, multiculturalism, and cultural competence in contribution to a progressive change in ourselves, schools, and society. The website provides information on workshops and training opportunities, consulting, research and publications, and free handouts for downloading.

Topic: Preparing for the Real Life Classroom

http://www.latinoteca.com

Latinoteca is a website published by Arte Publico Press. It contains information about Latino/a culture, history, music, literature, art, and current issues. Extensive free excerpts from books published by the Press may be downloaded and used for class discussion. Students may also use the website to search for books published by the Press.

Topic: Preparing for the Real Life Classroom

http://www.asiannation.org

Asian Nation is created by Dr. C. N. Le, a sociologist and director of Asian Studies at the University of Massachusetts–Amherst. The website consists of a series of articles by Dr. Le that introduce students to Asian American history, culture, and sociopolitical issues.

LEARNING ACTIVITIES AND ASSIGNMENTS

Over the course of 19 years, 57 semesters, and with approximately 900 students, the activities and assignments presented below have helped students (a) construct a culturally intentional, competent, and ethical counseling foundation and (b) make decisions about human rights, equality, and justice while serving multicultural and diverse clients.

Consultation Presentation

The consultation presentation is a major engagement activity and assignment designed to help students create a plan for moving a fictional counselor from cultural incompetence to competence when serving a client/student that self-identifies as a member of one of the American communities (ethnicity, gender, sexuality, social class, religion, and communities with special abilities) studied during the semester. Each team must consult with the counselor within a culturally appropriate context. Teams must research the core cultural values, worldviews, and life experiences of the community they have been assigned. They must (a) identify a counseling problem and (b) diagnose the problem within the cultural context of the client/student. Finally, each team must research four dimensions of cultural competence and divide their presentation into sections corresponding to each dimension.

- Dimension Number One—Promoting Cultural Awareness and Sensitivity: Students engage in activities that help them identify what beliefs, attitudes, and biases they bring to counseling that may impact culturally appropriate services. One way students do this is to create a case scenario that depicts a counselor providing culturally incompetent services to a person different from him or her in culture, life experiences, values, and worldviews. Critical to this assignment is identifying the counselor's biases, prejudices, attitudes, and assumptions.
- Dimension Number Two—A Critical Analysis—Enhancing Cultural Knowledge: Students engage in activities to enhance their knowledge of worldviews, life experiences, and values of the population on which they are presenting. For example, students complete an in-depth analysis of the cross-cultural scenario, looking for cultural issues such as language,

class-bound variables, and culture-bound variables between the counselor and client/student.

- Dimension Number Three—Developing Introductory Skills: Students engage in a number of activities to (a) promote the development of introductory counseling skills such as racial identity development and communication across cultures; (b) enhance knowledge about working within the cultural context of the community on which they are presenting by generating a counseling theory and assessing culturally biased assumptions inherent to the theory; and (c) promote advocacy behaviors on behalf of their community.
- Dimension Number Four—Moving from Awareness to Action: Each team concludes with a PowerPoint teaching classmates ways to counsel within the cultural context of a person that self-identifies with the community the team has been assigned to study. The presentation is followed by a demonstration of (and opportunity to practice) one intervention that is culturally sensitive and appropriate for working within the cultural and social contexts of the team's community.

The rubric for grading this activity is provided in Appendix A.

Real-Life Classroom

The real-life classroom (RLC) is designed to intensify student's self-awareness about differences and enrich knowledge about multiculturalism and diversity. Students leave the academic classroom and venture into the *real-world classroom* to experience, first hand, the cultural values, worldviews, and life experiences of the communities studied. Students participate in real-life experiences that challenge multidimensions of their beings. They confront their cognitions (thoughts), emotions (feelings), and physical behaviors (behaviors that they engage in) regarding differences and similarities between the multicultural and diverse communities studied and themselves.

The timeframe for the RLC is one month or three 3-hour class periods. At the end of the RLC, students return to the university classroom. They process the RLC by sharing experiences, thoughts, feelings, and insights believed to impact their journey toward culturally intentional, competent, and ethical counseling services with multicultural and diverse clients/students.

The RLC consists of three assignments: one mini-internship, eight cultural immersions, and RLC processing. Students map out their three journeys as follows.

Mini-Internship

Each student participates in a 10-hour mini-internship that provides an opportunity to see, first hand, how counseling professionals operate within the cultural and social contexts of the persons and communities they serve. Students work in an agency or school setting where counselors work with populations that are racially and ethnically different from them. Students are expected to incorporate what they have learned into the experience and glean what they can from the experience to facilitate developing skills (personal and professional) that are ethical, intentional, and culturally appropriate. Emphasis is placed on students' awareness, knowledge, and skills, the three dimensions of cultural competence espoused by the AMCD.

Mini-internship assignments are made early in the semester, and students can complete mini-internship hours at any time during weeks 10–14 of the course. Students must communicate with a contact person at the mini-internship site to confirm their participation at the site and to identify dates and times for completion of mini-internship hours. They must then provide the course instructor with the following information by week 8 of the class: name of the contact person, her or his job title, her or his e-mail address and mailing address, name of the agency, and ethnocultural populations served by the site.

Before students begin the experience, they are also asked to review ethical and legal considerations that should guide their work, including confidentiality, privileged communication, and privacy concerns.

Mini-internship hours must be completed by week 14, and each student must ask his or her contact person at the site to complete a feedback form verifying the number of hours completed and commenting on the student's work; the contact person then e-mails the completed form directly to the course instructor.

Cultural Immersions

Students are instructed to engage in eight cultural immersions over the course of 3 weeks. Cultural immersions are defined as opportunities for students to physically, emotionally, and psychologically immerse themselves in the different communities studied. The purpose of the immersions is to provide opportunities for students to tap many dimensions of themselves (thoughts, feelings, beliefs, etc.) and apply what they have studied to the real world. As students select opportunities of interest to them (personally and professionally), they intentionally seek experiences among each of the racial and ethnic populations studied this semester. They are informed that they may also seek to experience other forms of diversity such as sexual orientation, religion, disability, and age. The key point is to ensure that diversity emphasizes the racial and ethnic populations studied this semester.

Students are reminded as they go through the RLC that no one ethnocultural group is homogeneous, yet their goal is to identify cultural themes (e.g., values, worldviews, life experiences) that emerge in readings, cultural immersions, mini-internship, research, etc., and use this information to assist in building a more culturally intentional, competent, and ethical helping foundation. Students are required to complete cultural immersions in the American communities studied during the semester. Upon completion of the RLC, students share the following information for each cultural immersion: date of the immersion; time devoted to the experience; and site (or event) with a brief description of what they did and the mailing address of the site.

Processing the Real-Life Classroom

At the end of the RLC, students return to the university classroom to reflect on, share, and discuss their experiences and insights relative to their individual and collective journeys toward culturally intentional, competent, and ethical counseling. A powerful discussion is often generated around differences and similarities between what students read about the ethnocultural populations and what they experienced. In this discussion, students respond to questions such as the following:

- What values were identified as thematic for this population in the literature?
- What did you observe and experience in terms of similarities and differences in values?
- What life experiences did you read about that were thematic to the people you experienced?
- What observations did you have about similarities, differences, and life experiences?
- What behaviors (cognitive, affective, and/or physical) do you need to:
    - capitalize on (i.e., continue as you serve people different from you?)
    - change/modify/improve on as you serve people different from you?

Culmination of the Semester Feast, Transition Ceremony, Giving of Gifts

In an effort to bring closure to the collective journey students have undertaken and to commit to accepting the challenges of a lifelong journey toward culturally intentional, competent, and ethical counseling/helping services, the class culminates with a 2- to 3-hour feast, transition, and gift-giving ceremony. All must contribute to the planning and implementation of this event. Family members and significant others may be invited.

The three parts of this culmination activity are listed below and briefly discussed.

The Feast

The feast is a time to break bread together and prepare for transition beyond the class. A menu is developed and reflects the cultures and communities studied during the semester and/or students' own cultures.

Transition Ceremony

The guiding force of the transition ceremony is "Moving from Awareness to Action" as it relates to what has been learned during the semester. The ceremony must (a) symbolize a transition from awareness to action and (b) promote a commitment to continuing the journey toward culturally competent, ethical, and intentional helping services upon completion of the course. The ceremony is to be taken from a cultural ritual (created or researched) and may reflect one culture and community or all cultures and communities studied during the semester.

Giving of Gifts

This is one of the most influential assignments for the multicultural course. This assignment has proven valuable for students leaving as well as entering the course. The purpose of the assignment is to have students reflect on their semester experiences (e.g., challenges, insights, and issues). Students then identify a gift (purchased or made) to be shared with an incoming student. Guidelines follow.

- Identify a gift that reflects your cumulative (physical, psychological, emotional, spiritual, etc.) experiences this semester.
- Attach a message to the gift (a) stating your wish for a future student striving toward success during her or his journey in the course and (b) explaining the meaning of the gift and its implications for success in the course.
- Put the gift into a package. You determine the package and how you will present the package and message.

VIGNETTES

- Derald Wing Sue's series on racism (all four parts). Derald Wing Sue, professor of psychology and education, Teachers College, Columbia University, presents a four-part series on racism. No matter what race or ethnic origin, the series challenges viewers to take an honest appraisal of themselves and their biases and prejudices and take steps to overcome racism. Each vignette (60 minutes). Microtraining and multicultural development; http://www.emicrotraining.com
- Vignettes of culturally different counseling: working with clients different than you. Donald Pope Davis, Loreto Prieto, Amy L. Reynolds, & Luis Vazquez, New Mexico State University, present live demonstrations of multicultural counseling and therapy exploring issues of religion, physical challenge, gender, age, and language. This vignette explores internal self-talk of interviewers engaging in multicultural dialogue (49 minutes). Microtraining and multicultural development; http://www.emicrotraining.com

AUDIOVISUAL MATERIAL

Topic: Racism, Oppression, and Difference

- *The Color of Fear*
  Eight men meet for a series of intense discussions about race and racism. These conversations between African American, Asian American, European American, and Latino participants illustrate the powerful impact of racism on all, and the dynamics of cross-racial interaction. (90 minutes). Available from Stirfry Productions, http://www.stirfryseminars.com, (510)-204-8840.
  Discussion Questions: Victor says, "There's a way in which being American and White and human become synonyms."
  1. How might a counselor express their way of perceiving the world in the counseling setting?
  2. If Victor was your client, how might you respond to the anger he expresses?

Topic: Racism, Oppression, and Difference

- Tim Wise on White Privilege
  Tim Wise, author of *White Like Me: Reflections on Race from a Privileged Son*, speaks about White privilege June 25, 2002, at Bloedel Hall, St. Mark's Cathedral, Seattle. (58 minutes). Available from Media Education Foundation, http://www.mediaed.org
  Discussion Questions:
  1. What were some of the resources and assets Tim Wise identified that he had that people of color did not?
  2. What are the consequences of adopting a "colorblind" perspective?

Topic: Cultural and Social Justice Competence

- *Yellow: Race in America Beyond Black & White*
  This is an interview with Frank Wu, author of *Yellow: Race in America Beyond Black and White*. New York: Basic Books (2002). The C-SPAN interview shares Dr. Wu's perspective on race and his experience as a Chinese American.
  Discussion Questions: During the interview, Frank Wu discusses how people need to stand up for civil rights regardless of whether or not they are directly attacked;
  1. As a counselor in training, how will you advocate for civil rights?

2. Frank Wu speaks about how Chinese Americans have had it easier than African Americans. How does Frank Wu speak of the difficulties African Americans have endured?

Topic: Multicultural and Advocacy Competence

- *In Whose Honor: American Indian Mascots in Sports*
  The film documents the struggle of one Native American graduate student, Charlene Teters, to resist appropriation of Native American cultural symbols (46 minutes). Available from New Day Films, 22-D Hollywood Ave., Hohokus, NJ. (201) 652-6590.
  Discussion Questions:
  1. How did Charlene Teters' struggle to end the practice of adopting American Indian mascots reflect thematic values of the Native American community?
  2. What other cultural products or symbols have been appropriated by privileged groups?
  3. What might you do as a counselor to advocate against cultural appropriation?

TENTATIVE COURSE OUTLINE

The following is a tentative schedule for a 15-week, 3-semester-hour introductory course. The course is divided into three sections. Each section emphasizes a specific dimension of the multicultural competencies as proposed by Arrendondo et al. (1996) through the Association for Multicultural Counseling and Development (AMCD) and endorsed by the American Counseling Association.

The first 5 weeks (inclusive of the precourse developing rapport assignment) of the semester emphasize dimension one of the multicultural competencies and promotes cultural and social justice competence. Students are taught that culturally skilled counselors possess knowledge and understanding of how oppression, racism, and other forms of discrimination affect their counseling. Students engage in experiences, dialogues, and assessments designed to promote awareness of their individual and collective biases, prejudices, stereotypes, and forms of discrimination that may impact their work with clients, students, or communities different from them in areas such as race, ethnicity, religion, gender, socioeconomic status, and sexual orientation. An emphasis is placed on differences in values, worldviews, and life experiences and the subsequent impact on personal attitudes, beliefs, and feelings regarding cultural intentionality, multicultural, social justice, and advocacy competence. The first section concludes with enhancing awareness of the impact of communication and racial identity development on providing culturally intentional, competent, and ethical counseling services.

SECTION 1 (4 WEEKS): CULTURAL AND SOCIAL JUSTICE COMPETENCE

ENHANCING COUNSELOR AWARENESS

WEEK	*FOCUS: CULTURAL AND SOCIAL JUSTICE COMPETENCE*
Precourse	Developing Rapport
Week 1	Cultural Intentionality Multicultural and advocacy competence • Identification of emergency notification system • Multicultural and social justice counseling and ethics In-class assignment: Complete the implicit test
Week 2	Cultural Intentionality Racism, oppression, and difference • Guidelines for consultation team presentations • Consultation team presentation assignments In-class assignment: Initiate plans for consultation presentation (team work)—Generate conference proposal Generate consultation team theory Generate outline for presentation
Week 3	Cultural Intentionality Racism, oppression, and difference • Multicultural and advocacy competencies (dominant [European American/Christian/heterosexual/middle class/male/nondisabled] worldview, values, and privileges) • Giving of gifts In-class exercise #1: Personal beliefs & attitudes (As a culturally intentional and competent counselor, I . . .)
Week 4	Cultural Intentionality Racism, oppression, and difference • Racial and sexual identity development • Cross-cultural communication

Section 2 of the semester is designed to advance cultural and social justice competence. During this time, students offer group presentations. Their primary purpose is to move from awareness to action in theory and practice when providing culturally intentional, competent, and ethical counseling services to communities and individuals different from them in values, worldviews, and life experiences.

SECTION 2 (5 WEEKS): CULTURAL AND SOCIAL JUSTICE

KNOWLEDGE AND INTRODUCTORY SKILLS

WEEK	*FOCUS: CULTURAL AND SOCIAL JUSTICE COMPETENCE*
Week 5	Skill Development (2 presentations) • Serving and advocating for the African American community • Serving and advocating for the Asian American community • Serving and advocating for the Latino/a American community
Week 6	Skill Development (two presentations) • Serving and advocating for the Native American community • Serving and advocating for the Middle Eastern American community • Serving and advocating for the biracial American community
Week 7	Skill Development (two presentations) • Serving and advocating for the varying sexual orientations of the American community • Serving and advocating for the varying socioeconomic standings of the American community • Serving and advocating for the varying religious American communities
Week 8	Skill Development (two presentations) • Serving and advocating for the gender American community • Serving and advocating for American communities with disabilities (don't "dis" my ability)
Week 9	Skill Development Social justice and multicultural counseling

During the final section of the course, students enter the RLC and advance their awareness (personal attitudes, biases, stereotypes, etc.); knowledge of the values, life experiences, and worldviews of the communities studied during the semester; and preliminary skills used by practitioners working with multicultural and diverse individuals and communities. By participating within communities and among community members, student counselors get a better sense of what they think, feel, and do when interacting with human differences and similarities. In addition to having first-hand opportunities to "get a glimpse" into the lives of the communities, students also get a sense of community and individual advocacy needs.

Over a period of 3 weeks, each student must immerse her- or himself into each community studied by completing assignments such as attending a church service, eating ethnic foods, participating in ethnic programming, and interviewing a person that self-identifies as a member of one of the communities studied. In addition, each student must complete a 10-hour mini-internship working within a mental health or school setting that serves one of the populations studied. The course concludes with a feast, transition ceremony, and giving of gifts. The purpose of the ceremony is to bring closure to thoughts, feelings, and insights gained throughout the semester and commit to ongoing culturally competent and ethical counseling behavior. Following is a tentative schedule for the last 6 weeks of the course.

SECTION 3 (6 WEEKS): KNOWLEDGE AND INTRODUCTORY SKILLS IN THE RLC

WEEK	*COURSE FOCUS*
	Enhancing knowledge/developing skills
	Experiencing "real" lives, value systems, and worldviews
Week 10	Preparing for the real-life classroom • Building a strong knowledge base: Preparation for – cultural immersions – mini-internships – initiating plans for advocacy project
Week 11	RLC: Cultural immersions • African American community (church) • Asian American community (your choice) • Latino/a American community (cuisine) • Native American community (your choice) • Middle Eastern American community (your choice) • Biracial American community (your choice)
Week 12	RLC: Cultural immersions • Gender American community (your choice) • American communities with disabilities (your choice) • American communities with different sexual orientations (your choice) • American communities with different religious beliefs (your choice) • American communities with socioeconomic standings
Week 13	Return to the university classroom • Processing RLC • Finalize plans for the feast and transition ceremony and giving of gifts • Tie up loose ends regarding the advocacy project
Week 14	Implementation of advocacy project
Week 15	Feast, giving of gifts, and transition ceremony

CONCLUSION

Counselor educators (seasoned and new) are encouraged to keep three critical points in mind when training culturally intentional, competent, and ethical counselors for the 21st century. First, embrace the idea that teaching about difference, deliberately and intensely, is a viable and ethical counseling tool. Next, acknowledge your own comfort level as it relates to posing and addressing controversial beliefs, attitudes, emotions, and physical behaviors and then increase your comfort with such topics. Finally, maintain an on-going awareness of the impact of culture, social justice, and advocacy on rapport building, process, and outcome. As we pose and respond to two questions to share our experience with teaching a multicultural counseling course, we hope the information will help your journey, as counselor educators, to be more productive and enjoyable for you and your students.

Why do we enjoy teaching a multicultural counseling course? Teaching multicultural counseling allows us to have meaningful dialogue with our students on race and how race affects us as a human race. These conversations create emotions, and sometimes resistance, as students grapple with knowledge. Others experience a moment of redefining belief systems; this is the place where change takes place. Teaching, presenting, and facilitating workshops engages students in examining prejudices and systems of oppression. This is hopeful work and gives us and students a chance to change how these systems operate by examining ourselves and applying new understanding to our work and our advocacy.

Pearls of wisdom that may facilitate the focus and success of your work with students aspiring to be culturally intentional, competent, and ethical counselors: Students do not have to be rescued while they are experiencing *their* process, which may include questioning materials from class, experiences in class, and you (the instructor) or themselves. Allow students to sit with their struggle and resistance; both will indeed be a part of the process and will challenge you and your students. Students may come to a conclusion of what they truly value, serving all people or the need to be needed (serving self). However, it is important to leave sufficient time for processing students' thoughts and feelings about course activities. As a busy master's student, Sarah found herself wanting to discuss her experiences in depth, especially cultural immersion activities, which often provoked strong emotional reactions and raised many questions for her. When class time or assignments were not devoted to processing, it was easy for her to neglect processing in favor of more pressing assignments. Finally, anticipate students' anxiety and discomfort about discussing sensitive topics like racism and cultural bias. Consider allowing students to share in dyads or small groups before discussing the topics with the entire class. Students are more comfortable sharing about sensitive topics in smaller groups. Remember, the ultimate goal is that the process should create culturally intentional, competent, and ethical counselors.

APPENDIX A

CONSULTATION TEAM: MOVING FROM CULTURAL INCOMPETENCE TO CULTURAL COMPETENCE

ITEM	*POSSIBLE POINTS*	*EARNED POINTS*
Destination I: Promoting Cultural Awareness and Sensitivity		
• Case scenario		
Destination II: Enhancing Cultural Knowledge		
Critical analysis of cross-cultural scenario		
• Cross-cultural issues		
• Value differences/conflicts		
• Analysis of three worldviews: counselor, client, consultation team		
• Compare and contrast racial identity status of the counselor and client		
Destination III: Awareness to Action		
Consultation team theory of counseling within a cultural and social justice context		
Theory assessment for cultural bias		
Mission of advocacy		
Destination IV: Moving from Awareness to Action		
PowerPoint presentation		
Intervention demonstration and practice		

REFERENCES

Achenbach, K., & Arthur, N. (2002). Experiential learning: Bridging theory to practice in multicultural counseling. *Guidance and Counseling, 17*, 39–45.

American Counseling Association. (2005). *ACA code of ethics*. Alexandria, VA: Author.

Arredondo, P., Toporek, R., Brown, S., Jones, J., Locke, D. C., Sanchez, J., & Stadler, H. (1996). Operationalization of the multicultural counseling competencies. *Journal of Multicultural Counseling and Development, 24*, 42–78.

Arthur, N., & Achenbach, K. (2002). Developing multicultural counseling competencies through experiential learning. *Counselor Education and Supervision, 42*, 2–14.

Constantine, M. G., Hage, S. M., Kindaichi, M. M., & Bryant, R. M. (2007). Social justice and multicultural issues: Implications for the practice and training of counselors and counseling psychologists. *Journal of Counseling & Development, 85*, 24–29.

C-SPAN (Producer), & Moore, G. (Director). (2002). *Yellow: Race in America beyond Black and White*. USA: National Cable Satellite Corporation.

DeRicco, J. N., & Sciarra, D. T. (2005). The immersion experience in multicultural counselor training: Confronting covert racism. *Journal of Multicultural Counseling and Development, 33*, 2–16.

Guerini, F. (Producer), & Wah, L. M. (Director). (1994). *Color of fear*. USA: Stirfry Production.

Hays, D. G., & Erford, B. T. (2010). *Developing multicultural competence: A systems approach*. Upper Saddle River, NJ: Merril Prentice Hall.

Hong, G. K. (1993). Contextual factors in psychotherapy with Asian Americans. In J. L. Chin, Liem, J. H., Domokos-Cheng Ham, M.A., & Hong, G. K. (Eds.), *Transference and empathy in Asian American psychotherapy* (pp. 3–13). Westport, CT: Praeger.

Jhally, S. (Producer). (2008). *Tim Wise: On White privilege: Racism, white denial and the costs of inequality*. USA: Media Education Foundation.

Kim, B. S. K., & Lyons, H. Z. (2003). Experiential activities and multicultural counseling competence training. *Journal of Counseling and Development, 81*, 400–408.

Locke, D. C., & Kiselica, M. S. (1999). Pedagogy of possibilities: Teaching about racism in multicultural counseling courses. *Journal of Counseling and Development, 77*, 80–86.

Microtraining Associates, Inc. (Producer). (2006). *Derald Wing Sue Four Part Series on Racism*. USA: Microtraining and Multicultural Development.

Operationalization of the multicultural counseling competencies. *Journal of Multicultural Counseling and Development, 24*, 42–78.

Pack-Brown, S. P., Thomas, T. L., & Seymour, J. M. (2008). Infusing professional ethics into counselor education programs: A multicultural/social justice perspective. *Journal of Counseling & Development, 86*, 296–302.

Pedersen, P. (1987). Ten frequent assumptions of culturally bias in counseling. *Journal of Multicultural Counseling and Development, 15*, 16–24.

Ponterotto, J. G., Utsey, S. O., & Pedersen, P. B. (Eds.) (2006). *Preventing prejudice: Racial, Biracial, Multiracial, and Lesbian/Gay Identity Development and the Multicultural Personality (Part II)*. (2nd ed., pp. 57–145). Thousand Oaks, CA: Sage.

Rosenstein, J. (Producer & Director). (1997). *In whose honor: American Indian mascots in sports*. USA: New Day Films.

Seto, A., Young, S., Becker, K. W., & Kiselica, M. S. (2006). Application of the triad training model in a multicultural counseling course. *Counselor Education and Supervision, 45*, 304–318.

Sue, D. W., Arredondo, P., & McDavis, R. J. (1992). Multicultural counseling competencies and standards: A call to the profession. *Journal of Counseling & Development, 70*, 477–486.

Villalba, J. A., & Redmond, R. E. (2008). Crash: Using a popular film as an experiential learning activity in a multicultural counseling course. *Counselor Education and Supervision, 47*, 264–276.

Legal and Ethical Issues

6

Promoting Responsible Practice and Commitment to Ethical Ideals

Elizabeth Reynolds Welfel and Daniel O'Donnell

Ethics education has as its goal the development of a comprehensive understanding of the standards, values, and ethical dilemmas that characterize professional practice as a counselor. As Handelsman, Gottlieb, and Knapp (2005) noted, ethics education is, at its core, a process of acculturation into the values of the profession and a catalyst for the development of an ethical identity. Because this is such an ambitious goal, ethics education must always go beyond the confines of a single course and must be infused in every training experience if programs are to succeed in graduating counselors committed to fully responsible practice. Obviously, the development of an ethical professional identity begins with an understanding of ethics codes—their evolution, current content, and philosophical base. This task seems simpler than it really is, because no professional really grasps the standards until he or she applies them to complex cases and becomes cognizant of the connection (or disconnection) between a standard and his or her own personal values and emotional stability. The ethics literature abounds with examples of mental health professionals who failed to comply with ethical standards because they did not recognize the application of a standard to the situation they were facing or could not bring themselves to comply because of conflicting values or character flaws. Students must comprehend not only what the codes imply for their professional practice but why the codes include these provisions. The most ineffective instruction in the codes amounts to nothing more than a "pray and spray" approach to teaching, where the instructor presents slides with each standard, reads it aloud, and mentions how frequently it has been violated. Such an approach fosters the mistaken belief that ethical practice is nothing more than arbitrarily changing rules.

Students also need to grasp the relationship between professional ethics and the law. A student entering an ethics course often worries about doing something that will get him or her disciplined by the state board or sued by a client. The task of the ethics instructor is to familiarize students with the laws and regulations that govern counseling and to help them comprehend that a predominant focus on laws and regulations rather than ethical values and ideals is actually counterproductive. Whenever counselors concentrate on avoidance of breaking rules, they are losing sight of the welfare of the client and giving priority to their own interests, an action that increases rather than decreases their risk of irresponsible actions. One of the most common refrains of ethics scholars is that commitment to professional ethics reduces almost to zero the risk of litigation or disciplinary actions. In other words, ethics education should not be boiled down to risk management but must keep its attention on professional values. If counselor educators do not feel competent to review laws and legal cases, they can invite faculty from the law school or staff members from state boards as guest lecturers on the topic.

One of the dilemmas of ethics education is that when done properly, with attention to the application of ethics standards to complex cases, it engenders anxiety in students as they realize that ethics is not simply about obvious rules such as "don't have sex with clients," "report suspected child abuse," and "keep client records secure." Thus, helping students to develop a tolerance for ambiguity and offering them a model for ethical decision making to organize their thinking and emotional response to complex issues is a central task for the instructor. All of the texts listed below present helpful models for ethical decision making.

This approach to ethics education also raises internal conflicts when professional ethical values appear at odds with their personal moral values. For example, when students learn that in many states counselors must keep client disclosures of criminal acts confidential, they feel uneasy, as though they are not meeting their responsibilities as citizens to report known crimes to authorities. Or students who conceive of themselves as helpful people find some of the boundaries that must be kept in counseling difficult to honor. They also sometimes wonder why they cannot loan their clients money or why they cannot counsel a friend when these seem like humane actions to take. To respond to this dilemma it is important for instructors to foster open discussion of the students' views about such standards and to affirm the value of both personal and professional beliefs. Ultimately, the goal of ethics education is to help students integrate both personal and professional values and appreciate the role of each in professional practice (Handelsman et al., 2005). As a practical note, we frequently offer our students "bonus points" toward whenever they bring up such difficult questions in class. Faculty self-disclosure and guest presentations from practitioners about their own journeys to an ethical professional identity also help students wrestling with this conflict. (We leave the classroom when practitioners are presenting about the ethical issues in their work and their experiences along the way so that students feel free to ask questions without the presence of the ethics experts in the room.)

All ethics courses should include the following:

- Discussion and reading of the literature on ethical principles, virtues, and ethical theory so that students appreciate the source of the provisions in the codes and guidelines and deal effectively with those ethical issues in practice not directly addressed by the codes.
- Review of the types of ethical issues that have most troubled counselors over the years, including the ethical violations that have occurred and the ethical questions practitioners experience that do not result in disciplinary action against them.
- Review and application of a model of ethical decision making.
- Review of standards and research on the major dimensions of ethical practice: competence, confidentiality, informed consent, boundaries, practice with diverse populations, relationships with third-party payers and other professionals, diagnosis and assessment, multiple client situations, supervision, and practice in particular settings—for example, school, community, rehabilitation settings—and with particular age groups—for example, children, older adults, those with developmental disabilities.
- Review of self-care issues and strategies for managing the stress of coping with ethical and legal issues in practice, including practices for effective consultation with other professionals in the face of ethical questions.
- Discussion of personal accountability when one becomes aware of unethical practice, either one's own or that of other counselors.

OBJECTIVES AND CACREP STANDARDS

The standards of the Council for Accreditation of Counseling and Related Educational Programs (CACREP) and the ethics of the counseling profession have as their primary goal the promotion of ethical behavior through knowledge and critical thinking. Out of these factors flow our professional identity and a deep vision of our purpose and actions in society. The ethics course plays a vital role in developing the foundation for ethical behavior and its objectives are to assist students to:

1. Develop a thorough understanding of the ethical standards of the American Counseling Association (ACA) and the American School Counselors Association (ASCA) and their implications for programming and service delivery. (Section II.G.1.a.; Section II.G.1.g.; Section II.G.1.j.)
2. Become familiar with major legal rulings that affect the work of counselors and see the interplay between ethics and the law. (Section II.G.1.j.)

3. Understand the broader ethical principles underlying ethics codes so that students can make responsible ethical decisions about "cutting-edge" or complex ethical issues. (Section II.G.1.a.; Section II.G.1.j.)
4. Become familiar with research findings on ethical behavior of counselors and other mental health professionals. (Section II.G.1.c.)
5. Understand the relationship between personal values, emotional stability, and ethical actions as professionals. (Section II.G.1.d.; Section II.G.1.f.)
6. Become aware of emerging ethical issues and the responsible use of technology in counseling and psychotherapy and address special topics (counseling subspecialities, research, supervision, technology, teaching, etc.). (Section II.G.1.b.; Section II.G.1.c.; Section II.G.1.e.; Section II.G.1.h.)

CRITERIA FOR EVALUATING A TEXT

Instructors may have multiple considerations when choosing a text for an ethics course. Emerging technologies and the development of open-source texts may increase the number of options instructors have when choosing a text in the future and seem likely to influence how texts are used in classrooms. Though the delivery methods for content may change, the content of any text should include:

1. Accurate and comprehensive discussion of ethical standards and guidelines.
2. Discussion of the relationship between counseling ethics and relevant laws.
3. The development and history of counseling ethics.
4. An engaging perspective on current and emerging issues and research in ethics.
5. Exploration of professional identity and interdisciplinary issues.
6. Sufficient case examples and activities for self-reflection to make the topic come alive.
7. Attention to special settings such as school counseling and related topics; that is, ethics of supervision.

MOST POPULAR TEXTS

The following texts were selected by examining results of popular texts at Amazon.com and Google search results of syllabi for counseling ethics courses and all meet the criteria listed above. The texts are listed in alphabetical order.

Corey, G., Corey, M. S., & Callanan, P. (2011). *Issues and ethics in the helping professions* (8th ed.). Belmont, CA: Brooks Cole.

Remley, T., & Herlihy, B. (2010). *Ethical, legal, and professional issues in counseling* (3rd ed.). Boston, MA: Merrell.

Sommers-Flanagan, R., & Sommers-Flanagan, J. (2007). *Becoming an ethical helping professional: Cultural and philosophical foundations*. Hoboken, NJ: John Wiley & Sons.

Welfel, E. R. (2010). *Ethics in counseling & psychotherapy: Standards, research, & emerging issues* (4th ed.). Belmont, CA: Cengage.

SUPPLEMENTAL READING

We believe that no single text can fully describe the complexity and subtlety of ethical issues in practice, nor can one book explore some of the unique ethical issues in specific settings or with specific populations. There are many journals such as *Ethics and Behavior*, *Journal of Counseling and Development*, *Journal of Mental Health Counseling*, *Psychological Reports*, *Professional Psychology: Research and Practice*, and *Psychotherapy: Theory, Research, Practice, Training* that provide supplemental material. We recommend assigning some of the supplemental readings listed below.

Resources on the ACA Code of Ethics (2005)

Barnett, J. E., & Johnson, B. W. (2010). *Ethics desk reference for counselors*. Alexandria, VA: American Counseling Association.

Herlihy, B., & Corey, G. (Eds.). (2006). *ACA ethical standards casebook* (6th ed.). Alexandria, VA: American Counseling Association.

Introduction to the Course – Why Bother About Ethics

Anderson, S. K., & Handelsman, M. M. (2010). *Ethics for psychotherapists and counselors: A proactive approach*. Chichester, England: Wiley-Blackwell.

Phelan, J. E. (2007). Membership expulsions for ethical violations from major counseling, psychology, and social work organizations in the United States: A 10-year analysis. *Psychological Reports, 101*, 145–152.

Skovholt, T. M. (2001). *The resilient practitioner: Burnout prevention and self care strategies for counselors, therapists, teachers and health professionals*. Boston, MA: Allyn & Bacon.

Tjeltveit, A. C. (2006). To what ends? Psychotherapy goals and outcomes, the good life, and the principle of beneficence. *Psychotherapy: Theory, Research, Practice, Training, 43*, 186–200.

Nature and Scope of Unethical Practice

Gibson, W. T., & Pope, K. S. (1993). The ethics of counseling: A national survey of certified counselors. *Journal of Counseling and Development, 71*, 330–336.

Ponton, R. F., & Duba, D. (2009). The ACA code of ethics: Articulating counseling's professional covenant. *Journal of Counseling & Development, 87*, 117–121.

Current Ethical Standards and the Interplay of Law and Ethics

Baerger, D. R. (2001). Risk management with the suicidal patient; lessons from case law. *Professional Psychology: Research and Practice, 32*, 359–366.

Barsky, A. E., & Gould, J. W. (2002). *Clinicians in court: A guide to subpoenas, depositions, testifying and everything else you need to know*. New York: Guilford Press.

Kennedy, P. F., Vandehey, M., Norman, W. B., & Diekhoff, G. M. (2003). Recommendations for risk-management processes. *Professional Psychology: Research and Practice, 34*, 309–311.

Wheeler, A. M., & Bertram, B. (2008). *The counselor and the law*. Alexandria, VA: American Counseling Association.

Models of Ethical Decision Making

Birrell, P. J. (2006). An ethic of possibility: Relationship, risk, and presence. *Ethics & Behavior, 16*, 95–115.

Cottone, R. R. (2000). Ethical decision-making models: A review of the literature. *Journal of Counseling & Development, 78*, 275–283.

Cottone, R. R. (2007). Paradigms of counseling and psychotherapy, revisited: Is social constructivism a paradigm? *Journal of Mental Health Counseling, 29*, 189–203.

Competence to Practice

Engels, D. W. (2010). *The professional counselor: Portfolio, competencies, performance guidelines, and assessment* (4th ed.). Alexandria, VA: American Counseling Association.

Rosenberg, J. I., Getzelman, M. A., Arciune, F., & Oren, C. Z. (2005). An exploratory look at students' experiences of problematic peers in academic professional psychology programs. *Professional Psychology: Research and Practice, 36*, 665–675.

Confidentiality and Privilege

Committee on Legal Issues of the American Psychological Association. (2006). Strategies for private practitioners coping with subpoenas or compelled testimony for client records or test data. *Professional Psychology: Research and Practice, 37*, 215–222.

Glosoff, H. L., Herlihy, B., & Spence, E. B. (2000). Privileged communication in the counselor: client relationship. *Journal of Counseling and Development, 78*, 454–462.

Mitrevski, J. P., & Chamberlain, R. (2006). Psychotherapist–patient privilege: Applying *Jaffee v. Redmond*: Communications to a psychotherapist are not privileged if they occur outside the course of diagnosis or treatment. *Journal of the American Academy of Psychiatry and the Law, 34*, 245–246.

Limits of Confidentiality with Clients at Risk of Violence to Self or Others

Benjamin, G. A. H., Kent, L., & Sirikantraporn, S. (2009). A review of duty to protect statutes, cases, and procedures for positive practice. In J. L. Werth, E. R. Welfel, & G. A. H. Benjamin (Eds.), *The duty to protect: Ethical, legal, and professional responsibilities of mental health professionals* (pp. 9–28). Washington, DC: APA Press.

Jobes, D. A., & O'Connor, S. S. (2009). The duty to protect suicidal clients: Ethical, legal and professional considerations. In J. L. Werth, E. R. Welfel, & G. A. H. Benjamin (Eds.), *The duty to protect: Ethical, legal, and professional responsibilities of mental health professionals* (pp. 163–182). Washington, DC: APA Press.

Jobes, D. A., Rudd, M. D., Overholser, J. C., & Joiner, T. E. (2008). Ethical and competent care of suicidal patients. *Professional Psychology: Research and Practice, 39*, 405–413.

Kress, V. E., Protivnak, J. J., & Sadlak, L. (2008). Counseling clients involved with violent intimate partners: The mental health counselor's role in promoting client safety. *Journal of Mental Health Counseling, 30*, 200–210.

Confidentiality with Minors

Capuzzi, D. (2002). Legal and ethical challenges in counseling suicidal students. *Professional School Counseling, 6*, 36–45.

Gustafson, K. E., & McNamara, J. R. (1987). Confidentiality with minor clients: Issues and guidelines for therapists. *Professional Psychology: Research and Practice, 18*, 503–508.

Lazovsky, R. (2008). Maintaining confidentiality with minors: Dilemmas of school counselors. *Professional School Counseling, 11*, 335–346.

Lehrer, J. A., Pantell, R., Tebb, K., & Shafer, M. (2007). Forgone health care among U.S. adolescents: Associations between risk characteristics and confidentiality concern. *Journal of Adolescent Health, 40*, 218–226.

Lyren, A., Kodish, E., Lazebnik, R., & O'Riordan, M. A. (2006). Understanding confidentiality: Perspectives of African American adolescents and their parents. *Journal of Adolescent Health, 39*, 261–265.

Stone, C., & Isaacs, L. (2003). Confidentiality with minors: The need for policy to promote and protect. *Journal of Educational Research, 96*, 140–150.

Confidentiality and Mandated Reporting of Abuse and Neglect of Vulnerable Persons

Bryant, J. K. (2009). School counselors and child abuse reporting: A national survey. *Professional School Counseling, 12*, 333–342.

MacNair, R. R. (1992). Ethical dilemmas of child abuse reporting: Implications for mental health counselors. *Journal of Mental Health Counseling, 14*, 127–136.

Mathews, B., & Kenny, C. (2008). Mandatory reporting legislation in the United States, Canada, and Australia: A cross-jurisdictional review of key features, differences, and issues. *Child Maltreatment, 13*, 50–63.

Mitchell, C. W., & Rogers, E. (2003). Rape, statutory rape, and child abuse: Legal distinctions and counselor duties. *Professional School Counseling, 6*, 332–338.

Welfel, E. R., Danzinger, P. R., & Santoro, S. (2000). A primer on elder maltreatment for counselors: Legal and professional responsibilities. *Journal of Counseling and Development, 78*, 284–292.

Informed Consent: Ethical and Legal Dimensions

Center for Ethical Practice. (2008). *Sample adolescent informed consent form*. Retrieved from http://www.centerforethicalpractice.org/Form-AdolescentConsent.htm

Croarkin, P., Berg, J., & Spira, J. (2003). Informed consent for psychotherapy: A look at therapists' understanding, opinions, and practices. *American Journal of Psychotherapy, 57*, 384–400.

Somberg, D. R., Stone, G. L., & Claiborn, C. D. (1993). Informed consent: Therapists' beliefs and practices. *Professional Psychology: Research and Practice, 24*, 153–159.

Sexual Misconduct

Anonymous. (1991). Sexual harassment: A female counseling student's experience. *Journal of Counseling and Development, 69*, 502–506.

Bates, C. M., & Brodsky, A. M. (1989). *Sex in the therapy hour: A case of professional incest*. New York: Guilford Press.

Bonitz, V. (2008). Use of physical touch in the "talking cure": A journey to the outskirts of psychotherapy. *Psychotherapy: Theory, Research, Practice, Training, 45*, 391–404.

Committee on Women in Psychology of the American Psychological Association. (1989). If sex enters into the psychotherapy relationship. *Professional Psychology: Research and Practice, 20*, 112–115.

Hartl, T., L., Zeiss, R. A., Marino, C. M., Zeiss, A. M., Regev, L. G., & Leontis, C. (2007). Clients' sexually inappropriate behaviors directed towards clinicians: Conceptualization and management. *Professional Psychology: Research and Practice, 38*, 674–681.

Pope, K. S., Sonne, J. L., & Holroyd, J. (1993). *Sexual feelings in psychotherapy: Explorations for therapists and therapists-in-training*. Washington, DC: American Psychological Association.

Multiple Relationships and Nonsexual Boundary Violations

Austin, W., Bergum, V., Nuttgens, S., & Peternelj-Taylor, C. (2006). A re-visioning of boundaries in professional helping relationships: Exploring other metaphors. *Ethics & Behavior, 16*, 77–94.

Barnett, J. E., Lazarus, A. A., Vasquez, M. J. T., Moorehead-Slaughter, O., & Johnson, W. B. (2007). Boundary issues and multiple relationships. *Professional Psychology: Research and Practice, 38*, 401–410.

Brown, C., & Trangsrud, B. (2008). Factors associated with acceptance and decline of client gift giving. *Professional Psychology: Research and Practice, 39*, 505–511.

Gottlieb, M. C., & Younggren, J. (2009). Is there a slippery slope? Considerations regarding multiple relationships and risk management. *Professional Psychology: Research and Practice, 40*, 564–571.

Herlihy, B., & Corey, G. (2006). *Boundary issues in counseling: Multiple roles and responsibilities* (2nd ed.). Alexandria, VA: American Counseling Association.

Kessler, L. E., & Waehler, A. (2005). Addressing multiple relationships between clients and therapists in lesbian, gay, bisexual, and transgender communities. *Professional Psychology: Research and Practice, 36*, 66–72.

Moleski, S. M., & Kiselica, M. S. (2005). Dual relationships: A continuum ranging from the destructive to the therapeutic. *Journal of Counseling and Development, 83*, 3–11.

Younggren, J., & Gottlieb, M. C. (2004). Managing risk when contemplating multiple relationships. *Professional Psychology: Research and Practice, 35*, 255–260.

Testing, Assessment, and Diagnosis

Anastasi, A. (1992). What counselors should know about the use and interpretation of psychological tests. *Journal of Counseling and Development, 70*, 610–615.

Braun, S. A., & Cox, J. A. (2005). Managed mental health care: Intentional misdiagnosis of mental disorders. *Journal of Counseling and Development, 83*, 425–433.

Bush, S. S., & Martin, A. (2006). The ethical and clinical practice of disclosing raw test data: Addressing the ongoing debate. *Applied Neuropsychology, 13*, 115–124.

Eriksen, K., & Kress, V. E. (2004). *Beyond the DSM story: Ethical quandaries, challenges, and best practices.* Thousand Oaks, CA: Sage.

Kress, V. E., Eriksen, K. P., Rayle, A. D., & Ford, S. J. W. (2005). The *DSM-IV-TR* and culture: Considerations for counselors. *Journal of Counseling and Development, 83*, 97–104.

Pope, K. S. (1992). Responsibilities in providing psychological test feedback to clients. *Psychological Assessment, 4*, 268–271.

Group Counseling

Bernard, H., Burlingame, G., Flores, P., Greene, L., Joyce, A., Kobos, J. C., et al. (2008). Clinical practice guidelines for group psychotherapy. *International Journal of Group Psychotherapy, 58*, 455–542.

Brabender, V. M., & Fallon, A. (2009). Ethical hot spots of combined individual and group therapy: Applying four ethical systems. *International Journal of Group Psychotherapy, 59*, 127–147.

Fallon, A. (2006). Informed consent in the practice of group psychotherapy. *International Journal of Group Psychotherapy, 56*, 431–453.

Knauss, L. K. (2006). Ethical issues in recordkeeping in group psychotherapy. *International Journal of Group Psychotherapy, 56*, 415–430.

Lasky, G. B., & Riva, T. (2006). Confidentiality and privileged communication in group psychotherapy. *International Journal of Group Psychotherapy, 56*, 455–476.

Family Counseling

Gladding, S. T., Remley, T. P., & Huber, C. H. (2003). *Ethical, legal, and professional issues in the practice of marriage and family therapy* (3rd ed.). Upper Saddle River, NJ: Merrill.

Southern, S. (2006). Ethical code for the International Association of Marriage and Family Counseling. *The Family Journal, 14*, 92–98.

Zimmerman, J., Hess, A. K., McGarrah, N. A., Benjamin, G. A. H., Ally, G. A., Gollan, J. K., & Kaser-Boyd, N. (2009). Ethical and professional considerations in divorce and child custody cases. *Professional Psychology: Research and Practice, 40*, 539–549.

Technology in Counseling

Collins, L. H. (2007). Practicing safer listserv use: Ethical use of an invaluable resource. *Professional Psychology: Research and Practice, 38*, 690–698.

Gore, P. A., & Leuwerke, W. C. (2008). Technological advances: Implications for counseling psychology research, training, and practice. In S. D. Brown & R. D. Lent (Eds.), *Handbook of counseling psychology* (4th ed., pp. 38–53). Hoboken, NJ: John Wiley & Sons.

Heinlen, K. L., Welfel, E. R., Richmond, E. N., & Rak, C. F. (2003). Ethical issues in Web counseling: Do practitioners comply with current standards? *Journal of Counseling and Development, 81*, 61–69.

Vaccaro, N., & Lambie, W. (2007). Computer-based counselor-in-training supervision: Ethical and practical implications for counselor educators and supervisors. *Counselor Education and Supervision, 47*, 46–57.

Wilczenski, F. L., & Coomey, M. (2006). Cyber-communication: Finding its place in school counseling practice, education, and professional development. *Professional School Counseling, 9*, 327–331.

Multicultural Considerations in Counseling

Arrendondo, P. M., Toporek, R., Brown, S. P., Jones, J., Locke, D., Sanchez, J., & Stadler, H. (1996). Operationalization of the multicultural counseling competencies. *Journal of Multicultural Counseling and Development, 24*, 42–78.

Constantine, M. G., & Sue, D. W. (Eds.). (2005). *Strategies for building multicultural competence in mental health and educational settings*. New York: Wiley.

Cornish, J. A. E., Gorgens, K. A., Monson, S. P., Olkin, R., Palombi, B. J., & Abels, A. V. (2008). Perspectives on ethical practice with people who have disabilities. *Professional Psychology: Research and Practice, 39*, 488–497.

Cramer, R. J., Golom, F. D., LoPresto, C. T., & Kirkley, S. M. (2008). Weighing the evidence: Empirical assessment and ethical implications of conversion therapy. *Ethics & Behavior, 18*, 93–114.

Fowers, B. J., & Davidov, J. (2006). The virtue of multiculturalism: Personal transformation, character, and openness to the other. *American Psychologist, 61*, 581–594.

Herlihy, B., & Watson, Z. E. (2003). Ethical issues and multicultural competence in counseling. In F. D. Harper & J. McFadden (Eds.), *Culture and counseling: New approaches* (pp. 363–378). Needham Heights, MA: Allyn & Bacon.

Pack-Brown, S. P., & Williams, C. B. (2003). *Ethics in a multicultural context*. Thousand Oaks, CA: Sage.

Pope, K. S. (2005). Disability and accessibility in psychology: Three major barriers. *Ethics & Behavior, 15*, 103–106.

Pope-Davis, D. B., Coleman, H. L. K., Liu, W. M., & Toporek, R. L. (2003). *Handbook of multicultural competencies in counseling and psychology*. Thousand Oaks, CA: Sage.

Sadeghi, M., Fischer, J. M., & House, S. G. (2003). Ethical dilemmas in multicultural counseling. *Journal of Multicultural Counseling and Development, 31*, 179–191.

Schank, J. A., & Shovholt, T. M. (2006). *Ethical practice in small communities: Challenges and rewards for psychologists*. Washington, DC: APA Press.

Sobinski, M. R. (1990). Ethical principles in the counseling of gay and lesbian adolescents: Issues of autonomy, competence and confidentiality. *Professional Psychology: Research and Practice, 21*, 240–247.

Watson, Z. E. P., Herlihy, B. R., & Pierce, L. A. (2006). Forging the link between multicultural competence and ethical counseling practice: A historical perspective. *Counseling and Values, 50*, 99–107.

Whaley, A. L., & Davis, E. (2007). Cultural competence and evidence-based practice in mental health services: A complementary perspective. *American Psychologist, 62*, 563–574.

Yarhouse, M. A., & Tan, E. S. N. (2005). Addressing religious conflicts in adolescents who experience sexual identity confusion. *Professional Psychology: Research and Practice, 36*, 530–536.

Supervision and Consultation

Gottlieb, M. C. (2006). A template for peer ethics consultation. *Ethics & Behavior, 16*, 151–162.

Haynes, R., Corey, G., Moulton, P., & Muratori, M. (2010). *Clinical supervision in the helping professions: A practical guide* (2nd ed.). Alexandria, VA: American Counseling Association.

Warren, E. S. (2005). Future colleague or convenient friend: The ethics of mentorship. *Counseling and Values, 49*, 141–146.

Community Counseling

Danzinger, P. R., & Welfel, E. R. (2001). The impact of managed care on mental health counselors: A survey of perceptions, practices, and compliance with ethical standards. *Journal of Mental Health Counseling, 23*, 137–150.

Walfish, S., & Watkins, M. (2005). Readability level of Health Insurance Portability and Accountability Act notices of privacy practices utilized by academic medical centers. *Evaluation & the Health Professions, 28*, 479–486.

Teaching and Research

Haverkamp, B. E. (2005). Ethical perspectives on qualitative research in applied psychology. *Journal of Counseling Psychology, 52*, 146–155.

Zakrzewski, R. F. (2006). A national survey of American Psychological Association student affiliates' involvement and ethical training in psychology educator–student sexual relationships. *Professional Psychology: Research and Practice, 37*, 724–730.

School Counseling

American School Counselors Association. (2004). *Ethical standards for school counselors.* Retrieved from http://www.schoolcounselor.org/content.asp?contentid=136

Auger, R. W. (2006). Delivering difficult news to parents: Guidelines for school counselors. *Professional School Counseling, 10*, 139–145.

Bodenhorn, N. (2006). Exploratory study of common and challenging ethical dilemmas experienced by professional school counselors. *Professional School Counseling, 10*, 195–202.

Fischer, L., & Sorenson, G. P. (1996). *School law for counselors, psychologists, and social workers* (3rd ed.). White Plains, NY: Longman.

Glosoff, H. L., & Pate, R. H. (2002). Privacy and confidentiality in school counseling. *Professional School Counseling, 6*, 20–27.
Hermann, M. A. (2002). A study of legal issues encountered by school counselors and perceptions of their preparedness to respond to legal challenges. *Professional School Counseling, 6*, 12–19.
Huss, S. N., Bryant, A., & Mulet, S. (2008). Managing the quagmire of counseling in a school: Bringing the parents onboard. *Professional School Counseling, 11*, 362–367.
Lambie, G. W. (2005). Child abuse and neglect: A practical guide for professional school counselors. *Professional School Counseling, 8*, 249–258.
Lehr, R., Lehr, A., & Sumarah, J. (2007). Confidentiality and informed consent: School counsellors' perceptions of ethical practices. *Canadian Journal of Counselling, 41*, 16–30.
McFarland, W. P., & Dupuis, M. (2001). The legal duty to protect gay and lesbian students from violence in school. *Professional School Counseling, 4*, 171–179.
Merlone, L. (2005). Record keeping and the school counselor. *Professional School Counseling, 8*, 372–376.
Stone, C. (2002). Negligence in academic advising and abortion counseling: Court rulings and implications. *Professional School Counseling, 6*, 28–35.
Stone, C. B. (2005). *School counseling principles: Ethics and law*. Alexandria, VA: American School Counselor Association.

Ethics Complaints

Chauvin, J. C., & Remley, T. P., Jr. (1996). Responding to allegations of unethical conduct. *Journal of Counseling and Development, 74*, 563–568.
Cobia, D. C., & Pipes, R. B. (2002). Mandated supervision: An intervention for disciplined professionals. *Journal of Counseling and Development, 80*, 140–144.
Welfel, E. R. (2005). Accepting fallibility: A model for personal responsibility for nonegregious ethics infractions. *Counseling and Values, 49*, 120–131.

Termination of the Therapy Relationship

Davis, D. D., & Younggren, J. (2009). Ethical competence in psychotherapy termination. *Professional Psychology: Research and Practice, 40*, 572–578.
Rappleyea, D. L., Harris, S. M., White, M., & Simon, K. (2009). Termination: Legal and ethical considerations for marriage and family therapists. *American Journal of Family Therapy, 37*, 12–27.
Younggren, J. N., & Gottlieb, C. (2008). Termination and abandonment. *Professional Psychology: Research and Practice, 39*, 498–504.

Electronic Resources

Changes in federal law preclude bundling of textbooks and learning supplements (Higher Education Opportunity Act, 2008). This seems likely to influence the delivery method for supplemental materials, because CD-ROMs will no longer be packaged with accompanying textbooks. Increasingly, authors and publishing companies have provided access to supplemental materials through the World Wide Web. Separate resource materials are often available to instructors and students through these online sources. Publishing companies may offer students free supplemental resources, but any resources for which there is a fee must be offered separately, whether CD-ROMs or online supplements. Instructors must register and have their registration validated prior to using the instructor resources on the site.

- Corey, Corey, and Callanan (2011). *Issues and ethics in the helping professions* (8th ed.).

  Online student resources for Corey et al.'s (2011) textbook include a glossary of terms, web-based flashcards, and tutorial quizzes of each chapter, as well as a downloadable study guide. Students may access free resources at http://www.cengage.com/counseling/corey. Instructor resources include test banks data for use with Blackboard and WebCT and a downloadable instructor manual. The instructor manual provides multiple resources, including a guide for integrating the textbook and online resources, a practice and final exam, a glossary of terms, a sample course outline (syllabus, activities, cases, scoring rubrics, and additional reading suggestions), a glossary of terms, student course evaluation, a reprint of an article on teaching an ethics course, and PowerPoint slides.

- Remley and Herlihy (2010). *Ethical, legal, and professional issues in counseling* (3rd ed.).

  Online resources for Remley and Herlihy's (2010) text include a downloadable instructor's manual and test bank.

- Sommers-Flanagan and Sommers-Flanagan (2007). *Becoming an ethical helping professional: Cultural and philosophical foundations.*

  Online resources for Sommers-Flanagan and Sommers-Flanagan's (2007) text include the instructor's manual and PowerPoint slides, which may each be downloaded chapter by chapter or in consolidated form. A test bank with questions for each chapter is also available for download.

- Welfel (2010). Ethics in counseling and psychotherapy: Standards, research, and emerging issues (4th ed.).

  Online resources for Welfel's (2010) text are combined within an instructor's download at http://www.cengage.com/counseling/welfel. Instructors benefit from chapter summaries, class exercises and assignments, discussion questions, additional cases and suggested questions, essay questions and multiple-choice questions with an included answer sheet, and an additional list of recommended readings.

In addition to electronic resources provided by authors and publishers, there are additional websites that provide thoughtful analysis on ethics issues for mental health professionals.

WEBSITES

- American Counseling Association
  http://www.counseling.org/Resources/CodeOfEthics/TP/Home/CT2.aspx
  The ethics page of the ACA provides how-to information on seeking an ethics consultation from the ACA Ethics and Professional Standards Department, links to download the most recent ethics code for counselors and educational materials, as well as additional materials to assist students in developing ethical understanding.

- Articles, Research, and Resources in Psychology
  http://kspope.com/
  Though this site, "designed to be fully accessible to people with disabilities," (Pope, 2010, para. 1), is focused on psychology, it addresses challenging issues that counselors must consider as well, such as boundaries, informed consent, end-of-life concerns, and advocacy for people with limited resources and opportunity. In addition, the website provides resources for professional practice and for consumers.

AUDIOVISUAL MATERIAL

Toman and Rak (2000) suggested that the "use of motion pictures as a teaching tool can bring the personable and intimate study of human issues directly into the classroom, providing dialogue in the context of film characters' life circumstances" (p. 105). Their comment that films have provided ample opportunities for discussion of unethical behavior remains true today (Toman & Rak). Kurianski, Vallarelli, DelBuono, and Ortman (2010) reiterated this view and explored the use of film across a number of professional settings. The seeming ubiquity of visual media from traditional delivery mechanisms of television and theaters to mail-order DVDs to streaming television and films suggests that media is not only a popular form of communication but a useful medium for educational purposes. The examples of unethical behavior in television and film are abundant, so we will point out only a few.

Instructors may encourage students to view films and respond with written analysis or use the films and shows to stimulate classroom discussion. Additional exercises may be developed using visual media as well. Students can exercise their ethical sensitivity to develop a list of television or films in which characters face ethical questions and analyze the ethical dimensions and their personal responses to the issue and the character's response.

- West and Neufield (1999). *The general's daughter.*
  A film exploring the mysterious death of a high-ranking military officer's daughter. In the resulting investigation a military psychiatrist wrestles with the confidentiality of the woman's disclosures.

- Paris Barclay, et al. (2008). *In treatment.*
  This television series follows the professional work of a psychoanalytic therapist and the decisions he makes in service to his clients. The therapist is faced with multiple issues throughout the series, including sexual attraction, multiple relationships, mandated reporting, and self-care. Two seasons of the series have been produced. Every episode contains ethical issues, some of which the therapist handles appropriately and some he does not.

- Kasdan, Okun, and Kasdan (1999). *Mumford.*
  A film about a man finding a new start in life by faking a license and career as a psychologist. Addresses issues of professional identity and motivation to help others, training and education, licensure, and multiple relationships.

- Mitchell (2006). *Short bus.*
  This film follows the lives of several residents of New York City and their struggle to address issues of sexuality and relationships. The role of therapy and therapist is explored in this movie, and the issues of self-care, countertransference, boundaries, and multiple relationships as well as sexual diversity issues are prominent. (Please be advised: this film is sexually explicit.)

- Streisand, Karsch, and Streisand (1992). *The Prince of Tides.*
  A film about overcoming the psychological trauma of a dysfunctional upbringing. Addresses multiple relationships and sexual relationships with a client's family members.

Scholars in psychology and psychiatry have also discussed the use of film in ethics education. Schoener (2008) has identified a number of excellent popular and professional films and television productions that highlight subtle and complex ethical issues for mental health professionals. For example, Schoener provided detailed instructions for use of the HBO television series *In Treatment* (Levinson et al., 2008) as a springboard for discussion of boundary issues and competent psychotherapy. Gabbard and Gabbard (2001) have also published a resource that explores more broadly the use of film in psychiatry.

LEARNING ACTIVITIES

The following activities have been utilized in ethics courses taught by the authors and have resulted in positive student reactions and evidence of increased knowledge and ethical sensitivity.

- Extensive reading of current scholarship in addition to assignment of a text and the relevant ethics codes. This reading reinforces the perspective that ethics is more than applying a code.
- Substitution of weekly test cases for traditional midterm examination. Prior research suggests that case applications promote learning, and this method gives students extra incentives for staying current with the course readings. Also, the course includes frequent discussion of other cases in small groups.
- Use of an assignment that allows students to analyze an unresolved ethical issue the profession is currently facing—the ethics of providing counseling exclusively via the Internet. Students seek online counseling sites and analyze their compliance with current ACA standards and then discuss the results of their analysis in class and debate the ethics of online services.
- A role-play of an informed consent to counseling using both an adult client and a parent of a child client. A role-play of a situation in which a counselor needs to explain boundaries and/or respond to a client who requests that the counselor use a diagnosis for insurance eligibility even though the symptoms the client describes do not meet diagnostic criteria.
- A demonstration by the instructor of how he or she conducts an informed consent, screening interview for group counseling, or other activities that show ethical practice.
- Use of an assignment that "gives psychology away"—the development of consumer brochures on ethical issues and client rights. Students who succeed in getting the brochures implemented in their placements receive extra credit for the assignment.
- Inclusion of an adaptation of a mock ethics hearing. The instructor has developed written materials and students role-play participants in the hearing. Then they decide whether discipline is necessary and what level of discipline is appropriate. This experience not only familiarizes students with disciplinary procedures but gives them some exposure to the emotions involved in facing a hearing and of making judgments about the ethics of a colleague's practice.
- Development of a portfolio in which students keep copies of ethics codes and guidelines, supplemental readings, cases, state laws, and other assignments. This portfolio can be either in paper or electronic format. It is meant to be a resource for them after they complete the ethics course and graduate training.

TENTATIVE SCHEDULE

WEEK	*TOPIC*
Week 1	Introduction to the course—why bother about ethics? The nature and scope of unethical practice Current ethical standards and the interplay of law and ethics
Week 2	Models of ethical decision making
Week 3	Competence to practice Portfolio check #1
Week 4	Confidentiality and privilege Test case #1
Week 5	Limits of confidentiality with clients at risk of violence to self or others
Week 6	Confidentiality with minors Test case #2
Week 7	Confidentiality and mandated reporting of abuse and neglect of vulnerable persons Test case #3
Week 8	Informed consent: Ethical and legal dimensions
Week 9	Sexual misconduct Portfolio check #2
Week 10	Multiple relationships/nonsexual boundary violations Test case #4
Week 11	Ethics of testing, assessment, and diagnosis Ethics of group and family counseling Test case #5
Week 12	Ethical and legal dimensions of the use of technology in counseling Web counseling paper due
Week 13	Ethical counseling in a multicultural society Test case #6
Week 14	Ethical and legal dimensions of supervision Ethical and legal dimensions of community counseling HIPAA and community counseling
Week 15	Ethics of teaching and research Ethics and legal issues of school counseling Consumer brochure due Test case #7 distributed
Week 16	Ethical and legal issues in school counseling (continued) Ethics complaint process Mock ethics hearing Test case #7 due Portfolio check #3

CONCLUSION

Teaching ethics is an immensely rewarding endeavor when taught using some of the approaches mentioned in this chapter. Once students recognize that ethics is more than rules and regulations and that it deals with the fundamental issues in practice, they get very involved in the course and appreciate its value for their professional lives. As long as instructors design the course to include cases, discussion, and analysis of the codes and the literature, they will likely enjoy the course as much as the students profit from it.

REFERENCES

American Counseling Association. (2005). *2005 ACA code of ethics*. Retrieved from www.counseling.org.

Bernard, H., Burlingame, G., Flores, P., Greene, L., Joyce, A., Kobos, J. C., ... Feirman, D. (2008). Clinical practice guidelines for group psychotherapy. *International Journal of Group Psychotherapy, 58*, 455–542.

Corey, G., Corey, M.S., & Callanan, P. (2011). *Issues and ethics in the helping professions*. (8th ed.). Belmont, CA: Thompson/Brooks/Cole.

Downes, A., Favila, L., Kern, L., Krane, J. D., Leopold, S., Leopold, S., & Neufeld, M. (Producers), & West, S. (Director). (1999). *The general's daughter* [Motion picture]. United States: Paramount Pictures.

Gabbard, G. O., & Gabbard, K. (1999). *Psychiatry and the cinema*. Washington, D.C.: American Psychiatric Association

Handelsman, M. M., Gottlieb, M. C., & Knapp, S. (2005). Training ethical psychologists: An acculturation model. *Professional Psychology: Research and Practice, 26*, 59–65.

Kasdan, L., & Okun, C. (Producers), & Kasdan, L. (Director). (1999). *Mumford* [Motion picture]. United States: Touchstone Pictures.

Kurianski, J., Vallarelli, A., DelBuono, J., & Ortman, J. (2010). Cinematherapy: Using movie metaphors to explore real relationships in counseling and coaching. In M. Gregerson & M. Banks (Eds.), *The cinematic mirror for psychology and life coaching* (pp. 89–122). New York: Springer.

Levinson, S., Leight, W., Wahlberg, M. Garcia, R., Barclay, R., & Levi, H. (Producers) - Barclay, P., Garcia, R., McKay, J., Mayron, M., Fleck, R., Selim, A., Misiano, C., Hunt, C., George, T., de Segonzac, J., & Levi, H. (Directors). (2008). *In Treatment* [Motion picture]. United States: HBO .

Mitchell, J. C. (Producer & Director). (2006). *Short bus* [Motion picture]. United States: THINKFilm.

Pope, K. S. (2010). *Ethics in psychotherapy and counseling: A practical guide* (4th ed.). Hoboken, NJ: Wiley.

Remley. T. P., & Herlihy, B. (2010). *Ethical, legal, and professional issues in counseling* (3rd ed.). Upper Saddle River, NJ: Merrill Prentice Hall.

Schoener, G. (2008, May). *Making training in ethics and professional boundaries effective and dynamic*. Paper presented at the annual meeting of the American Psychiatric Association.

Sommers-Flanagan, R., & Sommers-Flanagan, J. (2007). *Becoming an ethical helping professional: Cultural and philosophical foundations*. New York: Wiley, Johnson & Sons.

Streisand, B., Karsch, A. (Producers), & Streisand, B. (Director). (1992). *The prince of tides* [Motion picture]. United States: Columbia Tristar.

Toman, S. M., & Rak, F. (2000). The use of cinema in the counselor education curriculum: Strategies and outcomes. *Counselor Education and Supervision, 40*, 105–114.

Welfel. E. R. (2010). *Ethics in counseling and psychotherapy: Standards, research, and emerging issues* (4th ed.). Belmont, CA: Thompson/Brooks/Cole.

West, S., & Neufield, M. (1999). *The general's daughter* [Motion picture]. United States: Paramount Pictures.

Zimmerman, J., Hess, A. K., McGarrah, N. A., Benjamin, G. A. H., Ally, G. A., Gollan, J. K., & Kaser-Boyd, N. (2009). Ethical and professional considerations in divorce and child custody cases. *Professional Psychology: Research and Practice, 40*, 539–549.

7 Theories of Counseling

If You Don't Have a Map You Might Get Lost

Nancy L. Murdock and Chia-Chih D. C. Wang

The challenge in teaching counseling theory is to show students how to use it. Kurt Lewin (1951) is reported to have said, "There is nothing so practical as a good theory" (p. 169), but in our observation, many students are more apt to follow the philosophy expressed by Mark Twain: "How empty is theory in the presence of fact" (Think Exist, 1999, Mark Twain section, p. 1). Our philosophy is that we truly learn the value of theory when we know how to apply theory to understand client presentations.

Yet no one theory is right for all students, nor is there one "correct" theory (Wampold, 2001). Surveys of professionals in the field indicate that many (but not a pure majority; Murdock, 2009) draw from multiple theoretical perspectives. A question often posed by students is "Why do I have to have a theory?" Our answer is that a theory is like a map. If you were walking across campus or driving to a distant destination, you'd probably want a map so that you could see the various routes you could take. Trying to do counseling without a theory is like driving without a map. Continuing the analogy, maps (theories) do not absolutely dictate which route you choose, but they do give you some idea which route might be the most efficient and the locations of landmarks of note along the way.

Therefore, there are at least two major aspects of a basic counseling theory course. First, students need to be exposed to a broad range of theoretical perspectives. Second, they need practice in the application of these theories.

A perennial question involves which theories to teach. Although some theories may seem more immediately applicable, or are more in vogue, we maintain that a basic theory course should survey approaches ranging from psychoanalysis to postmodern, social constructivist systems. A glance at the major texts in this area will allow you to review what these writers consider to be the important theoretical approaches and in the suggested class schedule at the end of this chapter, we provide our own list.

Aside from deciding which theories to address, there are several other topics that can be considered in teaching a basic theories course. These other possibilities include a review of psychotherapy outcome research and the empirically supported treatment controversy and material about individual and cultural diversity.

Some instructors ask students to practice particular skills related to theoretical approaches. This activity has the great benefit of behavioral learning related to the theory. However, because these activities are necessarily role-playing tasks, they have the drawback of feeling contrived to students. Another possible drawback is related to time constraints—fitting in lecture, role-playing, and case conceptualization practice in an already crowded schedule is difficult. Given that most counseling training programs offer a separate course for counseling skills, we are cautious about spending too much time on techniques and would recommend only focusing on those that illustrate the fundamental change mechanisms proposed by a particular theory.

A common assignment in theories class is the "my theoretical orientation" paper. In this assignment, students are asked to write about their personal philosophies, with or without reference to existing theoretical systems. A question to be considered here is whether students who have not yet seen a client are realistically capable of forming their own theoretical approaches. The plus side of such assignments is that they allow students to critically reflect upon theoretical systems and to examine their own value systems.

Reading from the original theory material is also considered helpful, to give students a deeper understanding of particular theories. A drawback to this approach (which is why we do not recommend using *only* original text material for a basic course) is that some of the original authors are not easy to read, and the material, in many cases, will be historically bound. The sheer amount of reading required to fully capture an approach is also an issue, particularly in a survey course that covers a large number of theoretical systems. We would advocate for brief readings that give students a sense of the original proponent's style instead. Original source readings of this nature can then focus on one important aspect of the theory.

Finally, we urge you to offer students material on how to apply theory. This process is one of the most difficult aspects of counseling for neophyte counselors. Most theories texts contain application examples, but few provide guidelines or structures for the application of theory. Later in this chapter we describe one such system.

Critical topics in a basic theories course are, of course, the theories. Students need an understanding of the three major branches of counseling theory: psychoanalysis, behavioral/cognitive–behavioral, and humanistic/person-centered theory. Most instructors will teach the classic approaches in these three general areas and then will add other systems such as Gestalt therapy, feminist approaches, solution-focused therapy, existential therapy, narrative therapy, or family systems theory. If you are teaching school counseling students, approaches can be selected or emphasized that suit that setting (e.g., cognitive–behavioral, solution focused). The counseling profession's emphasis on the importance of issues of individual and cultural diversity mandates that theories be considered in the light of their applicability to diverse clients. In addition, many theoretical approaches seem to emphasize dysfunction over health—instructors can correct this bias by bringing to students an awareness of this bias, as well as material or activities focusing on strengths and healthy functioning.

We generally use a lecture format to present core theory material. If you choose this approach, you will want to first present a uniform structure that will be used to present the theory. We like the following outline:

- Background (founders' history, social context, major proponents)
- Human motivation
- Central constructs
- Theory of the person and development of the individual
- Health and dysfunction
- Nature of therapy
    - Assessment
    - Overview of the therapeutic atmosphere
    - Roles of the client and counselor
    - Goals
    - Change mechanisms
- Therapeutic techniques
- Evaluation of the theory
    - Research support
    - Issue of individual and cultural diversity

OBJECTIVES AND CACREP STANDARDS

The Council for the Accreditation of Counseling and Related Educational Programs (CACREP) 2009 standard most clearly related to counseling theories is Section II.G.5. Helping Relationships. This standard specifies that programs should include "studies that provide an understanding of the counseling process in a multicultural society" (p. 12) including (a) an orientation to wellness and prevention as desired counseling goals; (b) counselor characteristics and behaviors that influence helping processes; (c) essential interviewing and counseling skills; (d) counseling theories that provide the student with models to conceptualize client presentation and that help the student select appropriate counseling interventions. Students will be exposed to models of counseling that are consistent with current professional research and practice in the field so they begin to develop a personal model of counseling; and (e) a system perspective that provides an understanding of family and other systems theories and major models of family and related interventions. Standards G2 and G3 in Section II are also relevant.

The following are sample objectives for a basic theories course:

1. Knowledge of the basic constructs and concepts of selected counseling theories. (Section II.G.3.a.; Section II.G.3.b.; Section II.G.3.d.; Section II.G.3.f.; Section II.G.3.h.; Section II.G.5.a.; Section II.G.5.d.; Section II.G.5.e.)
2. Knowledge of the history and current systems of thought about counseling and change mechanisms in the traditions of Western practice and philosophy. (Section II.G.3.a.; Section II.G.3.b.; Section II.G.3.d.; Section II.G.3.f.; Section II.G.3.h.; Section II.G.5.a.; Section II.G.5.d.; Section II.G.5.e.)
3. Skills in applying the major theories of counseling to form adequate case conceptualizations. (Section II.G.3.a.; Section II.G.3.b.; Section II.G.3.d.; Section II.G.3.f.; Section II.G.3.h.; Section II.G.5.a.; Section II.G.5.d.; Section II.G.5.e.)
4. Knowledge of cultural biases embedded in theories and the impact of cultural factors (e.g., gender, racial/ethnic, sexual orientation, socioeconomic status) on applications of existing theories on underrepresented populations in a multicultural society. (Section II.G.2.e.; Section II.G.2.f.; Section II.G.5.d.; Section II.G.5.e.)
5. Development of a preliminary personal theoretical model of counseling that draws from existing theories and is consistent with personal values and multicultural awareness. (Section II.G.2.e.; Section II.G.2.f.; Section II.G.5.d.; Section II.G.5.e.)

CRITERIA FOR EVALUATING A TEXT

The best texts in theories of counseling present comprehensive reviews of theory written in an accessible, student-friendly manner. We look for clear explanation of theoretical constructs, underlying philosophy, processes, and techniques along with examples of application of the theory. Discussions of research support and diversity issues are also important. Coverage of a wide range of theories is essential; instructors can then choose which theories they want to teach.

MOST POPULAR TEXTS

An informal survey of counseling programs and publishers indicated that the following were the top textbooks used in counseling theories courses.

Corey, G. (2009). *Theory and practice of counseling and psychotherapy* (8th ed.). New York: Cengage Learning.

Day, S. (2008). *Theory and design in counseling and psychotherapy* (2nd ed.). New York: Cengage Learning.
Murdock, N. L. (2009). *Theories of counseling and psychotherapy: A case approach* (2nd ed.). Upper Saddle River, NJ: Pearson/Merrill.
Seligman, L. (2010). *Theories of counseling and psychotherapy: Systems, strategies, and skills* (2nd ed.). Upper Saddle River, NJ: Prentice Hall.
Sharf, R. C. (2008). *Theories of psychotherapy and counseling: Concepts and cases* (4th ed.). New York: Cengage Learning.

Another helpful resource is Rochelin's (2007) *Applying counseling theories: An online, case-based approach.* The chapters in this edited book are written in a pragmatic style that focuses on case conceptualization. An accompanying website presents three client case studies, including a 12-minute video clip of the practice clients. In the text chapters, authors comment on the process of conceptualizing these cases. The student then goes to the website, selects a case and a theory, and writes a practice conceptualization (which can also be routed to the instructor) guided by questions that structure the assignment. After the case conceptualization is submitted, students can read the chapter expert's conceptualization of the same client.

SUPPLEMENTAL READING

There are many journals dedicated to research and position papers on theories of counseling. Some counseling-related journals include *Journal of College Counseling, Journal of Counseling & Development*, and *Journal of Humanistic Counseling.*

Topic: Outcomes of Counseling and Psychotherapy

D'Andrea, M., & Heckman, E. F. (2008). A 40-year review of multicultural counseling outcome research: Outlining a future research agenda for the multicultural counseling movement. *Journal of Counseling & Development, 86*, 356–363.
Draper, M. R., Jennings, J., Baron, A., Erdur, O., & Shankar, L. (2002). Time-limited counseling outcome in a nationwide college counseling center sample. *Journal of College Counseling, 5*, 26–38.
Whiston, S. C., & Sexton, T. L. (1998) A review of school counseling outcome research: Implications for practice. *Journal of Counseling and Development, 76*, 412–426.

Topic: Theories and Counseling in a Pluralistic World

Atkinson, D. R., Thompson, C. E., & Grant, S. K. (1993). A three-dimensional model for counseling racial–ethnic minorities. *The Counseling Psychologist, 21*, 257–277.
Palma, T. V., & Stanley, J. L. (2002). Effective counseling with lesbian, gay, and bisexual clients. *Journal of College Counseling, 5*, 74–89.

Pedersen, P. (2005). The importance of cultural psychology theory for multicultural counselors. In R. T. Carter (Ed.), *Handbook of racial–cultural psychology and counseling: Theory and research* (pp. 3–16). Hoboken, NJ: John Wiley.

Sue, D. W., Arredondo, P., & McDavis, R. (1992). Multicultural counseling competencies and standards: A call to the profession. *Journal of Counseling and Development, 70*, 477–485.

Topic: Psychoanalysis

Bornstein, R. F. (2005). Reconnecting psychoanalysis to mainstream psychology: Challenges and opportunities. *Psychoanalytic Psychology, 22*, 323–340.

Westen, D. (1998). The scientific legacy of Sigmund Freud: Toward a psychodynamically informed psychological science. *Psychological Bulletin, 124*, 333–371.

Yalom, I. D. (2003). *The gift of therapy: An open letter to a new generation of therapists and their patients*. New York: HarperCollins.

Topic: Person Centered Therapy

Heppner, P. H., Rogers, M. E., & Lee, L. A. (1990). Carl Rogers: Reflections on his life. In P. P. Heppner (Ed.), *Pioneers in counseling and development: Personal and professional perspectives* (pp. 54–59). Alexandria, VA: American Association for Counseling and Development.

Rogers, C. (1967). *On becoming a person*. Boston, MA: Houghton Mifflin.

Rogers. C. (1980). *A way of being*. Boston, MA: Houghton Mifflin.

Topic: Behavior Therapy

Bandura, A. T., Ross, D., & Ross, S. A. (1963). Imitation of film-mediated aggressive models. *Journal of Abnormal and Social Psychology, 67*, 3–11.

Lazarus, A. A. (1996). The utility and futility of combining treatment in psychotherapy. *Clinical Psychology: Science and Practice, 3*, 59–68.

Wilson, K. G. (1997). Science and treatment development: Lessons from the history of behavior therapy. *Behavior Therapy, 28*, 547–558.

Topic: Rational Emotive Behavior Therapy

Ellis, A. (2004). Why I (really) became a therapist. *Journal of Rational–Emotive Cognitive Behavior Therapy, 22*, 73–77.

Weinrach, S. G. (1990). Unconventional therapist: Albert Ellis. In P. P. Heppner (Ed.), *Pioneers in counseling and development: Personal and professional perspectives* (pp. 60–66). Alexandria, VA: American Association for Counseling and Development.

Topic: Cognitive Therapy

Beck, A. T. (1991). Cognitive therapy: A 30-year retrospective. *American Psychologist, 46*, 368–375.

Beck, A. T. (2005). The current state of cognitive therapy: A 40-year retrospective. *Archives of General Psychiatry, 62*, 953–959.

Topic: Feminist Theory

Brown, L. S. (2006). Still subversive after all these years: The relevance of feminist therapy in the age of evidence-based practice. *Psychology of Women Quarterly, 30*, 15–24.

Enns, C. Z. (1993). Twenty years of feminist counseling and therapy: From naming biases to implementing multifaceted practice. *The Counseling Psychologist, 21*, 3–87.

WEBSITES

- American Psychoanalytic Association
  http://www.apsa.org
  This is the official site of the American Psychoanalytic Association, which provides information for the general public and professionals who are interested in learning more about psychoanalysis. Contents of this website include Freud quotes, recommended reading lists, psychoanalytic perspectives on common mental health diagnoses, training and outreach programs, and a ZIP code–based directory search to find an analyst.

- Carl Rogers.info
  http://www.carlrogers.info/
  Saybrook University sponsors this site, which includes a bibliography of Rogers' work, excerpts from his daughter Natalie's DVD about her father, and links to other person-centered websites.

- The Association for Behavioral and Cognitive Therapists
  http://www.abct.org
  The official website for the Association for Behavioral and Cognitive Therapies (ABCT), this site includes information about cognitive–behavioral therapy, psychological symptoms, evidence-based treatments, and self-help books. You can also find a link to watch archived ABCT videos and podcasts including interviews with Aaron Beck, Albert Bandura, Albert Ellis, and Arnold Lazarus.

- Albert Ellis Institute
  http://www.rebt.org
  The official site of the Albert Ellis Institute, formerly the Institute for Rational Emotive Therapy, which includes content for the public and professionals, historical and current information about REBT, therapy services and training offered by the center, a searchable research database, and an "Ask the Therapist" section facilitated by one of the institute's therapists.

- Beck Institute
  http://www.beckinstitute.org
  This website provides information about the establishment and development of the Beck Institute for Cognitive Therapy and Research as well as a basic introduction to cognitive therapy. It also contains several useful links for students, professionals, and consumers.

- The Association for Women in Psychology
  http://www.awpsych.org
  This is the official website of the Association for Women in Psychology, a professional organization promoting feminist psychological education, theory, research, and activism. A link on this website, "Bias in Psychiatric Diagnosis" leads to several articles addressing gender and cultural biases embedded in the *Diagnostic and Statistical Manual of Mental Disorders* (*DSM*) system of the American Psychiatric Association.

- The William Glasser Institute
  http://www.wglasser.com/
  This link leads to the official website of the institute, which offers information about the Glasser Approach, also known as *reality therapy*. Descriptions of choice theory/reality therapy, lead management, and Glasser quality schools are provided along with information about training and certification.

- The Association for Advancement of Gestalt Therapy
  http://www.aagt.org/
  This website provides rather detailed descriptions about the structure, basic tenets, and key concepts of Gestalt therapy. It also contains links to various Gestalt organizations and journals in several countries.

- North American Society of Adlerian Psychotherapy
  http://www.alfredadler.org/
  This website provides information about Adler and his theory. It also includes links for materials, papers, and slides presented in the organization's annual conferences from 2008 to 2011.

- Solution Focused Brief Therapy Association
  http://www.sfbta.org/

This is the website of the association founded by Steve de Shazer and Insoo Kim Berg to promote solution-focused therapy. It offers information about the approach, training events, and conferences.

LEARNING ACTIVITIES AND ASSIGNMENTS

Conceptualization Practice

One of the most useful class activities is asking students to conceptualize a client case from various theoretical perspectives. Sample cases are included at the end of this chapter. Using small groups, this activity can take many forms: students conceptualize (a) the same case with one theory, (b) different cases using the same theory, or (c) the same case using different theories. As described earlier, Rochelen's (2007) online system can also be used for this assignment. Appendix A contains the outline for this assignment (adapted from Murdock, 1991).

Poster Presentation

Another engaged learning activity we have used with positive feedback from students is poster presentations of assigned theories. In the beginning of the semester, students are asked to review a set of counseling theories that are not covered by the instructor's lecture and to turn in a preference list that indicates their interest ranking of studying these theories (the instructor provides a list of possible theories). Based on the class size and the preference lists turned in by students, the instructor assigns students to 8–12 small groups. Each group consists of students who share interest in the selected/assigned theory; they are asked to complete two tasks: (a) write a paper summarizing the important elements of this theory and (b) develop a poster presentation to introduce the theory to peers. On the presentation day, the class period is divided into two sections with each containing approximately a half of the total scheduled poster presentations (we use a 2 hour and 40-minute block for this course). Students presenting in the second half of the class visit different poster presentations in the first half of the class, and then the roles of students (i.e., presenters and visitors) switch in the second half. These poster presentations are given in a free-flow, town hall meeting format, so presenting students are encouraged to use handouts or multimedia means to illustrate their theories. Presenting students give a brief introduction of the theory to those who approach their poster and answer questions raised by the visitors. Students' presentations are evaluated on the quality of the poster, handouts, and responses to audiences' inquiries. The evaluation form used for this activity is included at the end of this chapter.

Cultural Reflection Paper and Discussion

The instructor can arrange several reflection papers as preclass writing assignments to increase students' multicultural awareness of how their personal characteristics, orientations, and values influence the helping process. The reflection paper consists of organized essay questions assigned by the instructor the week prior to the scheduled in-class discussion. The main purposes of this assignment are to give students the opportunity to reflect on their personal background and learning experiences and to prepare students for in-class discussion activities. The instructor may use the same set of questions to facilitate in-class small-group discussions. The following are some questions we have used:

1. Describe yourself, with regard to your values, abilities, goals, and what you believe are most important.
2. Choose two racial/ethnical/cultural groups that are different from your own and describe your stereotypes of people from those two cultures.
3. Do you have some personal experiences to back up your thoughts about the two groups? Share some of your positive and negative experiences interacting with different groups of people on the list. What happened? How did you feel?
4. How have these experiences affected your views of other people with the same cultural backgrounds?
5. How might your stereotypes and previous experiences affect you as a counselor when working with clients from these two cultural groups?
6. On a personal level, what have been your experiences of being oppressed (based on your gender, race/ethnicity, religion, social class, age, etc.)? What actions might you have taken in these situations?
7. When might you have oppressed someone else, on a personal level? What was the basis for your oppression?

Instructors can also add questions that specifically relate diversity issues to theories, using questions such as the following:

1. Which theories fit best with your personal values and background and why?
2. Which theories are the worst fit for you and why?
3. How might your personal values, goals, and upbringing affect the way you use theories?

AUDIOVISUAL MATERIAL

There are many good video sources that demonstrate the major theoretical approaches.

Shostrom, E. L. (1965). *Three approaches to psychotherapy I*. Corona Del Mar, CA: Psychological and Educational Films. (Carl Rogers, client-centered psychotherapy; Fritz Perls, Gestalt therapy; and Albert Ellis, rational emotive therapy)

Shostrom, E. L. (1977). *Three approaches to psychotherapy II*. Orange, CA: Psychological Films. (Carl Rogers, client-centered psychotherapy; Everett L. Shostrom, actualizing therapy; Arnold Lazarus, multimodal behavior therapy)

Shostrom, E. L. (1986). *Three approaches to psychotherapy III*. Corona Del Mar, CA: Psychological and Educational Films. (Hans H. Strupp, dynamic psychotherapy; Donald Meichenbaum, cognitive–behavioral modification; Aaron T. Beck, cognitive therapy)

Another useful resource is

Murdock, N. L. (2009). *Theories in action* [video/DVD]. Upper Saddle River, NJ: Pearson/Merrill.

This video series shows the same client, Helen, in 20-minute excerpts of a counseling session with six therapists of different theoretical orientations (psychoanalytic, Gestalt therapy, cognitive therapy, feminist therapy, family systems therapy, and narrative therapy). After each session, the author discusses the session with the therapist. Like the *Three Approaches* series, it is useful for students to see how a different client presentation manifests with different theoretical approaches.

VIGNETTES

A common and helpful exercise in theories classes is to use counseling theory to conceptualize client cases. It is helpful to give a structure for this exploration, such as that described above. The following are three vignettes that could be used for this exercise.

Vignette 1

Ginny is a 24-year-old single Caucasian female who was required by her boss to come to counseling for a drinking problem. Ginny described missing work a few times in the past month because she drank too much the night before. She reported experiencing panic attacks regularly (three times in the past 2 months), depression, and an extreme fear of men and said that drinking helps her to cope with her emotions. She also reported engaging in binge eating and purging behaviors periodically, usually when feeling stressed. In addition, Ginny mentioned feeling compulsive about keeping her apartment "neat and spotless," often spending hours cleaning. Recently, Ginny started feeling worthless, lonely, losing control of her drinking, and disliking herself. However, she said she was reluctant to ask others for help because she believes she has to be strong and considers showing emotions as a sign of being weak.

Ginny is the oldest of three siblings (with twin sisters 5 years younger). Her father was an alcoholic and was not home most of time. Ginny's mother raised three children on her own after her father left the family when Ginny was 5. Ginny described witnessing her mother struggling with depression and sadness and using alcohol to "forget" those pains. She said her mother was very strict and often expressed resentment toward men and her husband to Ginny, saying that "no man is reliable," "be strong, never depend on men," and "all they want is your body." Ginny reported being raped by a classmate in high school when on a date. Client stated feeling scared, dirty, and angry about the boy but was too afraid to tell her mother because she knew her mother would blame her for agreeing to go out with the boy. Ginny said that she did not get a chance to confront the boy because he transferred to another school soon after that incident.

Vignette 2

Mary is a 16-year-old Hispanic female high school student who was referred by her teacher to see you for her emotional and behavioral problems. Mary described experiencing depression, sleep disturbance, and anxiety symptoms. Her grades have dropped dramatically from B+ to D in the past two semesters. Mary reported feeling very unhappy about her current life. She stated that her mother was killed in a terrible car accident 14 months ago during their last family trip. As the oldest child of four (with siblings aged 13, 10, and 7) in her family, she believes she has to assume the role her mother left in the family. Mary reported that her father began to date a woman about 3 months ago, which has made her feel very angry because she thinks her father has betrayed her mom. As a result, she has distanced herself from her father by not talking to him for about 2 months. Mary reported feeling lonely, worthless, and losing control of her life but she dislikes herself being so emotional and weak. "I wish I could be stronger, like my mom."

Mary's family immigrated to the states about 4 years ago and she had a hard time adjusting to the U.S. school system in the first couple years but was doing better until her mother died. She stated not wanting to continue her education because "in school nobody likes me anyway!" Mary says that she has been picked on a lot by other kids in her school, which is very White dominant, and that the only Hispanic teacher in her high school who seemed to care about her moved away last year. Mary appears to blame herself for what happened to her (the teasing and being picked on by other kids). She stated that if she could be stronger, more aggressive, and outgoing, those White kids would not have picked on her. She stated, "Maybe White is superior to us but I am so tired of being teased and looked down upon!"

Vignette 3

Stan is a 25-year-old Caucasian male client with chronic drug-abusing and drinking problems. Last week, he attempted suicide and was found by his current girlfriend, who rushed him to the hospital. Stan comes from an intact family but his parents fought most of the time. He characterized his mother as dominant and continually bitching at his father. On a few occasions when he was a child, he saw his mother physically assault his father. Stan described his father as a weak, passive, person who would never stand up to his mother. Stan reports that his mother often treated him the way she treated his father, saying things like "Why can't you grow up and be a man? You were a mistake—I wish I hadn't had you." Stan feels overwhelmed around strong and attractive women and he said he has trouble seeing himself being adequate as a man. He reports often feeling a great amount of anxiety and guilt about being a failure. Stan was married for 6 months 5 years ago. The marriage ended when his wife left him. He says that his wife was a strong and dominant woman who was always unhappy with him.

TENTATIVE COURSE OUTLINE

WEEK	*TOPIC*	*ASSIGNMENTS*
Week 1	Introductions; review of course syllabus Recent trends in counseling	
Week 2	How to use theory Counseling in a pluralistic world Theories and empirically supported interventions	Palma and Stanley (2002) Pedersen (2005) Sue, Arredondo, and McDavis, (1992) D'Andrea and Heckman (2008) Draper et al. (2002) Whiston and Sexton (1998)
Week 3	Psychoanalysis	Bornstein (2005) Western (1998) Yalom (2003)
Week 4	Person-centered therapy	Heppner, Rogers, and Lee (1990) Rogers (1967, 1980)
Week 5	Gestalt therapy	Bandura, Ross, and Ross (1963) Lazarus (1996) Wilson (1997)
Week 6	Behavior therapy	
Week 7	REBT	Weinrach (1990) Ellis (2004)
Week 8	Exam 1	
Week 9	Cognitive therapy	Beck (1991, 2005)
Week 10	Poster presentation	
Week 11	Solution-focused therapy	
Week 12	Family systems theory	
Week 13	Family systems theory (continued)	
Week 14	Feminist theory	Brown (2006) Enns (1993)
Week 15	Integration of theories Multicultural counseling model	Atkinson, Thompson, and Grant (1993)
Week 16	Exam 2	

CONCLUSION

Perhaps the most important tip we can give a new instructor is to *be prepared and organized*. There is a lot of material to cover in a theories of counseling course and it is often difficult to get through the material and still leave time for other class activities. Finding yourself anxious because of time constraints will probably lead to a less than enjoyable teaching experience, which will in turn have an impact on the experiences of your students.

As noted earlier, we have found that using video examples is extremely helpful in making the theory come alive for students. One question that surfaces with regard to video material is whether to show the video prior to a lecture (and then allowing students to brainstorm about the nature of the theory and its assumptions) or after (so that students can consolidate the material presented). We have used both approaches with apparent success.

Finally, we would suggest that you become as familiar with a wide range of theories as possible before you teach the class. Study your textbook, and when you have time, read a little original source material. However, the more you teach the course, the more comfortable you will become, so you do not have to go overboard the first time you teach it.

Students are generally very interested in the course content and are easily engaged in learning opportunities offered by the instructor. For this reason, we find that teaching counseling theory is one of our favorite, most rewarding assignments.

APPENDIX A

How to Use Theory

The goal of this exercise is to learn how to apply a theory to a client case study.

Steps in applying theory:

1. Know your theory: Answer the following questions:
   a. What is the core motivation of humans?
   b. What is healthy from this theoretical perspective? In this section you should review each of the theory's central constructs.
   c. How do we get unhealthy?
   d. Which developmental stages are important in this theory (if any)?
   e. Who are the key individuals or entities according to this theory? Consider at the levels of individual, family, society.
   f. What are the relative importance of affect, cognition, and behavior from this perspective?

2. Know your client: Answer the following questions:
   a. Describe the client's demographics, current living situation, and the specifics of the presenting problem.
   b. List theory-related information evident in the client's presentation. Take the perspective of this theorist: what things in the case are of interest to you?
3. Integrate: Answer the following questions:
   a. How do the details of the presenting problem fit with the theory's postulates concerning health and dysfunction?

      Here you should review the core constructs of the theory and determine how each applies to the current case. In essence, you are to *explain* the presenting problem, using the language of the theory.

      Be sure to take into account the background of the client and current living situation (e.g., social/cultural/race–ethnicity factors/sexual orientation, disability status, age).
   b. How do other aspects of the client's presentation fit with the postulates of the theory?

      Consider where information does not seem to fit in with the theory. Why? Please keep in mind that sometimes you have to extend the case material to understand the client presentation; you will probably have to hypothesize some things about the client to do this.
   c. Based on this theory, where does the client need to go?

      Here you are to establish theory-based goals for this client, keeping in mind cultural and other factors.
   d. How do I help the client get there?

      Decide the key change mechanisms proposed by the theory and which techniques will help the client reach the above goals and speculate, based on the case study, how the client might react to them.
   e. How will I know when the client is better?

      Review this theory's version of the healthy personality. How does it translate for this client and presenting problem?

APPENDIX B

Major Theory Paper and Presentation Grading Sheet

Theory: ______________________________ Rater: ____________________________

Presenters: ____

1. Quality of poster/handout content (7.5 points): ______/7.5
   a. The poster presentation is well organized and easy to follow.

b. The poster provides an appropriate amount of information covering all key concepts of the theory.
c. The poster clearly identifies the change mechanism proposed by the theory.
d. The poster adequately addresses limitations and multicultural and diversity considerations.
e. The presentation provides case conceptualizations of the theory.

Key:

- Were the descriptions of key concepts/terms clearly worded and understandable?
- Were interpretations of the theory's change mechanism and its relations with other important concepts adequately addressed?
- Were the multicultural/diversity issues adequately addressed?
- Did the case conceptualization demonstrate the key concepts and change mechanism proposed by the theory?

Narrative feedback ______________________________________

____

____

2. Oral presentation and responses to inquiries (7.5 points). ______/7.5
   a. Oral presentation provides concise introduction of the theory.
   b. Abstract theoretical concepts are explained with appropriate real-life examples.
   c. Responses to inquiries demonstrate accurate understanding of the theory.
   d. Presentations and Q&A are equally shared by each team member.

Narrative feedback ______________________________________

____

____

3. Team work, interaction with audience, and supplementary materials (5 points). Grade point: ______/5
   a. Team members work together as a cohesive whole.
   b. Members support and help each other during the presentation.
   c. Presentation facilitates mutual interactions between the presenter and audience.
   d. Supplementary materials/methods (e.g., handouts, PowerPoint, or pictures) are utilized to increase the clarity and effect.

Narrative feedback ______________________________________

____

____

Total Grade Point: ______/20

REFERENCES

American Psychiatric Association (2006). *Diagnostic and statistical manual of mental disorders* (4th ed. text revision). Washington, DC: Author.

Atkinson, D. R., Thompson, C. E., & Grant, S. K. (1993). A three-dimensional model for counseling racial–ethnic minorities. *The Counseling Psychologist, 21*, 257–277.

Bandura, A. T., Ross, D., & Ross, S. A. (1963). Imitation of film-mediated aggressive models. *Journal of Abnormal and Social Psychology, 67*, 3–11.

Beck, A. T. (1991). Cognitive therapy: A 30-year retrospective. *American Psychologist, 46*, 368–375.

Beck, A. T. (2005). The current state of cognitive therapy: A 40-year retrospective. *Archives of General Psychiatry, 62*, 953–959.

Bornstein, R. F. (2005). Reconnecting psychoanalysis to mainstream psychology: Challenges and opportunities. *Psychoanalytic Psychology, 22*, 323–340.

Brown, L. S. (2006). Still subversive after all these years: The relevance of feminist therapy in the age of evidence-based practice. *Psychology of Women Quarterly, 30*, 15–24.

Council for Accreditation of Counseling and Related Educational Programs. *2009 Standards*. Retrieved from http://cacrep.org/doc/2009%20Standards%20with%20cover.pdf

D'Andrea, M., & Heckman, E. F. (2008). Contributing to the ongoing evolution of the multicultural counseling movement: An introduction to the special issue. *Journal of Counseling & Development, 86*, 259–268.

Draper, M. R., Jennings, J., Baron, A., Erdur, O., & Shankar, L. (2002). Time-limited counseling outcome in a nationwide college counseling center sample. *Journal of College Counseling, 5*, 26–38.

Ellis, A. (2004). Why I (really) became a therapist. *Journal of Rational–Emotive Cognitive Behavior Therapy, 22*, 73–77.

Enns, C. Z. (1993). Twenty years of feminist counseling and therapy: From naming biases to implementing multifaceted practice. *The Counseling Psychologist, 21*, 3–87.

Heppner, P. H., Rogers, M. E., & Lee, L. A. (1990). Carl Rogers: Reflections on his life. In P. P. Heppner (Ed.), *Pioneers in counseling and development: Personal and professional perspectives* (pp. 54–59). Alexandria, VA: American Association for Counseling and Development.

Lazarus, A. A. (1996). The utility and futility of combining treatment in psychotherapy. *Clinical Psychology: Science and Practice, 3*, 59–68.

Lewin, K. (1951). *Field theory in social science: Selected theoretical papers*. D. Cartwright (Ed.). New York: Harper & Row.

Murdock, N. L. (1991). Case conceptualization: Applying theory to individuals. *Counselor Education and Supervision, 30*, 355–365.

Murdock, N. L. (2009). *Theories in action* [video/DVD]. Available from www.pearsonhighered.com/educator/academic/product/0,3110,0132286521,00.html

Murdock, N. L. (2009). *Theories of counseling and psychotherapy: A case approach* (2nd ed.). Upper Saddle River, NJ: Pearson/Merrill.

Palma, T. V., & Stanley, J. L. (2002). Effective counseling with lesbian, gay, and bisexual clients. *Journal of College Counseling, 5*, 74–89.

Pedersen, P. (2005). The importance of cultural psychology theory for multicultural counselors. In R. T. Carter (Ed.), *Handbook of racial–cultural psychology and counseling: Theory and research* (pp. 3–16). Hoboken, NJ: John Wiley.

Rochelin, A. (2007). *Applying counseling theories: An online, case-based approach*. Upper Saddle River, NJ: Pearson/Merrill.

Rogers, C. (1967). *On becoming a person*. Boston, MA: Houghton Mifflin.
Rogers, C. (1980). *A way of being*. Boston, MA: Houghton Mifflin.
Shostrom, E. L. (Producer). (1965). *Three approaches to psychotherapy I* [video/DVD]. Available from http://www.psychedfilms.com/
Shostrom, E. L. (Producer). (1977). *Three approaches to psychotherapy II* [video/DVD]. Available from http://www.psychedfilms.com/
Shostrom, E. L. (Producer). (1986). *Three approaches to psychotherapy III* [video/DVD]. Available from http://www.psychedfilms.com/
Sue, D. W., Arredondo, P., & McDavis, R. (1992). Multicultural counseling competencies and standards: A call to the profession. *Journal of Counseling and Development, 70*, 477–485.
Think Exist. (2009). Mark Twain quotes [Quote 1]. Retrieved from http://en.thinkexist.com/quotation/howemptyistheoryinthepresenceof/198683.html.
Wampold, B. (2001). *The great psychotherapy debate*. Mahwah, NJ: Lawrence Erlbaum.
Weinrach, S. G. (1990). Unconventional therapist: Albert Ellis. In P. P. Heppner (Ed.), *Pioneers in counseling and development: Personal and professional perspectives* (pp. 60–66). Alexandria, VA: American Association for Counseling and Development.
Westen, D. (1998). The scientific legacy of Sigmund Freud: Toward a psychodynamically informed psychological science. *Psychological Bulletin, 124*, 333–371.
Whiston, S. C., & Sexton, T. L. (1998). A review of school counseling outcome research: Implications for practice. *Journal of Counseling and Development, 76*, 412–426.
Wilson, K. G. (1997). Science and treatment development: Lessons from the history of behavior therapy. *Behavior Therapy, 28*, 547–558.
Yalom, I. D. (2003). *The gift of therapy: An open letter to a new generation of therapists and their patients*. New York: HarperCollins.

Counseling Skills
Building the Pillars of Professional Counseling

8

John Sommers-Flanagan and Nicholas Heck

Teaching an introductory counseling or "helping" skills course is one of the most exciting and daunting tasks required of counselor educators. It is exciting because teaching and learning counseling skills is foundational to the counseling profession and because, for many students, the helping skills course is a first opportunity to directly practice their new counseling skills. It is daunting because counselor educators must balance substantial course content with experiential activities, skill acquisition, interpersonal observation, feedback, and supervision. These tasks become all the more challenging because counselor educators are usually teaching a diverse, entry-level, counseling student cohort; this cohort arrives at their helping skills course with very different skill sets and lived experiences. Facilitating self-awareness and intentionality within this diverse group requires competence, patience, and compassion.

Regardless of whether this is your first or 50th time teaching a skills course, a new or renewed sense of excitement will be in the air. This is especially true for students. Many students will feel fortunate to be in your class and may be both excited and nervous about developing or sharpening their clinical skills. Having empathy for where counseling students are in their counseling skill developmental process helps model the empathy you want them to have for the clients with whom they will soon be working.

From selecting a text to implementing class activities, this chapter will help you plan a successful helping skills course. However, the ideas and resources provided are intended to facilitate, not dictate, your skills course. Every counseling program is unique and every professor will have distinct strengths and perspectives. You are the best expert on your course objectives and we hope this chapter will help you constructively address those objectives.

WHAT STUDENTS NEED: A GENERAL INSTRUCTIONAL MODEL

The question of what students need from an introductory counseling skills course can be answered on many levels. From a general or macro view, virtually all counseling skill instructional models emphasize four components: (a) exposure to helping skills knowledge and information (including theoretical and skill-based material); (b) observation of counseling skills in action; (c) practice and experience; and (d) feedback and supervision.

Helping Skills Knowledge and Information

To establish minimal helping skills competence, students need exposure to a substantial knowledge base; they need to be taught, usually through lecture and reading, basic information associated with counseling skill development. Although the knowledge base for counseling skill development is continually evolving, there is substantial agreement within training curricula and textbooks regarding appropriate and essential course content (Hill, 2009; Ivey, Ivey, & Zalaquett, 2010; MacCluskie, 2009; Young, 2009).

Observation of Counseling Skills

Students also need to see and hear effective counseling skills in action. Instructors should organize class demonstrations and video presentations to illustrate more appropriate and less appropriate counseling skills. When instructors model specific counseling skills, student learning is enhanced.

Practice and Experience

Knowledge, information, and observation are not enough to help students develop specific skills. Students also need to practice their developing counseling skills. Helping skills courses in counseling should be experiential. Repeated opportunities to practice new skills may include painful moments of self-reflection and self-evaluation, but progress toward more comfortable self-awareness and counselor intentionality eventually occurs. This is one reason why many of us still vividly recall our very first counseling skills course experiences.

Feedback and Supervision

To facilitate optimal skill development, students need more than self-reflection and self-evaluation; they need individualized, encouraging, and constructive feedback from peers and instructors. Such feedback is essential for developing natural or automatic counselor behaviors.

Substantial research supports student needs for knowledge, modeling, practice, and feedback. Ivey et al. (2010) claimed that 450 empirical studies support their microskills approach to counselor skill development. This research base emphasizes that counseling students can learn complex helping skills more efficiently if the skills are broken into small behavioral components.

Qualitative research also supports this instructional and learning process. In a phenomenological study, Woodside, Cole, Olberman, and Carruth (2007) investigated prepracticum counseling student experiences. Overall, students described the learning process as a growth journey infused with self-doubt. In particular, with regard to learning counseling skills, the researchers identified three core learning or instructional experiences: (a) classroom learning (including observations of counseling skills); (b) practice or experience; and (c) the challenge of developing self-awareness. These qualitative findings are consistent with helping skills textbook content and previous and ongoing empirical research (Hill, 2009; Hill, Stahl, & Roffman, 2007; MacCluskie, 2009; Young, 2009).

As implied in the Woodside et al. (2007) study, the road to learning effective counselor behaviors or skills is necessarily bumpy. This is partly because counseling skills constitute a systematic and sometimes awkward variation from normal social behavior. For example, students naturally feel strong impulses to offer reassurance, give advice, and validate their clients' feelings. Consequently, a major challenge inherent in teaching counseling skills involves gently guiding students toward an awareness and partial inhibition of their normal social impulses, while simultaneously helping them use therapeutic listening and intervention responses more consistently. Having students practice these new behaviors in front of their peers and having them watch video recordings of themselves will nearly always increase self-consciousness and self-doubt. This is why students also need support, encouragement, and reassurance throughout this learning process.

WISDOM FROM TWO MASTERS

As we explored teaching components associated with a general instructional model, we found ourselves immersed in the long and storied history of helping skill development within the counseling field. This inspired us to contact two master helping skills teachers, Drs. Allen Ivey and Mark Young. Together, they have taught helping skills for over 65 years. While reflecting on general instructional components of teaching counseling skills we asked them to provide a brief and essential tip for teaching and learning helping skills.

Mark Young

> The biggest issue in learning techniques of counseling is anxiety. When we are anxious, we cannot get off of ourselves. And getting off yourself is the definition of

> empathy. Students need to learn alternatives when they get stuck, blocked or the mind goes blank. The cure is focusing on the client's words and finding a way to paraphrase, reflect or summarize to get back on track. Anxiety diminishes when your focus is on the client rather than how you are doing. That is why I spend a good deal of time on getting the group comfortable with each other so they can practice with others watching. I try to normalize the stages of learning and highlight common problems so that students don't get anxious about being unable to learn the technique. In addition, I face this issue of anxiety head on through class discussion, comments on their transcripts and help them develop strategies through psychodramatic and other techniques to develop empathy as an alternative to anxiety. (M. Young, personal communication, January 11, 2010)

Allen Ivey

> The biggest challenge in teaching counseling skills is to help students realize that it isn't as easy as it looks. For example, attending behavior—culturally appropriate eye contact, vocal tone, body language, and verbal following—is simple. But, it is very different when one actually practices and has to keep the interview going. And, just going through practice is not enough, repeat practice is required until each skill becomes natural and spontaneous. And, obtaining feedback around each skill is necessary. You may think that you have competence, but do the observers feel the same way? Fortunately, the skills build on each other and beginners get to practice attending again and again. But as they move on to other skills such as reflection of feeling and competent confrontation, more practice is necessary. The concepts of the basic skills are clear, but using them in the session requires mastery. It is much easier to pass that exam than it is to demonstrate that one can do it in a live session. (A. Ivey, personal communication, January 7, 2010)

In his e-mail message, Ivey also provided a summary statement that captures much (but not all) of the helping skills teaching and learning process. He wrote: "All of this boils down to practice, practice, practice, and feedback, feedback, feedback!!" To this we would add: The counselor educator provides an intellectually stimulating, multiculturally sensitive, and interpersonally safe academic environment where all this practice, feedback, and personal and professional growth is most likely to occur.

COMMON INSTRUCTIONAL DILEMMAS AND DECISIONS

The biggest dilemmas associated with helping skills courses involve decisions pertaining to depth and content emphasis. For example, the question is not whether to integrate multicultural and social justice concepts into the counseling skills course curriculum but, rather, how much, how often, and in what way to weave in these essential threads. This section identifies several dilemmas and decisions associated with teaching counseling skills.

Multiculturalism, Diversity, and Social Justice

How shall I infuse multicultural, diversity, and social justice issues into my helping skills course? In the 1970s, multiculturalism became recognized as a fourth force influencing the practice of counseling and psychotherapy. When this occurred, most counseling curricula and textbooks responded by inserting a multicultural theory chapter into each text and multicultural learning unit into each curriculum. More recently, there has been a movement away from this learning unit approach and toward an approach that integrates multicultural, diversity, and social justice perspectives throughout curricula and textbooks (Brooks-Harris, 2008; Ivey, D'Andrea, Ivey, & Simek-Morgan, 2007). The 2009 Counseling and Counseling Related Educational Programs (CACREP) standards follow this trend. For example, CACREP describes the Helping Relationships knowledge base as: "HELPING RELATIONSHIPS—studies that provide an understanding of the counseling process in a multicultural society . . ." (p. 11). This statement clearly indicates that multiculturalism should no longer be viewed as a separate component but infused throughout counseling curricula. In a recent symposium, Sue (2009) and others echoed this view, emphasizing that we should not study a series of "White" theories and then a multicultural theory but that to be relevant, all theoretical perspectives must address multicultural, diversity, and social justice issues.

Providing a multicultural lens or platform at the beginning of a skills course and then referencing it throughout the course is one way counselor educators can address diversity issues. Several excellent multicultural models are available. These include (a) the multicultural competency model endorsed by the American Counseling Association and the American Psychological Association (see Sue, Arrendondo, & McDavis, 1992); (b) two models that use acronyms to emphasize that multiculturalism is about more than race and ethnicity (see D'Andrea & Daniels, 2001, for information on the respectful model and Hays, 2008, for information on the addressing model); (c) an anthropologically based model developed by Hofstede (2001; see MacCluskie, 2009, for more information on Hofstede's model).

Theory Versus Skill Development

How much do I focus on helping theory versus skill development? The microskills movement has, in some ways, streamlined counseling skill acquisition. When instructors isolate helping skills, provide practice opportunities, and give feedback to shape helping behaviors, most students are able to enact the skills. However, as Rogers (1942, 1961, 1980) repeatedly articulated, effective helping behavior is about more than technical skill acquisition.

Rogers (1942, 1961, 1980) formulated the core conditions of counseling and psychotherapy as counselor or psychotherapist attitudes, not behaviors. He believed that counselors should trust clients and adopt attitudes of congruence, unconditional positive regard, and empathic understanding. Our point is that overemphasizing technical application of helping skills, without an understanding of underlying theoretical concepts, may produce lower quality learning outcomes. This is partly what Natalie Rogers meant when she stated "Most . . . students . . . don't really understand in any depth what the person-centered approach is about" and "People are using the words 'methods' and 'techniques' which always puts me off, because although there certainly are methods that we use, it's much bigger than that" (as cited in J. Sommers-Flanagan, 2007, p. 123).

Clearly, counseling students need to understand person-centered (and other) theory at some point in their educational experience. We recommend that you intentionally decide how to balance theory and skill development in your helping skills course.

Practice Opportunities for Students

What is the most efficient means through which I can provide students with counseling practice opportunities? There are three options for resolving this dilemma: (a) using role-play or "acting" situations where students from within or outside class allow your students to practice their skills; this can include hiring actors or gathering volunteers (including yourself) to role-play client situations; (b) using analogue clients (e.g., introductory psychology students who receive extra credit for volunteering to be clients or having your students conduct real sessions with each other); or (c) using real clients from a campus or departmental clinic.

Each of these options has advantages and disadvantages. Early or initial counseling skill practice probably works best with role-play or acted-out client scenarios. This approach offers maximum safety and minimum risk, which is very important with neophyte counseling students. Later, it may be best to have analogue clients. For example, at the University of Montana we have mental health counseling students conduct eight different "clinical" or counseling interviews with eight different volunteers from introductory psychology courses. These volunteers are encouraged to be open to benefiting from an analogue counseling experience. The challenges of this approach arise when (a) volunteer students do not show up; (b) disinterested or unmotivated volunteers make practice counseling sessions rather difficult; or (c) working with volunteers feels artificial.

For the most part, we advise against using real clients for students in an introductory skills course. The risks are too high and potential benefits too small.

Providing Students Feedback

How shall I handle the student feedback process? A safe and systematic procedure for giving and receiving feedback in helping skills courses is especially important because risk taking, which intensifies student sensitivity and self-doubt, is required. Many or most students will feel vulnerable displaying their underdeveloped skills in front of their peers and instructor. However, the sooner and more often students expose themselves to outside scrutiny, the sooner they will be able to at least partially desensitize themselves from self-consciousness and performance anxiety. Consequently, we recommend providing guidelines for safely giving and receiving feedback on the first day of class. We offer several guidelines or norms regarding the giving and receiving of feedback. For example,

1. When students practice skills in front of peers, they control whether they receive feedback. They should be asked something like, "Do you want feedback on this?"
2. Students are free to give each other positive feedback, but constructive or corrective feedback is the responsibility of the instructor.
3. Although general positive feedback (e.g., "You did a good job!") is nice, specific feedback (e.g., "You looked calm and your paraphrases were very accurate") is more helpful.
4. Students may want to begin with a self-evaluation (e.g., "I thought my eye contact was about right and I was able to keep myself from asking too many questions").
5. The instructor may provide minor constructive feedback by telling students what they might have done instead, but more significant constructive feedback is given privately.
6. When/if trust levels in class are high, it may be appropriate for students to share minor constructive feedback with each other.

As the course instructor, you are the group's leader, role model, and mentor; students will generally follow your lead (Yalom & Leszcz, 2005). If you want students to show intentionality in their counseling skill development, it helps if you model intentionality in your decision making about the preceding instructional dilemmas. Similarly, if you value self-awareness and multicultural perspectives as teaching outcomes, your students will benefit when you model these values as you deliver your helping skills course content.

OBJECTIVES AND CACREP STANDARDS

Students will:

1. Be able to integrate wellness and prevention principles as they mutually formulate counseling goals with clients. (Section II.G.5.a.)
2. Understand and articulate how counselor characteristics such as age, gender, ethnicity, and class can influence the helping process. (Section II.G.5.b.)
3. Develop greater awareness about how counselor attitudes and behaviors affect the helping process. (Section II.G.5.b.)
4. Develop, apply, and evaluate the effectiveness of interviewing and counseling skills designed to promote client growth. (Section II.G.5.c.)

5. Articulate their understanding of counseling theories that provide models for case conceptualization and appropriate counseling interventions. (Section II.G.5.d.)
6. Begin developing their personal model of counseling by integrating general counseling techniques and specific solution-focused, cognitive, behavioral, emotion-focused, and interpersonal interventions with current professional research. (Section II.G.5.d.)
7. Develop a greater awareness of social and cultural attitudes, beliefs, and acculturative experiences by engaging in specific experiential learning activities designed to foster their understanding of self and culturally diverse clients. (Section II.G.2.b.)
8. Articulate how a systems perspective in general, and family systems perspective in particular, can lead to intervention strategies that help both the individual and system grow. (Section II.G.5.e.)
9. Learn and demonstrate crisis intervention (psychological first aid) and suicide prevention skills. (Section II.G.5.g.)

Overview of Critical Course Content

Helping skills course content will be primarily driven by CACREP standards, counseling program needs, instructor preferences, and available course materials. Given these forces, we identify five course content areas to be addressed in a general helping skills course.

- Professional and ethical issues. Although most counseling programs have a course dedicated to ethics and professional issues, courses that emphasize counseling skill application also must include at least minimal information about professional ethics (R. Sommers-Flanagan & Sommers-Flanagan, 2007). This is especially the case for introductory helping skills courses because informed consent is relevant and necessary, even during role-plays. At the very least, instructors should provide readings (usually included in helping skills texts) and discussion of confidentiality, boundaries, informed consent, competence, and self-care.
- Cultural and diversity awareness. We have already discussed the importance of infusing counseling skills courses with multicultural content. Among other reasons, our pluralistic society requires that counselors obtain training and education in multicultural competence and multicultural humility (Sue et al., 1992).
- Counseling identity, focus, and goals. CACREP standards emphasize that counselors-in-training be oriented toward "wellness and prevention as desired counseling goals" (2009, p. 11). This focus implies that counseling programs have theoretical foundations with more of an emphasis on positive personal development and less of an emphasis on psychopathology (e.g., more person-centered and solution-focused but less psychoanalytic). However, to completely ignore basic psychoanalytic principles like transference, counter-

transference, and the working alliance could be unethical because it would adversely affect counselor competency.

- Counseling skills training. Skills training is the obvious central focus of helping skills courses; most of your teaching time should be devoted to this content area. Students who complete counseling skills courses should be able to identify and use (a) attending skills (i.e., eye contact, body posture, voice tone, and verbal tracking); (b) silence; (c) paraphrasing or reflection of content; (d) reflection of feeling and feeling validation; (e) questions; (f) interpretation and/or reframing; (g) confrontation/challenging; (h) explanation; (i) advice giving; and other listening and influence strategies and techniques. Additionally, to some extent, counseling skill training should include a substantial focus on client observation or assessment—and an understanding of counseling process versus counseling content.
- Intake interviewing and other assessment/treatment-oriented training. Counseling students eventually develop their helping skills to the point where they provide professional counseling. But because counseling implies assessment, at least some skills training on how to conduct intake interviews, structured diagnostic assessment/treatment planning, suicide assessment interviews, and possibly mental status examinations is necessary.

The extent to which counselor educators cover intake interviewing and other assessment procedures within basic skills courses will vary considerably. This variability is also true within helping skills textbooks, because some texts dedicate only a few pages to intake interviewing, suicide assessment interviewing, and mental status examinations (see Hill, 2009; Ivey et al., 2010; MacCluskie, 2009), whereas others devote entire chapters to these topics (see J. Sommers-Flanagan & Sommers-Flanagan, 2009; Young, 2009). Nevertheless, understanding and experiencing advantages and disadvantages of interviewing as assessment and exploring case formulation and treatment planning models is crucial training content for counseling students.

CRITERIA FOR EVALUATING A TEXT

CACREP-accredited counseling programs utilize a variety of different textbooks and resources to address critical helping skills/interviewing and counseling content areas. For example, on the Association for Counselor Education and Supervision syllabus clearinghouse website, ten different textbooks are listed in 15 different helping skills syllabi; on this website, Mark E. Young's (2009) *Learning the Art of Helping* is listed most frequently.

Depending on your professional perspective, you may find yourself selecting a textbook based on a combination of the following factors:

1. Coverage of what you consider the most important course content areas.
2. Organization, tone, and delivery of the helping skills information.

3. Readability or student friendliness.
4. Integration of diversity and social justice principles and practice.
5. An empirical or evidence-based foundation.
6. Supplementary instructor resource materials (e.g., instructor's resource manual, DVDs).
7. Primary theoretical roots or orientation emphasized in the text.

MOST POPULAR TEXTS

The following textbooks (listed alphabetically) all include substantial core counseling skill coverage. They were selected for inclusion based on sales figures from Amazon.com, BarnesandNoble.com, listing on the ACES syllabus clearinghouse, and Google searches of additional counseling syllabi. This is a very short list; many other texts may be well suited for your course and program.

Hill, C. E. (2009). *Helping skills: Facilitating exploration, insight, and action* (3rd ed.). Washington, DC: American Psychological Association.

Ivey, A. E., Ivey, M., & Zalaquett, C. P. (2010). *Intentional interviewing and counseling facilitating client development in a multicultural society* (7th ed.). Belmont, CA: Brooks/Cole.

Sommers-Flanagan, J., & Sommers-Flanagan, R. (2009). *Clinical interviewing* (4th ed.). Hoboken, NJ: Wiley.

Young, M. E. (2009). *Learning the art of helping: Building blocks and techniques* (4th ed.). New York: Merrill.

Additional notable and popular helping textbooks include the following:

Cormier, S., Nurius, P., & Osborn, C. (2009). *Interviewing and change strategies for helpers*. Belmont, CA: Brooks/Cole.

MacCluskie, K. (2009). *Acquiring counseling skills: Integrating theory, multiculturalism, and self-awareness*. Upper Saddle River, NJ: Prentice Hall.

Murphy, B., & Dillon, C. (2008). *Interviewing in action in a multicultural world*. Belmont, CA: Brooks/Cole.

SUPPLEMENTAL READING

Individual counselor educators may use book chapters or journal articles to supplement textbook and class material. A few examples follow.
Readings on counseling theory:

Rogers, C. R. (1942). *Counseling and psychotherapy*. Boston, MA: Houghton Mifflin.

Rogers, C. R. (1961). *On becoming a person. A therapist's view of psychotherapy*. Boston, MA: Houghton Mifflin.
Rogers, C. R. (1980). *A way of being*. Boston, MA: Houghton Mifflin.

Readings on crisis assessment and management (including psychological first aid):

Jobes, D. A. (2006). *Managing suicidal risk: A collaborative approach*. New York: Guilford Press.
Ruzek, J., Jacobs, A. K., Layne, C. M., Vernberg, E. M., & Watson, P. (2007). Psychological first aid. *Journal of Mental Health Counseling, 29*, 17–49.
Sommers-Flanagan, J., & Sommers-Flanagan, R. (2009). *Clinical interviewing* (4th ed.). Hoboken, NJ: Wiley.
Williams, M. B. (2006). How schools respond to traumatic events: Debriefing interventions and beyond. In J. Garrick & M. B. Williams (Eds.), *Trauma treatment techniques: Innovative trends* (pp. 57–81). London: Haworth Press.

Readings on empirical helping skills research:

Claiborn, C. D., Goodyear, R. K., & Horner, P. A. (2002). Feedback. In J. C. Norcross (Ed.), *Psychotherapy relationships that work* (pp. 217–233). Oxford, UK: Oxford University Press.
Hill, C. E., & Knox, S. (2002). Self-disclosure. In J. C. Norcross (Ed.). *Psychotherapy relationships that work* (pp. 255–265). Oxford, UK: Oxford University Press.

Readings on mental status examinations and diagnosis and treatment planning:

Lazarus, A. (2007). *Brief but comprehensive psychotherapy: The multimodal way*. New York: Springer.
Seligman, L. (2005). *Diagnosis and treatment planning in counseling*. New York: Springer.
Sommers-Flanagan, J., & Sommers-Flanagan, R. (2009). *Clinical interviewing* (4th ed.). Hoboken, NJ: Wiley.

WEBSITES

- My Helping Lab
  http://www.myhelpinglab.com
  My helping lab is a website associated with Merrill/Pearson products. To access this website, students need a code that comes with purchasing a textbook and instructors need to obtain permission within the system. My Helping Lab includes access to instructional videos, test items, and other learning tools.

- The Association for Counselor Education and Supervision syllabus clearinghouse
  http://www.counseling.org/Resources/TP/SyllabusClearinghouse/CT2.aspx
  This website has many different CACREP course content area syllabi. You must be an ACES member to access the syllabus clearinghouse.

- CourseSmart
  http://instructors.coursesmart.com/learnmore
  This website includes access to a large variety of e-textbooks from several publishers. This website gives you nearly instant access to course materials.

LEARNING ACTIVITIES

Exploring potential learning activities and assignments for helping skills courses can be overwhelming. We recommend that you build your own set of learning activities and assignments based on your unique needs and preferences. The best resources for compiling learning activities and assignments are (a) the textbooks themselves (you can peruse most of them by using the CourseSmart website or by requesting examination copies) and (b) syllabi listed on the ACES syllabus clearinghouse or posted on the Internet.

The following learning activity list and description is necessarily limited.

Interview the Instructor

This activity is used during the first helping skills class meeting to set a positive tone and model risk taking associated with in-class practice and feedback. The instructor divides students into small groups and students generate questions, ranging from professional to personal, to ask the instructor. Students then take turns coming up to the front of the class to ask the instructor questions. This activity gives you a chance to role model your preferred level of openness while setting a "We get up in front of the class and practice" norm (J. Sommers-Flanagan & Sommers-Flanagan, 2009).

Exaggerating Poor Listening

To get an experiential sense of the power of attending behaviors, Ivey et al. (2010) suggested that students pair up and role-play negative attending behaviors (e.g., leaning backwards, folding or crossing one's arms, etc.). This process gives students a chance to be playful as they practice skills in front of each other.

No Questions Asked and Asking Nothing but Questions

Many beginning students ask too many questions in their early interviews. Consequently, it can be helpful for them to have repeated assignments where they spend 15–30 minutes or more interviewing each other or volunteers relying on less-directive listening skills instead of questions. Students can also be assigned short interview experiences where, similar to highly structured diagnostic interviews, they only ask questions and are not allowed to use basic listening skills (Ivey et al., 2010; J. Sommers-Flanagan & Means, 1987).

Responding to Personal Questions

It is very challenging for beginning interviewers to respond to personal questions. These questions can focus on virtually anything, but common questions include: "Are you married?" or "Do you have children?" or "How would you handle this problem?"

To practice responding to personal questions, Murphy and Dillon (2008) recommended that students gather in small groups (three to four students each) and ask each other personal questions. Students then practice responding in different ways and share their experiences and give each other feedback.

In-Class Interview Tag Teams

For more complex assessment interviews it may be less threatening for students to practice as teams. For example, groups of four or five students can team together to provide an in-class intake interview or suicide assessment interview with the instructor as a role-play client. Each student is assigned a portion of the interview and can call time out or "tag" his or her teammate as the interview proceeds.

Using Counseling Vignettes

Most texts include many specific vignettes for analysis and learning. These vignettes may include children with depressive symptoms, adults struggling with anxiety, adolescents who wear their anger on their sleeves, etc. Vignettes also vary by client ethnic orientation and many other factors. The key to using vignettes, whether in written, oral, or role-play format, is to closely analyze the unique responses of diverse clients in diverse situations facing diverse life problems. Using counseling vignettes helps students and instructors increase the breadth of their counseling training experiences.

AUDIOVISUAL MATERIAL

There is a plethora of audiovisual material available to augment your helping skills course. For example, many theories texts (see Archer & McCarthy, 2006; Corey, 2009) and many helping skills texts (see Hill, 2009; Ivey et al., 2010; Young, 2009) include accompanying DVD material. Regardless of the quality of these video products, watching and analyzing these demonstration videos can be beneficial. Additionally, there are many counseling skills video clips and comedy counseling spoofs available on YouTube and Google video. For example, a Mad TV clip with Bob Newhart as a counselor provides a sarcastic display of solution-focused counseling (see http://www.youtube.com/watch?v=T1g3ENYxg9k). The decisions you make regarding accompanying video material will be unique to your counselor training background, theoretical orientation, program needs, and many other factors.

Popular Media

- *In Treatment* (on HBO)
- *Shrink*
- *Ordinary People*
- *Good Will Hunting*
- *Prince of Tides*
- *Analyze This*

ASSIGNMENT

Oral Examinations

After repeatedly engaging in practice helping interviews throughout a semester, students may be given an experiential examination that focuses on either enacting counseling skills or on course content. Developing a simple evaluation rubric is the biggest challenge to oral examination options (see Appendix A for rubric).

Overall, the big outcomes question is "What will it look like when students can display adequate counseling skills or interviewing techniques?" The answer to this question almost always includes awareness and intentionality. As a teacher and evaluator, one of your greatest challenges is to develop clear criteria for evaluating student progress toward intentional and competent counseling skills.

TENTATIVE COURSE OUTLINE

WEEK	*TOPIC*
Week 1	Syllabus distribution, discussion, and course overview. Interview the instructor activity. Ethical expectations. Procedures for giving and receiving feedback. Multicultural principles
Week 2	Exploring attending and observational skills. Negative and positive attending skills role-plays. Multicultural perspectives on attending behaviors. Self-awareness and developing intentionality. The physical arrangements and preparations needed for a counseling session

WEEK	*TOPIC*
Week 3	Nondirective (less directive) listening skills. Today we focus on using silence, clarification, paraphrasing, nondirective feeling reflections, and summarization in counseling sessions
Week 4	Directive listening responses. Today we focus on using interpretive reflection of feelings, interpretation (including reframing), feeling validation, and confrontation or challenging in counseling sessions
Week 5	Using questions and action skills. Today we focus on using questions (including solution-focused or therapeutic questions), explanation or role induction, suggestion, agreement–disagreement, approval–disapproval, advice, and urging
Week 6	Using immediacy and self-disclosure. Handling client questions and challenges. Multicultural perspectives
Week 7	Interviewing as assessment I: The intake interview
Week 8	Interviewing as assessment II: The suicide assessment interview
Week 9	Interviewing as assessment III: The mental status examination
Week 10	Interviewing as assessment IV: Diagnostic interviewing and treatment planning
Week 11	Interviewing as influence: Counseling and therapeutic interviewing strategies with resistant or difficult clients
Week 12	Advanced counseling techniques I: Interviewing children and adolescents
Week 13	Advanced counseling techniques II: Interviewing techniques with couples and families
Week 14	Advanced counseling techniques III: The interview and counseling interventions with diverse populations
Week 15	Course overview

CONCLUSION

In conclusion, we love teaching basic helping skills courses for three main reasons: (a) students in the course are developmentally ready to learn; they are excited about finally getting a chance to apply counseling and psychological techniques with real people; (b) basic skills are basic for a reason; even after teaching this material many times, we find that whenever key issues or conflicts or challenges emerge in a counseling session, returning to the basic listening skills is nearly always the best strategy; (c) due to the focus on practice and feedback noted by Ivey (1971), teaching this course allows us to begin deep and lasting connections with students as they struggle to master the skills of the counseling trade.

It is impossible to become a perfect counselor. Consequently, in addition to the preceding recommendations in this chapter, we strongly recommend that helping skills instructors actively and repeatedly demonstrate specific interviewing and counseling techniques in class. We also recommend that students be allowed to provide instructors with both positive and constructive feedback. By doing so, you—the instructor—will become the best kind of role model who, as a lifelong learner, is willing to continuously acknowledge and learn from successes as well as mistakes; if we can inspire our students to be similarly open to learning throughout their professional counseling lives, we will have accomplished a very good thing.

APPENDIX A

Sample Oral Examination Evaluation Rubric

This rubric is designed for a content-focused oral examination. Students are provided a large list (40–50 items) of short-answer questions in advance and then are asked four questions in a small-group format. Student responses are evaluated on a 5-point scale (0–4 points).

- 4 Points (*excellent*)—The student articulates all details associated with the question and further elaborates on cultural diversity issues, application challenges, or research implications.
- 3 Points (*very good*)—The student provides a detailed answer that includes all major components associated with the question.
- 2 Points (*adequate*)—The student provides over half of the detailed content associated with the question but misses at least one significant content area.
- 1 Point (*marginal*)—The student articulates some essential information but provides less than 50% of the information that should have been included.
- 0 Points (*unacceptable*)—The student does not respond accurately to any portion of the question content.

As long as five distinct and ratable counselor behavioral responses can be operationalized, this rubric can be modified to evaluate counselor skill development in role-plays.

REFERENCES

Archer, J. J., & McCarthy C. J. (2006). *Theories of counseling and psychotherapy: Contemporary applications*. Upper Saddle River, NJ: Prentice Hall.

Bender, L., Armstrong, S., Weinstein, B., Weinstein, H., Gorden, J., Moore, C., Mosier, S., Smith, K. (Producer), & Van Sant, G. (Director). (1997). *Good will hunting* [Motion picture].

Berman, B., Chris Brigham, C., Crystal, B., Rosenthal, J., Weinstein, P., Amato, L., & Herrington, S., (Producers), & Ramis, H. (Director). (1999). *Analyze this* [Motion picture]. USA: Village Roadshow Pictures, NPV Entertainment, Baltimore Pictures, Spring Creek Productions, Face Productions, & Tribeca Productions.

Brooks-Harris, J. (2008). *Integrative multitheoretical psychotherapy*. Boston, MA: Houghton-Mifflin.

Burns, M., Brunetti, D., Pope, B., Saviano, J., & James, P. (Producer), & Pate, J. (Director). (2009). *Shrink* [Motion picture]. USA: Ignite Entertainment.

Corey, G. (2009). *Theory and practice of counseling and psychotherapy* (8th ed.). Belmont, CA: Brooks/Cole.

Council for Accreditation of Counseling and Related Educational Programs. (2009). *2009 Standards*. Retrieved from http://www.cacrep.org/template/index.cfm

D'Andrea, M., & Daniels, J. (2001). Respectful counseling: An integrative model for counselors. In D. Pope-Davis & H. Coleman (Eds.), *The interface of class, culture and gender in counseling* (pp. 417–466). Thousand Oaks, CA: Sage.

Hays, P. A. (2008). *Addressing cultural complexities in practice: Assessment, diagnosis, and therapy* (2nd ed.). Washington, DC: American Psychological Association.

Hill, C. E. (2009). *Helping skills: Facilitating exploration, insight, and action* (4th ed.). Washington DC: American Psychological Association.

Hill, C. E., Stahl, J., & Roffman, M. (2007). Training novice psychotherapists: Helping skills and beyond. *Psychotherapy: Theory, Research, Practice, Training, 44*, 364–370.

Hofstede, G. (2001). *Culture's consequences, comparing values, behaviors, institutions, and organizations across nations*. Thousand Oaks, CA: Sage.

Ivey, A. E. (1971). *Microcounseling: Innovations in interviewing training*. Oxford, USA: Charles C. Thomas.

Ivey, A. E., D'Andrea, M., Ivey, M. B., & Simek-Morgan, L. (2007). *Theories of counseling and psychotherapy: A multicultural perspective* (6th ed.). Boston, MA: Allyn & Bacon.

Ivey, A. E., Ivey, M. B., & Zalaquett, C. P. (2010). *Intentional interviewing and counseling: Facilitating client development in a multicultural society*. Belmont, CA: Brooks/Cole.

Levinson, S., Leight, W., Wahlberg, M., Garcia, R., Barclay, R., & Levi, H. (Producers) & Barclay, P., Garcia, R., McKay, J., Mayron, M., Fleck, R., Selim, A., Misiano, C., Hunt, C., George, T., de Segonzac, J., & Levi, H. (Directors). (2008). *In treatment* [Motion picture]. United States: HBO.

MacCluskie, K. (2009). *Acquiring counseling skills: Integrating theory, multiculturalism, and self-awareness*. Upper Saddle River, NJ: Pearson.

Rogers, C. R. (1942). *Counseling and psychotherapy*. Boston, MA: Houghton Mifflin.

Rogers, C. R. (1961). *On becoming a person. A therapist's view of psychotherapy*. Boston, MA: Houghton Mifflin.

Rogers, C. R. (1980). *A way of being*. Boston, MA: Houghton Mifflin.

Schwary, R. (Producer), & Redford, R. (Director). (1980). *Ordinary people* [Motion picture]. USA: Paramount Pictures &Wildwood Enterprises.

Sommers-Flanagan, J. (2007). The development and evolution of person-centered expressive art therapy: A conversation with Natalie Rogers. *Journal of Counseling and Development, 85*, 120–125.

Sommers-Flanagan, J., & Means, J. R. (1987). Thou shalt not ask questions: An approach to teaching interviewing skills. *Teaching of Psychology, 14*, 164–166.

Sommers-Flanagan, J., & Sommers-Flanagan, R. (2009). *Clinical interviewing* (4th ed.). Hoboken, NJ: Wiley.

Sommers-Flanagan, R., & Sommers-Flanagan, J. (2007). *Becoming an ethical helping professional: Cultural and philosophical foundations*. Hoboken, NJ: Wiley.

Streisand, B., Roe III, J. T., Corman, C., & Schorager, S., (Producers), & Streisand, B. (Director). (1991). *Prince of Tides* [Motion picture]. USA: Longfellow Pictures, Barwood Films, & Columbia Pictures.

Sue, D. W. (August, 2009). Discussant. Interviewing diverse clients. In J. Sommers-Flanagan (Chair) *The initial interview: Essential principles and techniques with diverse clients.* Symposium conducted at the 117th annual meeting of the American Psychological Association, Toronto.

Sue, D. W. (2009). Discussant: The initial interview: Essential principles and techniques with diverse clients. In Symposium conducted at the annual meeting of the American Psychological Association, Toronto.

Sue, D. W., Arrendondo, P., & McDavis, R. J. (1992). Multicultural competencies and standards: A call to the profession. *Journal of Multicultural Counseling and Development, 26*, 254–272.

Williams, M. B. (2006). How schools respond to traumatic events: Debriefing interventions and beyond. In J. Garrick & M. B. Williams (Eds.), *Trauma treatment techniques: Innovative trends* (pp. 57–81). Gloucestershire, UK: Haworth Press.

Woodside, M., Cole, K., Oberman, A., & Carruth, E. (2007). The experience of learning to be a counselor: A pre practicum perspective. *Journal for Counselor Education and Supervision, 47*, 14–28.

Yalom, I. D., & Leszcz, M. (2005). *The theory and practice of group psychotherapy* (5th ed.). New York: Basic Books.

Young, M. E. (2009). *Learning the art of helping: Building blocks and techniques* (4th ed.). New York: Merrill.

Group Work
Standards, Techniques, Practice, and Resources 9

Samuel T. Gladding and Nathaniel N. Ivers

A course in group work is a fundamental requirement for graduating from a counselor education program with a master's degree, especially one accredited by the Council for the Accreditation of Counseling and Related Educational Programs (CACREP). There are a number of essentials that students must take from such a course. There are also some common decisions and dilemmas instructors face when presenting a course with this content. Furthermore, there are some absolutely critical components a course of this nature must contain.

Learning to work in groups and how to work in groups is essential. Counseling students must master group skills principally because in almost any employment setting counselors will be asked to work with groups of clients and with groups of professionals for the overall good of everyone. Counselors who do not know how groups work or what to expect will not only be lost in what they do; they will also be ineffective. Thus, in taking a course on group work, counseling students need to gain the following:

- Knowledge of the stages groups go through, that is, forming, storming, norming, performing, and adjourning (Section II.G.6.a).
- Awareness that there are four main types of groups: psychoeducational, task/work, counseling, and psychotherapy (Section II.G.6.d).
- Information about the various associations and organizations for group workers (Section II.G.1.f).
- Research and resources available to group workers in leading or participating in groups (Section II.G.6.c).
- Ethical guidelines and legal pitfalls involved in leading or participating in groups, especially counseling and psychotherapy groups (Section II.G.1.j).

COMMON DILEMMAS AND DECISIONS INSTRUCTORS NEED TO MAKE

There are a number of dilemmas and important decisions faced by instructors of a group work course. Each of these will be addressed below.

The first dilemma is simply how much of the course they will devote to lecture and how much to experiential exercises. In making the decision regarding this matter, instructors are torn between how much factual knowledge students should master and how much actual group experience they should have. There is no easy solution. The answer is found in the composition of the class and what students intend to do afterwards.

A second dilemma instructors face is whether to role-play situations or to actually run a growth group. The answer again is dependent on what the ultimate goals of the course are in addition to time and ethical concerns. Role-playing is always easier and in most cases it can be just as enlightening. Students may actually increase their empathy and even gain insight into themselves through role-playing. Do they gain as much as they might through actually being group members? Probably not, but they also do not face as much peer pressure to perform and they avoid many of the ethical dilemmas that may accompany growth groups when group members accidentally or purposefully talk about what is happening in their group.

THINGS THAT ARE ABSOLUTELY CRITICAL FOR A GROUP WORK COURSE

First, it is essential that counseling students are able to differentiate the similarities and differences between working therapeutically with individuals and families and working therapeutically with groups.

Second, there are a number of group leadership techniques that must be mastered, such as linkage, cutting off, and drawing out, which are endemic to group work. Application of these skills, as well as determining when and how to apply them, are essentials that those enrolled in a group work course must master.

A third critical component of a group work course is an ability to anticipate and recognize the developmental stages most groups exhibit and what group dynamics are typical in each of those stages. Students must also learn how to help a group move from one stage to another.

A fourth factor that is essential to master in a group work course is the different skills needed in various types of groups. This factor is specifically related to leadership proficiencies. Knowing that authoritarian, democratic, and laissez-faire leadership leads to strikingly dissimilar results is important for someone in a group work course.

Finally, the research that defines how leaders should act when, for example, they are giving feedback is a significant component that should be taken from a course on this subject.

OBJECTIVES AND CACREP STANDARDS

The following is a list of some of the main ideas and skills students should learn in a group work course. These objectives are based on the 2009 standards of the Council on Accreditation of Counseling and Related Educational Programs.

- Advantages and disadvantages of group counseling, assessment procedures and circumstances under which it is indicated or contraindicated; that is, when other referrals should be made. (Section II.G.7.f.)
- Ethical guidelines and problems related to group work. (Section II.G.1.j.)
- Various theoretical approaches to group counseling. (Section II.G.6.c.)
- Group stages—process and dynamics. (Section II.G.6.a.)
- Characteristics of group leaders that affect group process; personal awareness of own strengths, weaknesses, values, prejudices, etc., and the effects on others. (Section II.G.6.b.)
- Theoretical rationales that support the use of various group counseling procedures or techniques. (Section II.G.6.d.)
- Research on group counseling that informs evidence-based practice. (Section II.G.8.e.)
- Development of a personal, carefully thought-out theory of group counseling. (Section II.G.6.c.)
- Ability to facilitate group process from a member's standpoint. (Section II.G.6.e.)
- Methods to continue learning about group process and group leadership. (Section II.G.6.d.)

In their 2009 standards, CACREP defined group work as "studies that provide both theoretical and experiential understandings of group purpose, development, dynamics, theories, methods, skills, and other group approaches in a multicultural society," including the following five components: (a) "principles of group dynamics," (b) "group leadership or facilitation styles and approaches," (c) "theories of group counseling," (d) "group counseling methods," and (e) "direct experiences in which students participate as group members in a small group activity" (p. 12). In this section, each of these CACREP standards is described in detail with the aim of creating clear and well-defined objectives for the overall group course and individual lesson plans. It is important to reiterate that course objectives based on these standards should aim to elicit both a theoretical and experiential understanding of the material.

- Students will understand components of group process including methods for facilitating therapeutic and healthy interactions among group members. (Section II.G.6.a.)

  According to CACREP (2009), the principles of group dynamics include an understanding and knowledge of "group process components, developmental stage theories, group members' roles and behaviors, and therapeutic factors of group work" (p. 12). *Group process* refers to the interactions between group members. Particular components of group process may include the following types of interactions between group members: contagion, conflict, anxiety, consensual validation, universality, family reenactment, and instillation of hope (Donigian & Malnati, 1997; Gladding, 2012).

- Students will understand developmental stage theories and be able to describe stage appropriate strategies for facilitating group movement through these stages. (Section II.G.6.a.)

  In regard to developmental stage theories, there are a number of competing, yet similar, models, including Tuckman and Jensen's (1977) stages of forming, storming, norming, performing, and adjourning; Ward's (1982) stages of power, cohesiveness, working, and termination; Kormanski and Mozenter's (1987) stages of awareness, conflict, cooperation, productivity, and separation; and Trotzer's (1999) stages of security, acceptance, responsibility, work, and closing.

- Students will become familiar with common group member behaviors and roles, and strategies for addressing them appropriately. (Section II.G.6.a.)

  With regard to group members' roles and behaviors, it is important that students understand common disruptive group member behaviors and roles such as monopolizing, manipulating, resisting, remaining silent, using sarcasm, focusing on others, and creating subgroups (Gladding, 2012).

- Students will be able to describe each of the 11 therapeutic factors listed and defined by Yalom and Leszcz (2005) and demonstrate ways in which these therapeutic factors could be used to help group members make positive changes. (Section II.G.6.a.)

  In regard to therapeutic factors, it is important that students understand the dynamics that affect therapeutic change. Yalom and Leszcz (2005) stated that a therapeutic factor is the "intricate interplay of human experiences" (p. 1) that is necessary for therapeutic change. They listed the following therapeutic factors: instillation of hope, universality, imparting information, altruism, the corrective recapitulation of the primary family group, development of socializing techniques, imitative behavior, interpersonal learning, group cohesiveness, catharsis, and existential factors. It is important that students gain familiarity with these factors, as well as methods by which they can utilize these factors to affect therapeutic change.

- Students will become familiar with the strengths and limitations of each leadership style, and they will know the qualities of an effective group leader and demonstrate these qualities through written exercises (e.g., written case studies) and experiential activities. (Section II.G.6.a.)

  The CACREP (2009) standards state that students should understand "group leadership or facilitation styles and approaches including characteristics of various types of group leaders and leadership styles" (p. 12). Chen and Rybak (2004) stated that an effective group leader possesses "conceptual and technical knowledge," "self knowledge and balance," "cultural sensitivity," "trustworthiness and honesty," "self-compassion and compassion for others," a "relaxed attitude (humor and flexibility)," and "intuition and discovery-oriented practice" (p. 33). In addition, Gladding (2008) listed six group leadership styles that are prevalent: authoritarian, democratic, laissez-faire, leaderless, interpersonal, and intrapersonal.

- Students will become familiar with various group counseling theoretical perspectives such that they can describe commonalities, distinguishing characteristics, and pertinent research and literature pertaining to each theory. (Section II.G.6.b.)

  CACREP (2009) states that students should learn theories of group counseling, "including commonalities, distinguishing characteristics, and pertinent research and literature" related to each theory (p. 12). For example, students should be familiar with aspects of the following theoretical orientations: psychoanalytic, person-centered, existential, transactional analysis, Adlerian, reality, gestalt, psychodynamic, cognitive (including rational emotive behavioral therapy), and behavioral.

- Students will understand and be able to demonstrate group counseling methods based on different group counseling orientations. (Section II.G.6.c.)

  The CACREP (2009) standards state that students should understand "group counseling methods, including group counselor orientations and behaviors, appropriate selection criteria and methods, and methods of evaluation of effectiveness" (p. 12). Therefore, students should not only be familiar with group counseling theories (as described in the previous section) but also group counselor orientations and behaviors related to specific theories.

- Students will demonstrate an understanding of appropriate pregroup screening steps, along with a familiarity with group inclusion and exclusion criteria. (Section II.G.6.d.)

  Concerning appropriate selection criteria and methods, students should demonstrate comprehension of appropriate screening techniques, including exclusion and inclusion criteria. Regarding screening techniques, Couch (1995) listed four steps to conducting a prescreening interview, including identifying needs, expectations, and commitment; challenging myths and misconceptions about the group; conveying information (e.g., limits of confidentiality, group stages, roles); and selecting members. Related to inclusion and exclusion criteria, Yalom and Leszcz (2005) stated that group members must possess motivation, self-awareness, and a desire to examine their interpersonal behaviors. They also stated that clients with interpersonal problems (e.g., shyness, passivity, aggressiveness) or clients who overintellectualize often are appropriate for and benefit from group work. In addition, they stated that group members who are willing and able to self-disclose and who can give and receive feedback are appropriate for group work.

- Students will be familiar with various methods for evaluating the effectiveness of a group, and they will demonstrate an ability to administer and interpret group effectiveness evaluations. (Section II.G.6.d.)

  Regarding group effectiveness evaluations, it is important that students understand methods for assessing the outcomes of a group. These evaluations can be accomplished in many ways depending on the group's focus. For example, in a cognitive–behavioral psychoeducation group, the administration of the Beck Depression Inventory (BDI) during the initial group session and again at the final group session can provide an important indicator of the effectiveness of the group. An anonymous, brief survey that elicits feedback about the group, given directly after the final session of a group, also is a means of assessing the group's effectiveness (Chen & Rybak, 2004). Other methods, such as follow-up contacts, may be utilized to assess the group's effectiveness, too.

- Students will participate as members of a small group during the course of the semester to gain an experiential understanding of the group process and what it is like to be a group member. (Section II.G.6.e.)

  The CACREP 2009 standards require that students engage in "direct experiences in which [they] participate as group members in a small group activity, approved by the program, for a minimum of 10 clock hours over the course of one academic term" (p. 12). This experiential activity is important because it gives students the opportunity to understand what it is like to be a member of a group and it provides them with models (i.e., the group facilitators' behaviors) of how to facilitate or cofacilitate a group.

CRITERIA FOR EVALUATING A TEXT

- Inclusion of CACREP Content Requirements

  The process of determining the appropriate criteria for evaluating a text for a group work course is similar to that of developing strong course objectives—in both, the CACREP standards should be consulted. A text that contains most if not all of the components of the CACREP group work standards is helpful because it ensures that these standards, at least the theoretical elements of them, are being met in the course. Aside from the text containing the theoretical content mandated by CACREP, other criteria are important to consider when evaluating and choosing a book for a group course.

- Inclusion of Experiential Activities
  Because CACREP (2009) requires both a theoretical and experiential understanding of group work (e.g., group dynamics, purpose, theory, multicultural issues), a text that includes at the end of every chapter experiential activities (e.g., classroom exercises, journal writing activities, and homework assignments) can be helpful.

- Inclusion of Case Studies
  The texts that contain clearly written case studies of, for example, group leaders engaging with monopolizing clients or group work at particular developmental stages (e.g., forming stage) can be helpful. Well-written case studies are probably beneficial for all courses but particularly for the group course because group work is very different than other counseling modalities. Group work texts with good case studies can help students better comprehend the content of a group course and understand how to apply this content in practice.

- Discussion of Cultural Diversity
  It is important to choose group texts that contain discussions of group work with culturally diverse populations.

- Other Criteria
  - It should have approximately the same number of chapters as there are weeks in the term. If not, an instructor will have to use two or more books or leave a lot of the materials in a book unassigned.
  - It should cite recent and significant research from the most prestigious journals in the field. If it does not, the book is essentially historical and irrelevant.
  - It should cover common dilemmas that occur in group settings, such as the group turning on the leader. In addition, it should define and delineate the uniqueness and overlap in the various types of groups that students will be involved in over their careers.

MOST POPULAR TEXTS

Corey, M., Corey, G., & Corey, C. (2010). *Groups: Process and practice* (8th ed.). Belmont, CA: Thomson/Brooks Cole.

Gladding, S. T. (2012). *Group work: A counseling specialty* (6th ed.). Upper Saddle River, NJ: Merrill Prentice Hall.

Jacobs, E. E., Masson, R. L., Harvill, R. L., & Schimmel, C. J. (2012). *Group counseling: Strategies and skills* (7th ed.). Belmont, CA: Brooks Cole.

Yalom, I. D., & Leszcz, M. (2005). *The theory and practice of group psychotherapy* (5th ed.). New York: Basic Books.

SUPPLEMENTAL READING

Professional journals that contain excellent research for supplementing textbooks include *Journal for Specialists in Group Work*, *Group Psychotherapy*, *Group Dynamics*, *Journal of Group Psychotherapy, and Psychodrama*, and *Sociometry*.

As an alternative to having to search the literature for supplemental articles one at a time, the Association for Specialists in Group Work (ASGW) has collected many such articles in volumes. Three of the most popular collections published by the ASGW are as follows:

Carmen, F., & Salaza, C. F. (2009). *Group work experts share their favorite multicultural activities*. Alexandria, VA: Association for Specialists in Group Work.

DeLucia-Waack, J., Bridbord, K. H., Kleiner, J. S., & Nitza, A. G. (Eds.). (2006). *Group work experts share their favorite activities* (Rev. ed.). Alexandria, VA: Association for Specialists in Group Work.

Foss, L. L., Green, G., Wolfe-Stiltner, K., & DeLucia-Waack, J. L. (2008). *School counselors share their favorite group activities*. Alexandria, VA: Association for Specialists in Group Work.

WEBSITES

Along with textbooks and supplemental articles, there are helpful websites available that are dedicated to group work. Along with the specific websites provided below, instructors may find it beneficial to look up group textbook publishers' websites, because often these websites contain supplemental group work resources.

- Association for Specialists in Group Work
  http://www.asgw.org/
  A variety of group resources are available, including instrumentation, training videos, podcasts, the *Journal for Specialists in Group Work* (JSGW), and the Group Standards Brochure. Concerning instrumentation, ASGW provides a free copy of *The Core Group Work Skills Inventory—Importance and Competence* (CGWSI-IC Inventory) and its complementary technical manual for use in training, practice, and research settings. A list of ASGW training videos also is provided on the website, along with contact information for

ordering and purchasing these videos. Available ASGW books also are listed under the training videos tab. Archived issues with full-text articles of the *Journal for Specialists in Group Work* from 1997 to 2005 are available on the website along with the full-text versions of the Group Standards Brochure and the ACA Governing Council Report.

- Division 49 of APA: Group Psychology and Group Psychotherapy
  http://www.apa49.org/
  This site contains group resources, including a link to the journal *Group Dynamics: Theory, Research, and Practice*, a list of professional associations related to group work, and a list of journals, books, and miscellaneous websites dedicated to group work. The website also contains a link to the full-text version of *The Group Psychologist* newsletter.

- Group Dynamics Resource Page
  https://facultystaff.richmond.edu/~dforsyth/gd/
  This site was created and is updated by Dr. Donelson R. Forsyth, a professor at the University of Richmond. It contains group resources such as song lyrics about the history of group research; experiential learning activities; information about research methods; examples of case studies by topic (e.g., cohesion development, formation); links to information on decision making, leadership, conflict, and intergroup relations; links to other online resources (e.g., online books, online readings); teaching resources (e.g., PowerPoint files on 16 group-related topics, classroom activities), links to group journals; and information about group-related conferences, meetings, and symposia.

LEARNING ACTIVITIES

Groups progress or regress depending on their membership and leadership. In order to make good progress it is helpful for group leaders to have learning activities readily available. Many of these activities are most appropriately enacted during the forming and adjourning stages of the group, with a few others specifically designated for the storming phase of the group. It is seldom that activities and assignments are needed or necessary for the norming and performing phases of the group.

Because there are literally dozens of exercises available for working with groups, counselor educators are well advised to refer to specialized books in this area as well as to consult with experienced colleagues when considering the use of a technique. Some of the most consulted books in the field are as follows:

Belmont, J. A. (2006). *103 Group activities and tips*. Eau Claire, WI: Pesi.
Bevilacqua, L. J. (2002). *Group therapy homework planner*. New York: Wiley.

Carrell, S. E. (2000). *Group exercises for adolescents: A manual for therapists* (2nd ed.). Thousand Oaks, CA: Sage.

Jones, A. (2000). *Team-building activities for every group*. Richland, WA: Rec Room Publishing.

Khalsa, S. S. (1999). *Group exercises for enhancing social skills and self-esteem*. Sarasota, FL: Professional Resource Press.

Liebmann, M. (2004). *Art therapy for groups: A handbook of themes and exercises* (2nd ed.). New York: Routledge.

Shea, E., & Dossick, J. (1988). *Creative therapy: 52 Exercises for groups*. Sarasota, FL: Professional Resource Press.

Shea, E., & Dossick, J. (1990). *Creative therapy II: Fifty-two more exercises for groups*. Sarasota, FL: Professional Resource Press.

Shea, E., & Dossick, J. (1995). *Creative therapy III: Fifty-two more exercises for groups*. Sarasota, FL: Professional Resource Press.

Viers, D., Krafchick, J., Aberle, J. T., & Zimmerman, T. S. (2006). *The group therapist's notebook: Homework, handouts, and activities for use in psychotherapy*. Philadelphia, PA: Haworth Press.

VIGNETTES

In this section, two vignettes and accompanying questions associated with different aspects of group work are presented. These vignettes can be used in training settings to help students understand and master group work concepts and strategies for addressing specific group-related problems. The first vignette describes a problem that several group members are experiencing and asks students to think of appropriate group leader responses using the skill of "linkage." The second vignette illustrates a "monopolizing" group member and asks students to think of strategies for addressing the inappropriate behavior in a therapeutic way. Along with these two vignettes, instructors can find helpful group-related vignettes in Yalom and Leszcz's (2005) text, Gladding's (2012) text, and on the Group Dynamics Resource Page created and updated by Dr. Donelson R. Forsyth (see Websites section for the URL to this site).

Vignette One: Linkage

In a psychoeducation group for Latina women with depression, Norma, one of the two coleaders of the group, describes a behavioral technique called *activity scheduling*. After describing how scheduling healthy and fun activities can facilitate positive feelings, Norma asks the group to write down one or two activities they would like to do before the next week's group meeting. She also asks them to write down things that might hinder them from performing these activities. Alicia states that she would like to go window shopping and work out; however, she is not sure when she could schedule the activities because of her parenting obligations. Tania reports that she would like to go on a date with her husband and jog at a park, but she is unsure about whether she can find time for these activities because she and her husband work a lot. Maria does not write down anything and states that it is hard for her to find time for herself because she has two young children and no family around to help her take care of them. Gabriela says that she also has had difficulty figuring out how to make time for herself since moving away from her friends and family 2 years ago.

1. What are some common themes described by the group members?
2. As a group leader, how might you respond to the group members' comments?
3. More specifically, how might group leaders use the skill of linkage to help group members in this situation?
4. How could linkage help group members begin to brainstorm ways to circumvent their perceived barriers to engaging in healthy activities?

Vignette Two: Responding to Monopolizing Group Members

In a process group, Michelle, the group facilitator, has been struggling to get some of her group members to participate actively. One of the problems has been that Alex, a group member, has taken up much of the past 3 weeks discussing his sadness, embarrassment, and anger concerning his recent divorce. Although his topic (an interpersonal problem) is potentially appropriate for the group, he has taken up a full hour of each of the past two group meetings. Additionally, he has apparently not recognized that other group members are getting restless with the topic and have not had opportunities to work on their own issues. In the present group, Michelle decides to invite a different group member, Rachel, to discuss a problem. Timidly, Rachel says she has an issue she would like to discuss and begins describing how her mother never listens to or cares about what she has to say. Before Rachel can finish discussing her problems with her mom, Alex says, "I know exactly what you're going through. My ex-mother-in-law acted the same way. One time . . ."

1. What are some disruptive group behaviors and characteristics that Alex is exhibiting?
2. Do you think he is appropriate for group at this time? Why or why not?
3. If you were the leader of this group, how might you respond to Alex?
4. Do you think it would be better to address this issue in the group or alone with Alex after the group? What are the advantages and disadvantages to each approach?

ASSIGNMENTS

- A minimum of 10 e-mail reflections for the main textbook and a minimum of 15 for the supplemental text are expected to be submitted on a regular and timely basis. Some chapters may be combined, and information about which chapters may be combined will be offered in class.
- A final paper, which will be an examination of a particular issue, figure, or theory in group work.
- The 10-hour experiential component is broken down into one-hour experiences at the end of each class starting in the third week of the semester. The experiential part of the group will be of a psychoeducational/task group nature. A class member (or two) will be asked to lead all but the first (Week 3) and last (Week 12) group meetings of the group. These meetings will revolve around the SCAMPER (i.e., substitute, combine, adopt/adapt, modify, put to other uses, eliminate, and reverse/rearrange) model for working with groups. The leader will receive the appointed time as a leader within 2 weeks with additional information on the SCAMPER model.

AUDIOVISUAL MATERIAL

There are a number of audiovisual materials available for teaching group work. Some are specific to certain types of groups.

Irvin Yalom Tape

Understanding Group Psychotherapy consists of three different DVDs: *Outpatients*, *Inpatients*, and *An Interview* (where Yalom discusses his existential approach to working as a psychotherapist). Information on this video is available from Psychotherapy.net in DVD format and may be found at http://www.yalom.com/video/home.

Gerald Corey Tape

Gerald Corey also has a commercially available 2-hour video featuring himself and his wife, Marianne, as they demonstrate their integrative approach to group work. This audiovisual features a real group and shows how it moves through its various stages. There is an accompanying workbook. The video is available for purchase from Brooks Cole Publishing, now part of Cengage Learning (http://www.cengage.com/).

Other excellent choices have been produced that deal especially with group counseling. Though some of these audiovisual materials were filmed in the 1980s and 1990s, most are still relevant.

Peg Carroll Tapes

These tapes from the mid-1980s show a group at work and the dynamics within the group quite well. This three-tape series (*Part I. The Initial Stage Order*; *Part II. Reassessing Goals—Transition and Flight*; and *Part III. The Group in Conflict and in Summation*) demonstrates how group members learn to participate in the "here and now process." Carroll periodically stops the group and dialogues with a group of outside observers regarding the meaning of her interventions. The tapes (60 minutes each) demonstrate the setting of norms, how to deal with resistance, the establishment of trust, scapegoating, and negative feelings.

Rex Stockton Tapes

The same format of learning to identify the different roles in group dynamics and gaining a solid foundation for leading groups is found in the three-part Rex Stockton tape series (*Part I. Early Development*; *Part II. Moving Through the Transition to the Working Stage*; and *Part III. The Working Stage and Termination*). Each of these tapes is 45 minutes in length.

Association for Specialists in Group Work Tapes

The Association for Specialists in Group Work has produced a number of other audiovisual resources. In addition to the Carroll and Stockton tapes, the following videos are available:

- *Leading Groups With Adolescents*—Presented by Janice DeLucia-Waack, Allen Segrist, and Arthur M. Horne
- *Celebrating Cultural Diversity: A Group for Fifth Graders*—Presented by Sheri Bauman and Sam Steen

Information on ordering these products can be gleaned from the American Counseling Association and found on the ASGW website (http://www.asgw.org/asgw_training_videos.asp).

POPULAR MEDIA

In addition to DVDs that have been produced to show particular types of groups or specific skills, there are a number of movies that instructors can use that illustrate important points.

- *Twelve Angry Men*—Both versions show the dynamics involved in a task group
- *Apollo 13*—The importance of cooperation and creativity in groups
- *The Breakfast Club*—The evolution of an unstructured group
- *Metallica: Some Kind of Monster*—The band works out interpersonal issues
- *Remember the Titans*—Overcoming stereotypes, developing teamwork

Instructors can use these audiovisuals through showing them in class or assigning them as homework for students to view, critique, and then discuss in class. Regardless, questions related to these materials revolve around a number of topics, such as: What happened that brought the group closer together or made it more divisive? What did the leader do? What else could the leader have done? What interventions proved most effective? How do you think you would have handled the situation?

TENTATIVE COURSE OUTLINE

WEEK	*TOPIC*
Week 1	Introduction: History and models
Week 2	Therapeutic factors and group dynamics
Week 3	Group leadership and beginning a group
Week 4	Multicultural factors to consider in group work
Week 5	Psychoanalytic groups
Week 6	Norming and storming stages of a group
Week 7	The working and ending stages of a group
Week 8	Ethical and legal issues in group work
Week 9	Gestalt and psychodrama
Week 10	Groups for children and adolescents
Week 11	Groups for adults and elderly
Week 12	Person-centered and existential groups
Week 13	Adlerian and reality therapy groups
Week 14	Rational–emotive behavioral and behavioral therapy groups
Week 15	The termination stage of a group

CONCLUSION

Group work is a multifaceted and complex activity that results in participants improving or regressing in their behaviors and interpersonal functioning. We have found that those who would work in groups on any level should be aware that groups are developmental and that there are multiple stages to groups. They should also be cognizant of the myriad dilemmas that come with deciding how to teach group work.

Fortunately, CACREP has provided standards that counselor educators must meet if their programs are to be accredited. In addition, scholars in the group field have produced texts, DVDs, and other professional and popular media that counselor educators can use in teaching. This chapter has examined a variety of resources that can be employed in helping counseling students master information and techniques essential to becoming an exemplary group worker on a number of levels.

We like teaching group work because it is an energizing experience as well as an essential course for counseling students to master. We have found out through the years that this course, regardless of the time allotted to it, is best taught when the instructor engages students in group activities that illustrate factual information; for example, having class members participate in small groups that mirror different stages of groups. Furthermore, it is essential for instructors to read widely and often offer the class information from recent outside findings that supplement what they are learning from classroom assignments and activities.

Being mindful of oneself as well as being attuned to the lives of others in a group setting is the key to working effectively in teaching group work.

REFERENCES

American Psychological Association. (2009). Division 49 of APA: Group psychology and group psychotherapy. Retrieved from http://www.apa49.org/

Association for Specialists in Group Work (2000). *Professional Standards for the Training of Group Workers*. Alexandria VA: Author.

Association for Specialists in Group Work (n.d.). *The group standards brochure: What every counselor must know about group work.* Alexandria VA: Author. Retrieved from http://asgw.org/pdf/Group_Stds_Brochure.pdf

Bauman, S., & Steen, S. (2009). *Celebrating cultural diversity: A group for fifth graders* [video/DVD]. Hanover, MA: Microtraining Associates. Available from http://www.asgw.org/asgw_training _videos.asp

Beck, A. T., Steer, R. A., Brown, G. K., (1996). *Manual for Beck Depression Inventory II (BDI-II).* San Antonio: TX, Psychology Corporation.

Berlinger, J., Sinofsky, B, Kamen, J., Scherma, F., Bonifiglio, M., Dawson, R., (Producers) & Berlinger, J., Sinofsky, B. (Directors). (2004). *Metallica: Some Kind of Monster* [Motion picture]. USA: Radical Media & Third Eye Motion Picture.

Carroll, P. (Producer). (1980). *Group work: Leading in the here and now.* [video/DVD]. Available from http://www.asgw.org/asgw_training_videos.asp

Chen, M., & Rybak, C. J. (2004). *Group leadership skills.* Belmont, CA: Brooks/Cole.

Corey, G. (Producer). (2012). *Theory and Practice of Group Counseling* [video/DVD]. Available from http://www.cengage.com/

Couch, R. D. (1995). Four steps for conducting a pregroup screening interview. *Journal for Specialists in Group Work, 20*, 18–26.

Council for the Accreditation of Counseling and Related Educational Programs (CACREP, 2009). 2009 standards. Retrieved from http://cacrep.org/doc/2009%20Standards%20with%20cover.pdf

DeLucia-Waack, J., Segrist, A., & Horne, A. M. (2009) *Leading groups with adolescents* [video/DVD]. Hanover, MA: Microtraining Associates. Available from http://www.asgw.org/asgw_training_videos.asp

Donigian, J., & Malnati, R. (1997). *Systemic group therapy.* Pacific Grove, CA: Brooks/Cole.

Fonda, H., Justin, G., Rose, R. (Producers), & Lumet, S. (Director). (1957). *Twelve angry men* [Motion picture]. USA: Fox Movie Studio.

Gladding, S. T. (2008). *Group work: A counseling specialty* (5th ed.). Upper Saddle River, NJ: Merrill Prentice Hall.

Gladding, S. T. (2012). *Groups: A counseling specialty* (6th ed.). Upper Saddle River, NJ: Merrill/Prentice Hall.

Hallowell, T., Valis, L., Gracer, B., Orleans, L., Porter, A. L., (Producers) & Howard, R. (Director). (1995). *Apollo 13* [Motion picture]. USA: Universal Studios.

Jacobs, E. E., Masson, R. L., Harvill, R. L., &. Schimmel, C. J. (2012). *Group counseling: Strategies and skills* (7th ed.). Belmont, CA: Thomson Brooks/Cole.

Jacobs, E. E., Robert, L. L., Masson, R. L., & Harvill, R. L. (2008). *Group counseling: Strategies and skills* (6th ed.). Belmont, CA: Brooks Cole.

Kormanski, C. L., & Mozenter, A. (1987). A new model of team building. A technology for today and tomorrow. In J. W. Pfeiffer (Ed.), *The 1987 annual: Developing human resources* (pp. 255–268). San Diego, CA: University Associates.

Meyer, A., Friesen, G., Hughes, J., Manning, M., Tanen, N. (Producers), & Hughes, J. (Director). (1998). *The breakfast club* [Motion picture]. USA: Universal Pictures.

Stenson, M., Flynn, M., Bruckheimer, J., Oman, C., Sandston, P., Worthington, J. K. (Producers) - & Yakin, B., Hutcheson, J. (Director). (2000). *Remember the Titans* [Motion picture]. USA: Walt Disney Studios Motion Pictures.

Stockton, R. (1995). *Developmental aspects of group counseling* [video/DVD]. Available from http://www.asgw.org/asgw_training _videos.asp

Trotzer, J. P. (1999). *The counselor and the group* (3rd ed.). Philadelphia, PA: Taylor & Francis.

Tuckman, B. W., & Jensen, M. A. C. (1977). Stages of small-group development revisited. *Group and Organizational Studies, 2*, 419–427.

Ward, D. E. (1982). A model for the more effective use of theory in group work. *Journal for Specialists in Group Work, 7*, 224–230.

Wilson, F. R., Newmeyer, M. D., Rapin,L. S., & Conyne, R. K. (2007). *The Core Group Work Skills Inventory—Importance and Competence (CGWSI-IC Inventory).* Alexandria VA: Association for Specialists in Group Work. Retrieved from http://www.asgw.org/PDF/CGWSI-IC%20Inventory.pdf

Yalom, I. (Producer). (2006). *Understanding Group Psychotherapy* [video/DVD]. San Franicisco: CA: PsychotherapistResources.com.

Yalom, I. D., & Leszcz, M. (2005). *The theory and practice of group psychotherapy* (5th ed.). New York: Basic Books.

Career Counseling

10

A Process-Based Teaching Approach for Training Career Counselors

Sarah Toman

Of all of the required counselor education courses, the career development or career counseling course is often one of the most dreaded by students. Based on their self-disclosures, my perception of their dread is that the course will be boring, dry, contain repetition of materials they learned in high school through school-to-work programs, or that the course will consist of 15 weeks of learning to write a résumé. Argh! Who would want to teach that course? I have had the pleasure, though, of also hearing from students that they learned through the career development class that helping others with career development and career choices can be exciting, that career counselors have measurable and obvious markers of change, that career assessments can be affirming and not just numbers, and that this is a course that blends well with the other courses in the counseling curriculum.

A career development class contains many goals for students. The Council for the Accreditation of Counseling and Related Educational Programs (CACREP) standards require knowledge of theories (4a), labor market and informational resources (4b), program development (4c), life roles and multicultural factors (4d), career and educational steps from planning through evaluation (4e), assessment and techniques (4f), and the process of career counseling (4g). In addition to these goals, my goals for students include gaining an appreciation for the *art* of career counseling, resources to match the unique needs/wants and readiness of each client as an individual, an understanding of career as a developmental process or unfolding, and a realization that the career topic is possible content in any setting where the counselor finds employment. Ultimately, I would like for students to feel confidence in their knowledge and competence in performing their art. I want students to love the process.

I feel I must diverge here to include a bit about my teaching philosophy and how that intertwines with facilitating a 15-week career development course with graduate counseling students. Because I consider myself a Gestalt therapist, I believe in the power of bringing to the classroom, the Gestalt theory beliefs about (a) relationship, (b) development, and (c) change.

As in Gestalt therapy, the I–Thou relationship (Buber, 1923/1958) is key to developing trust between student and instructor. In the classroom, this means believing that nurturing a quality relationship is as important as the quality of the course content. I ask students to be willing to examine their own career stories as a part of understanding career development as a process. The quality of the relationship between us fosters thoughtful, honest, and self-exploratory class discussion and career papers submitted during the last third of the semester.

Not only does one's career develop over his or her life span, but I also believe that we, as instructors, can assist our students' awareness of their development over the span of a 15-week semester. Exercises and course experiences can be developmentally graded to aid students in advancing their sophistication and understanding of the career development process. From week 1 through week 15 of the semester, the complexity of the career development theories, interventions, and experiential class activities grows, not only due to the increased complexity of each theory but also due to the cumulative effect and contrast/comparison between theoretical perspectives. As a Gestaltist might explain, development is possible due to the support of the relational field (McConville, 1995). In a career counseling class, a mixture of individual, group, and student-suppporting-student activities can assist with the growth that is possible in the classroom setting. I also make every attempt to include experiences for visual learners, auditory learners, and kinesthetic learners. As stated by Dunn and Griggs (2000), "Learning style theory recognizes that learners' cognitive, affective, physiological and sociological patterns determine their academic outcomes" (p. 8).

The Gestalt theory of change influences not only my teaching style but also my beliefs about creating change in one's career. As Yontef (2005) explained, "In Gestalt therapy theory, the therapist is not a change agent that makes change happen. The Gestalt therapist is an agent in the quest to create conditions that maximize conditions for growth, conditions that allow growth to happen when it has been arrested or limited, conditions that focus attention where needed for healing and growth" (p. 82). I would like to suggest that creating an environment where students appreciate learning and appreciate the uniqueness of their own career stories is one way to influence their interest in the field of career development and counseling. Rosenblatt (1975/1994) offered a Gestalt-oriented series of questions to assist clients in making meaning of their careers: "If I want to experience my job, to find out its meaning, to create a new whole, I might ask what it is, and what it is not; what I like about it and what I do not like; what jobs I gave up for this job and what jobs might still be open to me" (p. 37). He then described how reaching a more complete gestalt (or whole view) creates "excitement, a feeling of aliveness, a potential for growth" (p. 48), whether the result is a realization of a new contentment with work or a desire to change careers. The same realizations can occur for students in their career development class when we include the foundational Gestalt elements of awareness to the relational field, making meaning of career as a developmental process, and creating an environment for change. In the paragraphs that follow, I will highlight the aspects of my syllabus and class structure that coincide with my Gestalt teaching philosophy and with the demand of our program credentialing bodies.

OBJECTIVES AND CACREP STANDARDS

When students want to familiarize themselves with the goals and the objectives of a career development/career counseling course, they can locate them in both a college catalogue description and the course syllabus. Although both descriptions need to adhere to the content required by accreditation boards, it is also possible to reflect a process-focused teaching philosophy in such phrases as "consider the role of the counselor in facilitating the career development of clients and self," or "to provide classroom experiences which encourage partners in learning." To follow is an example of both documents.

Catalogue Description:

CNS 624 Career Development and Information Services (3 credits). Intensive study of the psychological and social factors in career development, as well as major theories of career development and how they influence the use of career and educational information in schools and agencies. Includes a review of major assessment tools and computer packages to assist in career decision-making. Discussion of the relationship of career to other facets of development. (Cleveland State University, 2008)

- To gain basic knowledge of individual and group career counseling interventions and consider the role of the counselor in facilitating the career development of clients and self. (Section II.G.4.a.; Section II.G.4.g.)
- To introduce and provide an overview of the major vocational theories and interventions and assessment materials. (Section II.G.4.a.; Section II.G.4.f.; Section II.G.4.g.)
- To consider the unique career development needs of women and populations of diversity, addressing preventative and remedial career concerns. (Section II.G.4.d.; Section II.G.4.g.)
- To provide classroom experiences which encourage partners in learning in promoting a better understanding of the career development process. (Section II.G.4.)

- To instruct students in professional program management of career guidance facilities, whether at the school, agency, or private setting. (Section II.G.4.c.; Section II.G.4.e.)
- To assist future school counselors with the knowledge and skills needed to assist young people in planning and entering a career. (Section II.G.4.c.; Section II.G.4.d.)
- To assist future agency counselors with the knowledge and skills needed to assist career-concerned individuals across the life span. (Section II.G.4.c.; Section II.G.4.d.)
- To provide a historic perspective to the area of career choice, career readiness, and development. (Section II.G.4.d.)
- To become familiar with the multitude of resources available in print, online, and in the workforce for assisting clients with gathering labor market information and possibilities. (Section II.G.4.b.)

CRITERIA FOR EVALUATING A TEXT

No one textbook can contain all elements of career theory, career interventions, multiculturalism, labor market information, up-to-date web sources, and career change and development necessary to thoroughly cover all aspects of a graduate-level class. However, it may also be financially unreasonable to expect students to purchase multiple texts. One of the first criteria I consider is the cost of the textbook weighed against its offerings in relation to the course goals. I then require supplemental materials, which may be made available on reserve in the library or online.

Another evaluation criterion I employ is the accessibility of the material for the graduate-level student. I do not want a text that is too simplistically written as to insult the adult student, nor do I want a text that is academically too challenging at the master's level in referencing advanced comparisons, vocabulary, research, or constructs. Advanced manuscripts and original publications can be included as supplemental readings.

When choosing a textbook, I also consider the balanced report of theories and interventions across all chapters. I am not interested in assigning a book that highlights one or two major theories at the expense of so many other approaches. Students who have an opportunity to gain exposure and experience with a variety of theorists' specialties can then become more flexible practitioners in meeting the individual needs/wants of each client they serve and have the opportunity to develop their own theoretical perspective.

MOST POPULAR TEXTS

The books that I have found most closely align with the course objectives and criteria evaluations listed above are as follows:

Brown, S. D., & Lent, R. W. (Eds.). (2005). *Career development and counseling: Putting theory and research to work*. Hoboken, NJ: John Wiley & Sons.

Niles, S. G., & Harris-Bowlsby, J. G. (2009). *Career development interventions in the 21st Century* (3rd ed.). Columbus, OH: Merrill.

Sharf, R. (2010). *Applying career development theory to counseling* (5th ed.). Pacific Grove, CA: Brooks/Cole Thompson Learning. Retrieved from http://www.cengage.com/highered/

SUPPLEMENTAL READING

There are journals dedicated to career. Some of these journals include *Journal of Career Development*, *Career Development Quarterly*, and *Journal of Vocational Behavior*. I have found that assigning students the following supplemental texts is helpful in meeting both CACREP standards and course objectives:

Savickas, M. L. (1989). Career-style assessment and counseling. In T. J. Sweeney (Ed.), *Adlerian counseling: A practical approach for a new decade* (pp. 289–320). Muncie, IN: Accelerated Development.

Savickas, M. L. (1993). Career counseling in the Postmodern era. *Journal of Cognitive Psychology, 7*, 205–215.

Swanson, J. L., & Fouad, N. A. (2010). *Career theory and practice: Learning though case studies* (2nd ed.). Thousand Oaks, CA: Sage.

Swanson, J. L., & Fouad, N. A. (2010). *Career theory and practice: Learning though case studies* (2nd ed.). Thousand Oaks, CA: Sage.

The following supplemental texts may be of use for the course instructor, when preparing background or supplemental information, or for the student, in reading original sources:

Dawis, R. V., & Lofquist, L. H. (1976). Personality style and the process of work adjustment. *Journal of Counseling Psychology, 23*, 55–59.

Holland, J. (1973). *Making vocational choices*. Englewood Cliffs, NJ: Prentice Hall.

Herr, E. L., Cramer, S. H., & Niles, S. (2004). *Career guidance and counseling through the lifespan* (6th ed.). Boston, MA: Pearson Education.

Lent, R. W., Brown, S. D., & Hackett, G. (1994). Toward a unifying social cognitive theory of career and academic interest, choice and performance. *Journal of Vocational Behavior, 45*, 79–122.

Parsons, F. (1909). *Choosing a vocation*. Boston, MA: Houghton Mifflin.

Salomone, P. (1996). Tracing Super's theory of vocational development: A 40-year restrospective. *Journal of Career Development, 22*, 167–184.

Sampson, J. P., Reardon, R. C., Peterson, G. W., & Lenz, J. G. (2004). *Career counseling and services: A cognitive information processing approach*. Belmont, CA: Brooks/Cole Thompson Learning.

Spokane, A. (1991). *Career intervention*. Englewood Cliffs, NJ: Prentice Hall.

Swanson, J. L., & Fouad, N. A. (2010). *Career theory and practice: Learning through case studies* (2nd ed.). Thousand Oaks, CA: Sage.

WEBSITES

- The National Career Development Association
  http://www.ncda.org
  This is the professional organization for career counselors and career counselor educators. It contains resources for the student and professional, links to locating a career counselor, information about career development facilitators, the *Career Development Quarterly*, and professional conferences.

- Kuder
  http://www.kuder.com
  This website contains three vocational assessments, Kuder Career Search With Person Match, Kuder Skills Assessments, and Super's Work Values Inventory. Their Kuder Career Planning System contains the Kuder Galaxy (containing exploration activities for elementary school-aged students), Kuder Navigator (containing career planning activities for middle and high school-aged students), and Kuder Journey (to assist with the job search process). The website also offers two career curricula, Develop Your Future and Take Hold of Your Future.

- Career Path
  http://www.careerpath.com
  At Career Path, individuals can complete six free career assessments, obtain guidance resources, and begin a job search.

- Keisey
  http://www.keisey.com
  This site contains many links for free career and personality assessments. LiveCareer assesses interests, values, personality, and knowledge/skills/abilities. ClassesUSA assists with the college search process. The Highlands Ability Battery and Halogen's Employee Assessment are available for employers.

Sites for job searches include the following:

- http://www.bls.gov/OCO/ for the *Occupational Outlook Handbook*
- http://www.acinet.org/ for America's Career Info-net
- http://www.jobbankinfo.org/ for America's job bank, listed state by state
- http://www.monster.com
- http://www.job.com

LEARNING ACTIVITIES

The in-class activities listed below reflect teaching this career class from a Gestalt perspective, while taking into account students' various learning styles. Along with utilizing the Gestalt therapy concepts of relationship, development, and change noted in the introductory paragraphs of this chapter, the engaged learning activities listed below also highlight the Gestalt concept of learning in the here and now, with a focus on the learning process rather than the content. Various learning activities are planned for each class section yet, frequently, spontaneous learning experiments can emerge during class discussion. I recommend being prepared to present more learning activities than there is possibly time for and selecting those activities that fit best with the class discussion and the class members' degree of sophistication and enthusiasm. Though I have used the following learning activities in multiple class sections, I have not included every activity every time I taught the career development class. I encourage you to experiment with what works best for you with each offering of the class. The learning activities are listed and described by topic.

Introduction

1. Student introductions—Have class members divide into pairs, with one student functioning as an employer and the other as an employee engaged in a job interview. Ask the employer to collect the information he or she believes might be relevant to hiring this student. As all return to large-class format, have the employers introduce each "applicant" to the class, as if the class were the hiring committee.
2. Play a film clip from the film, *Working Girl*, where Tess is meeting with the employee assistance program counselor to place her in a new position. Follow the clip with class discussion about the counselor's style and what other career interventions might be useful for Tess.

Trait and Factor Theory

1. Administer the Strong Interest Inventory (Strong, Hansen, & Campbell, 1994) during this class section. Answer sheets and scoring are typically available through the college/university counseling center or through the career services office.
2. Career development steps—This activity consists of four steps; the bottom step, mobilization of energy, consists of all of the confusion and experiences that prompt individuals to wonder about how to change their career direction. Step 2 is the phase of self-exploration in which individuals learn about themselves and what they bring to their careers. Step 3, career exploration, includes learning about aspects of careers. The final step, match and fit,

combines everything learned through taking the previous steps to arrive at potential career choices or a direction. These steps can be assigned to discuss in small groups (sharing experiences), included in a whole-class discussion (offering examples from class members), or provided as an overview to trait and factor theory concepts.

Holland Typology of Careers

1. Strong Interest Inventory explanation followed by students having the opportunity to work in pairs to discuss/brainstorm the meaning of their own results
2. Discuss "The Party," from Bolles' (2009) *What Color Is Your Parachute?* The graphic can be drawn on the chalkboard or SMART board or displayed on computer screens. Following discussion of each corner of the party, students can be asked to place themselves in actual corners of the room to illustrate the Holland (1973) typology of the class makeup.
3. Play Hollywood film or television clips that depict characters of each of the six Holland types. Some examples are Dr. House or CSI characters for investigative type.
4. Ask students to complete the self-directed search at the college/university counseling center or career services.

Theory of Work Adjustment

1. Values cards shuffle. Prepare a deck of cards that consists of work values (e.g., having steady employment, working independently, leading others). With class members sitting in a circle, ask one student to volunteer to participate with you in a class demonstration. Ask the student to make his or her initial card sort to be a pile of "must-have" values and a pile of cards of "can live without." Ask the student to take the must-have pile of cards and divide again into "preferable" and "cannot live without" values. Ask the student to describe how examples from each final stack fit or did not fit with his or her previous jobs and which should be possible in his or her next career (presumably counseling). Ask the student to identify the absolute top five cards and the meaning of those values to them. The students in the circle can do the activity on paper while watching the demonstration. One resource for card decks is *Deal Me In* (1992) by Career Systems, Inc.
2. Although not an activity based on the theory of work adjustment, a career visualization can be designed that includes elements of visualizing job satisfaction as obtained through correspondence between one's abilities and the abilities reinforced in the work environment. The visualization can be presented as a whole-class activity that begins with a very brief muscle relaxation and follows with a story of picturing themselves in a work setting of

satisfaction. What outcomes do they experience being in a correspondent and satisfying job?

Developmental Career Theory

1. Super's Work Values Inventory, revised. This can be assigned and completed online at http://www.kuder.com (Zytowski, 2006). This activity can be completed in the university computer lab during class time.
2. Timeline. Ask students to construct, on large paper, a visual depiction of their career history, beginning with first job, typically as an adolescent, and concluding with their current position. Ask students to depict in words or pictures elements they believe were influential for their growth at each job point. Following a brief class discussion of any patterns they noticed, ask students to continue the timeline with predictions of their next jobs/careers.
3. Rainbow. Prepare a handout of Super's rainbow graphic (1980), containing lines for home life, work life, citizen, leisure life, student, and child across the developmental stages of birth, growth, exploration, establishment, maintenance, and disengagement. Ask students to shade in their graphs according to the importance of each role during each stage. Following a brief discussion of any patterns they noticed, ask students to continue their graphs through the disengagement stage.

Psychodynamic Approaches

1. Career styles questions explanation and demonstration. Savickas (1989) published a series of questions based in Adlerian theory that can help identify underlying, perhaps unconscious, motivations for the meaning of careers in individual lives. Ask for a student volunteer and demonstrate the type of career interview in the style of Savickas' questions.
2. Early recollections. Ask students to write their three first early recollections (not career recollections but early life recollections). Ask students to explore in pairs, or small groups, any patterns or themes they find across the three recollections that may influence how they function in a work setting, what they find important in the workplace, or about their career choices.
3. Role models. In pairs, ask students to identify a fictitious, real, or early childhood role model. Ask each student to describe the elements of that role model that most caught their attention. The other student in the pair takes notes about how those descriptions may also apply to the individual now and shares and discusses his or her observations.

Constructivist and Narrative Approaches

1. Career history as a book. Ask students to develop a table of contents for their own personal story. Each chapter should be identified with a title and several sentences about the contents of the chapter. Ask students to write a chapter title(s) for any future chapter(s). The final task is to provide a title for their book.
2. Provide a graphic of a picket fence. Ask students to write on each picket an example of something they experienced as a barrier to their career development. In small groups, ask students to compare the effects of those barriers on their career choices.

Social Learning Theory

1. Explain the construction of a family genogram and assist students in preparing genograms that depict their family, adding family members' careers. Although genograms are not necessarily a social learning theory intervention, the charts can assist with understanding and including the aspect of genetic endowment.
2. Administration and explanation of the Career Beliefs Inventory.

Social Cognitive Career Theory

1. Present a career case in class in which students can discuss the cognitive behavior therapy notion of challenging irrational beliefs, as pertaining to the case. Ask students to identify, through aspects of the case, the client's sense of self-efficacy and subsequent actions.
2. Ask students to complete the Kuder Skills Assessment at http://www.kuder.com (Zytowski & Luzzo, 2002) and engage the class in a discussion of assessment of skills versus beliefs about skills.

Relational Approaches to Career Development

1. Return to genogram activity of class 7 and ask students to focus on the section of the graph that depicts their immediate family. Ask students to identify the parenting style they experienced growing up and create hypotheses about influences of that style on their career history and that of their siblings.

Career Development of Women

1. Career myths. As a class, generate a list on the board/SMART board or computer of myths that women and minorities have encountered in the past that have affected their career development. Discuss in what ways those myths may or may not be prevalent today.
2. In small groups, ask students to create designs of future research projects on the topic of career development of women and/or minorities. Ask students to base their research questions on any of the theories discussed in class over the semester.

Career Decision-Making Approaches

1. In *Take Hold of Your Future*, by Harris-Bowlsbey (2004), the author describes three types of decisions: decisions with certainty, decisions with measured risks, decisions with uncertainty. Ask students to discuss their perceptions of returning to school for a degree in counseling. This activity can be completed as a whole class, in small groups, or in pairs.
2. Ask students to make a graph of current decisions and the internal and external obstacles standing in the way of those decisions. Ask them to make a second graph of past decisions and internal and external obstacles, with a column for the outcomes of those decisions. Discuss any repeating themes or patterns of obstacles.
3. Write a letter: Ask students to write themselves a letter that includes a pep talk for something they would like to accomplish in the next 6 months. Provide mailing envelopes for the letters; ask students to address and seal the envelopes. Mail each class member's letter 6 months after the conclusion of the class.

Occupations: Information and Theory

1. Discussion and demonstration of online resources generated by the students.
2. Library resources. Provide copies of the Directory of Occupational Titles (DOT), *Occupational Outlook Handbook*, etc., for students to review.

Theories in Combination

1. Prepare a grid on the board that places aspects of each theory within Ken Wilber's (2000) quadrants of internal (subjective), external (behavioral), cultural, and social.

AUDIOVISUAL MATERIAL

The book, *What Color Is Your Parachute?* (Bolles, 2009), has additional programs available for the career counselor, educator, or client. Bolles' website (http://www.jobhuntersbible.com) offers DVDs of his workshops. He has also published a Career Center edition of his book on CD-ROM for use at career workstations, appropriate for use with high school students and adults.

On the National Career Development Association website (http://www.ncda.org), Marilyn Brink offers a page called Hands-On Career Awareness Activities for Early Elementary Students. She provides lesson plans for four career stations that blend well with the elementary school curriculum.

The website Monster Worldwide (n.d.) offers the following recommendations of movies that can "make you see your career or your job search in a different light and move you to action." They suggest renting: *All the President's Men* (1976), *Coal Miner's Daughter* (1980), *Elizabeth* (1997), *Fields of Dreams* (1989), *Invincable* (2006), *It's a Wonderful Life* (1946), *Rudy* (1993), *Seabiscuit* (2003), and *Working Girl* (1988).

In addition to the list of films from Yahoo, in Toman and Rak, (2000a), we suggested using the films *On the Waterfront* (1954) and *Mrs. Doubtfire* (1994). Also in Toman and Rak (2000b), we discussed the use of films for teaching counseling theories. *Spellbound* (1945) is helpful for teaching psychodynamic theories, *Ordinary People* (1979) and *What's Love Got To Do With It* (1994) for family and relational theories, and *Silent Fall* (1995) for cognitive behavioral therapy.

VIGNETTES

I firmly believe in using the career stories of unidentifiable clients, published case studies, and characters from film and fiction to help increase the understanding and application of career development theories. The case studies used in class for essays and discussions came from a variety of sources:

- The "Getting Down to Cases" feature in the *Career Development Quarterly*.
- Case examples from Swanson and Fouad's (2010) textbook, *Career Theory and Practice: Learning Through Case Studies*.
- Case example of "Anna" from MacCluskie, Welfel, and Toman (2002), *Using Assessment in Clinical Practice*, which includes case material and career assessments.

ASSIGNMENTS

This course contains four main grade assessment elements.

1. One element is to assess your application and understanding of career development theory.
2. One element is to assess your knowledge and skills in using career development theory to entertain your choice of career interventions.
3. One element is to explain your own career development through the theories and interventions.
4. One element is to search, evaluate, and share web information with the class.

Case Essay Tests

During five selected class meetings, you will receive five different career case studies. Your essay (approximately two hand-written pages) will address the following points based on the assignment readings for that class:

1. Conceptualization of the case based on the assigned chapter/reading using at least three theory concepts.
2. Describe three career counseling interventions you would use with this client, based on the client's presenting concerns and the theory's concepts.

Career Development Project

Maximum of 15 double-spaced pages:

1. You are the subject of this case study—introduce yourself (such as: basic demographics, family, work history, personal development, educational background, health, social development, or other pertinent factors).
2. Describe your career situation by using concepts and terminologies from at least three of the career development theorists discussed in class.
3. Include scores from three career assessment instruments.
4. Indicate at least three steps/interventions that might be considered in your career counseling sessions.
5. Conclude with a prognosis for your future and career goals.

Online Resources Handout

Please make enough copies of your handout for each student and the instructor. You are to locate, identify, and briefly evaluate two online career web sources. Please format your handout in the following manner:

- Online resource handout
  - Online address
  - The population this site would fit the best (e.g., age group)
  - Your evaluation of its usefulness and your recommendation for how to assign this site to a client or class

Repeat the above points for the second web address. Both addresses and descriptions should fit on one typed page.

Final Exam

The final, in-class examination consists of multiple choice questions covering all class lectures, textbook chapters, and supplemental reading assignments.

TENTATIVE COURSE OUTLINE

WEEK	*TOPIC AND ASSIGNMENTS*
Week 1	Introductions and syllabus review Explanation of all class assignments/projects Case study #1 and group discussion Introduction to trait and factor theory
Week 2	Trait and factor theory (chapters 1 and 2) Case study #2, first essay test Strong Interest Inventory administration Career development steps
Week 3	Holland typology of careers (chapter 5) Case study #3 and group discussion Strong Interest Inventory explanation Self-directed search
Week 4	Theory of work adjustment (chapter 4) Case study #4, second essay test Values card shuffle; career visualization
Week 5	Developmental career theory (chapters 7, 8, 9, 10) Case study #5 and group discussion Work Values Inventory administration and explanation

WEEK	*TOPIC AND ASSIGNMENTS*
Week 6	Psychodynamic approaches (reading #1) Case study #6 and third essay test Career styles questions explanation and demonstration
Week 7	Constructivist and narrative approaches (chapter 11) Case study #7 and group discussion
Week 8	Social learning theory cognitive career theory (chapter 13) Case study #8 and group discussion Introduction of genograms Career Beliefs Inventory
Week 9	Social cognitive career theory (chapter 14) Case study #9 and fourth essay test Career Beliefs Inventory
Week 10	Relational approaches to career development (chapter 12) Case study #10 and group discussion Genograms
Week 11	Career development of women (reading #2) Career development of special populations (#3) Career project due Case study #11 and group discussion Career myths
Week 12	Career decision-making approaches (chapter 15) Case study #12 and fifth essay test Career decision exercises Online resources project due
Week 13	Occupations: Information and theory (chapter 3) Case study #13 and group discussion Discussion and demonstration of online resources
Week 14	Theories in combination (chapter 16) Supplemental reading #4 Case study #14 and group discussion Review for final exam
Week 15	Final exam

CONCLUSION

Facilitating many sections of our career development class has been some of the most rewarding teaching of my career, because I was able to function in the classroom in a way that was congruent with my philosophies of teaching. I was able to offer experiential learning activities in every class meeting that could capture the various preferred learning style of each student. I proceeded in a relational style, creating safety in sharing personal material, discussing perspectives, and modeling the I–Thou stance of Gestalt therapy. The students' development from believing that career counseling is about writing resumes to believing in the application of career theory and assessment was exciting to witness. And, of course, the most exciting change was student gains in knowledge, confidence, self-efficacy, and abilities to perform the art of career counseling. They did learn how to love the process, by experiencing elements of the process themselves.

My "pearls of wisdom" are to believe in the process yourself. If you have never directly experienced the art of counseling, hire a counselor. Even as college/university faculty members, we have plenty to talk about with counselors. I would also recommend having a vast personal library of career development resources. Read, read, read, and share what you read with your students. Watch Hollywood films with an eye for use in the classroom, because many films depict aspects of the film characters at work. Finally, do not hesitate to write your own case vignettes for your students. Every career story can be a teaching tool for the student and the instructor. And I hope you find you love the process, too.

APPENDIX A

RUBRIC FOR CASE ESSAY TESTS (6 POINTS PER ESSAY)

CASE NAME AND ASSIGNED THEORY	*NEEDS IMPROVEMENT (0–2 POINTS)*	*COMPETENT (3–4 POINTS)*	*OUTSTANDING (5–6 POINTS)*
	Student did not use the concepts or interventions from the assigned theory/chapter/s Student used only one theory concept during conceptualization section of essay Student used only one intervention during counseling intervention section of the essay	Student used and demonstrated understanding of the assigned theory but only incorporated one or two theory concepts during the conceptualization section of essay Student used only one or two interventions during the intervention section of the essay	Student used and demonstrated understanding of the assigned theory Student accurately used three theory concepts during the conceptualization section of the essay Student appropriately used three interventions during the intervention section of the essay

RUBRIC FOR CAREER DEVELOPMENT PROJECT

UNACCEPTABLE (<8 POINTS)	*ACCEPTABLE (9–15 POINTS)*	*PROFICIENT (15–22 POINTS)*	*EXEMPLARY (22–30 POINTS)*
Student may adequately present his or her career story but only uses one career theory during the conceptualization section (Part II) Student includes only one career assessment instrument (Part III) Student indicates only one step or career counseling intervention (Part IV) Student does not include a prognosis or future career goals	Student adequately presents his or her career story but only uses two career theories during the conceptualization section (Part II) Student includes less than three career assessments (Part III) Student indicates less than three steps or career counseling interventions (Part IV) Student includes only brief prognosis or future goals	Student adequately presents his or her career story but does not provide all elements of Parts II through VI, missing one or more career theories or one or more career assessment or one or more steps or interventions Student provides prognosis or future goals that fit with the client history, conceptualization, assessments, and counseling steps/interventions	Student adequately presents his or her story, provides at least three career theories in the conceptualization, includes at least three career assessments, offers three or more counseling steps or interventions, and provides a prognosis or future goals that fit with the client history, conceptualization, assessments, and counseling steps/interventions

RUBRIC FOR ONLINE RESOURCES HANDOUT (10 POINTS)

NEEDS IMPROVEMENT (0–3 POINTS)	*COMPETENT (4–7 POINTS)*	*OUTSTANDING (8–10 POINTS)*
Student did not bring to class enough copies for all class members Student did not provide web addresses Student did not describe the population for this website Student did not offer his or her evaluation of the site	Student brought enough copies for all class members but only completed information for one web address or did not include web addresses or did not include population recommendation or did not evaluate the sites	Student brought enough copies for all class members Student included web addresses for two sites, described the populations recommended for each site, and offered an evaluation of both sites

REFERENCES

Alison Owen, A., Fellner, E., Bevan, T. (Producers), & Kapur, S. (Director). (1998). *Elizabeth* [Motion picture]. USA: Shepperton Studio.

Bolles, R. N. (2009). *What color is your parachute? A practical manual for job hunters and career changers.* North Berkley, CA: Ten Speed Press.

Brink, M. (2008). *Hands-on career awareness activities for early elementary schools.* Retrieved from www.ncda.org

Buber, M. (1958). *I and Thou.* New York: Charles Scribner's Sons. (Original work published 1923)

Capra, F. (Producer), & Capra, F. (Director). (1946). *It's a wonderful life* [Motion picture]. USA: Liberty Films.

Chapin, D., Krost, B. (Producer), & Gibson, B. (Director). (1993). *What's love got to do with it* [Motion picture]. USA: Touchstone Pictures.

Ciardi, M., Gray, G., Mok, K. (Producers), & Core, E., (Director). (2006). *Invincible* [Motion picture]. USA: Walt Disney Studios Motion Pictures.

Cleveland State University. (2008). Graduate catalogue. Retrieved from http://www.csuohio.edu

Coblenz, W. (Producer), & Pakula, A. J. (Director). (1976). *All the president's men* [Motion picture]. USA: Warner Brothers & Wildwood.

Cohen, J., Farren, J., and Farren, C. (1992). *Deal me in.* Washington, D.C.: Career Systems, Inc.

Dunn, R., & Griggs, S. A. (2000). *Practical approaches to using learning styles in higher education.* Santa Barbara, CA: Praeger Publishers.

Frankish, B. E., Levin, L. (Producers), & Robinson, P. A. (Director). (1989). *Field of dreams* [Motion picture]. USA: Gordon Company and Universal.

Fried, R. N., Woods, C. (Producers), & Anspaugh, D. (Director). (1993). *Rudy* [Motion picture]. USA: Columbia TriStar.

Greenhut, R., Mark, L., Wick, D. (Producers), & Nichols, M. (Director). (1988). *Working girl* [Motion picture]. USA: Twentieth Century Fox Film.

Harris-Bowlsbey, J. (2004). *Take hold of your future* (5th ed.). New York: National Career Assessment Services.

Kennedy, K., Marshall, F., Ross, G., Sindell, J. (Producers), & Ross, G. (Director). (2003). *Seabiscuit* [Motion picture]. USA: Universal Pictures

Krumboltz, J. D. (1991). *Career Beliefs Inventory (CBI).* Available at http://www.mindgarden.com/products/cbi.htm

MacCluskie, K., Welfel, E., & Toman, S. (2002). *Using assessment in clinical practice.* Thousand Oaks, CA: Sage.

McConville, M. (1995). *Adolescence.* Oakland, CA: Analytic Press.

Monster Worldwide (n.d.). Movies to inspire your career goals. Retrieved from http://career-advice.monster.com/in-the-office/work-life-balance/movies-to-inspire-your-career-goals-hot-jobs/article.aspx

Robinson, J. G. (Producer), & Beresford, B. (Director). (1995). *Silent fall* [Motion picture]. USA: Warner Home Video.

Rosenblatt, D. (1995). *The Gestalt therapy primer.* Southhold, NY: Yurisha. (Original work published 1975)

Sampson, J. P., Reardon, R. C., Peterson, G. W., & Lenz, J. G. (2004). *Career counseling and services: A cognitive information processing approach.* Belmont, CA: Brooks/Cole Thompson Learning.

Savickas, M. L. (1989). Career-style assessment and counseling. In T. J. Sweeney (Ed.), *Adlerian counseling: A practical approach for a new decade* (pp. 289–320). Muncie, IN: Accelerated Development.
Schwartz, B., (Producer), & Apted, M. (Director). (1980). *Coal miner's daughter* [Motion picture]. USA: Universal Studios.
Schwary, R. L. (Producer), & Redford, R. (Director). (1979). *Ordinary people* [Motion picture]. USA: Paramount Pictures.
Selznic, D. O. (Producer), & Hitchcock, A. (Director). (1945). *Spellbound* [Motion picture]. USA: Selznic International Pictures and Vanguard Films.
Spiegel, S. (Producer), & Kazan, E. (Director). (1954). *On the waterfront* [Motion picture]. USA: Columbia Pictures and Horizon Pictures.
Strong, E.K., Hansen, J., & Campbell, D.P. (1994). *Strong interest inventory*. Thousand Oaks, CA: Stanford University Press/Consulting Psychologists Press.
Super, D.E. (1980). A life-space, life-span approach to career development. *Journal of Vocational Behavior, 16*, 282–298.
Swanson, J. L., & Fouad, N. A. (2010). *Career theory and practice: Learning through case studies* (2nd ed.). Thousand Oaks, CA: Sage.
Toman, S., & Rak, C. F. (2000a). Teaching career development theories using cinema. In M. Pope & C. W. Minor (Eds.), *Experiential activities for teaching career counseling and facilitating groups* (pp. 53–55). Columbus, OH: National Career Development Association.
Toman, S., & Rak, C. F. (2000b). The use of cinema in the counselor education curriculum: Strategies and outcomes. *Counselor Education and Supervision, 40*, 105–114.
United States Department of Labor (2010). *Dictionary of occupational titles with O*NET definitions*. Baton Rouge, LA: Claitors Publishing.
U.S. Department of Labor Statistics (2010–2011). *Occupational outlook handbook (OOH)*. Washington, DC: Office of Occupational Statistics and Employment Projections.
Wilber, K. (2000). *Integral psychology*. Boston, MA: Shambhala.
Williams, R., Williams, R., Radcliffe, M.A., Williams, M. G. (Producers), & Columbus, C. (Director). (1994). *Mrs. Doubtfire* [Motion picture]. USA: Blue Moon & Twentieth Century Fox Films.
Yontef, G. (2005). Gestalt therapy theory of change. In A. L. Woldt & S. Toman (Eds.), *Gestalt therapy: History, theory and practice* (pp. 81–100). Thousand Oaks, CA: Sage.
Zytowski,, D. (2006). *Super Work Values Inventory-Revised (SWVI-Revised)*. Available at http://www.kuder.com/solutions/kuder-assessments.html#supers_work_values_inventory
Zytowski, D. G. & Luzzo, D. A. (2002). *Kuder Skills Assessment*. Available at http://www.kuder.com/solutions/kuder-assessments.html#kuder_skills_assessment

11 Assessment

Teaching Assessment in Counselor Education

John M. Laux, Carrie A. VanMeter, Stephanie A. Calmes, and Holly L. Harper

Assessment lays the groundwork for good counseling. Without a foundation in assessment education, counselors run the risk of misdiagnosing and subsequently mistreating their clients (Laux & Perera-Diltz, 2008). The Council for Accreditation of Counseling and Related Educational Programs (CACREP, 2009) recently outlined both general and program-specific guidelines relevant to the knowledge, skills, and practices associated with assessment in counseling.

OBJECTIVES AND CACREP STANDARDS

Students will:

1. Demonstrate understanding of the history of assessment. (Section II.G.7.a.)
2. Demonstrate understanding of standardized and nonstandardized testing and other assessment techniques. (Section II.G.7.b.)
3. Demonstrate understanding of statistical concepts such as reliability and validity. (Section II.G.7.c.; Section II.G.7.d.; Section II.G.7.e.)
4. Demonstrate understanding of ethics in assessment. (Section II.G.7.g.)
5. Demonstrate understanding of the social and cultural assessment related factors. (Section II.G.7.f.)

The school counseling and the clinical mental health counseling specialty areas each have sections in which CACREP prescribes knowledge and skills and practices requirements that are unique to their respective disciplines (CACREP, 2009). School counseling students' knowledge base should include an understanding of the role that multiple factors may play in school-age students' personal, social, and academic functioning. These factors include the following: abuse, violence, eating disorders, attention deficit hyperactivity disorder, and childhood depression. School counseling graduate students should know the signs and symptoms of school-aged personal substance abuse as well as those signs and symptoms associated with living in a home where substance abuse is present. Finally, CACREP expects school counseling students to know how to undertake and complete needs assessments for academic, career, and personal/social development.

The 2009 CACREP standards explicitly state that students in school counseling programs are expected to demonstrate skills and practices across five domains:

1. Assessment and interpretation of students' needs and strengths in the context of their students' culture, language, values, backgrounds, and abilities
2. Selection of appropriate strategies to assess academic, career, and personal/social development
3. Valid interpretation of students' assessment results as well as evaluation of the effectiveness of educational programs and interventions
4. Referral to other school professionals and community resources when necessary
5. Assessment of obstacles that hinder students' academic, career, and personal/social development.

Like school counselors, clinical mental health counselors must demonstrate specific knowledge and skills and practices competencies. Clinical mental health counselors (CMCH) must know the "... principles and models of assessment, case conceptualization, theories of human development, and concepts of normalcy and psychopathology leading to diagnoses and appropriate counseling treatment plans" (CACREP, 2009, p. 32). Clinical mental health counselors understand clinical evaluation, including diagnostic interviews, mental status examinations, symptom inventories, and psychoeducational and personality assessments. CMHCs sufficiently understand psychopharmacological medications such that they can initiate referrals for medical evaluations and identify the common unintended effects of these medications. Finally, CMHCs can identify standardized instruments used to assess substance use disorders and process addictions.

CMHCs are charged with four sets of skills and practices (CACREP, 2009). Guided by an awareness of cultural biases, CMHCs select, implement, and interpret assessment interventions to assist in the diagnosis and treatment planning of their clients. CMHCs "demonstrate skill in conducting an intake interview, a mental status evaluation, a biopsychosocial history, a mental health history, and a psychological assessment for treatment planning and caseload management" (CACREP, p. 33). CMHCs are able to screen for addiction, aggression, danger to self and/or others, and cooccurring mental disorders. Finally, CMHCs assess clients' stages of dependence, change, or recovery in order to employ the appropriate treatment approach along the continuum of care.

CRITERIA FOR EVALUATING A TEXT

Textbook selection can be a daunting and time-consuming task. Unfortunately, there is a paucity in the counseling literature regarding textbook selection at the graduate level. Nevertheless, selecting a textbook is an important component in designing a course on assessment in counseling (Angell, DuBravac, & Gonglewski, 2008). Textbooks are not only important for the students but also provide a way for new educators to increase their professional development (Newton & Newton, 2009). Inevitably, novice counselor educators, who are in the earlier stages of skill development and knowledge attainment, will be called upon to teach courses for the first time. The right textbook will serve as a guide in this process.

- Comprehensiveness. An assessment textbook's comprehensiveness is a function of both breadth of material covered and the literature cited. At minimum, any textbook under consideration will cover the assessment domains as prescribed by CACREP. It may be the case that a text adequately covers large portions of the CACREP domains while neglecting others. In such cases, it will be the counselor educator's responsibility to provide students with supplemental readings or learning opportunities in order to cover these omitted content areas. Further, a current textbook will contain information on those assessments and procedures that are considered state of the art among practicing clinicians. When evaluating the depth of discussion, an educator looks for how well the text explains the material and asks the following questions. Does the text go into enough detail on the subject matter? Will students be able to understand material fully or is the text vague? Are new concepts introduced and fully explained? A comprehensive assessment textbook will cite the most up-to-date psychometric research on existing assessments. A good selection criterion is that the textbook's chapters should include both seminal citations as well as any psychometric research from the most recent 10-year period.
- Textbook organization. Chapter structure is another important consideration. Organization can be evaluated first by examining the table of contents. This is a quick way to see whether the material in the textbook is presented in an order that makes sense with the counselor educator's teaching pedagogy. Another place to investigate in the text is the page layout. Quickly glance through the headings and subheadings to determine the degree to which they are informative to the reader. Read through the first several pages of randomly selected chapters to determine whether or not the writing style is appropriate for the intended readers.
- Available textbook bundles/supplementation. Currently, many textbook publishers "bundle" their books with optional media components such as CD-ROMs and links to online learning opportunities. The services offered by these packages can range from support and resources on websites to

interactive multimedia to further engage students. These ancillary materials also need to be evaluated for usability and relevance to the course before choosing them. Such packages are intended to add to the overall effectiveness of the course and to entice a counselor educator into choosing that textbook.

MOST POPULAR TEXTS

The following list of frequently used assessment texts was compiled from a review of syllabi for courses taught in CACREP accredited master's programs. It may be used as a starting point for the textbook review process and should not be interpreted as an endorsement by the chapter's authors or this text's editors or publishers.

Hood, A. B., & Johnson, R. W. (2007). *Assessment in counseling: A guide to the use of psychological assessment procedures*. Alexandria, VA: American Counseling Association.
Neukrug, E. S., & Fawcett, R. C. (2010). *Essentials of testing and assessment: A practical guide for counselors, social workers, and psychologists* (2nd ed.). Belmont, CA: Brooks/Cole.
Walsh, W. B., & Betz, N. E. (2001). *Tests and assessments* (4th ed.). Upper Saddle River, NJ: Prentice Hall.

In addition to whichever text(s) are selected, we suggest that counselor educators consider adding Matarazzo's (1992) "Psychological Testing and Assessment in the 21st Century" and Helms' (1992) "Why Is There No Study of Cultural Equivalence in Standardized Cognitive Ability Testing?" to the reading list of any master's-level assessment course.

SUPPLEMENTAL MATERIAL

There are journals dedicated to assessment, such as *Measurement and Evaluation in Counseling and Development* and *Journal of Personality Assessment*. Other prominent journals that discuss assessment include *Journal of Counseling and Development*, *American Psychologist*, *Journal of College Counseling*, *Journal of Addictions and Offender Counseling*, and *Journal of Studies on Alcohol*. The following are two articles we frequently use when teaching this course in assessment.

Helms, J. E. (1992). Why is there no study of cultural equivalence in standardized cognitive ability testing? *American Psychologist, 47*, 1083–1101.
Matarazzo, J. D. (1992). Psychological testing and assessment in the 21st century. *American Psychologist, 47*, 1007–1018.

WEBSITES

There are a variety of websites appropriate for use in an assessment course as a supplement to course materials and to enhance student learning. All of the following will provide students with information that may be helpful in the use and interpretation of testing instruments.

- The American Counseling Association
  http://www.counseling.org
  This website is a comprehensive site that includes information and resources for counselors and counseling students on the topics of publications, press releases, public policy, and careers. The ACA website also includes a section on counseling ethics, an online library, online learning options, and a job center. Assessment students may find helpful the website's available ethics guidelines related to the use of testing and instrumentation, as well as the publications and relevant research information related to the use of assessments.

- The ACA Code of Ethics
  http://www.counseling.org/Resources/CodeOfEthics/TP/Home/CT2.aspx
  This site includes the ACA code of ethics-specific language with respect to evaluation, assessment, and interpretation. These ethical guidelines are available at www.counseling.org (above).

- The Association for Assessment in Counseling and Education
  http://www.theaaceonline.com/home.htm
  This association is a division of the American Counseling Association. According to the AACE website, "The Association for Assessment in Counseling and Education (AACE) is an organization of counselors, educators, and other professionals that advances the counseling profession by providing leadership, training, and research in the creation, development, production, and use of assessment and diagnostic techniques." The purposes of the AACE include promoting professional development, professionalization, research and knowledge, and public awareness and support, all related to the use of assessments. Assessment students may find beneficial the resources page, including a full library of test reviews.

- The American Educational Research Association
  http://www.aera.net
  This association "is concerned with improving the educational process by encouraging scholarly inquiry related to education and evaluation and by promoting the dissemination and practical application of research results." Information is available on the AERA website to address publications,

employment, grants, and education research and research policy. Assessment students may find helpful the section on "Research Points," the AERA's quarterly series, as well as the available grants, special interest groups, and publications on the site.

- The American Evaluation Association
  http://www.eval.org/
  This professional organization is dedicated to the use and study of testing instruments and evaluations. The AEA identifies its mission as: "To improve evaluation practices and methods, increase evaluation use, promote evaluation as a profession, and support the contribution of evaluation to the generation of theory and knowledge about effective human action." Assessment students may find particularly beneficial the training directory, links to related resources, and information on publications and research.

- The Joint Committee on Testing Practices
  http://www.apa.org/science/jctpweb.html
  This committee was established by the American Educational Research Association, the American Psychological Association, and the National Council on Measurement in Education in 1985. The JCTP website provides information on school testing, fair testing practices, responsible test use, and other ethical assessment issues. Though the JCTP disbanded in 2007, publications and resources are still available online. Assessment students may find most beneficial the information on research ethics, responsible conduct of research, and testing-related resource links.

- The National Council on Measurement in Education
  http://www.ncme.org/
  This website states that its purpose is to encourage scholarly efforts to advance the science, scoring, and use of testing instruments and to disseminate knowledge about instrumentation, interpretation, and application of educational measurement. Information is available on the NCME website for publications, career opportunities, and links and resources related to testing and measurement. Assessment students may most benefit from the available testing-related guidelines, the code of professional responsibilities in measurement, and the option to join the NCME listserv.

- Buros Center for Testing
  http://www.unl.edu/buros/
  According to its website, the Buros Center for Testing has a focus of "improving the science and practice of testing." The Buros Center for Testing includes two separate institutes, the Buros Institute of Mental Measurements (BIMM), and the Buros Institute for Assessment Consultation and Outreach (BIACO). The BIMM is well known for its publications, including the *Mental Measurements Yearbook*, a commonly used tool by professionals for the

selection and use of testing instrumentation. Most useful to the assessment student are the online test reviews, articles on testing and instrumentation, and assessment-related resources and tools.

LEARNING ACTIVITIES

- Group project. This requires students to form working groups of three to four in order to collaborate on the production of a mock assessment. The purpose of the mock assessment is to familiarize the students with the methods and procedures involved with creating a standardized assessment. The group assignment could be used to demonstrate CACREP's school counseling assessment skills and practices 1–5. This project may be used to cover the clinical mental health counseling assessment knowledge 2 and the skills and practices 1 and 2. The mock assessments constructed by the group may be unitary in nature (such as a measure of depression) or they may be multidimensional (such as a measure of intelligence). Completed proposals should be formatted according to American Psychological Association (APA) style. The assessment project should address (a) the title and purpose of the instrument, (b) the domain assessed, (c) administration and interpretation procedures, (d) the manner in which results are communicated to the test-taker, (e) how items were selected and constructed, (f) item response format (e.g., true/false, Likert, yes/no/maybe, reading comprehension), (g) a minimum of 10 items to represent the selected domain, (h) methods to be employed to standardize the instrument including two sources of reliability data and three types of validity data to be used, and (i) mock normative sample data (e.g., age, sex, ethnicity, education, socioeconomic status).
- Presentation. Each student will make a presentation that introduces and reviews an assessment instrument relevant to their future work setting. Whenever possible, each presentation should begin with a brief demonstration of the instrument. In addition, each student will prepare an outline for their presentation that will double as a handout for the entire class. The presentation and handout should cover the following information: the student's name, the name of the instrument, current edition and year published, a brief discussion on why this assessment was chosen, the assessment's author(s) and publisher, the purpose of the assessment and the domain it covers, the manner in which the assessment was standardized, the target population, and the assessment's strengths and weaknesses. In addition, the presentation should include a review of the instrument's available reliability and validity data and a critical review of at least five peer-reviewed empirical articles in which the instrument was either the subject of the investigation or was used to operationally define a trait of interest. Provide full citations and an abstract for each article. Student's clarity of presentation and professionalism will be evaluated.

TENTATIVE COURSE OUTLINE

WEEK	*TOPICS AND ASSIGNMENTS*
Week 1	Introduction to the course: review course requirements
	Fundamental and current issues in measurement
	Assessment: historical perspectives concerning the nature and meaning
	Assessment theory
	Activities: group test, group formation, topic selection
Week 2	Basic statistical concepts (scales of measurement, measures of central tendency, indices of variability, shapes and types of distributions, types of correlation coefficients)
	Activities: work on group presentations
Week 3	Important qualities in any measurement procedure
	Reliability (theory of measurement error, types of reliability, how to use reliability data)
	Validity (types of validity, evidence of validity, the relationship between reliability and validity)
	Activities: work on group presentations
	Turn in group membership composition
Week 4	TEST: Basic statistical concepts
Week 5	Case conceptualization, the assessment interview, and the relationship between assessment and diagnosis of mental and emotional disorders
Week 6	Cognitive tests: Theories on intelligence
	Assessment of intelligence
	Assessment of aptitudes
	Strategies for selecting, administering, and interpreting cognitive tests in counseling
	Activities: define *intelligence*
Week 7	Education decisions and achievement tests
	Strategies for selecting, administering, and interpreting achievement tests in counseling
Week 8	Assessment of personality theories
	Objective personality assessment
	Projective personality assessment
	Behavioral measures of personality
	Turn in rough draft of group project
Week 9	Assessment of personality (continues)
	Strategies for selecting, administering, and interpreting personality tests in counseling
Week 10	Assessment of interest and career
	Strategies for selecting, administering, and interpreting interests and career variables tests in counseling

WEEK	TOPICS AND ASSIGNMENTS
Week 11	Ethical standards and legal considerations
Week 12	Race, ethnicity, culture, and demographic variables in tests and achievements
	In-class presentations
Week 14	In-class presentations
Week 15	In-class presentations/exam review
Week 16	Final exam

ADVANCED ASSESSMENT COURSE

Some counselor education programs, particularly those that offer a 60-semester-hour clinical mental health counseling degree, require their students to successfully complete an advanced course in assessment that builds upon the education and skills obtained at an introductory level. The advanced assessment course is designed to teach students knowledge, skills, and abilities in the administration and interpretation of standardized, objective personality assessments that cover both the normal and abnormal range of personality, including *Diagnostic and Statistical Manual of Mental Disorders* (*DSM*) Axis I and II disorders, with an additional special focus on substance abuse and dependence disorders. Reading assignments are made using a common advanced text (Groth-Marnat, 2009) and several peer-reviewed journal articles.

MOST POPULAR TEXTS

Butcher, J. N. (Ed.). (2006). *MMPI-2: A practitioner's guide*. Washington, DC: American Psychological Association.

Groth-Marnat, G. (2009). *Handbook of Psychological Assessment* (5th ed.). New York: John Wiley & Sons.

SUPPLEMENTAL READING

Association for Assessment in Counseling and Education. (2003). *Responsibilities of users of standardized tests* (3rd ed.). Retrieved from http://aac.ncat.edu/Resources/documents/RUST2003%20v11%20Final.pdf

Caldwell, A. B. (2001). What do the MMPI scales fundamentally measure? Some hypotheses. *Journal of Personality Assessment, 76*, 1–17.

Clawson, T. W. (1997). Control of psychological testing: The threat and a response. *Journal of Counseling & Development, 76*, 90–93.

Clements, R. (2002). Psychometric properties of the Substance Abuse Subtle Screening Inventory—3. *Journal of Substance Abuse Treatment, 23*, 419–423.

Feldstein, S. W., & Miller, W. R. (2007). Does subtle screening for substance abuse work? A review of the Substance Abuse Subtle Screening Inventory (SASSI). *Addiction, 102*, 41–50.

Hansen, N. D. (2002). Teaching cultural sensitivity in psychological assessment: A modular approach used in a distance education program. *Journal of Personality Assessment, 79*, 200–206.

Ivey, A. E., & Ivey, M. B. (1998). Reframing *DSM-IV*: Positive strategies from developmental counseling and theory. *Journal of Counseling & Development, 76*, 334–350.

Keiller, S. W., & Graham, J. R. (1993). The meaning of low scores on MMPI-2 clinical scales of normal subjects. *Journal of Personality Assessment, 61*, 211–223.

Laux, J. M., Perera-Diltz, D., Smirnoff, J., & Salyers, K. M. (2005). The SASSI-3 Face-Valid Other Drug Scale: A psychometric investigation. *Journal of Addictions and Offender Counseling, 26*, 15–23.

Laux, J. M., Salyers, K. M., & Kotova, E. (2005). A psychometric evaluation of the SASSI-3 in a college sample. *Journal of College Counseling, 8*, 41–51.

Long, K. A., Graham, J. R., & Timbrook, R. E. (1994). Socioeconomic status and MMPI-2 interpretation [Special issue]. *Measurement & Evaluation in Counseling & Development, 27*, 158–177.

McCrae, R. R., & Costa, P. T. (1991). The NEO Personality Inventory: Using the five-factor model in counseling. *Journal of Counseling & Development, 69*, 369–372.

McCrae, R. R., & Costa, P. T. (1997). Personality trait structure as a human universal. *American Psychologist, 52*, 509–516.

Morasco, B. J., Gfeller, J. D., & Elder, K. A. (2007). The utility of the NEO-PI-R validity scales to detect response distortion: A comparison with the MMPI-2. *Journal of Personality Assessment, 88*, 276–283.

Myerholtz, L., & Rosenberg, H. (1998). Screening college students for alcohol problems: Psychometric assessment of the SASSI-2. *Journal of Studies on Alcohol, 59*, 439–446.

Nichols, D. S. (2006). Tell me a story: MMPI responses and personal biography in the case of a serial killer. *Journal of Personality Assessment, 86*, 242–262.

Ridley, C. R., Li, L., & Hill, C. L. (1998). Multicultural assessment: Reexamination, reconceptualization, and practical application. *The Counseling Psychologist, 26*, 827–910.

Schinka, J. A., Kinder, B. N., & Kremer, T. (1997). Research validity scales for the NEO-PI-R: Development and initial validation. *Journal of Personality Assessment, 68*, 127–138.

Timbrook, R. E., & Graham, J. R. (1994). Ethnic differences on the MMPI-2? *Psychological Assessment, 6*, 212–217.

Tsai, D. C., & Pike, P. L. (2000). Effects of acculturation on the MMPI-2 scores of Asian American students. *Journal of Personality Assessment, 74*, 216–230.

Widiger, T. A., & Costa, P. T. (1994). Personality and personality disorders. *Journal of Abnormal Psychology, 103*, 78–91.

ASSIGNMENTS

- Precompleted instrument interpretation. Each student could interpret a set of precompleted instruments provided along with accompanying mock background demographic information chosen from the Minnesota Multiphasic Personality Inventory-2 (MMPI-2; Butcher, Dahstrom, Gramm, Tellegen, &

Kaemmer, 1989), NEO-Personality Inventory—Revised (NEO-PI-R; Costa & McCrae, 1992), Millon Clinical Multiaxial Inventory—III (MCMI-III; Millon, Davis, & Millon, 1997), and Substance Abuse Subtle Screening Inventory 3 (SASSI-3; Miller, Roberts, Brooks, & Lazowski, 1997) as take-home interpretation assignment. Students will produce a written clinical assessment report of each take-home assessment complete with clinical interpretation of the assessment results, diagnoses, and treatment recommendations. These assignments may be used to cover the CACREP clinical mental health counseling assessment knowledge 1, 2, and 4 and the skills and practices 3 and 4.

- Administer and interpret instruments. Students are expected to administer and interpret one MMPI-II, one NEO-PI-R, one MCMI-III, one SASSI-3, and an assessment interview. Further, students are required to select, administer, and interpret an additional standardized assessment of the student's choice. This choice should be made after taking into consideration the appropriateness of the assessment based on the mock client's cultural background. The results of these assessments and interview will be used to produce an integrated combined final report. These assignments may be used to cover the CACREP clinical mental health counseling assessment knowledge 1, 2, and 4 and the skills and practices 1–4.
- Final examination. Students will complete a comprehensive final exam on the last day of the course that will cover material presented in the course discussion and assigned readings. The final exam will cover clinical mental health counseling assessment knowledge 1, 2, and 4.

WEEK	*TOPICS AND ASSIGNMENTS*
Week 1	Introduction
Week 2	The clinical interview
	The assessment report
	Development of MMPI
Week 3	MMPI, MMPI-2
Week 4	MMPI-2/RC
	Take-home MMPI 1 due
Week 5	MMPI
	Score MMPI
Week 6	NEO-PI-R
	MMPI #2 due
Week 7	NEO-PI-R
Week 8	Score NEOs
	NEO I due
Week 9	Start MCMI
Week 10	MCMI III
	Score MCMI-IIIs
	NEO #2 due

(continued)

WEEK	*TOPICS AND ASSIGNMENTS*
Week 11	Start SASSI
	MCMI-1 due
Week 12	Finish SASSI
	Score SASSIs
	Take-home MCMI-2 due
Week 13	Multicultural assessment
Week 14	Ethics/professional issues
	Both take-home SASSIs due
Week 15	Course review
Week 16	Final exam
	Final integrated report due

CONCLUSION

Faculty teaching assessment courses must consider that some counselor education students may be intimidated by the course material. Assessment courses should be practical and interesting to students. Integrating students' areas of clinical interest into assignments makes this course less intimidating and potentially more effective for the students. Assessment is a fun course!

REFERENCES

American Psychiatric Association. (2000). *Diagnostic and statistical manual of mental disorders* (4th ed. text revision). Washington, DC: Author.

Angell, J., DuBravac, S., & Gonglewski, M. (2008). Thinking globally, acting locally: Selecting textbooks for college-level language programs. *Foreign Language Annals, 41*, 562–573.

Butcher, J. N., Dahlstrom, W. G., Graham, J. R., Tellegen, A., & Kaemmer, B. (1989). *Minnesota Multiphasic Personality Inventory-2 (MMPI-2): Manual for administration, scoring, and interpretation, revised.* Minneapolis: University of Minnesota Press.

Costa Jr., P. T., & McCrae, R. R. (1992). *Revised NEO Personality Inventory (NEO-PI-R) and NEO Five-Factor Inventory (NEO-FFI) Professional Manual.* Lutz, Florida: Psychological Assessment Resources.

Council for Accreditation of Counseling and Related Educational Programs. (2009). *2009 Standards.* Retrieved from http://www.cacrep.org/2009standards.html

Groth-Marnat, G. (2003). *Handbook of psychological assessment* (4th ed.). Hoboken, NJ: John Wiley & Sons.

Helms, J. E. (1992). Why is there no study of cultural equivalence in cognitive ability testing? *American Psychologist, 47*, 1083–1101.

Laux, J. M., & Perera-Diltz, D. M. (2008). Assessment and diagnosis of addictions. In D. Capuzzi & M.Stauffer (Eds.), *Foundations of Addictions Counseling* (pp. 101–125). Boston, MA: Allyn and Bacon.

Matarazzo, J. D. (1992). Psychological testing and assessment in the 21st century. *American Psychologist, 47*, 1007–1018.

Miller, G. A., Roberts, J., Brooks, M. K., & Lazowski, L. E. (1997). *SASSI-3 user's guide.* Bloomington, IN: Baugh Enterprises.

Millon, T., Davis, R., & Millon, C. (1997). *Millon Clinical Multiaxial Inventory-III: MCMI-III Manual* (2nd ed.). Minneapolis: NCS Pearson, Inc.

Newton, D. P., & Newton, L. D. (2009). A procedure for assessing textbook support for reasoned thinking. *The Asian Pacific Education Researcher, 18*(1), 109–115.

Spies, R. A. Carlson, J. F., & Geisinger, K. F. (2010). *The Eighteenth Mental Measurements Yearbook.* Lincoln: The University of Nebraska Press.

12 Diagnosis, Pathology, Wellness, and Evidence-Based Practices for Counselors

Figuring Out What's Wrong, What's Right, and the Best Way to Help

Dale-Elizabeth Pehrsson, Mary Amanda Graham, Kerry A. Bartlett, and Asti Sproul

Mary sat staring at the blank computer screen; her department chair had just left her office not 10 minutes earlier. The chair just proposed to Mary that she teach the *DSM* class, claiming Mary's background made her "just perfect" and besides, she just found out that Dr. Smith's sabbatical application was approved and there was no one else who could teach it. Mary's breathing quickened . . . and then she thought, "Where do I begin?" For many neophyte counselor educators, this scene looms in recent memory and is all too familiar.

As new professors and instructors, planning for a new course initially seems exciting. This excitement can be followed by a deep sense of foreboding. When we begin planning we examine program curriculum, outcomes and Council for the Accreditation of Counseling and Related Educational Programs (CACREP) standards. We ask questions like "What do I know about this topic?" "How can I deliver this in a stimulating and comprehensive manner?" "What is the best text to use?" "If I decide on a text, where is the best place to find it?" "What makes me an expert in this area?" and " What is the best method of instruction, face to face, lecture, forum, hybrid or online?" Over time our anxiety lessens as we tackle new courses. However, the questions and the need for thoughtful delivery of curriculum and course planning remain.

Good teaching requires strategy. In many ways, pedagogy is like planning a 10- to 15-act play; the content, delivery, readings, activities, outcomes, projects, and examinations all require a flow and balance that builds toward a culmination or final act. In the end, instructors should have a good sense of what has been delivered and whether students have gained the knowledge and skills necessary to move to the next leg of their learning journey or their own opening act.

Most students who enroll in coursework focusing on diagnosis, pathology, wellness, and treatment interventions are either in a mental health counseling program or have a passionate interest in the topic. As clinical mental health, family, and school counselors, we believe that all counselors need to be conversant and knowledgeable in the use of the mental health diagnostic and pathology tools as well as in how to locate and use professional literature about research supported treatments. All counselors may not use the *Diagnostic and Statistical Manual of Mental Disorders* (*DSM*; American Psychiatric Assocation [APA], 2000) in their daily practice with clients. Nevertheless, an overall understanding of pathological categories provides a useful framework from which to draw when working with interdisciplinary teams, making referrals, or reading academic or clinical reports. Knowing the common clinical language that intersects academic, medical, and mental health professions builds our professional competence and better serves our clients.

In a course such as this, students should achieve several outcomes based on the content and delivery of the course. This course should include an overview of the *Diagnostic and Statistical Manual* (APA, 2000), an understanding of the various classifications, the diagnoses and related symptoms that clients present in general society, predominant diagnoses that manifest along the life continuum, current research-based treatment interventions, medications and wellness strategies, and diversity factors that influence and impact diagnosis and treatment. This type of course readies students for entry into practice.

There are several common dilemmas that instructors encounter as they make decisions related to course preparation. First, we think instructors should apply a consistent pedagogical approach. For us, this really depends on the course subject, the expected outcomes, and student development. This course is usually taught during the second year of a graduate program, so information as well as application to practice is critical in the planning process. Class size impacts teaching style and curriculum development. Assignments will differ depending on class size. When course sections have 60 students rather than 15, assignments will differ. It is very challenging for instructors to read and critique 60 weekly case analyses and planned treatment interventions; a multiple-choice examination might be more appropriate for larger class sections. The professor's budget also presents a concern. In times of lean finances, departments often limit paper copies or if professors have gone green and use a form of electronic delivery, a difference is created in how a course is prepared. Another important aspect to consider when preparing the course is whether the instructor is teaching on a quarter or semester system. Planning the course for an 11-week quarter term is vastly different from planning for a 15-week semester. There is more of a pressing need for the instructor to determine the core and necessary concepts students must learn from the class in 11 weeks versus 15 weeks. The instructor must be organized, focused, and meticulous when planning for an 11-week course in order to meet all course objectives and CACREP standards in a condensed time frame. When teaching within a shorter quarter term, we recommend the use of technology to support learning (Blackboard, WebCT, etc.). When there is a large body of information to synthesize, it may be beneficial to offer the course completely online or use a hybrid format. These formats can enhance independent learning outside of the traditional face-to-face format.

Hybrid class structures have many benefits. The online portion of a course offers students the flexibility of "attending" when convenient to the student's schedule. Many graduate students are working adults and nontraditional students. Having the flexibility to complete the online portion of the course is supportive of student employment and family and personal needs. The online portion of the hybrid course not only creates flexibility but offers students a relaxed, safe, and comfortable environment in which to pose discussion questions, give feedback, and participate. Students have a solid amount of time between face-to-face classes to read material, research cases, and prepare for class discussions. Hybrid and online classes require thoughtful planning for students and instructors. Students are more responsible and must manage priorities. Instructors considering an online or hybrid approach need to be technologically savvy beyond the basics. Instructors need training for use of technologically sophisticated tools such as Skype, Webinar software, podcasting, and editing mechanisms for embedding and uploading video clips. University technological designers and support staff are major resources and provide essential support. Contact them early in your planning and rely on them often. Instructors also need to be diligent in screening texts, articles, assignments, and assessments for multicultural responsiveness. Materials and activities, as discussed below, should be engaging, thought provoking, experiential, and current. This course is often daunting to students, and if instructors are unable to engage students in the learning process, students will be less likely to understand and integrate the material. No matter what format the instructor chooses in the delivery of this type of course, it is essential to understand and implement critical content components related to course delivery.

Several critical content components and related course topics are essential for this kind of class, including the following:

1. Knowledge, use, and familiarity with the *DSM* (APA, 2000)
2. Knowledge, use, and familiarity with the Global Assessment of Functioning (GAF) (DSM, 2000)
3. Knowledge, use, and familiarity with the development of master treatment plans
4. Knowledge, use, and familiarity with the current research-based counseling interventions
5. Knowledge, use, and familiarity with wellness plans
6. Knowledge, use, and familiarity with major pathological concerns and diagnosis for each developmental stage of the life span
7. Knowledge, use, and familiarity with the diversity and cultural matters that affect assessment, treatment, and outcome of clients
8. Knowledge and familiarity with the current medications or psychopharmacology prescribed with common diagnoses
9. Knowledge and familiarity of the potential for chemical and substance abuse disorders to mimic and often coexist with some medical and/or psychological disorders
10. Knowledge, use, and familiarity with assessment of suicide risk and prevention and treatment

Beyond these critical content components, instructors must be cognizant of meeting CACREP standards when constructing course syllabi and assignments.

OBJECTIVES AND CACREP STANDARDS

There are several course and student learning objectives related to this course, no matter the counseling degree (school, mental health, college counseling, etc.). Each degree requires that students learn mental health-related knowledge that is foundational for all counselors. The critical components listed above also match the CACREP standards. For the purposes of this course the clinical mental health counseling program requirements and standards (CACREP, 2009) are most appropriate. These standards state clearly that graduates will demonstrate knowledge, skills, and practices necessary to deal with a wide array of situations within the context of mental health counseling. The clinical mental health counseling (CMHC) standards put forth by CACREP require that students who are preparing for clinical mental health counseling work demonstrate entry level professional knowledge. That said, a common core of curriculum is outlined in Section II.G. Within the context of this specific course, the following standards identify what should be considered in course planning and delivery.

- Understands ethical and legal considerations specifically related to the practice of clinical mental health counseling. (CMHC A.2.)
- Understands a variety of models and theories related to clinical mental health counseling, including the methods, models, and principles of clinical supervision. (CMHC A.5.)
- Recognizes the potential for substance use disorders to mimic and coexist with a variety of medical and psychological disorders. (CMHC A.6.)
- Understands the impact of crises, disasters, and other trauma-causing events on people. (CMHC A.9.)
- Understands the operation of an emergency management system within clinical mental health agencies and in the community. (CMHC A.10.)
- Demonstrates the ability to apply and adhere to ethical and legal standards in clinical mental health counseling. (CMHC B.1.)
- Knows the etiology, the diagnostic process and nomenclature, treatment, referral, and prevention of mental and emotional disorders. (CMHC C.2.)
- Knows the disease concept and etiology of addiction and cooccurring disorders. (CMHC C.4.)
- Knows the principles, models, and documentation formats of biopsychosocial case conceptualization and treatment planning. (CMHC C.7.)
- Recognizes the importance of family, social networks, and community systems in the treatment of mental and emotional disorders. (CMHC C.8.)
- Understands professional issues relevant to the practice of clinical mental health counseling. (CMHC C.9.)
- Uses the principles and practices of diagnosis, treatment, referral, and prevention of mental and emotional disorders to initiate, maintain, and terminate counseling. (CMHC D.1.)
- Applies multicultural competencies to clinical mental health counseling involving case conceptualization, diagnosis, treatment, referral, and prevention of mental and emotional disorders. (CMHC D.2.)
- Promotes optimal human development, wellness, and mental health through prevention, education, and advocacy activities. (CMHC D.3.)
- Demonstrates appropriate use of culturally responsive individual, couple, family, group, and systems modalities for initiating, maintaining, and terminating counseling. (CMHC D.5.)
- Demonstrates the ability to use procedures for assessing and managing suicide risk. (CMHC D.6.)
- Provides appropriate counseling strategies when working with clients with addiction and cooccurring disorders. (CMHC D.8.)
- Demonstrates the ability to recognize his or her own limitations as a clinical mental health counselor and to seek supervision or refer clients when appropriate. (CMHC D.9.)
- Understands how living in a multicultural society affects clients who are seeking clinical mental health counseling services. (CMHC E.1.)
- Understands the effects of racism, discrimination, sexism, power, privilege, and oppression on one's own life and career and those of the client. (CMHC E.2.)

- Understands current literature that outlines theories, approaches, strategies, and techniques shown to be effective when working with specific populations of clients with mental and emotional disorders. (CMHC E.3.)
- Understands the implications of concepts such as internalized oppression and institutional racism, as well as the historical and current political climate regarding immigration, poverty, and welfare. (CMHC E.5.)
- Demonstrates the ability to modify counseling systems, theories, techniques, and interventions to make them culturally appropriate for diverse populations. (CMHC F.3.)
- Knows the principles and models of assessment, case conceptualization, theories of human development, and concepts of normalcy and psychopathology leading to diagnoses and appropriate counseling treatment plans. (CMHC G.1.)
- Understands various models and approaches to clinical evaluation and their appropriate uses, including diagnostic interviews, mental status examinations, symptom inventories, and psychoeducational and personality assessments. (CMHC G.2.)
- Understands basic classifications, indications, and contraindications of commonly prescribed psychopharmacological medications so that appropriate referrals can be made for medication evaluations and so that the side effects of such medications can be identified. (CMHC G.3.)
- Identifies standard screening and assessment instruments for substance use disorders and process addictions. (CMHC G.4.)
- Demonstrates skill in conducting an intake interview, a mental status evaluation, a biopsychosocial history, a mental health history, and a psychological assessment for treatment planning and caseload management. (CMHC H.2.)
- Screens for addiction, aggression, and danger to self and/or others, as well as cooccurring mental disorders. (CMHC H.3.)
- Applies the assessment of a client's stage of dependence, change, or recovery to determine the appropriate treatment modality and placement criteria within the continuum of care. (CMHC H.4.)
- Knows evidence-based treatments and basic strategies for evaluating counseling outcomes in clinical mental health counseling. (CMHC H.3.)
- Develops measurable outcomes for clinical mental health counseling programs, interventions, and treatments. (CMHC J.2.)
- Knows the principles of the diagnostic process, including differential diagnosis, and the use of current diagnostic tools, such as the current edition of the *DSM*. (CMHC K.1.)
- Understands the established diagnostic criteria for mental and emotional disorders and describes treatment modalities and placement criteria within the continuum of care. (CMHC K.2.)
- Knows the impact of cooccurring substance use disorders on medical and psychological disorders. (CMHC K.3.)
- Understands the relevance and potential biases of commonly used diagnostic tools with multicultural populations. (CMHC K.4.)

- Understands appropriate use of diagnosis during a crisis, disaster, or other trauma-causing events. (CMHC K.5.)
- Demonstrates appropriate use of diagnostic tools, including the current edition of the *DSM*, to describe the symptoms and clinical presentation of clients with mental and emotional impairments. (CMHC L.1.)
- Is able to conceptualize an accurate multi-axial diagnosis of disorders presented by a client and discuss the differential diagnosis with collaborating professionals. (CMHC L.2.)
- Differentiates between diagnosis and developmentally appropriate reactions during crises, disasters, and other trauma-causing events (adapted from CACREP standards 2009). (CMHC L.3.)

When constructing the course utilizing the critical components and integrating CACREP standards and objectives into the syllabus, it is essential for instructors to select texts and materials that will be engaging, practical, and supportive of the course content.

CRITERIA FOR EVALUATING A TEXT

Despite the potential time commitment, instructors must choose textbooks that will ultimately support and enhance student learning while addressing various course and CACREP standards. According to Wolfe (2004), the most critical question to consider when selecting a textbook is whether or not the text supports the course objectives that have been developed. Once the course objectives are clear, instructors can begin the search for a beneficial textbook. One might wonder how to make an informed decision about selecting the optimum textbook available. There are several desirable characteristics to consider during this quest.

To begin, textbooks should possess relevant information and be written by credible authors. An appropriate book elaborates on the scope of the course and provides pertinent information that can be applied to the class. When selecting a textbook, request the most recent edition. A recent publication most likely includes the newest research, studies, and information available to both students and the profession. Outdated information can lead to more work for the instructor and student confusion and impact the instructor's credibility. "A well chosen textbook allows the instructor to elaborate on or reinforce what students have read, rather than contradict or correct it" (Chatman, 1985, p. 150). To determine whether the authors are considered a credible source, it is often helpful to contact various publishing companies, research the source, and ask for feedback from more seasoned colleagues such as the instructor's department chair, peers and faculty members (Wolfe, 2004). Publishing companies such as Pearson, Brooks/Cole, and Sage can provide information about the most frequently used texts. Some methods of researching the text may include posting on the Association for Counselor Educators and Supervisors (ACES) listserv called CESNET (https://listserv.kent.edu/cgi-bin/wa.exe?A0=CESNET-L), reviewing the syllabi on the collaboratively sponsored

American Counseling Association (ACA) and ACES Syllabus Clearinghouse website (http://www.counseling.org/Resources/TP/SyllabusClearinghouse/CT2.aspx), and even perusing websites such as Amazon to see which texts are the biggest sellers. Further, Ornstein (1994) recommended reviewing textbooks that have been "scrutinized by scholars, educators, and minority groups" (p. 70). These existing reviews and ratings help support a decision to consider a specific textbook. Once the selection of books that meet the above listed criteria points has been identified, instructors can review materials based on more specific qualifications.

An important consideration in textbook selection is determining whether the textbook suits the student population it will serve. The book must be written at the knowledge level, developmental level, and critical thinking level of the students who will be reading it. Concept difficulty can affect whether students will benefit from the text or become frustrated with it. Ornstein (1994) proposed the following question: "Does it provide the student with a sense of accomplishment because it can be mastered and is still challenging?" (p. 71). Though many courses incorporate various learning modalities, textbooks should offer the students additional visual or audio aids that support multiple learning needs and styles. A quality textbook addresses issues of interest to the student population (Chatman, 1985). For example, if students enrolled in a course are also on a school counseling graduate track, examples of mental health relevant to the school setting will engage students. Considering the student population will further narrow an instructor's textbook search.

Selecting a textbook entails examining chapter organization, visual appeal, and the supplemental materials included. Organization enhances student readability (Ade-Ridder, 1989). Navigation of the textbook is easy when the publisher includes proper content and index sections. Major concepts and themes should be easily identifiable as well. Ade-Ridder also suggested using a text that provides identification by using headings, pictures, tables, informative table sections, and separate case studies within the book. According to Wolfe (2004), visually appealing charts and pictures "can motivate and stimulate students to learn more about the topic" (p. 59). Books that contain prereading questions in the beginning of each chapter as well as summaries at the end are useful due to their ability to reinforce what the student should read or has previously read. For instructor and student benefit, many course developers search for a textbook that provides supplemental materials or instructional aides. These can include, but are not limited to, instructional manuals, study guides, test banks, discs with short films, case studies, exercise books, reinforcement and enrichment activities, and example lesson plans (Ornstein, 1994). Instructional aides have the ability to inspire and support the development and delivery of a course and provide first-time instructors many tools. This cuts down on preparation time.

Now that the vital characteristics of a textbook are outlined, instructors might ask themselves where they should go or look for these textbooks. Contacting publishing companies allows for advisement from knowledgeable professionals and helps narrow the search. Many publishing companies send out sample textbooks to instructors (Wolfe, 2004). This allows for thorough review. Textbook displays at national or regional conferences offer opportunities for instructors to talk with publishers or their representatives, often resulting in even more resources for instructors. Speaking with sales representative in person allows for exceptional assistance. Another route to consider is personally building a textbook. "Course packets and customized textbooks are becoming more common. Customized textbooks allow an instructor to choose chapters from different books and have them bound together as one book" (Wolfe, p. 59). This would ensure that the course textbook is comprehensive and caters to needs of the course and students. Another new route to consider is digital or e-textbooks that would be solely accessed online using a computer. Directly selecting the sections of a textbook can create an inclusive book with lower costs, eliminating the need for students buying multiple textbooks. Students are more likely to invest in a textbook when it has utility and is cost-effective.

Instructors evaluate textbooks for sensitivity to multicultural matters; books should have an unbiased nature. Competent instructors use materials to promote student competency in multicultural and advocacy counseling strategies. Therefore, texts should portray underrepresented populations accurately. These could include, but are not limited to, women; governmentally designated minorities; various social classes; physically, mentally, auditorily, or visually challenged individuals, among others; and the gay, lesbian, bisexual, transgendered, and queer (GLBTQ) community (Ade-Ridder, 1989). To ensure a more unbiased text, examine whether the author discusses viewpoints in a fulsome manner, including pros and cons of topics and theories. As educators, we are responsible for providing students with precise and comprehensive information.

Considering these many factors will assist course developers in making informed decisions regarding textbooks and thus promote the best learning opportunities for students. Though a perfect book may not exist, considering these factors will help the instructor make the best choice. These criteria help instructors select textbooks that have the most beneficial attributes and will balance out any of the existing shortcomings that may exist (Ornstein, 1994). As addressed later in this chapter, it is often possible to overcome any textbook shortcomings by providing students with supplemental articles, websites, case vignettes, and audio materials.

MOST POPULAR TEXTS

American Psychiatric Association. (2000). *Diagnostic and statistical manual of mental disorders* (4th ed., text rev.). Washington, DC: Author.

Eriksen, K., & Kress, V. E. (2000). *Beyond the DSM story: Ethical quandaries, challenges, and best practices*. Thousand Oaks, CA: Sage.

Morrison, J. (2007). *Diagnosis made easier: Principles and techniques for mental health clinicians*. New York: Guilford Press.

Seligman, L., & Reichenberg, L. W. (2007). *Selecting effective treatments: A comprehensive, systematic guide* (3rd ed.). San Francisco, CA: Wiley.

Zimmerman, M. (1994). *Interview guide for evaluating DSM-IV psychiatric disorders and the mental status exam*. Philadelphia, PA: Psych Products Press.

Using the current edition of the *DSM* as the main text for this course is generally recommended. Each of the subsequently listed texts addresses frequent student concerns that arise as they familiarize themselves with the *DSM*.

SUPPLEMENTAL READING

Providing supplemental articles to students is a great way to enhance course textbooks. Journal articles may expand upon issues briefly discussed in the course textbook(s), introduce an alternative point of view, or provide more current information. Furthermore, assigning scholarly journal readings to students can augment lecture comprehension, increase classroom participation, and even enhance examination performance of students (Lei, Bartlett, Gorney, & Herschbach, 2010). There are many excellent journals that provide articles on the varying topics of psychopathology. Two of the counseling-related journals are *Journal of Counseling and Development* and *Journal of Mental Health Counseling*. Researching articles can become yet another time-consuming process; therefore, we include a few suggested articles addressing topics most frequently covered in this type of course. These articles give a brief overview, identify a critique, or highlight a specific component of a related area. The suggested articles are given as examples, but new instructors are encouraged to tailor the articles to the design of their course.

Creating supplementary learning experiences requiring that students research beneficial articles assists in the development of research skills, a critical skill that is essential to their future competence. During this process students become familiar with reviewing literature and in turn build confidence to seek out information for future clients when necessary. Instructors have the freedom to provide students with journal articles, require students to locate relevant articles themselves, or include a combination of both approaches when designing their courses.

Diagnosis: Becoming Familiar With the Diagnostic and Statistical Manual

Hinkle, J. (1994). Psychodiagnosis for counselors: The *DSM-IV*. Retrieved from ERIC database. (EDO-CG-94-06)

Provides an overview of the *DSM-IV* discussing the major features, sociocultural implications, and the multi-axial system.

Lopez, S. J., Edwards, L. M., Pedrotti, J. T., Prosser, E. C., LaRue, S., Spalitto, S. V., & Ulven, J. C. (2006). Beyond the *DSM-IV*: Assumptions, alternatives, and alterations. *Journal of Counseling and Development, 84*, 259–267.

Critiques the *DSM-IV* and mentions the challenges clinicians may face when using the *DSM* while offering some alternative suggestions on how to approach diagnosis and treatment.

Smart, D., & Smart, J. (1997). *DSM-IV* and culturally sensitive diagnosis: Some observations for counselors. *Journal of Counseling & Development, 75*, 392–398.

Reviews the evolution of cultural sensitivity within the *DSM-IV* including the newest features. Contains a discussion of the glossary of culture-bound syndromes and reviews cultural formation. Also speaks about V-code, V62.4. This addresses cultural sensitivity.

Topic: Schizophrenia and Psychotic Disorders

McGorry, P., Killackey, E., Elkins, K., Lambert, M., & Lambert, T. (2003). Summary Australian and New Zealand clinical practice guideline for the treatment of schizophrenia. *Australian Psychiatry, 11*, 136–147.

Provides thorough outlines discussing the definition, diagnosis of, and treatment approaches to schizophrenia at various stages according to the Australian and New Zealand protocol.

Topic: Mood Disorders

Jonas, B. S., Brody, D., Roper, M., & Narrow, W. E. (2003). Prevalence of mood disorders in a national sample of young American adults. *Social Psychiatry and Psychiatric Epidemiology, 38*, 618–624.

Examines the prevalence of mood disorders (major depressive episode, dysthymia, and bipolar disorder) reported from the Epidemiological Catchments Area Study from 1980 to 1985 and compares these results with the Third National Health and Nutrition Examination Survey conducted from 1988 to 1994.

Koran, L. (2007). Diagnosing and treating comorbid mood disorders and obsessive compulsive disorder. *Current Medical Literature: Psychiatry, 18*, 73–81.

Discusses the diagnosis of and subtypes of obsessive–compulsive disorder (OCD), the prevalence of mood disorders in OCD patients, and treatment considerations for comorbid OCD with either major depression disorder (MDD), dysthymia, or bipolar disorder.

Chung, H., Culpepper, L., De Wester, J., Grieco, R., Kaye, N., Lipkin, M., Ross, R. (2007). Recognizing and understanding bipolar disorder. *Journal of Family Practice, 56*, S5–S10.

Presents a case study of a man initially diagnosed with depression later to be diagnosed with bipolar disorder. The authors implied that bipolar disorder is often misdiagnosed due to depressive symptoms normally presented by bipolar patients.

Topic: Anxiety Disorders

Pontoski, K. E., & Heimberg, R. G. (2010). The myth of the superiority of concurrent combined treatments for anxiety disorders. *Clinical Psychology Science and Practice, 17*, 107–111.

Pontoski and Heimberg comment on the effectiveness and different factors associated with combination treatment for patients diagnosed with an anxiety disorder.

Fong, M., & Silien, K. (1999). Assessment and diagnosis of *DSM-IV* anxiety disorders. *Journal of Counseling & Development, 77*, 209–217.

Reviews the assessment and diagnosis of anxiety disorders based on the *DSM-IV*. The authors discuss the dominant symptoms of anxiety disorders and mention the high frequency with which these disorders are misdiagnosed.

Topic: Personality Disorders

Ling, H., & Qian, M.-Y. (2010). Relationships between attachment and personality disorder symptoms of Chinese college students. *Social Behavior and Personality, 38*, 571–576. doi:10.2224/sbp.2010.38.4.571

Examines how early childhood attachment, both good and bad, may be a predictor for the severity of a personality disorder.

Topic: Wellness, Alternatives and Supportive Approaches

Wallace, E. V. (2007). Managing stress: What consumers want to know from health educators. *American Journal of Health Studies, 22*, 56–58.

Discusses stress, what causes it, and how to reduce stress within a short amount of time.

Okonski, V. (2003). Exercise as a counseling intervention. *Journal of Mental Health Counseling, 25*, 45–56.

Discusses how to use exercise to contribute to a person's total well-being, explaining specific recommendations on how to include exercise in a holistic mental health treatment plan.

Myers, J., Sweeney, T., & Witmer, J. (2000). The wheel of wellness counseling for wellness: A holistic model for treatment planning. *Journal of Counseling & Development, 78*, 251–266.

Reviews the foundation, research, and implications of the modified version of Myers, Sweeny, and Witmer's holistic model of wellness and prevention over the life span.

Topic: Eating Disorders, Sexuality and Gender, Impulse Control

Myers, T. C., Swan-Kremeier, L., Wonderlich, S., Lancaster, K., & Mitchell, J. E. (2004). The use of alternative delivery systems and new technologies in the treatment of patients with eating disorders. *International Journal of Eating Disorders, 36*, 123–143.

Reviews the advances in technology that offer additional ways to provide counseling and what these might mean for treating eating disorders.

Keel, P. K., & Haedt, A. (2008). Evidence-based psychosocial treatments for eating problems and eating disorders. *Journal of Clinical Child & Adolescent Psychology, 37*, 39–61.

Discusses evidence-based treatment for children and adolescents with eating disorders while considering treatments known to be effective with adults. Two of the common forms of treatment include family-based therapy and self-guided cognitive–behavioral therapy.

Topic: Substance-Related Disorders

Bellack, A. (2007). Issues in understanding and treating comorbidity in people with serious mental illness. *Clinical Psychology: Science and Practice, 14*, 70–76. doi:10.1111/j.1468-2850.2007.00064.x

Reviews the prevalence of comorbid disorders and discusses factors in successful treatment and motivation for both change and treatment. Highlights the need to understand the intricacies of various comorbid combinations to effectively treat them.

Samet, S., Nunes, E., & Hasin, D. (2004). Diagnosing comorbidity: Concepts, criteria, and methods. *Acta Neuropsychiatrica, 16*, 9–18. doi:10.1111/j.1601-5215.2004.0062.x

Discusses the evolution of comorbidity, reviews the substance-related categorical terms of the *DSM* (primary, substance-induced, organic, nonorganic), and highlights instruments that assist counselors in distinguishing between psychiatric and substance disorders (Psychiatric Research Interview for Substance and Mental Disorders [PRISM]; Hasin, Trautman, Miele, Samet, Smith, & Endicott, 1996).

Topic: Childhood and Adolescent Disorders

Rowe, J. (2010). Dealing with psychiatric disabilities in schools: A description of symptoms and coping strategies for dealing with them. *Preventing School Failure, 54*, 190–198. doi:10.1080/10459880903217945

Provides an overview of common childhood disorders most often identified by teachers. Also discusses symptoms and teacher recommendations for improving the classroom environment. These issues may assist new counseling students in becoming familiar with the symptoms and adapt the teacher recommendations to be more fitting for the therapeutic setting.

Topic: Dissociative Disorders

Öztürk, E., & Sar, V. (2008). Somatization as a predictor of suicidal ideation in dissociative disorders. *Psychiatry & Clinical Neurosciences, 62*, 662–668. doi:10.1111/j.1440-1819.2008.01865.x

Finds that a history of both childhood trauma and a comorbidity between dissociative disorder and somatization disorder may predict suicide ideation.

WEBSITES

In a technologically savvy world, a way to increase student engagement and interest in a course such as this is to utilize the World Wide Web. There are numerous useful and content-supportive websites available for this course. Most students today are comfortable and quite adept at navigating the web and its treasure trove of resources. The advantage of web resources is that there are many and they are current. Two challenges in using the web can include questionable sources that lack credibility and links that are often broken. These challenges make it critical for instructors to ensure that sites are still live when pointing students to a website. That said, there are several sites we recommend for use by instructors. From the sites listed below, we would like to highlight *Get Information* (Mental Health America, 2010). This is an extremely comprehensive website that addresses a vast number of issues relating to mental health including details and descriptions of disorders and treatment, extensive resources for both clients and mental health professionals, and first-hand stories of people struggling with disorders. It is a website that students and professionals alike will find helpful.

- APA Diagnostic Classification *DSM-IV-TR*
  http://www.behavenet.com/capsules/disorders/dsm4TRclassification.htm
  A website listing the *DSM* diagnostic criteria online. Note: Psychiatryonline offers a virtual *DSM* library that consists of the *DSM-IV-TR*, *DSM-IV-TR Handbook of Differential Diagnosis*, and *DSM-IV-TR Cases*. This service is provided for a fee at http://www.psychiatryonline.com/dsmLibrary.aspx

- American Psychiatric Association: *DSM-5* Development
  http://www.dsm5.org/Pages/Default.aspx
  Information on the next edition of the *DSM* is described on this website, including proposed draft revisions.

- American Psychiatric Association: Mental Health Links
  http://www.psych.org/SpecialGroups/MentalHealthResources.aspx
  Provides a list and links to professional and consumer organizations associated with the mental health field.

- Anxiety Disorders Association of America
  http://www.adaa.org/
  An extensive and thorough resource concerning anxiety disorders that covers types of anxiety disorders, living with anxiety, taking action, and resources for professionals.

- Bibliotherapy Education Project
  http://www.library.unlv.edu/faculty/research/bibliotherapy/
  A searchable database that offers reviews and suggestions of books addressing specific issues and allows for additional evaluations to be made.

- Dr. Carlow P. Zalanquett's Page
  http://www.coedu.usf.edu/zalaquett/index.html
  Directs viewers to several sources of useful information featuring relaxation, screening, and an interview regarding treatment of victims of traumatic events. This is just one of many websites created by professors that are full of worthwhile information.

- Global Assessment of Functioning Scale
  http://depts.washington.edu/washinst/Resources/CGAS/Index.htm#below
  Outlines the GAF scale including scores and descriptions. Also provides a link to a companion online training page that supplies scenarios to practice assigning GAF rating scores.

- MayoClinic.com: Diseases and Conditions
  http://www.mayoclinic.com/health/DiseasesIndex/DiseasesIndex
  Presents comprehensive reviews of many disorders addressing several factors, including definition, symptoms, causes, risk factor, complications, tests

and diagnosis, treatment and drugs, lifestyle and home remedies, alternative medicine, coping and support, and prevention.

- Medscape Psychiatry & Mental Health
  http://www.medscape.com/psychiatryhome
  Offers "health professionals the most robust and integrated medical information and educational tools" consisting of information regarding current news, upcoming conferences, journals and resource centers (WEBMD, 2010b). Medscape requires viewers to create a free account.

- Mental Health America Get Information
  http://www.mentalhealthamerica.net/go/information
  Factsheets searchable by audience, issue, or disorders and treatments offer information and additional resources pertaining to the selected topic.

- National Alliance on Mental Illness
  http://www.nami.org/Template.cfm?Section=By_Illness
  A professional organization that shares comprehensive information regarding mental disorders and suggests further resources.

- National Eating Disorders Association
  http://www.nationaleatingdisorders.org/information-resources/
  Contains an information and resource section that defines eating disorders, provides informational videos and seminars, lists an abundance of additional resources, and contains informational documents for treatment professionals. This website also highlights current news and programs and events.

- SAMHSA's National Mental Health Information Center
  http://mentalhealth.samhsa.gov/topics/explore/
  Discusses multiple issues relating to mental health. Selecting "Treatment and Recovery" and "Online Publications" leads to websites devoted to specific disorders and their prevalence, cause, diagnosis, treatment, and additional resources.

- Substance Abuse and Mental Health Services Administration
  http://www.samhsa.gov/index.aspx
  SAMHSA is a government agency created to "focus attention, programs, and funding on improving the lives of people with or at risk for mental and substance abuse disorders" (SAMHSA, 2010b). This website, among many other services, offers a treatment locator and a web guide to other websites containing information regarding prevention and treatment of disorders.

- The Wellspring
  http://www.thewellspring.com/
  A site devoted to increasing the awareness of integrated wellness by reviewing the various aspects of wellness and how to achieve them.

- WebMD: Mental Health
  http://www.webmd.com/mental-health/default.htm
  Presents information on a wide array of mental health issues via a specialized health center for each particular issue.

- WHO Guide to Mental and Neurological Health in Primary Care
  http://www.mentalneurologicalprimarycare.org/index.asp
  This guide speaks to several areas of concern relating to child and adult disorders, including presenting concerns, diagnostic features (based upon the International Classification of Diseases [*ICD*-9]), differential diagnosis and coexisting conditions, essential information for patient and family, medication, referral, and resources for patients and families. A resource directory is provided for the United Kingdom as well as many downloadable pdf handouts for patients.

- World Health Organization: *International Classification of Diseases*
  http://www.who.int/classifications/icd/en/
  Presents a history and current edition of the *ICD*-10. Specific attention may be directed toward Chapter V: "Mental and Behavioral Disorders F00-F99."

LEARNING ACTIVITIES AND ASSIGNMENTS

In addition to having students utilize websites and related electronic media for learning, other meaningful learning activities and assignments assist students in applying knowledge into application for practice.

DSM Diagnosis Informational Paper (40 Points)

An important goal of this course is to familiarize counselors-in-training with the current *DSM* and diagnosis and treatment practices they will likely face as a professional counselor. Therefore, students will choose one Axis I or Axis II diagnosis and describe it in detail. The description should include not only descriptive information regarding the diagnosis but information regarding the diagnosis as it relates to life span development. Please provide at least two current therapies and/or empirically shown treatment modalities for the diagnosis discussed. Discussion regarding multicultural implications and considerations of the diagnosis and treatment approach must be included. The assignment must be 6–10 pages, American Psychological Association style (APA, 6th edition, 2nd printing, 2009), not including title page, abstract, references, and related materials. The grading rubric for this assignment should be broken up into five areas with point allocations for each area left to the discretion of the instructor. These areas include diagnosis explained in detail, discussion of life span, current therapies/treatments, multicultural implication/considerations, and correct APA formatting.

Mental Health Assessment and Treatment Plan (40 Points)

Students are expected to complete a diagnostic assessment and treatment plan for one client. Given the information learned during the class, students can complete this mental health assessment and treatment plan for a mock client. If students have access to clients via internship and/or practicum, they may facilitate an actual interview. The assignment must be 6–10 pages, APA style (6th edition, 2nd printing, 2009), not including title page, abstract, references, etc. Confidentiality protocol and procedures must be followed. The assessment and plan must include the following:

Client Information

This is presented in narrative form and includes the client's name (please change this if accessing real client information) and descriptive information such as social identity (race/ethnicity, gender, sexual orientation, economic status, disability status, religion, etc.). Other information to include would be applicable family information, age, past treatment services and/or diagnosis, and current or past medications and medical history.

Presenting Problem

This section is an addition to the client information section. Include client observations and or discoveries (via interview), current and past psychosocial stressors, and mental status. Summarize the main client symptoms and diagnosis using the *DSM*.

Prescriptive Information and Treatment Plan (Gathered From the Diagnosis of the Client)

This section is the treatment planning section. Use objective language and outline a thorough care plan given your knowledge of the *DSM*, the client's diagnosis, and applicable treatment modalities. The treatment plan should include but is not limited to:

- Diagnosis (primary and secondary)
- GAF score
- Client strengths and resources
- Goals of counseling
- Plan for helping client
- Client self-help strategies
- Types of intervention recommended

- Frequency and duration of intervention/counseling
- Multicultural considerations
- Prognosis
- Discharge plan and follow-up

The grading rubric for this assignment should be broken up into the related areas with point allocations for each area left to the discretion of the instructor. These areas include client information, presenting problem, prescriptive information and treatment plan, and correct APA formatting.

DSM Diagnosis Informational Presentation (40 Points)

Students in groups of three will choose one Axis I or Axis II diagnosis and describe it in detail. The presentation should not only include descriptive information regarding the diagnosis but information regarding the diagnosis as it relates to life span development. Please present at least two current therapies and/or empirically shown treatment modalities for the diagnosis discussed. Discussion regarding multicultural implications and considerations of the diagnosis and treatment approach must be included in the presentation. Presenters will be responsible for providing a detailed outline to the instructor and a condensed outline to their classmates. Presenters will have the opportunity to evaluate one another regarding contribution to the presentation. Following is a list of possible topics (this is not a limiting list; please select a diagnosis that you would like to examine in depth). Scholarly references must be utilized. Please let the instructor know which topic your group has selected so there will be no repeated presentations:

- Attention deficit/hyperactivity disorder
- Bipolar disorder
- Antisocial personality disorder
- Borderline personality disorder
- Schizophrenia (paranoid type)
- Delusional disorder
- Specific phobia
- Trichotillomania
- Conversion disorder
- Dementia
- Obsessive–compulsive disorder

The grading rubric for this presentation is for a group grade and should be broken up into five areas with point allocations in each area left to the discretion of the instructor. These areas include diagnosis explained in detail, discussion of life span, current therapies/treatments, multicultural implication/considerations, and presentation style. Each presenter should be given the opportunity to self-evaluate and evaluate their copresenters. This feedback can be taken into consideration when giving the final grade.

Movie Diagnostic (30 Points)

Students will be required to write a paper on a movie character, relating course material to the character chosen. Movies must be approved by the instructor prior to the paper being written. Students will use a diagnostic report format that includes client information, presenting problem, prescriptive information, and treatment plan. Students will be required to do an in-depth case conceptualization on the character they chose. Students must diagnosis the character using the *DSM* and include a written justification as to why such diagnosis was chosen. Students should include multicultural considerations for the client and the diagnosis of the client. The assignment must be 6–10 pages, APA style (6th edition, 2nd printing, 2009), not including title page, abstract, references, etc. Scholarly references must be included.

The grading rubric for this presentation should be broken up into five areas with point allocations in each area left to the discretion of the instructor. These areas include diagnostic report, case conceptualization, written justification, multicultural considerations, and APA formatting.

Prozac Nation Book Club Discussion (20 Points)

Over the course of the quarter students are assigned to read *Prozac Nation* (Wurtzel, 2002). During your readings, you are to keep an information journal to jot down thoughts, ideas, reflections, reactions, questions, favorite statements/actions, statements/actions you disagree with, questionable behavior of the therapists, personal reactions to family members, etc. These journals will serve as a reference and reminders for students during the class discussion about the book to facilitate a rich and detailed reflection of the reading. Students will hand in their informal journals at the end of the book discussion.

The grading rubric for this assignment should be broken up into two areas with point allocations in each area left to the discretion of the instructor. These include students providing a minimum of two discussion points, questions, concerns, ethical issues and/or comments per chapter, and discussion and participation points for the small group.

In addition to assignments, the use of counseling vignettes can assist the students in integrating material with real case scenarios. Students gain valuable experience by utilizing course material and case conceptualization skills while working through counseling vignettes. This can be done as a group activity or individually, inside or outside of the classroom. Below are some counseling vignettes students can use to apply knowledge and for the instructor to facilitate deep discussion around course material.

VIGNETTES

Counseling Vignette #1

VP, a 15-year-old African American female currently being evaluated at the local emergency department of the community hospital, is accompanied by her stepfather. She is sedate, smells of alcohol and marijuana, and is slurring her words. Two months ago she was caught with marijuana in school and suspended for 2 weeks. Legal charges are pending. Since that time she has been withdrawn from friends and despondent. She reports to her stepfather that she feels hopeless and fearful of going to juvenile. She has lost weight in the past month. She has started to cut. She denies suicidal ideation. She has had no previous counseling experience.

Counseling Vignette #2

Laura, a 22-year-old Caucasian female has a long history of psychological issues. She recently dropped out of college, one quarter before graduating. She is above intelligence on standardized tests. After Laura came home from college she started using alcohol frequently and began to engage in "odd" behaviors. She goes long hours without sleeping, she checks the doors frequently to see if they are locked, and states she fears someone is "out to get her." She reports hearing voices.

Counseling Vignette #3

DM is a 44-year-old single Asian American male. He was referred for a psychiatric evaluation by his primary counselor. He reports high levels of anxiety and worry. He engages in ritualistic behaviors daily such as checking to see whether he has locked his doors and windows. He reports that the behaviors are not only ritualistic but repetitive.

As you can note, there are many rich assignments and activities that can be utilized by instructors to support the learning in this course. Depending on the length of the course, the instructor can include, adapt, or integrate any or all of these activities as they outline develop the course.

In addition to the above assignments and vignettes, there are numerous videos that instructors can utilize to encourage insight and discussion among students.

AUDIOVISUAL MATERIAL

Supplemental videos offer a component unreachable by printed materials; they tap into an avenue that surpasses an individual's cognitive barriers allowing a more memorable and enriching experience. Videos/CDs provide students with more concrete examples and appeal to visual learners. Access to individual personal stories and professionals that might otherwise be unobtainable is made possible through videos. Incorporating videos into the course can enhance the course in several ways. Students can be shown a podcast, lecture, vignette, or film on topics relating to mental disorders and wellness. Showing videos, films or YouTube clips in class or as homework assignments increase students' awareness and understanding of the impact of mental illness on an individual and the individual's environment. An exercise that ultimately leads to enhanced class discussions resulting from intensified critical thinking, for example, screening *Rachel Getting Married*, can lead to a discussion regarding the recovery process of an addict. However, it can also provoke a discussion concerning the impact of an addiction on individual family members and the family unit as a whole. Likewise, viewing *A Beautiful Mind* can encourage several different types of discussions. These conversations may include detecting symptoms and signs of a disorder, gaining insight into a schizophrenic phenomenological viewpoint, and/or recognizing the significance of identifying support when coping with a mental illness.

Similar to supplemental articles, students may also be prompted to create their own video of a counseling session between a counselor and client exhibiting symptoms of a disorder. Regardless of the specific way you choose to integrate videos into your course, it is highly recommended that you do so. Tobolowsky (2007) supported the use of videos and commented, "Realize that it may help open doors for you students, their needs, and their understanding in ways that no book could" (p. 24). University libraries are terrific sources to begin searching for applicable videos. Below we highlight internet video sources you may also find useful.

- Association for Academic Psychiatry
  http://www.hsc.wvu.edu/aap/Video/video_page.htm
  Provides links to websites containing counseling vignettes.

- Cinematherapy.com
  http://www.cinematherapy.com/filmindex.html
  Provides an index of movies organized by relevant topic including a general mental illness category that can be suggested or shown to clients/students.

- Healthy Place: America's Mental Health Channel
  http://www.healthyplace.com/
  Gives access to films and mental health videos created by professionals and individuals with disorders. Videos can be downloaded into RealPlayer, and URL and embedded links are provided.

- National Eating Disorders Association
  http://www.nationaleatingdisorders.org/research-efforts/
  Videos of experts covering issues pertaining to eating disorders (e.g., fighting stigma with science, brain imaging and eating disorders, eating disorders in adolescents, and cognitive styles in eating disorders) are provided. These videos have embedding capabilities and can be downloaded.

- PANSS Training DVD, Volume 1
  http://www.hsc.wvu.edu/aap/Video/PANSS/index.htm
  Videos of sample counseling sessions are provided.

- Schizophrenia.com
  http://www.schizophrenia.com/video/index.htm
  Supplies audio and video files on diagnosis, symptoms, and treatment of schizophrenia.

- Symptom Media
  http://symptommedia.com/home/
  Videos created jointly by mental health professionals and the film community portray realistic sessions between counselor and client. Sample films are viewable; however, full-length films require a paid subscription. Videos are accompanied by content outlines.

- Videos of Psychiatric Disorders
  http://www.hsc.wvu.edu/aap/Video/flvVideoFiles/WVU-Videos/WVU-Videos.html
  Downloadable videos displaying sample counseling sessions involving mental disorders and related areas are available.

- WebMD Video
  http://www.webmd.com/a-to-z-guides/videos/default.htm
  Informational videos designed similar to news clips are available addressing some of the more popular disorders (e.g., anxiety, depression, emotional wellness). These videos are preceded by a short advertisement.

- YouTubeEDU
  http://www.youtube.com/education?b=400
  Provides a database of searchable videos encompassing lectures, personal anecdotes, etc., on a variety of topics, including diagnostic disorders and wellness. Videos should be reviewed for credibility and searches should be limited to the education category.

TENTATIVE COURSE OUTLINE

Laying out the course syllabus helps the professor plan for the entire term. Universities often have templates that are preferred; these also help guide the instructor in their development. Some universities have a format that is mandatory; pay attention to the recommendations of your program. Usually examples abound, so take advantage of that. Some faculty members are very generous with sharing information as well.

The course schedule is embedded in the syllabus and serves to keep the professor as well as the students on task and organized. Ideally, the syllabus and the course schedule are fixed and do not change but allow for some flexibility; student needs can change during a semester and the professor should attend to that and work with it but must cover what has been outlined. The syllabus is a contract offered by the university and both professors and students are responsible for the delivery of their agreed-upon parts. Usually, this course is taught in the second year of the students' courses of study. The emphasis is on integration of advanced knowledge and application to clinical work. Therefore, teaching, learning, and related assessments focus on these aims. When laying out the course schedule, discussing modules or chapters is best, moving from 1 through 15. This way, if one module overlaps with another it is less confusing. For example, if in week 1 the professor is covering module number one, "Introduction to the *DSM* Manual and Related Vocabulary," and the professor does not finish, the professor can carry it over to week 2 and then start module number two midway through the second 3-hour lecture. This is useful if the class is offered online as well, because students can move from one module to the next. However, some students like exact dates, so for illustration below dates are included. Below is a partial course outline that organizes the modules, readings, assignments, CACREP standards, learning outcomes, class format, and instructor/learner responsibilities.

Week 1 (Date TBA)
(Week 1 Has an Expanded Course Outline for Illustration)

Module one: Syllabus, intro to *DSM*, vocabulary, psychopathology, wellness, *DSM* class system readings:

Reading:

- All reading assignments are due prior to the start of class
- This week read the course syllabus and *DSM* table of contents

Class Format:

- Lecture, hands-on demonstration, question–answer session related to course contract

Learning Outcomes:

- Students will learn course requirements
- Students will gain understanding of course assignments and learning responsibilities
- Students will begin use of *DSM* as a tool

Student Expectations:

- Students to read syllabus and *DSM* table of contents
- Students will be prepared to engage in thoughtful discussion
- Students will bring course related materials, texts, and questions with them

Instructor Expectations:

- Instructor will have all course-related materials prepared and posted on web campus 48 hours prior to first class
- Instructor will present lecturette and hands-on activity related to introductory use of the *DSM*
- Instructor will clarify course requirements and answer questions related to student expectations

CACREP Standards:

- A.1, 2, 3, 6 and B.1, 2, 3, 4, 5

Assignments due this week:

- Online quiz submitted prior to class

Week 2 (Date TBA)
(Week 2 Has an Expanded Course Outline for Illustration)

Module two: Schizophrenia and psychotic disorders, diagnosis, treatments, psychopharmacology

Readings:[a]

American Psychiatric Association. (2000). *Diagnostic and statistical manual of mental disorders* (4th ed., text rev.). Washington, DC: Author.

First, M. B., & Tasman, A. (2006). *Clinical guide to the diagnosis and treatment of mental disorders*. Hoboken, NJ: Wiley.

Myers, J. E., & Sweeney, T. J. (Eds.). (2005). *Counseling for wellness: Theory, research, and practice.* Alexandria, VA: American Counseling Association.

Sinacola, R. S., & Peters-Strickland, T. S. (2006). *Basic psychopharmacology for counselors and psychotherapists.* Boston, MA: Pearson.

Class Format:

- Lecturette, case analysis, video presentation, vignette discussion, GAF analysis

Learning Outcomes:

- Students will learn criteria for diagnosis of specific *DSM* category (schizophrenia/psychotic)
- Students will demonstrate competent use of diagnostic criteria related to category
- Students participate in case analysis and development of master treatment planning

Student Expectations:

- Students to read related materials prior to class
- Students will be prepared to engage in thoughtful discussion

Instructor Expectations:

- Instructor will have related teaching materials prepared/posted on web campus one week prior to class
- Instructor will present lecturette and hands-on activity related to the module
- Instructor will have tests and case analysis critiqued and graded and returned to students within 7 days of submission

CACREP Standards:

- A.1, 2, 3, 6; B.1, 2, 3, 4, 5; C.2, 4, 7, 8, 9; D.1, 2, 3, 5, 6, 8, 9; E.1, 2, 3, 5; F.3; G.1, 2, 3, 4; H.2, 3, 4; I.3; J.2; K.1, 2, 3, 4, 5; and L1, 2

Assignments:

- Online quiz submitted prior to class

[a] Provide page ranges or chapters for all readings.

Week 3 (Date TBA)
(Week 3 Has an Expanded Course Outline for Illustration)

Module two continued: Schizophrenia and psychotic disorders, diagnosis, treatments, psychopharmacology

Readings:[a]

American Psychiatric Association. (2000). *Diagnostic and statistical manual of mental disorders* (4th ed., text rev.). Washington, DC: Author.

First, M. B., & Tasman, A. (2006). *Clinical guide to the diagnosis and treatment of mental disorders*. Hoboken, NJ: Wiley.

Myers, J. E., & Sweeney, T. J. (Eds.). (2005). *Counseling for wellness: Theory, research, and practice.* Alexandria, VA: American Counseling Association.

Sinacola, R. S., & Peters-Strickland, T. S. (2006). *Basic psychopharmacology for counselors and psychotherapists.* Boston, MA: Pearson.

Class Format:

- Lecturette, case analysis, video presentation, vignette discussion, GAF analysis

Learning Outcomes:

- Students will learn criteria for diagnosis of specific *DSM* category (schizophrenia/psychotic)
- Students will demonstrate competent use of diagnostic criteria related to category
- Students participate in case analysis and development of master treatment planning

Student Expectations:

- Students to read related materials prior to class
- Students will demonstrate competent use of diagnostic criteria related to category
- Students participate in case analysis and development of master treatment planning

Instructor Expectations:

- Instructor will have related teaching and module materials prepared and posted on web campus one week prior to class
- Instructor will present lecturette and hands-on activity related to the module
- Instructor will have tests and case analysis critiqued and graded and returned to students within 7 days of submission

CACREP Standards:

- A.1, 2, 3, 6; B.1, 2, 3, 4, 5; C.2, 4, 7, 8, 9; D.1, 2, 3, 5, 6, 8, 9; E.1, 2, 3, 5; F.3; G.1, 2, 3, 4; H.2, 3, 4; I.3; J.2; K.1, 2, 3, 4, 5; and L1, 2

Assignments:

- Online quiz submitted prior to class

[a] Provide page ranges or chapters for all readings.

Week 4 (Date TBA)

Module three: Depressive and bipolar disorders, diagnosis, treatments, and psychopharmacology

Readings: Completed prior to class

Class Format:

Learning Outcomes:

(continued)

Student Expectations:

Instructor Expectations:

CACREP Standards:

- A.1, 2, 3, 6; B.1, 2, 3, 4, 5; C.2, 4, 7, 8, 9; D.1, 2, 3, 5, 6, 8, 9; E.1, 2, 3, 5; F.3; G.1, 2, 3, 4; H.2, 3, 4; I.3; J.2; K.1, 2, 3, 4, 5; and L1, 2

Assignment:

- Online case analysis submitted prior to class

Week 5 (Date TBA)

Module three continued: Depressive and bipolar disorders, diagnosis, treatments, and psychopharmacology

Readings: Completed prior to class

Class Format:

Learning Outcomes:

Student Expectations:

Instructor Expectations:

CACREP Standards:

- A.1, 2, 3, 6; B.1, 2, 3, 4, 5; C.2, 4, 7, 8, 9; D.1, 2, 3, 5, 6, 8, 9; E.1, 2, 3, 5; F.3; G.1, 2, 3, 4; H.2, 3, 4; I.3; J.2; K.1, 2, 3, 4, 5; and L1, 2

Assignment:

- Online quiz submitted prior to class

Week 6 (Date TBA)

Module four: Anxiety disorders, diagnosis, treatments, and psychopharmacology

Readings: Completed prior to class

Class Format:

Learning Outcomes:

Student Expectations:

Instructor Expectations:

CACREP Standards:

- A.1, 2, 3, 6; B.1, 2, 3, 4, 5; C.2, 4, 7, 8, 9; D.1, 2, 3, 5, 6, 8, 9; E.1, 2, 3, 5; F.3; G.1, 2, 3, 4; H.2, 3, 4; I.3; J.2; K.1, 2, 3, 4, 5; and L1, 2

Assignment:

- Online case analysis submitted prior to class

Week 7 (Date TBA)

Module four continued: Anxiety disorders, diagnosis, treatments, and psychopharmacology

Readings: Completed prior to class

Class Format:

Learning Outcomes:

Student Expectations:

Instructor Expectations:

CACREP Standards:

- A.1, 2, 3, 6; B.1, 2, 3, 4, 5; C.2, 4, 7, 8, 9; D.1, 2, 3, 5, 6, 8, 9; E.1, 2, 3, 5; F.3; G.1, 2, 3, 4; H.2, 3, 4; I.3; J.2; K.1, 2, 3, 4, 5; and L1, 2

Assignment:

- Online quiz submitted prior to class

Week 8 (Date TBA)

Module five: Dissociative disorders, somatoform and factitious disorders, diagnosis, treatments, and psychopharmacology

Readings: Completed prior to class

Class Format:

Learning Outcomes:

Student Expectations:

Instructor Expectations:

CACREP Standards:

- A.1, 2, 3, 6; B.1, 2, 3, 4, 5; C.2, 4, 7, 8, 9; D.1, 2, 3, 5, 6, 8, 9; E.1, 2, 3, 5; F.3; G.1, 2, 3, 4; H.2, 3, 4; I.3; J.2; K.1, 2, 3, 4, 5; and L1, 2

Assignment:

- Online case analysis submitted prior to class

Week 9 (Date TBA)

Module six: Personality disorders, diagnosis, treatments, and psychopharmacology

Readings: Completed prior to class

Class Format:

Learning Outcomes:

Student Expectations:

Instructor Expectations:

CACREP Standards:

- A.1, 2, 3, 6; B.1, 2, 3, 4, 5; C.2, 4, 7, 8, 9; D.1, 2, 3, 5, 6, 8, 9; E.1, 2, 3, 5; F.3; G.1, 2, 3, 4; H.2, 3, 4; I.3; J.2; K.1, 2, 3, 4, 5; and L1, 2

Assignment:

- Online quiz submitted prior to class

Week 10 (Date TBA)

Module seven: *DSM* disorders—children/adolescents, diagnosis, treatments, and psychopharmacology

Readings: Completed prior to class

Class Format:

Learning Outcomes:

Student Expectations:

Instructor Expectations:

CACREP Standards:

- A.1, 2, 3, 6; B.1, 2, 3, 4, 5; C.2, 4, 7, 8, 9; D.1, 2, 3, 5, 6, 8, 9; E.1, 2, 3, 5; F.3; G.1, 2, 3, 4; H.2, 3, 4; I.3; J.2; K.1, 2, 3, 4, 5; and L1, 2

Assignment:

- Online case analysis submitted prior to class

Week 11 (Date TBA)

Module eight: Wellness models, addictions, strength-based, and crisis approaches to *DSM* disorders

Readings: Completed prior to class

(continued)

Class Format:

Learning Outcomes:

Student Expectations:

Instructor Expectations:

CACREP Standards:

- K.1; A.2, 5, 6, 9, 10; C.4; and L.3

Assignment:

- Online quiz submitted prior to class

Week 12 (Date TBA)

Module nine: Supportive/integrative treatments, biofeedback, stress management, nutrition, and diet

Readings: Completed prior to class

Class Format:

Learning Outcomes:

Student Expectations:

Instructor Expectations:

CACREP Standards:

- K.1; A.2, 5, 6, 9, 10; C.4; and L.3

Assignment:

- Online case analysis submitted prior to class

Week 13 (Date TBA)

Module nine continued: Supportive/integrative treatments, exercise, yoga, relaxation, meditation, life and career planning

Readings: Completed prior to class

Class Format:

Learning Outcomes:

Student Expectations:

Instructor Expectations:

CACREP Standards:

- K.1; A.2, 5, 6, 9, 10; C.4; and L.3

Assignment:

- Online quiz submitted prior to class

Week 14 (Date TBA)

Module ten: Spirituality, religious, and cultural approaches to mental wellness

Readings: Done prior to class

Class Format:

Learning Outcomes:

Student Expectations:

Instructor Expectations:

CACREP Standards:

- K.1; A.2, 5, 6, 9, 10; C.4; and L.3

Assignment:

- Online case analysis due

Week 15 (Date TBA)
Module eleven: Review for final exam
Readings: Done prior to class include online study guide, class and web materials
Class Format:
Online only
Learning Outcomes:
Student Expectations:
Instructor Expectations:
CACREP Standards:
- All previously listed for the course

Assignment:
- Due before last day of semester, final exam, final culminating case study

CONCLUSION

Over the years of teaching we have learned many lessons; here we share a few. First, instructors should avoid just handing out the syllabus cold and then hurriedly asking whether there are any questions. Often students will be too intimidated to ask questions or may not know what to ask. Also, they may not have read the syllabus yet. Students are busy. We recommend walking students through the syllabus, slowly, as if it is an informed consent tool. In a way this is informed consent, because the syllabus is a contract. With discussion, it provides opportunities to clarify and garner student "buy in" and further explain why a particular assignment was chosen and how it relates to their learning and eventual clinical practice. We have found that reviewing the syllabus prevents misunderstandings, establishes trust, and cements the teaching supervisory relationship. Second, professors do well to respond quickly to students' e-mails, phone inquiries, discussion board posts, and office hour appointments. This type of responsive practice avoids problems and actually will impact teaching evaluations in a positive manner. Third, if a professor receives more than two student inquiries asking for clarification on a topic, this generally indicates that there is more student confusion in the class as a whole. Professors do well to bring these questions or concerns back to the entire class in some format (like during the lecture or posting on the discussion board) so students have a chance to pose further questions. We have found that when two students speak up, generally there are about a dozen who follow. Fourth, we encourage all professors to perform a midsemester check in. Ask students what is going well and what they might want added or adjusted in the course. At midterm it is not too late because professors can tweak lectures and information presented in the class; this models flexibility and shows responsiveness and avoids end-of-semester negative evaluations. Fifth, avoid changing the syllabus in terms of assignments; if professors need to adapt the assignments, removing demands is acceptable; however, adding projects will never add positive votes to a faculty member's teaching evaluations. Students hate surprises (that mean more work for them) and doing so puts a faculty member's reputation at risk. Students appreciate a professor who follows the syllabus, the course outline, and the planned expectations as contracted. Adding more is never received well. Sixth, about 3 weeks before the end of the term, start reminding students of what was covered in the syllabus and how much they learned; this reminder bolsters awareness and when students rank you on evaluations, they are knowledgeable about what you covered in the course. On a final note, it is incumbent upon professors to check with colleagues in a program what the course expectations are among faculty. Programs usually work in concert and some even use a cohort model; students become upset and cranky if all assignments are due the Monday after Thanksgiving. When faculty members work together the students appreciate it and do better in terms of planning. This works better and gives positive feedback to the program and individual faculty members as well. These are just a few tips that have worked well for us and we hope they benefit you as well.

REFERENCES

Ade-Ridder, L. (1989). Textbook decisions: Making an informed decision. *Family Relations, 38*, 231–240.

American Counseling Association (ACA) & Association for Counselor Educators and Supervisors (ACES, 2011). *ACA-ACES Syllabus Clearinghouse*. Retrieved from http://www.counseling.org/Resources/TP/SyllabusClearinghouse/CT2.aspx

American Psychiatric Association. (2000). *Diagnostic and statistical manual of mental disorders* (4th ed., text rev.). Washington, DC: Author.

American Psychological Association (APA, 2009). *Publication manual of the American Psychological Association* (6th ed., 2nd printing). Washington, DC: Author.

American Psychiatric Association. (2010). *DSM-5 development*. Retrieved from http://www.dsm5.org/Pages/Default.aspx

American Psychiatric Association. (2010). *Mental health links*. Retrieved from http://www.psych.org/SpecialGroups/MentalHealthResources.aspx

American Psychiatric Publishing. (2010). *DSM library*. Retrieved from http://www.psychiatryonline.com/dsmLibrary.aspx

Anxiety Disorders Association of America. (2010). *ADAA anxiety disorders association of America*. Retrieved from http://www.adaa.org/

Armian, N., Demme, J., Platt, M. (Producer), & Demme, J. (Director). (1998). *Rachel getting married* [Motion picture]. USA: Sony Pictures Classics.

Association for Academic Psychiatry. (2010). *Psychiatry streaming video segments*. Retrieved from http://www.hsc.wvu.edu/aap/Video/video_page.htm

BehaveNet. (2010). *APA diagnostic classification DSM-IV-TR*. Retrieved from http://www.behavenet.com/capsules/disorders/dsm4TRclassification.htm

Bellack, A. (2007). Issues in understanding and treating comorbidity in people with serious mental illness. *Clinical Psychology: Science and Practice, 14*, 70–76. doi:10.1111/j.1468-2850.2007.00064.x

Capra, F. (Producer), & Capra, F. (Director). (1946). *It's a wonderful life* [Motion picture]. USA: Liberty Films.

Center for Disease Control and Prevention (n.d.). *Third National Health and Nutrition Examination Survey conducted from 1988 to 1994*. Retrieved from http://www.cdc.gov/nchs/surveys.htm

Chatman, S. (1985). Improving textbook selection. *Teaching of Psychology, 12*, 150–152.

Chung, H., Culpepper, L., De Wester, J., Grieco, R., Kaye, N., Lipkin, M., & Ross, R. (2007). Recognizing and understanding bipolar disorder. *Journal of Family Practice, 56*, S5–S10.

Council for the Accreditation of Counseling and Related Educational Programs (CACREP, 2009). *2009 standards*. Retrieved from http://cacrep.org/doc/2009%20Standards%20with%20cover.pdf

Eriksen, K., & Kress, V. E. (2000). *Beyond the DSM story: Ethical quandaries, challenges, and best practices*. Thousand Oaks, CA: Sage.

Findler, D., & West Virginia University Department of Behavioral Medicine and Psychiatry. (2008). *Videos of psychiatric disorders*. Retrieved from http://www.hsc.wvu.edu/aap/Video/flvVideoFiles/WVU-Videos/WVU-Videos.html

First, M. B., & Tasman, A. (2006). *Clinical guide to the diagnosis and treatment of mental disorders*. Hoboken, NJ: Wiley.

Fong, M., & Silien, K. (1999). Assessment and diagnosis of *DSM-IV* anxiety disorders. *Journal of Counseling & Development, 77*, 209–217.

Hasin D, Trautman K, Miele G, Samet S, Smith M, & Endicott J. (1996). Psychiatric Research Interview for substance and mental disorders (PRISM): Reliability for substance abusers. *American Journal of Psychiatry, 153*, 1195–1201.

HealthyPlace.com. (2010). *Healthyplace: America's mental health channel*. Retrieved from http://www.healthyplace.com/

Hinkle, J. (1994). Psychodiagnosis for counselors: The *DSM-IV*. Retrieved from ERIC database. (EDO-CG-94-06)

Howard, R., Grazer, B. (Producer), & Howard, R. (Director). (1946). *A beautiful mind* [Motion picture]. USA: Universal Studios and DreamWorks.

Jonas, B. S., Brody, D., Roper, M., & Narrow, W. E. (2003). Prevalence of mood disorders in a national sample of young American adults. *Social Psychiatry and Psychiatric Epidemiology, 38*, 618–624.

Keel, P. K., & Haedt, A. (2008). Evidence-based psychosocial treatments for eating problems and eating disorders. *Journal of Clinical Child & Adolescent Psychology, 37*, 39–61.

Kent State University (n.d). CESNET-L Home Page. Retrieved from https://listserv.kent.edu/cgi-bin/wa.exe?A0=CESNET-L

Koran, L. (2007). Diagnosing and treating comorbid mood disorders and obsessive compulsive disorder. *Current Medical Literature: Psychiatry, 18*, 73–81.

Lei, S., Bartlett, K., Gorney, S., & Herschbach, T. (2010). Resistance to reading compliance among college students: Instructors' perspectives. *College Student Journal, 44*, 219–229.

Ling, H., & Qian, M.-Y. (2010). Relationships between attachment and personality disorder symptoms of Chinese college students. *Social Behavior and Personality, 38*, 571–576. doi:10.2224/sbp.2010.38.4.571

Lopez, S. J., Edwards, L. M., Pedrotti, J. T., Prosser, E. C., LaRue, S., Spalitto, S. V., & Ulven, J. C. (2006). Beyond the *DSM-IV*: Assumptions, alternatives, and alterations. *Journal of Counseling and Development, 84*, 259–267.

Mayo Foundation for Medical Education and Research. (2010). *Diseases and conditions*. Retrieved from http://www.mayoclinic.com/health/DiseasesIndex/DiseasesIndex

McGorry, P., Killackey, E., Elkins, K., Lambert, M., & Lambert, T. (2003). Summary Australian and New Zealand clinical practice guideline for the treatment of schizophrenia. *Australian Psychiatry, 11*, 136–147.

Mental Health America. (2010). *Get information*. Retrieved from http://www.mentalhealthamerica.net/go/information

Morrison, J. (2007). *Diagnosis made easier: Principles and techniques for mental health clinicians*. New York: Guilford Press.

Myers, J. E., & Sweeney, T. J. (Eds.). (2005). *Counseling for wellness: Theory, research, and practice*. Alexandria, VA: American Counseling Association.

Myers, J., Sweeney, T., & Witmer, J. (2000). The wheel of wellness counseling for wellness: A holistic model for treatment planning. *Journal of Counseling & Development, 78*, 251–266.

Myers, T. C., Swan-Kremeier, L., Wonderlich, S., Lancaster, K., & Mitchell, J. E. (2004). The use of alternative delivery systems and new technologies in the treatment of patients with eating disorders. *International Journal of Eating Disorders, 36*, 123–143.

National Alliance on Mental Illness. (2010). *Mental illnesses*. Retrieved from http://www.nami.org/Template.cfm?Section=By_Illness

National Eating Disorders Association. (2010a). *Accurate information can light the path to prevention, treatment, hope and healing*. Retrieved from http://www.nationaleatingdisorders.org/information-resources/

National Eating Disorders Association. (2010b). *Research into eating disorders focuses on causes, prevention and cures*. Retrieved from http://www.nationaleatingdisorders.org/research-efforts/

O'Brien, D., & Scharber, C. (2010). Teaching old dogs new tricks: The luxury of digital abundance. *Journal of Adolescent & Adult Literacy, 53*, 600–603. doi:10.1598/JAAL.53.7.7

Okonski, V. (2003). Exercise as a counseling intervention. *Journal of Mental Health Counseling, 25*, 45–56.

Ornstein, A. (1994). The textbook-driven curriculum. *Peabody Journal of Education, 69*, 70–85.

Öztürk, E., & Sar, V. (2008). Somatization as a predictor of suicidal ideation in dissociative disorders. *Psychiatry & Clinical Neurosciences, 62*, 662–668. doi:10.1111/j.1440-1819.2008.01865.x

PANSS Institute, & Muskin, R. P. (2004). *PANSS training DVD, volume 1*. Retrieved from http://www.hsc.wvu.edu/aap/Video/PANSS/index.htm

Pontoski, K. E., & Heimberg, R. G. (2010). The myth of the superiority of concurrent combined treatments for anxiety disorders. *Clinical Psychology Science and Practice, 17*, 107–111.

Rowe, J. (2010). Dealing with psychiatric disabilities in schools: A description of symptoms and coping strategies for dealing with them. *Preventing School Failure, 54*, 190–198. doi:10.1080/10459880903217945

Samet, S., Nunes, E., & Hasin, D. (2004). Diagnosing comorbidity: Concepts, criteria, and methods. *Acta Neuropsychiatrica, 16*(1), 9–18. doi:10.1111/j.1601-5215.2004.0062.x

Schizophrenia.com. (2004). *Internet-based audio and video files on schizophrenia and related issues*. Retrieved from http://www.schizophrenia.com/video/index.htm

Seligman, L., & Reichenberg, L. W. (2007). *Selecting effective treatments: A comprehensive, systematic guide* (3rd ed.). San Francisco, CA: Wiley.

Sinacola, R. S., & Peters-Strickland, T. S. (2006). *Basic psychopharmacology for counselors and psychotherapists*. Boston, MA: Pearson.

Smart, D., & Smart, J. (1997). *DSM-IV* and culturally sensitive diagnosis: Some observations for counselors. *Journal of Counseling & Development, 75*, 392–398.

Substance Abuse and Mental Health Services Administration. (2010a). *Mental health topics*. Retrieved from http://mentalhealth.samhsa.gov/topics/explore/

Substance Abuse and Mental Health Services Administration. (2010b). *United States Department of Health and Human Services: Substance Abuse & Mental Health Services Administration*. Retrieved from http://www.samhsa.gov/index.aspx

Substance Abuse and Mental Health Services Administration. (2010c). *What is SAMHSA?* Retrieved from http://www.hhs.gov/samhsa/about/1336.html

Symptom Media. (2010). *Welcome to symptom media*. Retrieved from http://symptommedia.com/home/

Tobolowsky, B. (2007). In practice—Thinking visually: Using visual media in the college classroom. *About Campus, 12*, 21–24.

University of Nevada–Las Vegas. (2007). *Bibliotherapy education project: UNLV libraries and college of education*. Retrieved from http://www.library.unlv.edu/faculty/research/bibliotherapy/

Wallace, E. V. (2007). Managing stress: What consumers want to know from health educators. *American Journal of Health Studies, 22*, 56–58.

Washington Institute. (n.d.). *The Washington Institute on-line training and assessment*. Retrieved from http://depts.washington.edu/washinst/Resources/CGAS/Index.htm#below

WebMD. (2010a). *About Medscape from WebMD*. Retrieved from http://www.medscape.com/public/about

WebMD. (2010b). *Medscape psychiatry & mental health*. Retrieved from http://www.medscape.com/psychiatry

WebMD. (2010c). *Mental health*. Retrieved from http://www.webmd.com/mental-health/default.htm

WebMD. (2010d). *Videos a–z*. Retrieved from http://www.webmd.com/a-to-z-guides/videos/default.htm

Wellness Associates. (2010). *The wellspring*. Retrieved from http://www.thewellspring.com/

Wolfe, K. (2004). Course materials—Syllabus and textbooks. *Journal of Teaching in Travel & Tourism, 4*, 55–60. doi:10.1300/J172v04n04•05

Wolz, B. (2010). *The cinematherapy.com film index*. Retrieved from http://www.cinematherapy.com/filmindex.html

World Health Organization. (2004). *WHO guide to mental and neurological health in primary care*. Retrieved from http://www.mentalneurologicalprimarycare.org/index.asp

World Health Organization (2010). *International Statistical Classification of Diseases and Related Health Problems*, 9th revision (ICD-9). Retrieved from http://apps.who.int/classifications/apps/icd/icd9online/

Wurtzel, E. (2002). *Prozac nation*. New York: Riverhead Trade.

YouTube, LLC. (2010). *YouTube EDU*. Retrieved from http://www.youtube.com/education?b=400

Zalaquett, C. P. (n.d.). *Carlos P. Zalaquett, Lic, MA, PhD: University of South Florida*. Retrieved from http://www.coedu.usf.edu/zalaquett/index.html

Zimmerman, M. (1994). *Interview guide for evaluating DSM-IV psychiatric disorders and the Mental Status Exam*. Philadelphia, PA: Psych Products Press.

13 Teaching Research
Adventures in Wonderland

Paula R. Danzinger

Research is the basis of all we do in the social sciences. The theories we use, the techniques we hone, and the conceptualizations that we make about clients all have their bases in research (Monette, Sullivan, & DeJong, 2008). Without research we have no way of knowing whether what we do is effective and safe. Without research we are just guessing; with research we have a scientific grounding.

Counselors need to have a solid conceptual background in both quantitative and qualitative research. As practitioners, they will need to be capable of finding research that applies to their practice and they need to know how to read and understand research articles and their implications for practice (Monette et al., 2008). Moreover, counselors need to be consumers of research; that is, capable of evaluating research with a critical eye, understanding which research studies have validity and which are flawed (Jones & Kottler, 2005). Counselor educators must be able to train counseling students to do all this in a way that is understandable to students who do not have strong backgrounds in research and statistical analysis and, hopefully, make research approachable—maybe even fun.

Counseling students come from many diverse personal and educational backgrounds. Though some come out of undergraduate psychology programs, many other counselor education enrollees are entering counseling with undergraduate degrees in education, communications, and humanities. Most students will have had very limited exposure to research methods and statistics and many are intimidated by the very idea of research. Counselor educators are faced with the task of overcoming the anxiety many students feel when faced with the prospect of conducting and analyzing research, not to mention the fear of statistical computations.

Another challenge for the counselor educator is to present research in a manner relevant to what the student is learning in other courses. How does research apply to theory, group work, and clinical practice? Within the confines of a three-credit course, how does the instructor show the student the intricacies and beauty of research design? Within a three-credit course, how does the counselor educator present statistical concepts as well as design concepts and make it interesting to the student?

Any basic course in research for a graduate student must include the fundamentals of research design, statistical analysis, the mechanics of preparing research for publication or presentation, ethical issues related to research, program evaluation, and the fundamentals of being a competent consumer of research literature. Hopefully, this chapter will give counselor educators some ideas on how to incorporate these topics in a meaningful and interesting way.

OBJECTIVES AND CACREP STANDARDS

The Council for the Accreditation of Counseling and Related Educational Programs (CACREP) requirements for research are wide ranging and too comprehensive for one three-credit course. The use of research to inform practice must be incorporated throughout the counseling curriculum, along with the importance of research in advancing the counseling profession. Research methods, statistical methods, models of needs assessment and program evaluation, and ethical and culturally relevant strategies for interpreting and reporting research results are appropriate content for the research course.

The following are suggested objectives for a course using CACREP standards:

1. To introduce research design methods including quantitative statistics and design and qualitative design. (Section II.G.7.b; Section II.G.7.c.; Section II.G.7.d.; Section II.G.7.e.; Section II.G.7.g.; Section II.G.8.b.; Section II.G.8.c.)
2. To introduce basic data collection methods. (Section II.G.8.b.)
3. To introduce basic program development and evaluation. (Section II.G.8.d.; CMHC C.3.; CMHC H.2.)
4. To introduce the use of research to inform counseling practice. (Section II.G.8.a.; CMHC I.1.)
5. To introduce computerized data bases to access references and research documents. (Section II.F.)
6. To introduce the use of technology for statistical analysis. (Section II.F.; Section II.G.8.c.)
7. To provide knowledge of issues in research ethics. (Section II.G.8.f.)
8. To introduce the role that race, class, gender, and societal issues have in research approaches and findings. (Section II.G.2.a.; Section II.G.8.e.; Section II.G.8.f).

CRITERIA FOR EVALUATING A TEXT

Each counselor educator picks his or her textbooks based on personal criteria, but following are my suggestions for some general criteria that can be used to ensure that a research methods textbook is appropriate for the course content and for the educational level of the student using the book. One of the factors you need to consider before evaluating a textbook is whether or not this is a new or continuing course and, if it is a continuing course, is the course being modified at this time or are you looking for a text to fit within the established content of the course. If it is a new course or if you are modifying the course, you can tailor the course somewhat to the textbook chosen, but if it is an established course the text will need to conform to the course's current content.

The first criterion in picking a research methods text, whether for a new or continuing course, needs to be the readability of the text. A text's content might be superior, but if it is written in obtuse language, the content will be lost. Some research texts have excellent content but are not written in a style accessible to students. Though the book obviously needs to be written at a graduate student level, it is advisable to avoid a text that is written for an experienced researcher. In my experience, the texts that get the highest evaluation ratings from my students are those that are written in a clear and concise manner and that explain concepts in language that is appropriate for students without extensive research backgrounds.

The subsequent criterion for choosing the text would be degree of congruence between the text coverage and the planned course content. I have found many texts that are readable but only cover a portion of the planned course content. It is often difficult to find a research book that covers research design and statistical analysis in both qualitative and quantitative areas as well as program evaluation and needs assessment. Though it will probably be impossible to find one book that covers everything, some texts come closer than others. Necessary course topics that are omitted in the text must be covered by supplemental articles, which will be covered later in this chapter.

When evaluating content you need to make a decision about the emphasis of the course. The following questions are offered for consideration in evaluating suitability of a given text for the research course you will teach:

1. Will you be concentrating more on design or analysis?
2. Is the course mainly going to be concerned with quantitative design or will you be emphasizing qualitative design?
3. Does the course cover program evaluation and needs assessment or are those covered in another course in the program?
4. How much statistical background does the student have and how much emphasis will there be on statistics in this course?
5. What are the assignments of the course?
6. Will the students be designing and actually running a research project or is the class more in the realm of theory?

7. Finally, is this a beginning research course or will the students come into the class with previous experience in conducting research? The appropriateness of any given text will depend on the answers to these questions.

A final criterion for choosing your text should be the cost of the text. Many graduate students are going to school on loans, and many loans do not cover the total cost of their schooling, let alone textbooks. The cost of textbooks has increased along with every other college expense, and textbooks in research are no exception. Considering the impact that the text will have on the student's financial standing has to be part of the evaluation process.

POPULAR TEXTS

There are many textbooks that are published for research courses. The following are some of the most popular, best selling research texts as listed by Amazon.com (Amazon.com, 2010).

Babbie, E. R. (2011). *The basics of social research* (4th ed.). Belmont, CA: Wadsworth/Cengage.
Bordens, K., & Abbott, B. B. (2007). *Research design and methods: A process approach* (7th ed.). Columbus, OH: McGraw-Hill.
Heppner, P. P., Wampold, B. E., & Kivlighan, D. M. (2007). *Research design in counseling* (3rd ed.). Belmont, CA: Brooks/Cole.

The above texts offer readers a good overview of research design and the use of research in the social sciences and counseling. The publishers of these and most other texts offer supplemental materials for instructors that range from test banks and PowerPoint presentations covering the book's contents to support websites for the students and other supportive materials such as access to online journals and books. There are other books that offer a different slant and approach to using research, such as:

Jones, W. P., & Kottler, J. A. (2006). *Understanding research: Becoming a competent and critical consumer*. Upper Saddle River, NJ: Prentice Hall.

As stated above, your choice about the type of book to use will be governed by the type of research course and your intended content. There are many good texts being published that cover all aspects of research, and most publishers are more than willing to provide examination copies of their texts for your review.

SUPPLEMENTAL MATERIAL

As mentioned earlier, you may choose to organize your course content around a specific text. However, it has been my experience that determining the course content from the CACREP core curriculum area of research and the content of the other courses in the program, such as assessment and appraisal, is a more efficient approach to course design. That being said, you will probably need to find and make available other reading materials for your students.

The first approach to generating supplemental materials is to explore other textbooks that cover some of the material omitted by your chosen text. These supplemental books can be put on reserve at your school's library so they are available for the students. Online electronic reserve, available in many institutions, makes materials instantly available to many students at one time. Assignment of specific chapters that highlight the target area(s) gives the student access to more extensive information without incurring extra costs to the student. In addition, many publishers now offer instructors the ability to design their own text by using chapters from multiple texts and allowing the students to purchase these chapters electronically. In some cases the publishers can actually compile chapters for you and make them available to students in a comprehensive manner.

The next approach is to identify and obtain journal articles. Students need to know how to read and interpret research articles. Though part of the course content will be for the students to find research articles for a literature review, providing concrete examples of good, mediocre, and bad research articles is an excellent method to help students understand the elements that comprise a solid research design and a good write up of research.

Journals in the field of counseling such as *Journal of Counseling and Development* and *Counseling Research & Practice* can be scanned for supplemental articles. Some articles under specific topics that may be useful to integrate into this course are provided below.

Topic: Quantitative Research

Palinkas, L. A. (2011). Mixed method designs in implementation research. *Administration Policy in Mental Health & Mental Health Services Research, 38*, 44–53.

Walker, W. (2005). The strengths and weaknesses of research designs involving quantitative measures. *Journal of Research in Nursing, 10*, 571–582.

Topic: Qualitative Research

Abrams, L. S. (2010). Sampling hard to reach populations in qualitative research. *Qualitative Social Work, 9*, 536–550.

Berrios, R., & Lucca, N. (2006). Qualitative methodology in counseling research: Recent contributions and challenges for a new century. *Journal of Counseling and Development, 84*, 174–183.

Topic: Survey Research

Alessi, E. J. (2010). Conducting an Internet-based survey: Benefits, pitfalls, and lessons learned. *Social Work Research, 34*, 122–128.

Baruch, Y. (2008). Survey response rate levels and trends in organizational research. *Human Relations, 61*, 1139–1160.

Etchegaray, J. M. (2010). Understanding evidence-based research methods: Reliability and validity considerations in survey research. *Health Environments Research & Design Journal (HERD), 4*, 131–135.

Jankowski, N. W. (2006). Conducting online surveys. *Quality & Quantity, 40*, 435–456.

Umbach, P. (2005). Getting back to the basics of survey research. *New Directions for Institutional Research*, 91–100.

Topic: Methods and Results

Bell, A. (2007). Designing and testing questionnaires for children. *Journal of Research in Nursing, 12*, 461–469.

LEARNING ACTIVITIES AND ASSIGNMENTS

Quantitative Data Gathering

The first assignment of the course is the beginning of the quantitative project, which accounts for the bulk of the grade for the course. Each student is assigned a research group, a research question is designed by the group, and then the question is discussed with the entire class. Each group decides on their topic and they present the class with a quantitative research question covering that topic. The class then gives the group feedback on whether the question is measurable and observable and what types of statistics could be used to analyze the data. This exercise helps all of the students in the class come to a better understanding of the difficulties in designing a research question, and the discussion covers many of the pitfalls that researchers must be aware of when designing projects.

After the group decides on their topic and question, they must design a survey, complete a project protocol for approval by the University's Institutional Research Board (IRB), survey a minimum of 10 participants each, and then enter and analyze the data using the Statistical Package for the Social Sciences (SPSS) program (IBM Corporation, 2010). The whole project is done in collaboration with all members of the group and the instructor. Groups are given group discussion boards on Blackboard in order to work together, and class time is also allotted for group meetings.

The quantitative data collecting and analyzing assignment accounts for 25% of the grade. Though it is a group project, each student receives an individual grade based on his or her participation in Blackboard and class discussions, as well as the overall quality of the group's work. A rubric for grading this activity is provided in Appendix A.

Literature Review

Though the design, data collection, and data analysis is a group project, each student is required to write his or her own literature review. Each group member must pick a different aspect of the research question and focus his or her review on that aspect. Group members may share references and resources, but the review itself must be their own original work. The paper is worth 20% of the grade and is graded on American Psychological Association (APA, 2009) format (4 points), content (8 points), overall writing (6 points), and references (2 points). A rubric for grading is provided in Appendix A.

Methods and Results

The last component of the quantitative assignment is the methods and results section. Students follow the procedure for writing a methods section, explaining the participants and the instrument used and outlining how the surveys were administered. This assignment also includes writing up the results obtained through their analysis of the survey data using SPSS. This assignment is graded on APA format, content, and overall writing. A rubric for grading is provided in Appendix A.

Each group will write up a methods section based on the development of the survey and how data were gathered. After the data are analyzed in class the group will write a results section.

The combination of these three assignments helps give the student a feel for designing, implementing, and analyzing research in a comprehensive way that is manageable in one three-credit research course.

Qualitative Data Collecting

Though this course mainly focuses on quantitative design, qualitative methods are also discussed. This assignment consists of a naturalistic observation. Students are given very little input into the format for this assignment. They are told to do a naturalistic observation and to prepare a research report in APA format. They are reminded that this is a qualitative assignment, but no other information is given. A large portion of this assignment involves the student investigating what a naturalistic observation actually is and discovering how it differs from quantitative design. The assignment is worth 15% of the grade and is evaluated on appropriateness of the observation, overall writing, and whether or not it is a true qualitative observation. A rubric for this assignment is provided in Appendix A. Each student will be responsible for one naturalistic observation (qualitative data).

Program Evaluation

The final course assignment is a group project in program evaluation. Each group is given a different scenario of a program that is currently running in either a school or community setting. The programs range from programs for depressed adolescents and young adults to programs for academically disadvantaged youth. Each hypothetical program has encountered problems and the group has been called in to help discover some of the issues affecting the efficacy of the program. The groups meet both in class and online and each group submits one paper to the instructor. This will be an online group assignment outlining the steps for evaluation of a counseling program. Each group will be given a program scenario and will be required to produce a paper that answers the following questions:

1. What type of evaluation is appropriate for this program (formative/process, etc.)?
2. How will the program be monitored?
3. What steps are necessary to begin the evaluation? Who are the stakeholders? Whose input is desired? What are ways to secure that input?
4. What instruments/resources may help in evaluating the program?
5. What pragmatic issues need to be considered?
6. What is the plan for disseminating the results?

As with the quantitative project, each group participant receives an individual grade based on his or her participation and input and on the overall quality of the group paper. The assignment is worth 15% of the grade. For full credit, each of the above-listed six questions must be adequately addressed.

These assignments were developed and refined over time to fit the needs of our students and with the content of other courses in the program in mind. I tried many different approaches before arriving at one that gave students a wide range of experiences that could be tied together for a comprehensive experience in research without the students conducting individual studies. Though this model works for our program, each research course needs to be tailored to the specific program in which it is offered. I would encourage counselor educators to experiment with their assignments and to consider the research course a continual work in progress. Using feedback from one semester to another can help define the needs of the students and help the counselor educator fine-tune the course assignments and requirements.

TENTATIVE COURSE OUTLINE

WEEK	*TOPICS AND ASSIGNMENTS*
Week 1	Introduction and structure of class
Week 2	Developing group questions Developing the research topic Developing the research question
Week 3	Quantitative research and design Qualitative research and design
Week 4	Qualitative assignment due The research plan Participants, measurement, instruments
Week 5	Developing surveys Needs assessment and accountability
Week 6	Begin to write surveys in class
Week 7	Literature review due Finish writing surveys The methods section, descriptive studies
Week 8	Introduction to SPSS Discussion of methods and statistical analysis Creating data files for analysis Inferential statistics
Week 9	Program evaluation—Process vs. formative Picking research participants, discussion of random assignment of participants
Week 10	Quantitative data due Data analysis done in class, computer assistance: SPSS and SAS Reading and understanding results sections
Week 11	Group meeting time for results (each group will meet with instructor)
Week 12	Methods and result section due Group meeting for program evaluation
Week 13	Program evaluation group meeting Ethics of research
Week 14	Program evaluation due Finishing up the program evaluation
Week 15	Sharing your research with the class Discussion of final paper

CONCLUSION

Teaching research in a graduate counseling program can be intimidating but ultimately rewarding. I enjoy seeing students gain an understanding of the power of research from a different angle. Though all students in a graduate program have experience using research to inform their learning, very few of them have actually developed and implemented research studies. Asking questions by way of surveys and then finding some answers to those questions stimulates the students in new ways. By extension, it subsequently allows me to look at conducting research with a new eye.

Teaching this course has also informed me about graduate students in general and my students in particular. They are, for the most part, afraid of research. They come into the class like proverbial "deer in headlights." I have learned over the years to keep it simple while keeping it challenging. Presenting complex concepts in an understandable manner has been difficult at times and I have found that by putting the material in terms of everyday life, the students seem better able to grasp the material. I allow the students to form research questions that intrigue them, such as the use of social networking sites by different age groups and the connection between alcohol use and risky sexual behaviors. Helping the students develop simple surveys that can give them some insight into these questions whets their appetites to know more. Another thing that I have learned is that statistics do not have to be about math; statistics can be about ideas and concepts. Most of my students have little if any background in statistics, and I have found that by presenting statistical information in this way students are less anxious and more able to utilize and appreciate statistics.

Teaching research in a graduate counseling program can be as intimidating as taking a research course. Many students enter counseling programs with a preconceived notion that research will be their hardest course, and those who have no previous experience with research dread the prospect. The instructor is challenged to make the course interesting and engaging for the student, and the counselor educator has to choose his or her text and assignments with this in mind. Though this task can be daunting, it can also be rewarding, especially when you witness the students learning how to conduct and analyze research and how to apply research to their clinical practice.

APPENDIX A

RUBRIC FOR EVALUATING THE QUANTITATIVE RESEARCH PROJECT

QUANTITATIVE ASSIGNMENT

	MAXIMUM POSSIBLE POINTS	*UNACCEPTABLE*	*ACCEPTABLE*	*EXCELLENT*
Research question	2	Not measurable and/or observable. No clearly defined independent and/or dependent variables	Observable and measurable, somewhat defined independent and dependent variables	Observable and measurable and well-defined independent and dependent variables

SURVEY

	MAXIMUM POSSIBLE POINTS	*UNACCEPTABLE*	*ACCEPTABLE*	*EXCELLENT*
IRB form	1	Incorrectly filled out or partially filled out, not all requirements covered	Properly filled out with all requirements covered	Properly filled out, clear and concise language, all requirements covered
Consent form	1	Poorly written, not all areas covered	All areas covered	Clear and concise language, all areas covered
Survey	6	Poorly designed, unfocused, does not relate to research question	Adequately designed, focused, and addresses research question	Well (elegantly) designed, easy to fill out, focused, and on target in regards to research question
Discussion participation	5	Poor or infrequent participation	Adequate participation	Consistent, quality participation
Data analysis	5	Improper entering of data, no understanding of results	Proper entering of data, some understanding of results	Proper entering of data, good understanding of results

RUBRIC FOR EVALUATING THE LITERATURE REVIEW

	LITERATURE REVIEW			
	MAXIMUM POSSIBLE POINTS	*UNACCEPTABLE*	*ACCEPTABLE*	*EXCELLENT*
APA format	4	APA format not present or incorrect	APA format followed for the most part, minor mistakes	APA format followed to the letter
Content	8	Does not cover subject of research question adequately or is focused in an area different than the subject of the research question	Covers subject of research question adequately	Covers subject of research question in detail, covers all areas of research question
Overall writing	6	Poorly written, grammatical and/or spelling mistakes	Writing grammatically correct, spelling correct	Clear and concisely written, grammatically correct, spelling correct
References	2	Inadequate or out of date references	Adequate references, most within 10-year period	Comprehensive reference page, all (excepting seminal works) within 10 years

RUBRIC FOR EVALUATING METHODS AND RESULTS

		METHODS AND RESULTS		
	MAXIMUM POSSIBLE POINTS	*UNACCEPTABLE*	*ACCEPTABLE*	*EXCELLENT*
APA format	2	APA format not present or incorrect	APA format followed for the most part, minor mistakes	APA format followed to the letter
Content	8	Methods not clearly defined, results incorrectly or not reported	Methods adequately defined, results reported adequately	Methods spelled out in a clear and concise manner (study could be replicated), results reported clearly
Overall writing	5	Poorly written, grammatical and/or spelling mistakes	Writing grammatically correct, spelling correct	Clear and concisely written, grammatically correct, spelling correct

RUBRIC FOR EVALUATING THE QUALITATIVE DATA GATHERING

		NATURALISTIC OBSERVATION		
	MAXIMUM POSSIBLE POINTS	*UNACCEPTABLE*	*ACCEPTABLE*	*EXCELLENT*
Quality of observation	5	Observation has no detail and/or focus	Observation is focused but lacks detail	Observation is focused and detailed
Overall writing	5	Poorly written, grammatical and/or spelling mistakes	Writing grammatically correct, spelling correct	Clear and concisely written, grammatically correct, spelling correct
Qualitative content	4	Observation utilizes quantitative methods such as counting or percentages	Observation mostly qualitative in nature	Observation totally qualitative in nature
APA format	1	Not double spaced, if any references used they are not APA format	Double spaced, if references are used there are few APA mistakes	Double spaced, if references are used there are no APA mistakes

REFERENCES

American Psychological Association (2009). *Publication manual of the American Psychological Association* (6th ed., 2nd printing). Washington, DC: Author.

IBM Corporation (2010). *Statistical Package for the Social Sciences (SPSS) program*. Available at http://www-01.ibm.com/software/analytics/spss/

Jones, W. P., & Kottler, J. A. (2006). *Understanding research: Becoming a competent and critical consumer*. Upper Saddle River, NJ: Prentice Hall.

Monette, D. R., Sullivan, T. J., & DeJong, C. R. (2008). *Applied social research: A tool for human services* (7th ed.). Belmont, CA: Thompson/Brooks/Cole.

Umbach, P. (2005). Getting back to the basics of survey research. *New Directions for Institutional Research, 127*, 91–100.

14 Psychopharmacology Across the Life Span

Psychotropics Are Quite Complicated on Many Levels

Carl F. Rak, Dilani M. Perera-Diltz, and Kathryn C. MacCluskie

Psychopharmacology is an important topic in counselor education because of the vast number of clients on prescribed medication. Though this course is more likely to be a curricular requirement in a community mental health track, the content also has potential applicability for school counseling students as well, due to the likelihood of their students being on psychotropic medication.

At this introductory stage of the chapter, we must offer readers the following disclaimer and acknowledgment that we bring inherent biases to the topic. Our biases have developed over many collective years working in clinical settings, observing psychotropic medication being used, misused, and abused by consumers and by the individuals who prescribe them. For some clients, prescribed psychotropic medication is what enables them to be functional, contributing members of society. Unfortunately, though, for other clients, psychotropic medication seems to ultimately cause more problems than it solves. We feel ethically compelled to encourage faculty to fully consider teaching your students about psychopharmacology not only from the traditional "doctor knows best" context but also from a broader, sociopolitical, feminist, systemic perspective in which certain individuals hold more power than others. In keeping with the American Counseling Association's Code of Ethics, one of the main goals of counseling in general is to help clients achieve their potential and have life satisfaction through autonomy, social justice, and empowerment. In the scope of a Psychopharmacology for Counselors course, then, the ultimate goal is to teach future counselors how to empower their future clients to become educated consumers and partners in their own health care.

Psychopharmacology is a topic area in which it is critical that an instructor stay completely current on the emerging research related to psychotropic medication, including both effectiveness and adverse effects. The volume of research on medication continues to grow at an incredible rate.

Effective teaching of psychopharmacology demands an instructional approach that weaves together three strands of related content. The first strand consists of the biology, chemistry, and neuroanatomy of psychopharmacology. The second strand is the quagmire of discourse in the professional literature regarding the complex relationship between psychiatrists and other mental health practitioners. The third strand, which may actually be the most daunting to learn, is to understand the importance of presenting current information, challenging due to the burgeoning changes and research in the field of psychopharmacology.

Perhaps the biggest challenge in preparing to teach this vast content is deciding the extent to which one will teach psychopharmacology from a traditional vantage point versus how much one will explore the dynamic changes that have occurred over the last few years that contradict the traditional paradigm. This is not to trivialize the physiology of psychopharmacology, the pharmacodynamics, and the pharmacokinetics and the layers of adverse impact on consumers of psychotropic medication but rather to emphasize that our traditional understandings of pharmacological groups are changing dramatically.

For example, 25 years ago, Anafranil (clomipramine) was heralded as the drug for depression along with cognitive behavioral therapy. In 2011, we now understand that the relief from depression for many clients using Anafranil was temporary, and some negative effects included clients becoming highly suicidal or developing bipolar disorder. Similarly, 5 to 15 years ago, Celexa, Lexapro, Prozac, Luvox, Paxil, and Zoloft were touted to be the prime medical interventions for major depression and depressive anxiety (White et al., 2010). Now, research trials have demonstrated that these selective serotonin reuptake inhibitors (SSRIs) are no more efficacious than placebos, and some trials even contraindicated use of SSRIs to treat patients with depression (White et al., 2010). Some authors have alleged that studies which demonstrated the efficacy of placebos were actually suppressed from publication by pharmaceutical companies (Begley, 2010).

Yet another example of the complex ethical issues involving medication is the recent, seeming epidemic of children and adolescents diagnosed with bipolar disorder. There has been a veritable avalanche of studies and websites for parents coping with children and adolescents who ostensibly are afflicted with this disorder. However, though the diagnostic criteria do seem to capture the essence of the manifestation of this disorder, the diagnosis and subsequent medications usually prescribed result in labeling children for life. Moreover, the medication essentially becomes a form of chemical restraint, which often brings with it major adverse effects on their growth and development. Arriving at a medication decision that is truly in a child's best interest is a complex process of evaluating long and short term costs and benefits. Counselors are sometimes in a better position than a prescribing physician to do this type of problem-solving with clients, due to the additional time they may offer clients to engage in detail-oriented problem exploration. These are but a few brief examples of the ideological dilemmas that an instructor of this course will encounter as he or she prepares the course curriculum from year to year. Readers are referred to Murray (2009) for a comprehensive presentation of the complexities of contemporary psychotropic medication usage in the capitalistic American economy.

As a group of authors, our bias and collective clinical experience informs our call to counselor education faculty to consider moving beyond the traditional teaching of psychopharmacology, broadening the course scope to include the changing nature of pharmaceuticals and the changing nature of the pressure exerted by pharmaceutical companies to use their products in treatment. Ethical concerns about truly informed consent are especially salient when dealing with psychotropic medication because patients who are being treated for mental disorders may be compromised in their ability to objectively weigh the pros and cons of particular medications. This vulnerability may cause consumers to be correspondingly more dependent than they might be otherwise and result in counselors needing to be versed in client empowerment. Again, this could take the form of examining costs and benefits of medication with the client or perhaps with the client and his or her prescribing physician or helping clients by role-playing a dialogue with their physician.

OBJECTIVES AND CACREP STANDARDS

The Council for the Accreditation of Counseling and Related Educational Programs (CACREP, 2009) standards require that counseling students understands "basic classifications, indications, and contraindications of commonly prescribed psychopharmacological medications so that appropriate referrals can be made for medication evaluations and so that the side effects of such medications can be identified" (CMHC G.3.).

In keeping with the above standard requirement, the following objectives were developed for this course.

1. Understand the basic structure and function of the nervous system as it pertains to psychotropic medications.
2. Describe the means by which drugs are taken into the body, distributed, metabolized, and eliminated.
3. Identify examples of psychotropic medications that are used in the clinical treatment of commonly diagnosed psychological conditions of clients and describe impact on symptoms.

4. Identify principal classes of psychoactive drugs and the typical sites and mechanisms of action.
5. Understand the concepts of tolerance and dependence.
6. Increase awareness of drug interactions and the possible impact of recreational drugs on client functioning.
7. Be able to articulate the current debate about the appropriateness of psychotropic medications for children.
8. Understand the role of counselors in working with psychiatric consultation to help manage symptoms.
9. Understand the role of counselors in talking with clients who have questions about psychotropic medications.
10. Demonstrate ability to articulate basic findings of ethnopharmacotherapy and pharmacoeconomics.
11. Demonstrate ability to articulate the relationship between the pharmaceutical companies, the Food and Drug Administration, managed care, and the consumer.

CRITERIA FOR EVALUATING A TEXT

There are a number of criteria that we recommend considering in choosing a text for this course. Those criteria are as follows:

- Authors' background and experience. It is advisable for authors to have experience either in terms of knowledge from practice in psychopharmacology or knowledge from research and teaching psychopharmacology at an institution of higher learning.
- The author's grasp of biology, anatomy, biochemistry, pharmacokinetics (how the body reacts after the drugs have been taken), pharmacodynamics (how the drugs act on the body), and ability to explain those mechanisms in understandable language.
- Clear writing style with visuals/diagrams that truly aid student learning of processes and drug actions.
- Proactive stance on the relationship of the physician and the mental health professional and guidelines for best practices.
- Discussion of the adverse effects of all psychotropic drugs and their interaction effects with alcohol, prescribed medications, and illicit street drugs.

MOST POPULAR TEXTS

Ingersoll, R. E., & Rak, C. F. (2006). *Psychotropic medications for mental health professionals: An integral approach*. Pacific Grove, CA: Brooks/Cole.

Petersen, M. (2008). *Our daily meds: How the pharmaceutical companies transformed themselves into slick marketing machines and hooked the nation on prescription drugs*. New York: Sarah Crichton Books.

Preston, J. D. (2008). *Handbook of clinical psychopharmacology for therapists* (5th ed.). Oakland, CA: New Harbinger.

Stahl, S. M. (2008). *Stahl's essential psychopharmacology: Neuroscientific basis and practical applications* (3rd ed.). Cambridge, UK: Cambridge University.

SUPPLEMENTAL READING

There are many journals that provide excellent supplemental material for teaching this course. Some such journals include *Advances in Psychiatric Treatment, Archives of General Psychiatry, European Psychiatry, International Journal of Psychopharmacology, Journal of Clinical Psychiatry, Journal of the American Academy of Psychoanalysis and Dynamic Psychiatry, Journal of Psychopharmacology, and Psychiatric Annals.*

Topic: Physiology

Carlat, D. (2010, April). Mind over meds. *The New York Times*. Retrieved from http://www.nytimes,com/2010/04/25/magazine/25Memoir-t.html?_r=1&emc=eta1

Glannon, W. (2007). Psychopharmacology and memory. In W. Glannon (Ed.), *Defining right and wrong in brain science: Essential readings in neuroethics*. New York: Dana.

Hamilton, R. J. (Ed.). (2009). *Tarascon pocket pharmacopoeia* (10th ed.). Sadbury, MA: Jones and Bartlett.

Topic: Ethics and Politics

Abel-Horowitz, J. (1998). Psychopharmacotherapy during an analysis. *Psychoanalytic Inquiry, 18*, 673–701.

Begley, S. (2010, January). Studies suggest that the popular drugs are no more effective than a placebo: In fact, they may be worse. *Newsweek,* 35–41.

Catell, P. (2004). *Drugs and clients: What every psychotherapist needs to know*. Petaluma, CA: Solarium Press.

Correll, C. U. (2010). From receptor pharmacology to improved outcome: Individualizing the selection, dosing, and switching of antipsychotics. *European Psychiatry, 25*, S12–S21.

Crespo-Facorro, B., Rodrigues-Sanchez, J. M., Perez-Iglesias, R., Mata, I., Ayesa, R., Ramirez-Bonilla, M., et al. (2009). *Journal of Clinical Psychiatry, 70*, 1–12.

Ferrier, I. N., Ferrie, L. J., & MacCritchie, K. A. (2006). Old drug, new data: Revisiting lithium therapy. *Advances in Psychiatric Treatment, 12*, 256–264.

Meyer, D. J., & Simon, R. I. (1999). Split treatment: Clarity between psychiatrists and psychotherapists. *Psychiatric Annals, 29*, 241–245.

Meyers, B. S., Flint, A. J., Rothschild, A. J., Mulsant, B. H., Whyte, E. M., Peasley-Miklus, C., Heo, M. (2009). A double-blind randomized controlled trial of olanzapine plus sertraline vs. olanzapine plus placebo for psychotic depression. *Archives of General Psychiatry, 66*, 838–847.

Miller, R. R., & Smoot, R. L. (2005). Combining psychopharmacology and psychotherapy. In L. Vandercreek (Ed.), *Innovations in clinical practice, focus on adults*. Sarasota, FL: Professional Resource.

Murray, T. L. (2009). The loss of client agency into the psychopharmaceutical–industrial complex. *Journal of Mental Health Counseling, 31*, 283–308.

Olfman, S. (Ed.). (2007). *Bipolar children: Cutting-edge controversy, insights, and research.* Westport, CT: Praeger.

President's Council on Bioethics Staff. (2005). Better memories? The promise and perils of pharmacological interventions. In W. Glannon (Ed.), *Defining right and wrong in brain science: Essential readings in neuroethics* (pp. 237–257). New York: Dana.

Rickles, W. H. (2006). Listening to Prozac, with the third ear: A psychoanalytic theory of psychopharmacology. *Journal of the American Academy of Psychoanalysis and Dynamic Psychiatry, 34*, 709–733.

Roose, S. P., & Cabaniss, D. L. (2005). Psychoanalysis and psychopharmacology. In E. S. Person, A. M. Cooper, & G. O. Gabbard (Eds.), *Textbook of psychoanalysis* (pp. 255–266). Washington, DC: American Psychiatric Association.

Shannon, S. (2002). *Handbook of complementary and alternative therapies in mental health.* San Diego, CA: Academic Press.

Sinacola, R. S., & Peters-Strickland, T. (2006). *Basic psychopharmacology for counselors and psychotherapists*. Boston, MA: Allyn & Bacon/Prentice Hall.

Smith, F., Wittmann, C. W., & Stern, T. A. (2008). Medical complications of psychiatric treatment. *Critical Care Clinics, 24*, 635–656. doi:10.1016//j.ccc.2008.05.004

White, C., Wigle, P. R., Eichel, E., Albert, L. G., & Udom, L. (2010). Answers to your questions about SSRIs. *The Journal of Family Practice, 59*, 19–25.

Topic: Antidepressants and Mood Stabilizers

Edwards, H. (2006). Psychopharmacological considerations in anger management. In E. L. Feindler (Ed.), *Anger-related disorders: A practitioner's guide to comparative treatments* (pp. 189–202). New York: Springer.

Goldberg, J. F. (2010). Antidepressants in bipolar disorder: 7 Myths and realities. *Current Psychiatry, 9*, 41–49.

Goodman, M., Jeong, J. Y., & Triebwasser, J. (2009, July 13). Borderline personality disorder and bipolar disorder: Distinguishing features of clinical diagnosis and treatment. *Psychiatric Times,* 55–59.

Malhi, G. S., Adams, D., Lampe, L., Paton, M., O'Connor, N., Newton, L.A., & Berk, M. (2009). Clinical practice recommendations for bipolar disorder. *Acta Psychiatrica Scandinavica, 119*, 27–46.

Mallakh, R. S., Elmaadawi, A., Loganathan, M., Lohano, K., & Gao, Y. (2010). Bipolar disorder: An update. *Postgraduate Medicine, 122*, 24–31.

Yatham, L. N., & Kusumakar, V. (2009). *Bipolar disorder: A clinician's guide to treatment management* (2nd ed.). New York: Routledge.

Topic: Antipsychotic

Buchana, R. W., Kreyenbuhl, J., Zito, J. M., & Lehman, A. (2002). The schizophrenia PORT pharmacological treatment recommendations: Conformance and implications for symptoms and functional outcome. *Schizophrenia Bulletin, 28*, 63–73. Retrieved from http://schizophreniabulletin.oxfordjournals.org

Kane, J. M., Detke, H. C., Dieter, N., Sethuraman, G., Lin, D. Y., Bergstrom, R. F., & McDonnell, M. B. (2010). Olanzapine long-acting injection: A 24-week randomized, double-blind trial of maintenance treatment in patients with schizophrenia. *American Journal of Psychiatry, 167*, 181–189.

Lehman, A. F., Steinwachs, D. M., & Steinwachs, D. M. (2010). At issue: Translating research into practice: The schizophrenia Patient Outcomes Research Team (PORT) treatment recommendations. *Schizophrenia Bulletin, 24*, 1–10. Retrieved from http://schizophreniabulletin.oxfordjournals.org

Topic: Medicating Children

Chang, K. D., Saxena, K., Howe, M., & Simeonova, D. (2010). Psychotropic medication exposure and age at onset of bipolar disorder in offspring of parents with bipolar disorder. *Journal of Child and Adolescent Psychopharmacology, 20*, 25–32. doi:10.1089/cap.2009.0036

Einarson, A., & Boskovic, R. (2009). Use and safety of antipsychotic drugs during pregnancy. *Journal of Psychiatric Practice, 15*, 183–192.

Geller, B., Tillman, R., Bolhofner, K., & Zimerman, B. (2010). Pharmacological and non-drug treatment of child bipolar I disorder during prospective eight-year follow-up. *Bipolar Disorders, 12*, 164–171. doi:10.1111/j.1399-5618.2010.00791.x

Grier, B., Wilkins, M. L., & Jeffords, E. H. (2010). Diagnosis and treatment of pediatric bipolar disorder. In P. C. McCabe & S. R. Shaw (Eds.), *Psychiatric disorders: Current topics and interventions for educators* (pp. 17–27). Thousand Oaks, CA: Corwin.

Topic: Herbaceuticals

Ingersoll, R. E. (2005). Herbaceuticals: An overview for counselors. *Journal of Counseling and Development, 83*, 434–443.

WEBSITES

- United States National Library of Medicine: National Institutes of Health
  http://www.nlm.nih.gov/databases/databases_medline.html

  This site offers access to the National Library of Medicine's premier bibliographic database covering the fields of medicine, nursing, dentistry, veterinary medicine, the health care system, and the preclinical sciences.

- American Psychological Association
  http://www.apa.org/pubs/databases/psycinfo/index.aspx

  This site provides access to psychological literature from the 1800s to the present.

- American Society of Clinical Psychopharmacology
  http://www.ascpp.org/
  This is the home of the psychopharmacologists' society. It offers an explanation of psychopharmacology, educational opportunities, and information for patients.

- Journal of Clinical Psychopharmacology
  http://journals.lww.com/psychopharmacology/pages/default.aspx
  This is the home site for the journal. You have to subscribe to be able to read the journals.

- American Journal of Psychiatry
  http://www.ajp.psychiatryonline.org/
  This website offers recent research on controversial topics in psychopharmacology. It also provides new information about psychiatric diagnoses.

- Psychopharmacology Links
  http://www.ncpamd.com/psychopharm.htm
  This site provides links to medication information, free and reduced medication program information, and articles on psychopharmacology.

LEARNING ACTIVITIES

Group Presentation

The purpose of the group presentation is to provide students with the opportunity to explore a certain psychopharmacological agent in depth. Groups of no more than five will prepare a 30-minute presentation on a single psychopharmacological agent.

Analyze the protocol of how clients/patients receive psychiatric care at a mental health center or agency and interview one or two case counselors or clinicians about their understanding of and satisfaction with that procedure.

Review the literature on split treatment and analyze how a mental health professional can more easily engage a psychiatrist in the joint effort of assisting a client.

Consume a form of mass media and do a frequency count on ads for psychotropic medication. Analyze the ads and lead a class discussion about it.

Audiovisual Material

Grubin, D. (Producer). (2002). *The secret life of the brain: Parts 1–5*. Available at http://www.pbs.org/wnet/brain/about.html

Vignettes

There are 50 case vignettes in the Ingersoll and Rak (2006) textbook.

Assignments

Following are some possible assignments for this course.

- Literature Review: The literature review should include information gained from Medline and/or Psychinfo literature on a particular class of drugs.
- Term Paper: Write a paper on a chosen drug. The paper should include information that a counselor should know about indications, contraindications, actions, effects, side effects, how the drug is prescribed and administered, and the signs of an overdose. This information should be researched from professional literature such as the *Physicians' Desk Reference*, Psychinfo, or Medline.
- Quizzes: These could be either in-class in small groups or take-home open book. The time limit for these quizzes is normally 30 minutes.
- Midterm: This includes multiple-choice and short-answer questions.
- Comprehensive Final: This includes multiple-choice and short-answer questions.

TENTATIVE COURSE OUTLINE

WEEK	*TOPIC*	*ASSIGNMENTS DUE*
Week 1	Introduction	
Week 2	Physiology	
Week 3	Politics	
Week 4	Antidepressants	
Week 5	Anxiolytics	
Week 6	Catch up	Quiz 1
Week 7	Antipsychotics	Midterm
Week 8	Mood stabilizers	
Week 9	Medicating kids	Quiz 2
Week 10	Herbaceuticals	
Week 11	Catch up	
Week 12	Drugs of abuse	Quiz 3
Week 13	Cognitive enhancers	
Week 14	Catch up	
Week 15	Final/literature review	

CONCLUSION

Using medication with mental health clients is challenging, and discussing those challenges in an ethical and valuable way creates an atmosphere of honesty and humility in course dialogues and classroom interactions. What I (C.R.) love about teaching this course is that the outcome of medication on any given client is seldom simple and direct. The pearl of wisdom I might offer readers is that the first time you teach this course, teach only what you know about psychopharmacology but be prepared to spend an enormous amount of time updating your knowledge base and living with the uncertainty of an unfolding and confusing discipline. This is one topic in which truly the more you learn the less you know.

REFERENCES

American Counseling Association. (2005). *2005 ACA code of ethics*. Retrieved from www.counseling.org.

Balon, R. (1999). Positive aspects of collaborative treatment. In R. Balon & M. B. Riba (Eds.), *Psychopharmacology and psychotherapy: A collaborative approach* (pp. 1–32). Washington, DC: American Psychiatric Association.

Begley, S. (2010, January 29). Studies suggest that the popular drugs are no more effective than a placebo: In fact, they may be worse. *Newsweek*, 35–41.

Bhugra, D., & Bhui, K. (2001). *Cross-cultural psychiatry: A practical guide*. New York: Oxford University Press.

Bloom, F., Nelson, C. A., & Lazerson, A. (2001). *Brain, mind, and behavior* (3rd ed.). New York: Worth.

Bodenheimer, T. (2000). Uneasy alliance: Clinical investigators and the pharmaceutical industry. *The New England Journal of Medicine, 342*, 1539–1544.

Breggin, P. R. (1997). *Brain disabling treatments in psychiatry: Drugs, electroshock, and the role of the FDA*. New York: Springer.

Breggin, P. R., & Breggin, G. (1994). *Talking back to Prozac: What doctors aren't telling you about today's most controversial drug*. New York: St. Martins Paperbacks.

Carlson, N. R. (1997). *Physiology of behavior* (5th ed.). Boston, MA: Allyn & Bacon.

Churchland, P. S. (1999). Toward a natural science of the mind. In Z. Houshmand, R. B. Livingston, & B. A. Wallace (Eds.), *Consciousness at the crossroads: Conversations with the Dalai Lama on brain science and Buddhism* (pp. 17–32). Ithaca, NY: Snow Lion.

Churchland-Smith, P. (1995). *Neurophilosophy: Toward a unified science of mind/brain*. Cambridge, MA: MIT Press.

Colbert, T. (2000). *The four false pillars of biopsychiatry: One hundred years of medical nonsense*. Tustin, CA: Kevco.

Cooper, J. R., Bloom, F. E., & Roth, R. H. (2003). *The biochemical basis of neuropharmacology*. New York: Oxford University Press.

Council for the Accreditation of Counseling and Related Educational Programs (CACREP, 2009). *2009 standards*. Retrieved from http://cacrep.org/doc/2009%20Standards%20with%20cover.pdf

Crespo-Facorro, B., Rodrigues-Sanchez, J. M., Perez-Iglesias, R., Mata, I., Ayesa, R., Ramirez-Bonilla, M., . . . Vazquez-Barquero, J. L. (2009). Neurocognitive effectiveness of haloperidol, risperidone, and olanzapine in first-episode psychosis: a randomized, controlled 1-year follow-up comparison. *Journal of Clinical Psychiatry, 70*, 1–12.

Damasio, A. (2000). *The feeling of what happens: Body and emotion in the making of consciousness*. New York: Harvest.

Davis, K. L., Charney, D., Coyle, J. T., & Nemeroff, C. (Eds.). (2002). *Neuropsychopharmacology: The fifth generation of progress*. Philadelphia, PA: Lippincott Williams & Wilkins.

Edwards, H. (2006). Psychopharmacological considerations in anger management. In E. L. Feindler (Ed.), *Anger-related disorders: A practitioner's guide to comparative treatments* (pp. 189–202). New York: Springer.

El-Mallakh, R. S. (1996). *Lithium: Actions and mechanisms*. Washington, DC: American Psychiatric Association.

Feldman, R. S., Meyer, J. S., & Quenzer, L. F. (1997). *Principles of neuropsychopharmacology*. Sunderland, MA: Sinauer Associates.

Fisher, S., & Greenberg, R. P. (Eds.). (1997). *From placebo to panacea: Putting psychiatric drugs to the test*. New York: Wiley.

Gabbard, G. O. (Ed.). (1994). *Treatments of psychiatric disorders* (2nd ed.). Washington, DC: American Psychiatric Association.

Gardiner, H. W., & Kosmitzki, C. (2001). *Lives across cultures: Cross cultural human development* (2nd ed.). Boston, MA: Allyn & Bacon.

Goldenberg, M. M. (1990). *Pharmacology for the psychotherapist*. Muncie, IN: Accelerated.

Good, W. V., & Nelson, J. E. (1995). *Psychiatry made ridiculously simple*. Miami, FL: Medmaster.

Goodman, M., Jeong, J. Y., & Triebwasser, J. (2009, July 13). Borderline personality disorder and bipolar disorder—Distinguishing features of clinical diagnosis and treatment. *Psychiatric Times*, 55–59.

Grilly, D. M. (1994). *Drugs and human behavior*. Boston, MA: Allyn & Bacon.

Grubin, D. (Producer). (2002). *The secret life of the brain: Parts 1–5* [DVD]. Available at http://www.pbs.org/wnet/brain/about.html

Halbreich, U., & Montgomery, S. (2000). *Pharmacotherapy for mood, anxiety, and cognitive disorders*. Washington, DC: American Psychiatric Association.

Healy, D. (2000). *The creation of psychopharmacology*. Cambridge, MA: Harvard University Press.

Healy, M. (1996). *The antidepressant era*. London, England: Oxford University Press.

Healy, M., & Doogan, D. P. (Eds.). (1996). *Psychotropic drug development: Social, economic, and pharmacological issues*. London, England: Chapman & Hall Medical.

Heinrich, M., & Gibbons, S. (2001). Ethnopharmacology in drug discovery: An analysis of its role and potential contribution. *Journal of Pharmacy and Pharmacology, 53*, 425–432.

Ingersoll, R. E. (2000). Teaching a psychopharmacology course to counselors: Justification, structure, and methods. *Counselor Education and Supervision, 40*, 58–69.

Ingersoll, R. E. (2001). The nonmedical therapist's role in pharmacological interventions with adults. In E. R. Welfel & R. E. Ingersoll (Eds.), *The mental health desk reference* (pp. 88–93). New York: Wiley.

Ingersoll, R. E., & Rak, C. (2006). *Psychopharmacology for mental health professionals*. Belmont, CA: Wadsworth.

Janicak, P.G., Davis, J.M., Preskorn, S. H., & Ayd, F. J. (1997). *Principles and practice of psychopharmocotherapy* (2nd ed.). Baltimore, MD: Williams and Wilkins.

Jensvold, M. F., Halbreich, U., & Hamilton, J. (Eds.). (1996). *Psychopharmacology and women: Sex, gender, and hormones*. Washington, DC: American Psychiatric Press.

Kane, J. M., Detke, H. C., Dieter, N., Sethuraman, G., Lin, D. Y., Bergstrom, R. F., … McDonnell, M. B. (2010). Olanzapine long–acting injection: A 24-week randomized, double-blind trial of maintenance treatment in patients with schizophrenia. *American Journal of Psychiatry, 167*, 181–189.

Kaplan, H. I., & Saddock, B. J. (1991). *Synopsis of psychiatry* (7th ed). Baltimore, MD: Williams & Wilkins.

Kramer, P. D. (1993). *Listening to Prozac: A psychiatrist explores antidepressant drugs and the remaking of the self*. New York: Viking.

Lawson, W. B. (1999). The art and science of ethnopharmacotherapy. In J. M. Herrera, W. B. Lawson, & J. J Sramek (Eds.), *Cross cultural psychiatry* (pp. 67–73). New York: Wiley.

Lehman, A. F., Kreyenbuhl, J., Buchanan, R. W., Dickerson, F. B., Dixon, L. B., Goldberg, R., … Steinwachs, D. M. (2004). The schizophrenia Patient Outcomes Research Team (PORT) treatment recommendations 2003. *Schizophrenia Bulletin, 30*, 193–217. Retrieved from http://schizophreniabulletin.oxfordjournals.org

Lickey, M. E., & Gordon, B. (1991). *Medicine and mental illness: The use of drugs in psychiatry*. New York: W. H. Freeman & Co.

Longenecker, G. S. (1994). *How drugs work: Drug abuse and the human body*. Emoryville, CA: Ziff-Davis Press.

Malhi, G. S., Adams, D., Lampe, L., Paton, M., O'Connor, N., Newton, L.A., … Burk, M. (2009). Clinical practice recommendations for bipolar disorder. *Acta Psychiatrica Scandinavica, 119*, 27–46.

Marengell, L. B., & Martinez, J. M. (2006). *Concise guide to psychopharmacology*. Washington, DC: American Psychiatric Association.

Meyer, D. J., & Simon, R. I. (1999). Split treatment: Clarity between psychiatrists and psychotherapists. *Psychiatric Annals, 29*, 241–245.

Meyer, J. S., & Quenzer, L. E. (2005). *Psychopharmacology: Drugs, the brain, and behavior*. Sunderland, MA: Sinauer Associates.

Meyers, B. S., Flint, A. J., Rothschild, A. J., Mulsant, B. H., Whyte, E. M., Peasley-Miklus, C., ... Heo, M. (2009). A double-blind randomized controlled trial of olanzapine plus sertraline vs. olanzapine plus placebo for psychotic depression. *Archives of General Psychiatry, 66*, 838–847.

Murray, T. L. (2009). The loss of client agency into the psychopharmaceutical–industrial complex. *Journal of Mental Health Counseling, 31*, 283–308.

Nesi, T. (2008). *Poison pills: The untold story of the Vioxx drug scandal*. New York: St. Martins Press.

Olson, J. (1995). *Clinical pharmacology made ridiculously simple*. Miami, FL: Medmaster.

Preston, J., O'Neal, J., & Talaga, M. (1995). *Handbook of clinical psychopharmacology for therapists*. Oakland, CA: New Harbinger.

Rosenzweig, M. R., Breedlove, S. M., & Leiman, A. L. (2002). *Biological psychiatry* (3rd ed.). Sunderland, MA: Sinauer Associates.

Schatzberg, A. F., & Nemeroff, C. B. (1999). *Textbook of psychopharmacology* (2nd ed.). Washington, DC: American Psychiatric Association.

Siegel, R. K. (1989). *Intoxication*. New York: Pocket Books.

Snyder, S. H. (1996). *Drugs and the brain*. New York: Scientific American Library.

Sperry, L. (1995). *Psychopharmacology and psychotherapy: Strategies for maximizing treatment outcomes*. New York: Guilford Press.

Stahl, S. (2000). *Essential psychopharmacology: Neuroscientific basis and practical applications* (2nd ed.). Cambridge, MA: Cambridge University Press.

Stahl, S. (2005). *Evidence based psychopharmacology*. Cambridge: Cambridge University Press.

Stahl, S. (2006). *Essential psychopharmacology: The prescriber's guide*. Cambridge: Cambridge University Press.

Temin, P. (1980). *Taking your medicine: Drug regulation in the United States*. Cambridge, MA: Harvard University Press.

Werry, J. S., & Aman, M. G. (Eds.). (1999). *Practitioner's guide to psychoactive drugs for children and adolescents* (2nd ed.). New York: Plenum Press.

White, C., Wigle, P. R., Eichel, E., Albert, L. G., & Udom, L. (2010). Answers to your questions about SSRIs. *The Journal of Family Practice, 59*, 19–25.

Wilens, T. E. (1999). *Straight talk about psychiatric medications for kids*. New York: Guilford Press.

Field Placement *"Where the Rubber Hits the Road"* 15

Christopher M. Faiver, M. Cecile Brennan, and Paula J. Britton

The field placement component of counselor education programs is usually the culmination of the overall graduate academic experience. As such, students entering your courses ideally have a basic knowledge of individual, group, and career theory and practice; an understanding of the impact of human development; an appreciation of diversity; a sense of the importance of keeping up with research; fundamental skills in testing and assessment; and an appreciation of ethics and legalities. In essence, students registering for Practicum have completed the Council for the Accreditation of Counseling and Related Educational Programs (CACREP, 2009) core coursework. These national standards stipulate the parameters for the entire field placement component, which is divided into practicum and internship courses. However, you, as instructor, set the tone.

We have found that most students enter the course with a sense of excitement and anticipation but also some fear and trepidation. After all, this is where the "rubber meets the road." They must now prove themselves. Everything that they have learned in lecture and simulated experiences now becomes the real thing. Thus, beyond the competencies that students must get from the field placement component, students must also gain a true sense of accomplishment and self-assurance. This is where the instructor's knowledge and skills become critical.

Your job is a difficult one. In our estimation, you must walk the fine line between that of gate keeper of the profession and that of understanding nurturer of the student. As gate keeper, your duty is not only to protect the integrity of your program, its students, and faculty but, more important, to protect any future clients from potential harm. As an understanding nurturer, you take on an almost Rogerian stance of a nonjudgmental counselor for the student. Indeed, sometimes these roles can come into conflict, especially when there is a marginally acceptable intern in the course. To further complicate things, we have noticed that in some instances, students may have an excellent record in academic coursework but display worrisome behaviors when in placement with live clients.

Following CACREP standards, the practicum, comprised of 100 hours, is a more intensely supervised experience and serves as a transition from the techniques courses to the internship. The internship itself is 600 hours in total and can be likened to an apprenticeship in which students are almost ready to assume the role of counselor. Certainly, close supervision is a component of both courses, which require a 40% direct service component (e.g., of the 600 hours of internship, 240 hours must be in direct contact with clients).

A critical component to teaching these courses is preparation—your own and your students. It is very helpful to have a practicum/internship handbook or website that contains all of the essential information, evaluations, contracts, logs, etc., that should be referred to before, during, and after the completion of the course. Additionally, making sure that you are very specific and clear in your syllabi is essential. Because students are anxious, excited, and sometimes overwhelmed, they may not attend to details explained to them verbally in class. Instead, having checklists and charts allows them to get a handle on all of the activities, paperwork, and licensure requirements. We use the metaphor of taxes to enlist students help in keeping copies of everything pertaining to practicum/internship. In the same way that it is essential to retain all tax-related receipts, students need to retain all documents related to their fieldwork. We also encourage them to check the state's licensure websites regularly as the laws/rules change frequently. This underscores the importance of their ethical and legal responsibility to maintain awareness of the changing laws and rules and developing good professional habits.

Setting the stage for a process versus academic course is also essential. It is important to model, from the first day of the course, the importance of creating a community of support, safety, and respect. We talk about the importance of being vulnerable and not knowing versus being smart and all together. In fact, we mention early in the course that it is the students who think they have this all figured out who are the ones that create worry for us. Instead, we model our own uncertainty and fragility in working in such an amorphous field. Using clinical examples of how we struggled with particular clinical dilemmas gives permission for students to be more open about their own struggles. We also incorporate some early class demonstrations on how to give and receive feedback. Feedback should be offered, not given, and should be framed as an opinion and possibility rather than as fact. Moreover, it is important to always be specific, behavioral, and constructive.

We conduct these courses using a biweekly 3-hour meeting of the class led by the course instructor. During the courses, students are required to present case presentations, share tapes/and clinical material, and give/receive feedback in a group supervision format. Methods of instruction include lectures, discussion, small-group work, experiential exercises, guest speakers, and group consultation.

OBJECTIVES AND CACREP STANDARDS

Due to the experiential nature of these courses, we attempt to underscore basic CACREP standards that have been addressed in other courses. We see it as a chance to revisit some of the basics, this time in a real-life context. Thus, the objectives of the courses cross over many of the CACREP standards. At the end of the course, students will be able to:

- Demonstrate basic individual and group counseling skills as evidenced by case presentations and taped counseling sessions. (Section II.G.5c)
- Illustrate use of counseling theories that provide the models to conceptualize client presentation and assist student in selecting appropriate counseling interventions as evidenced by case presentations. (Section II.G.5.d.; CMHC C.7.)
- Display application of a variety of counseling approaches most appropriate for specific client problems and populations as evidenced by case presentations and individual supervision. (CMHC D.7.; CMHC F.3.)
- Show ability to develop effective case notes and treatment plans as evidenced by case presentations. (CMHC D.7.)
- Demonstrate application of multicultural competencies and use of culturally responsive counseling skills as evidenced by case presentations and taped counseling sessions. (Section II.G.2.d.; CMHC D.2.; CMHC D.4.)
- Exhibit ability to utilize self-care strategies and recognize one's own limitations as a counselor as evidenced by personal analysis logs, individual supervision, and evaluation of experience paper. (Section II.G.1.d.; CMHC D.9.)
- Display appropriate use of diagnostic tools and the *Diagnostic and Statistical Manual of Mental Disorders* (*DSM*; 2000) to describe the symptoms and clinical presentation of clients with mental and emotional impairments as evidenced by case presentations. (CMHC L.1.)
- Show ability to conceptualize an accurate multi-axial diagnosis of disorders presented by a client and discuss with colleagues as evidenced by case presentations. (CMHC D.1.; CMHC G.2.; CMHC K.2.; CMHC K.3.; CMHC L.2.)
- Illustrate ability to provide peer support and consultation as evidenced by class discussions. (Section II.G.5.f.)
- Provide evidence for comprehension and application of legal and ethical standards as evidenced by feedback from site supervisor and case presentations. (Section II.G.1.j.; CMHC A.2.; CMHC B.1.)
- Display understanding and application of crisis intervention and suicide prevention models as evidenced by role-played response to mock suicidal client. (Section II.G.5.g.; CMHC D.6.)
- Demonstrate application of research findings to inform the practice of mental health counseling. (CMHC J.1.)
- Show knowledge of professional roles, functions, and relationship with other human service providers, including strategies of interagency/interorganizational

collaboration and communication as evidenced by feedback from site supervisor. (Section II.G.1.c.)

- Present understanding of professional organizations including membership benefits, activities, services to members, ethical standards, and current professional issues as evidenced by discussion, reflection of course lecture on the topic, and course requirement to participate in local/state/national professional activity. (Section II.G.1.f.; Section II.G.1.g.; CMHC A.4.)
- Display comprehension of professional credentialing, including certification, licensure and accreditation practices and standards, ethical standards, and the effects of public policy on these issues evidenced by reaction to lecture on the topic as well as completion of course requirement to get involved in professional activity. (Section II.G.1.g.; Section II.G.1.j.; CMHC A.4.)
- Demonstrate awareness of the role and process of counselor advocacy on behalf of the profession and advocacy process needed to address institution and social barriers that impede access, equity, and success for clients as evidenced by course requirement to participate in one advocacy activity. (Section II.G.1.i.; CMHC D.3.; CMHC E.4.; CMHC F.2.)
- Provide application of research findings to inform the practice of mental health counseling. (CMHC J.1.)
- Provide evidence for a grasp of professional issues that affect clinical mental health counselors and the practice of counseling. (CMHC A.7.; CMHC C.9.)
- Demonstrate an appreciation of the management issues of mental health services, knowledge of public mental health policy, and financing and regulatory processes to improve service delivery opportunities in mental health counseling. (CMHC A.8.; CMHC B.2.; CMHC E.6.)

CRITERIA FOR EVALUATING A TEXT

When shopping for texts in the field placement coursework areas, we look first and foremost for practicality. In addition, a text that assists students in looking inward and examining themselves, their motivations, their defenses, and the effect of their own personal issues on interacting with clients and maintaining boundaries is needed. The text should also review codes of ethics and the law governing counseling and assist students in preparing for subsequent state and national licensure and certification examinations. Moreover, we find that it is helpful for students to have some knowledge of psychotropic medications, including familiarity with the *Physician's Desk Reference* (Physicians' Desk Reference, Inc., 2008). Finally, an understanding of crisis intervention techniques and chemical dependency is useful. You may wish to note that these two final areas are highlighted in the CACREP 2009 Section standards—and rightly so! In addition, the text is used differently from those used in traditional lecture courses. For instance, students are encouraged to read and learn in order to improve their clinical skills and abilities, rather than simple rote learning useful for examinations. We also encourage students to think about developing and expanding their own professional library and other resources.

MOST POPULAR TEXTS

Baird, B. N. (2008). *The internship, practicum, and field placement handbook: A guide for the helping professions* (5th ed.). Upper Saddle River, NJ: Prentice Hall.

Corey, G., Corey, M. S., & Callanan, P. (2007). *Issues and ethics in the helping professions* (7th ed.). Pacific Grove, CA: Brooks/Cole.

Corey, M. A., & Corey, G. (2007). *Becoming a helper* (5th ed.). Pacific Grove, CA: Brooks/Cole.

Faiver, C., Eisengart, S., & Colonna, R. (2004). *The counselor intern's handbook* (3rd ed.). Pacific Grove, CA: Brooks/Cole.

Kiser, P. M. (2008). *The human services internship: Getting the most from your experience* (2nd ed.). Pacific Grove, CA: Thomson Brooks/Cole.

Welfel, E. R. (2010). *Ethics in counseling and psychotherapy: Standards, research, and emerging issues* (4th ed.). Pacific Grove, CA: Brooks/Cole.

SUPPLEMENTAL MATERIAL

The supplemental material available for field experience coursework is endless. Some suggested American Counseling Association journals include *AdultSpan Journal*, *Career Development Quarterly*, *Counseling and Values*, *Journal of Addictions and Offender Counseling*, *Journal of Counseling and Development*, *Journal of Humanistic Counseling*, *Journal of Multicultural Counseling and Development*, *Journal of School Counseling*, and *Professional School Counseling*. Some specific suggestions are provided below.

Topic: Advocacy

Myers, J. E., Sweeney, T. J., & White, V. E. (2002). Advocacy for counseling and counselors: A professional imperative. *Journal of Counseling and Development, 80*, 394–402.

Roysicar, G. (2008). The big picture of advocacy: Counselor, heal society and thyself. *Journal of Counseling and Development, 87*, 288–294.

Topic: Crisis Counseling

Fein, A. H., Carlisle, C. S., & Isaacson, N. S. (2008). School shootings and counselor leadership: Four lessons from the field. *Professional School Counseling, 11*, 246–252.

Marshall, R. D., Amsel, L., Neria, Y., & Suh, E. J. (2006). Strategies for dissemination of evidence-based treatments: Training clinicians after large-scale disasters. In F. H. Norris, S. Galea, M. J. Friedman, & P. J. Watson (Eds.), *Methods for disaster mental health research* (pp. 226–239). New York: Guilford Pres.

Topic: Diagnosis

Geroski, A. M., Rodgers, K. A., & Breen, D. T. (1997). Using the *DSM-IV* to enhance collaboration among school counselors, clinical counselors, and primary care physicians. *Journal of Counseling & Development, 75*, 231–239.

Zalaquett, C. P., Fuerth, K. M. Stein, C., Ivey, A. E., & Ivey, M. B. (2008). Reframing the *DSM-IV-TR* from a multicultural/social justice perspective. *Journal of Counseling & Development, 86*, 364–371.

Topic: Diversity

Arredondo, P., Tovar-Blank, Z. G., & Parham, T. A. (2008). Challenges and promises of becoming a culturally competent counselor in a sociopolitical era of change and empowerment. *Journal of Counseling & Development, 86*, 261–268.

Portman, T. A. A. (2009). Faces of the future: School counselors as cultural mediators. *Journal of Counseling & Development, 87*, 21–27.

Topic: Documentation

Cameron, S., & Turtle-Song, I. (2002). Learning to write case notes using the SOAP format. *Journal of Counseling & Development, 80*, 286–292.

Myrick, R. D. (2003). Accountability: Counselors count. *Professional School Counseling, 6*, 174–179.

Topic: Ethics

Huss, S. N., Bryant, A., & Mulet, S. (2008). Managing the quagmire of counseling in a school: Bringing the parents onboard. *Professional School Counselor, 11*, 362–367.

Whittinghill, D., Bordeau, W. C., Whittaker, T. T., & Lusk, S. L. (2008). Only I can save my client. In L. E. Tyson, J. R. Culbreth, & J. R. Harrington (Eds.), *Critical incidents in clinical supervision: Addictions, community and school counseling* (pp. 77–83). Alexandria, VA: American Counseling Association.

Study Guides for Counselor Exams

- *Encyclopedia of Counseling Package: Complete Review Package for the National Counselor Examination, State Counseling Exams, and Counselor*

Preparation Comprehensive Examination (CPCE) by Howard Rosenthal (Hardcover, May 19, 2009)

- *NCE: National Counselor's Exam Complete Study Guide, Including Trial Exam for National Board of Certified Counselors and Licensed Professional Counselor Certification.* Complete study guide for the National Counselor's Exam, including trial exam.
- *NCE Secrets Study Guide: NCE Exam Review for the National Counselor Examination* by NCE Exam Secrets Test Prep Team (Paperback, 2009)
- *NCE Flashcard Secrets: NCE Test Practice Questions & Exam Review for the National Counselor Examination* by NCE Exam Secrets Test Prep Team (Cards, 2009)
- *Praxis School Guidance & Counseling 20420* by Sharon Wynne (Paperback, 2008)
- *Study Guide for the NCE Exam* by Dr. Linton Hutchinson (Paperback, January 1, 2009)
- *Vital Information and Review Questions for the NCE, CPCE and State Counseling Exams: Special 15th Anniversary Edition* by Howard Rosenthal (CDs, May 12, 2009)
- *Vital Information and Review Questions for the NCE and State Counseling Exams* [Sound Recording]: *Test Anxiety Prevention* by Howard Rosenthal. With 325 tutorial questions and answers, offers more material than any previous version.

Websites: Professional and Credentialing Associations

- American Association for Marriage and Family Therapy
  http://www.aamft.org
  The American Association for Marriage and Family Therapy (AAMFT) is the professional association for the field of marriage and family therapy. It represents the professional interests of more than 24,000 marriage and family therapists throughout the United States, Canada, and abroad. AAMFT facilitates research, theory development, and education and develops standards for graduate education and training, clinical supervision, professional ethics, and the clinical practice of marriage and family therapy.

- American Counseling Association
  http://www.counseling.org
  Dedicated to the growth and development of the counseling profession and those who are served, the site features the latest information on publications, public policy involvement, conferences, employment, and other related resources. Links to other counseling-related organizations are provided,

including CACREP, National Board for Certified Counselors (NBCC), and state licensure boards.

- American Psychological Association
  http://www.apa.org
  Based in Washington, DC, the American Psychological Association (APA) is a scientific and professional organization that represents psychology in the United States. With 150,000 members, APA is the largest association of psychologists worldwide. The mission of the APA is to advance the creation, communication, and application of psychological knowledge to benefit society and improve people's lives. The site has information available to its members as well as to students and the general public.

- American School Counselors Association
  http://www.schoolcounselor.org/
  The American School Counselors Association (ASCA) supports school counselors' efforts to help students focus on academic, personal/social, and career development so they achieve success in school and are prepared to lead fulfilling lives as responsible members of society. ASCA provides professional development, publications and other resources, research, and advocacy to more than 25,000 professional school counselors around the globe.

- Council for Accreditation of Counseling and Related Educational Programs
  http://www.cacrep.org
  CACREP is an independent agency recognized by the Council for Higher Education Accreditation to accredit master's degree programs in career counseling; college counseling; community mental health counseling; gerontological counseling; marital, couple, and family counseling/therapy; school counseling; student affairs; doctoral degree programs; and counselor education and supervision. This website is provided as a service to students, educators, and practitioners interested in what it means to be a CACREP accredited program. Of particular use to aspiring counselor educators, among others, is the availability of the 2009 accreditation standards.

- Education Trust: The National Center for Transforming School Counseling
  http://www2.edtrust.org/EdTrust/Transforming+School+Counseling/main
  The National Center for Transforming School Counseling works with a network of organizations, state departments of education, school counselor professional associations, institutions of higher education, and school districts across the country dedicated to transforming school counselors into powerful agents of change in their schools and in the lives of their students.

- National Board for Certified Counselors
  http://www.nbcc.org
  The National Board for Certified Counselors is the nation's premier professional certification board devoted to credentialing counselors who meet

standards for the general and specialty practices of professional counseling. The NBCC site has helpful resources for counselor education students, counselors, and the general public. NBCC publishes the national comprehensive examination used by many counselor education programs.

- U.S. Department of Health and Human Services
  http://www.os.dhhs.gov
  The U.S. government agency provides useful information about the agency itself and its numerous services.

LEARNING ACTIVITIES

The following are activities that enhance the experience of both practicum and internship students. Because these courses are experiential, the learning activities and assignments are less content based and more process oriented. Role-plays are used in every class to provide students with opportunities to demonstrate and practice counseling interventions. We suggest three formal role-play activities to augment these courses:

- Role-play of first session protocol. Because there are so many variables to be covered in an initial session with a client, students often struggle with getting the correct information communicated (e.g., confidentiality, supervisory status, etc.) while creating a therapeutic alliance with the client. We find it helpful to have students role-play an opening session and practice the delicate balance of providing ethical informed consent along with joining with the client (Paez & Britton, 2004).
- Role-play of "being present" with clients. We have noticed through the years that one of the major errors that new counselors make is early problem solving with their client versus empathically listening to clients and allowing the issues to emerge. This skill of being present can be promoted through an exercise where students role-play with a peer in two sessions. In the first session, students are instructed to discuss a real-life concern with their peer counselor. The peer counselor will be in a problem-solving mode and suggest solutions/answers to their dilemma. In the next role-play the peer counselor will instead sit with his or her client and focus on understanding what that person is thinking, feeling, and experiencing. We then process how the two role-plays differ and the impact it had on the client.
- Role-play of crisis client. In this activity, the instructor role-plays a suicidal/homicidal client to each student as the class observes. Each student is given a different scenario in which he or she must assess and act on the crisis at hand. These scenarios allow students to discuss and process both the necessary counseling interventions needed in each situation as well as the feelings/thoughts that they experienced while dealing with the crisis.

- Case presentations. Each student makes one case presentation to the class. A case presentation consists of a written summary of the client's presenting problem, assessment (including behavioral observations, environmental assessment, mental status exam, and results of appropriate test data), diagnostic impressions, treatment plan, treatment summary, prognosis, and recommendations. Students are given an outline but may adjust it according to their particular site. The total length of each written presentation is rather short, to reinforce the importance of being concise. Students make copies of the written summary for classmates and are instructed not to use any identifiable information. They are encouraged to present a challenging case they are having problems with or want some help with. Additionally, the students are required to bring to class an audible audio/videotape of the case, with sections picked out to play for the class, and are instructed to elicit feedback from the class and instructor. They are also asked to discuss current literature as it relates to the case; for example, theoretical conceptualization, intervention strategies, articles on the presenting concern, etc. One recent journal article that is directly related to the case is presented to the instructor at the time of the presentation. Students are given about 45 minutes for the presentation, leaving at least 20 minutes of that time for consultation and discussion with the class.
- Site visits. Students set up an onsite meeting every semester that includes their site supervisor, their instructor, and themselves. This is done early in the semester so that mutual responsibilities can be clarified. It is also a good way to maintain positive relationships with sites and site supervisors and provide a forum for problem management. During this meeting, specific goals and outcome expectations are discussed. Site supervisors are asked to document and communicate clearly to the student and instructor their assessment of the intern's progress toward outcome expectations and inform the intern and instructor of any substandard performance so that remedial plans can be made.

ASSIGNMENTS

Practicum Course Required Assignments

- Personal analysis log (PAL). Students are required to e-mail a PAL to the instructor and university supervisor each week. The PAL includes an update of their work for the week, including number of clients seen. It also includes reactions to class, the required readings, working with clients, and other pertinent reactions to their placement. The purpose of the PAL is to help students track their progress over the semester in terms of self-awareness and comfort level with the counseling process. It also serves as a mechanism to keep in touch with students and have some evidence of their progress and concerns.

- Practice video. Early in the course, students bring a practice videotaped role-play of a counseling session. Students work in dyads in order to create the video, taking turns being the counselor and client. Additionally, the video is played for the entire class. Emphasis is placed on relationship-building skills (e.g., listening, nonverbal behavior, empathy, etc.). This activity gets students used to the process of taping and giving and receiving feedback early on in the process.
- Professional goals. Students develop a set of professional goals they wish to pursue to refine their counseling knowledge and skills. These goals are shared with the class early on in the course and provide a specific direction for counselor development. We find that the activity also provides students with experience using goal setting that can be generalizable in their work with clients.
- University supervision. In addition to supervision with their site supervisors, students meet for individual supervision with an assigned university supervisor. In these meetings, the students play a minimum of one tape per week for the supervisor. They present areas they want help with in terms of understanding the client, defining the problem, enhancing their counseling skills, or developing a treatment plan. Students also discuss other cases each week.
    - The students are responsible to have an audible tape of a client ready to be played for each group supervision session. If unable to get a client tape, a role-played tape may be used.
    - Each tape must contain a counseling session of no less than 30 minutes (case management is not considered counseling).
    - Each tape is to be completely audible (both the student and the client).
    - A minimum of 10 tapes is required to pass the course.
- Evaluation of experience paper. This paper encourages students to explore the goodness of fit between their site opportunities and their learning goals as a counseling professional. They reflect on how the experience has been for them and explore ways that they can make the practicum/internship experience more profitable. They discuss the resources and limitations of their site, their self-perceptions of themselves as a therapist, their strengths and weaknesses, and goals for next semester.

Internship Class Required Assignments

- Session critiques. Two audio- or videotapes of sessions with corresponding critiques are required. The critique is an opportunity for students to demonstrate that they are being reflective and participate in self-supervision. They discuss why they picked the interventions and the strategies they used, their own reactions during the session, and their sense of process.

- Peer consultation and PAL. Students make e-mail entries at least once a week to all classmates as well as the instructor. The PAL includes reflections on activities in class, site placement, working with clients, and other pertinent reactions to their position as a counselor trainee. The purpose of the PAL is to help students track their progress over the semester in terms of self-awareness and comfort level with the counseling process. The secondary purpose is for us to create a peer consultation community where they can support each other and provide consultation.
- Resource notebook. Each class, students bring to class resource material to share with their fellow students. This may include handouts used in counseling, Internet resources, articles, poems, etc., that they have found helpful in working with clients. The intent of this activity is to help students expand their professional resource library and integrate literature, books, and ideas into their work as counselors.
- Participation in a professional activity/meeting/conference. Students are required to attend one professional activity during the semester. This may include attendance at a professional meeting, conference, or symposium, and they are asked to write a one-page reaction to the activity. The purpose of this activity is to encourage professional networking and continuing education.
- Advocacy activity. Students are required to complete one advocacy activity during the semester. This could include advocacy for the profession, such as writing a politician regarding a proposed legislation or advocacy on behalf of clients, such as runs/walks for a certain cause. Students should write a one-page description and reaction to the activity. This activity is meant to encourage the adoption of advocacy role as part of their responsibility as a professional counselor.
- Myself as a counselor paper. At the end of the semester, students are asked to write a short paper describing what they have learned about themselves over the past year, including their perceived strengths and weaknesses as a counselor. They discuss obstacles they encountered and what was helpful to them in their process of becoming a counselor. They also address strategies they have adopted for self-care. Students will share this information the last day of class with each other.
- Closing activity. During the last class, each student will reflect on the experience and share part of what they wrote in their myself as a counselor paper. Then each student will provide one reflection on the strengths of each classmate. It allows for positive affirmation and an encouragement of a sense of community, so essential in doing the work of counseling.

Evaluation of Students

Again, due to the process nature of the course, emphasis is not put on grades. As a result, we made these courses pass/fail. Students are informed early on that they will not be expected to be perfect but instead to demonstrate basic competencies expected for a counseling student at their developmental level and a progression of skills. We frame counselor development as an ongoing, evolving concept and that their completion of these courses and this program is just a step in their continual progression in developing their counselor identity. Students are also told early on that if they are not meeting minimum standards they will be referred back to the instructor for a formal remediation plan that involves the site supervisor, university supervisor, instructor and student. They are assured that there will be no surprises (Kress & Protivnak, 2009). However, evaluation is a critical part of these courses and is conducted through formative and summative evaluation processes:

- Formative evaluation. Students receive feedback after every supervision session involving areas of strength as well as competencies to work on. We take a strength-based approach focusing on their unique assets and assist students in processing feedback and beginning their own self-supervision.
- Summative evaluation. At the end of each semester, there is a more formal evaluation process. For practicum we use the professional performance fitness evaluation (Kerl, Garcia, McCullough, & Maxwell, 2002) and the university supervisor, site supervisor, and instructor will evaluate the student using this assessment tool. On the same form, students also do a self-evaluation, and all evaluations serve as a forum for discussion and development of further goals.

CONCLUSION

We find the practicum and internship to be challenging courses, in that students are now required to put into practice didactic and classroom experiential knowledge. The challenge extends to the professor, too! Leading students to make the leap from the academic to the professional can be a daunting task, especially with students who have little or no practical experience. But the task can be rewarding for those instructors who use their creativity, intuition, and knowledge of group process. This is exciting!

Teaching practicum and internship requires the instructor to have a bit of the talent of the improvisational actor. Though it is important to have a plan for the class, the material the students bring should become the focus. The instructor works with the material until insights have been gained and lessons have been learned by both the student presenting the case and by the entire class. This process can be exhilarating because it draws on past experience as a counselor and expertise as an educator. It is never boring, and the students are always engaged because each class addresses timely issues and concerns.

One of the rewards of teaching practicum and internship is the opportunity to be a part of the counselor identity development process. Witnessing students who often began with very insecure identities as counselors grow into more confident, self-aware clinicians who are finding their unique voice as a counselor is a joy. Analogous to parenting, to be part of the developmental process of others can promote a sense of connection to each other and the larger profession at hand.

Moreover, similar to being a therapist, teaching this course requires an ability to be present, mindful, and intuitive. We have found that being prepared and planned to deliver a lesson is helpful, but being able to set aside your plans and go with the process is critical. It is often in these moments that the real learning takes place. However, walking the fine line between doing therapy and teaching a class can often become blurred in these process classes. Remind yourself that personal material may come up in class as it relates to the clinical work and can be important to discuss; however, working that material would not be appropriate. Knowing how to walk this line is important. We find it helpful to have this conversation with the students early and often to be a helpful component as well as regular conversations with other faculty regarding keeping good boundaries. As with almost all that we do, it is best not done in a vacuum.

Finally, the insecurity many students feel about their counseling abilities can result in their wanting us to lower our expectations and standards. Their neediness and anxiety can trigger some of our own insecurities and result in our willing participation in their attempts to limit constructive feedback and the kind of challenge that, though difficult in the short run, encourages growth and professional development. Willingness to expect less, sometimes referred to as *idiot compassion*, which may appear to be empathetic, results in undermining the student's development and an overall enabling of the student. Our job as educators is to demand excellence. When we do this we affirm both our faith in the student and our commitment to our profession.

We trust that we have provided you with useful and detailed material for designing practicum and internship courses that will be practical, challenging, stimulating, and rewarding both for you as instructor and for your students. As we noted at the start of this chapter, CACREP delineates the course parameters, but it is your uniqueness, including your creativity, personality, and experiences, that sets the tone for this interactive experience. We wish you well in your journey.

REFERENCES

American Psychiatric Association (2000). *Diagnostic and statistical manual of mental disorders* (4th ed. text revision). Washington, DC: Author.

Arthur, G. (2005). *NCE : National counselor's exam complete study guide: Including trial exam for National Board of Certified Counselors, licensed professional counselor certification.* Atlanta, GA: St. Bartheémy Press

Council for the Accreditation of Counseling and Related Educational Programs (CACREP, 2009). *2009 standards.* Retrieved from http://cacrep.org/doc/2009%20Standards%20with%20 cover.pdf

Physicians' Desk Reference Inc. (2008). *Physicians' Desk Reference* (PDR) 2009. Montvale, NJ: Author.

Hutchinson, L. (2009). *Study guide for the NCE exam* (5th ed.). Winter Park: FL: Licensure Exams.

Kerl, S. B., Garcia, J. L., McCullough, C. S., & Maxwell, M. E. (2002). Systematic evaluation of professional performance: Legally supported procedure and process. *Counselor Education and Supervision, 41*, 321–334.

Kress, V. E., & Protivnak, J. J. (2009). Professional development plans to remedy problematic counseling student behaviors. *Counselor Education and Supervision, 48*, 154–166.

Loewenstein, S., & Wynne, S. (2008). *Praxis school guidance & counseling 20420.* Cambridge, MA: XAMOnline.com.

NCE Exam Secrets Test Prep Team (2009). *NCE flashcard study system: NCE test practice questions & exam review for the National Counselor Examination.* Beaumont, TX: Mometrix Media.

NCE Exam Secrets Test Prep Team (2009). *NCE Secrets Study Guide: Your key to exam success.* Beaumont, TX: Mometrix Media.

Paez, S. B., & Britton, P. J. (2004). Encouraging a student's voice in the informed consent process: A training model. *Journal of Systemic Therapies, 23*, 4–18. Rosenthal, H. (2005). *Encyclopedia of counseling package: Vital information and review questions for the NCE and state counseling exams with anxiety prevention* (rev. ed.) [CD-ROM]. New York: Taylor and Francis Group.

Rosenthal, H. (2008). *Encyclopedia of counseling: Master review and tutorial for the National Counselor Examination (NCE), State Counseling Exams, and Counselor Preparation Comprehensive Examination (CPCE).* New York: Taylor and Francis Group.

Rosenthal, H. (2009). *Human Services Dictionary: Complete review package for the National Counselor Examination (NCE), State Counseling Exams, and Counselor Preparation Comprehensive Examination (CPCE).* New York: Taylor and Francis Group.

Rosenthal, H. (2009). *Vital information and review questions for the NCE, CPCE, and state counseling exams (Special 15th anniversary ed.)* [Audio CD]. New York: Taylor and Francis Group.

Adapting Courses to the Online Format

16

Dilani M. Perera-Diltz

A resource book for counselor education is not complete without some discussion about and direction for online teaching influenced by the increased use of distance learning technologies. Online course work offers better access, convenience, and flexibility (Conceiçáo, 2007) for students pursuing a counseling degree. A quality online course does not simply emerge by converting and placing traditional classroom materials online. Design and delivery of online coursework, therefore, calls for rethinking the role of the learner, instructor, and the design within the new medium (Conceiçáo, 2007). This chapter will provide readers with an overview of online instruction, including strengths and weaknesses, guidelines for online course development, and guidelines for course management once the class is up and running.

CHARACTERISTICS OF LEARNERS

Characteristics of learners best suited for online coursework are those who are individual self-starters and who are highly motivated (Simonson, Smaldino, Albright, & Zvacek, 2006). Learner skills required to secure a successful online experience begin with basic computer literacy, access to a computer, and a reliable and efficient Internet connection. Learners must be able to manage their time; be disciplined to complete and submit assignments; generate a schedule for routine participation; dedicate approximately 3 hours per week per credit hour similar to a traditional class; be motivated to read, write, and participate as needed and requested; be flexible to address technology issues; and be able to ask questions and ask for help when needed (Conceiçáo, 2007).

ROLE OF THE INSTRUCTOR

The role of an instructor may vary depending on the involvement in design and delivery of the coursework. Online course work tends to be a partnership of teaching and learning, moving away from the instructor as the source of authority and knowledge to instructor as facilitator of the learning experience (Conceiçáo, 2007). Anderson, Rourke, Garrison, and Archer (2001) characterized the online instructor in yet another way: the designer of the educational experience, the facilitator of the social environment, and the expert on the subject matter.

Whether the online instructor chooses one of the above models or another model, the core remains that the online instructor's role is similar to yet different from that of the traditional instructor's role. Conceiçáo (2007) characterized the online instructor as (a) an instructional designer who designs, organizes, administers, and presents course content; (b) a facilitator who engages learners in the learning process; (c) a catalyst who activates conversation; and (d) a participant in learning. Coppola, Hiltz, and Rotter (2001) defined the role of the instructor as (a) facilitator of cognitive components of thinking, learning, storing information; (b) facilitator of affective components of interpersonal relationships among students, between the student and instructor, and between student and the online environment; and (c) course manager. Although these roles appear similar to that of the traditional classroom that utilizes an active learning model of teaching, the online instructor must be mindful in designing a course in which the consumer can navigate the learning experience without the presence of the designer. Facilitating discussion requires instructions as simple as "please use other student's name instead of responding as you" due to the lack of visual cues for discussion to more complex instructions on where to post the reply so that it is meaningful to group discussion. In addition, the instructor needs to determine the degree of involvement desired. Does the instructor plan to be present daily or on a casual check in basis? Based on the degree of involvement, the instructor has to design the course for the degree of independent functioning required. Furthermore, the instructor's role also needs to be communicated to students so they may adjust their expectations of the role of the instructor. Therefore, in offering online coursework, the role of the instructor must be carefully considered and delineated.

DESIGN CONSIDERATIONS

In considering the design, the partnership of teaching and learning results in a learner-centered environment. Therefore, the environment will need to evolve based on the needs of the learners present. The online course, then, must continuously change based on the learning styles and needs of the learners. The online classroom is similar to the traditional classroom in which there are students at different learning levels participating in the same room. Therefore, the online classroom should adhere to the seven principles of effective teaching, which include: (a) open dialogue between student and instructor; (b) encourage cooperative learning among students; (c) encourage active learning; (d) provide personal feedback within a reasonable time frame; (e) encourage time on task so students meet deadlines and avoid procrastination; (f) communicate high expectations; and (g) value and allow diverse talents and ways of learning (Graham, Cagiltay, Lim, Craner, & Duffy, 2001). To design a continuously evolving classroom based on learner styles, the design of the online course must have flexibility and a level of designer/instructor presence. As changes are made, these must be explicitly communicated with the students. The simple method of announcing course changes in the classroom in a traditional course must be preplanned in the online setting, so the learners are knowledgeable on how to acquire information on course changes. In an online environment, the instructor could use either e-mail and/or an announcement board as the vehicle.

Prior to undertaking the design, the development, and the delivery of an online course, it is beneficial to understand the strengths and limitations of online courses.

POINTS OF DIFFERENCE

Teaching Focus

In the online setting, the instructor's role changes from that of the traditional lecturer of knowledge to that of the facilitator of active learning. The online medium allows the instructor to provide individual student-focused learning, facilitating active learning in students at various levels of development as a counselor. However, such facilitation requires a significant additional time commitment in design, development, and delivery in the online environment (Conceiçáo, 2007; Grosjean & Sork, 2007). Online courses also require the instructor to have competence in technology.

Accessibility

Online coursework provides students the opportunity to learn from the convenience of home and at a speed mostly determined by the learner. However, the convenience depends on the student's available access to appropriate technology. At times, students may attempt to engage in online coursework with inadequate technology and Internet services, leading to frustration and inconvenience. At other times, the platform used to teach online coursework may not be available due to technology issues leading to anxiety in students.

Learning Pace

Online courses can be designed to be self-paced. Some instructors may choose to allow students to set their own pace and complete assignments prior to the end of semester. This method has both advantages and disadvantages. The obvious advantage is that students can take the time they need and be flexible in how and when they complete their learning within a semester. A possible disadvantage is that students have to be self-motivated, disciplined, and organized to complete a course that is entirely self-paced. In addition, students in a solely self-paced course miss out on the classroom learning community and the breadth and depth of knowledge gained from discussion. Therefore, it may be best to keep with the effective practices of education and to set time on task within the semester to prevent students from procrastinating and not completing the course as planned. Setting a time frame such as a week for discussion threads will create a sense of a learning community.

Creating a Community of Learners Who Share the Knowledge

Online coursework provides many opportunities for students to engage with each other and share information if tools available are used appropriately. Ability to post announcements, to publish student assignments so other students may view the content, to post in nonsynchronous threaded discussions, to engage in synchronous chat, to privately invite someone to discuss issues, to blog on a topic, to journal privately or publicly, and to e-mail both individually and to the entire group all provide excellent media to facilitate a community of learners who share their knowledge. The disadvantage is that facilitating and actively participating in such a course is time consuming for both the learner and the instructor. At times, the time required to complete a module may be longer than the typical classroom time frame to complete similar material.

Interpersonal Dynamics

The interpersonal dynamics between instructor and students are different in traditional than in online education settings. Some (Wilczenski & Coomey, 2006) have claimed that students may have less opportunity to ask questions because the logistics of interacting online are more difficult, considering challenges such as the timing of questions, typing speed, coordination of multiple questions, and the need to keep the discussion flowing. Student-to-student interaction, although technically possible, is limited by the same set of logistical hindrances. In addition, students may censure their communication because it is recorded or it may be inappropriate in online discussion because it is depersonalized. However, the instructor has some control over the interpersonal dynamics in a class.

Wider Audience

Online coursework provides the opportunity to facilitate counselor education for students nationally and even internationally. The convenience of using the Web to take a course makes it possible for students who were unable to get to a campus location to take the course. Widening the audience of counselor education is beneficial in the current economic climate. A wider audience also may bring more diversity into the classroom setting.

Below is a chart that provides some of the differences between traditional and online teaching.

	TRADITIONAL	*ONLINE*
Instructor focus	Group; accommodation of different learner styles is limited	Individual; different learner styles can be better accommodated
Instructor time	Limited	Time consuming
Instructor competence	Topic/area	Topic and technology
Accessibility to instructor	Limited to class time or office hours	Dependent on design: Can be boundless
Accessibility to course	Class time	Dependent on design; week to entire semester
Learning pace	Group	Dependent on design; mostly self-regulated
Student requirements	Attendance and participation	Attendance, participation, self-motivation, discipline, and organization
Student learning time	Limited	Boundless
Student interaction	Public and limited to class time	Public or private (among limited number of students) and boundless
Audience	Limited to geographic region	Unlimited
Social rules/ boundaries	Discussed and processed	Written and described; discussion is possible dependent on design
Networking	Limited among students	Boundless among students
Going green	Paper assignment submission	Paperless assignment submission
Bullying	Limited access	Open access

A good online course requires the instructor to invest time in two main components: development and management. I bring to this discussion my experiences from designing and teaching online classes. I will provide below some of my insights from my experiences and from the literature available.

TIPS FOR DEVELOPING AN ONLINE COURSE

There are two types of online course development: converting a traditional course to the online medium and developing a new course in the online medium. Similar to planning to deliver a traditional course, reflecting on how to integrate new information and experience to prior learning and how to form collaborative discussion (Conceiçáo, 2007) is essential for either type of online course design. The goal in each form of online course development is to maintain the pedagogical integrity. Prior to course development, first, a decision of who develops the course will need to be made. Some prefer a team approach, whereas others prefer an individual approach. If using a team approach, who should be involved and when and why they should be involved needs to be predetermined (Grosjean & Sork, 2007). Next, it is also important to establish realistic time lines for the conversion of or original development of an online course (Grosjean & Sork, 2007). Online course development takes more time than planning for a traditional class. It is beneficial to design, develop, and upload the entire course prior to the beginning of the semester in which it is offered because course management will require the instructor's time, making ongoing course development and upload an unrealistic goal. The standard online course format includes (a) aims and objectives; (b) content; (c) model of delivery; (d) active learning; and (e) assessment (Grosjean & Sork, 2007).

Determine the Essential Topics for the Course

Determining topics is not much different than what is done for preparation for a traditional class. However, what is provided for resources and classroom activities will have to be appropriate for the online medium. In determining topics, difference due to medium of delivery needs to be considered.

Example 1

Some audiovisual tape production companies will not give permission to upload their material to the online environment, even if placed on reserve through the library. Therefore, if audiovisual information is to be used, you may want to first check whether it can be uploaded. If not, decisions need to be made on if it is essential for the student's learning or if it can be eliminated from the course content. If it is deemed essential, is it feasible for students to come to campus and watch it at a designated location?

Example 2

If you have a group activity during which you ask students to freeze and process, this cannot be done in the online medium without making some adjustments. One possible adaptation is to tape these segments and then have students discuss each segment.

Determine What Tools Are Available in Your Online Course Delivery Program

Tools may come in a variety of categories. Following are possible tools available for an online course under the Blackboard platform. Some online course delivery programs may offer different tools than discussed below.

- Organization tool—calendar, search, and syllabus
- Communication tools—announcement, chat, discussions (blog, thread, journal), mail, roster, and who's online
- Student learning activity tools—assessments, assignments, and goals
- Content tools—learning modules, local content, media library, Sharable Content Object Reference Model (SCORM), and web links
- Student tools—my files, my grades, my progress, and notes

Determine Which Tools Are Best Suited to Present the Course

It is necessary to learn and determine which tools are best suited to present which components of your course. Some tools I have used frequently are provided below.

- Announcements—This tool is useful to communicate with the entire class about information necessary to complete an assignment, updates on changes in requirements, or to make general announcements on upcoming counseling-related activities. By providing such announcements, the students receive information they may receive in a classroom as announcements, thus creating a classroom atmosphere. A pop-up feature as well as time frame during which to display a message is available.
- Assignments—This tool offers the option to set a cutoff for the due date as well as for a late assignment. Assignments through this tool may be hidden or shown and released as needed.
- Calendar—This tool is useful to provide an overview of what is expected each week. The calendar can be modified by each student to set their personal deadlines.
- Chat—This tool is good for synchronous class or small-group discussion. Using chat provides the instructor and/or group of students the opportunity to be online simultaneously, engaging in a written discussion. Facilitating such a written discussion is necessary to ensure that meaningful discussion can take place. For instance, when students have a comment or question, they need to be able to inform the facilitator that they are waiting to provide input. Then the facilitator would call on those students depending on whether the facilitator wants to take a question or comment at that point of

the discussion. Being online at the same time tends to create a pseudo-classroom environment.

- Discussions—Three different types of discussions may be available to you.
  - Threaded discussion is appropriate to pose questions to widen and deepen students' understanding of a topic covered within a week. These discussion topics can be locked and/or hidden so no one can respond in them. Locking modules is useful if your design is to move students through modules in a predetermined time frame. For instance, I leave each module open for one week during which I expect each student to complete the module. This allows me to keep all students focused on one topic to deepen the discussion of that topic through meaningful reading of and commenting on peer comments. Hiding future modules from student view has reduced feelings of being overwhelmed for some students. These features can be implemented based on instructor and student preferences.
  - Blog is useful to write about findings from exploring websites related to the topic of the week. Students are able to comment on findings from a similar site and have a dialogue with each other through the use of blog discussion. These blogs may also be locked and/or hidden.
  - Journal discussion is useful to maintain a continuous dialogue with each student individually. I utilize this thread as a means for securing formative feedback about the module and to answer individual questions about each module.
- Learning Modules—This tool is useful for organizing the topics of the course. Organizing a semester course in 16 modules provides a useful tool to move the students through the content in a timely manner within a semester. Moving the entire class from topic to topic weekly has been beneficial for building a sense of community and for meaningful discussion through the above discussion tools.
- Mail—Similar to e-mail, the tool is useful to engage in individual dialogue with students on their inquiries and requests. This tool can be directed to one's personal e-mail.
- Roster—This tool provides students with the opportunity to introduce themselves and build a sense of community. It has capabilities of uploading pictures, if needed.
- Syllabus—Either a traditional or modified syllabus can be uploaded through this tool.
- Who's Online—This tool provides the opportunity for those online simultaneously to dialogue with each other if needed. This tool also allows a student or instructor to make him- or herself unavailable if deemed necessary. The dialogue through this invited communication is private and cannot be viewed by the instructor.
- Web Links—This tool provides the opportunity to upload relevant websites for the course so students may explore the vast amount of information available on the web.

In addition to the above tools, students have tools available that allow them to save their own files and notes, and view their grades and/or progress.

Overall Organization of the Course

In addition to choosing the topics, material, and tools, it is essential that the online course is organized so students can locate the necessary information without having to hunt through clutter. Appendix A provides an overview of how I organize my courses. My online courses are built on a 16-module format if the course is to be offered during a regular semester. Each module can hold a different topic or it could be part of a series within a topic. If each module does not hold a different topic leading to 16 topics, then I utilize modules to contain the main themes and unit folders within the modules to contain the 16 weeks of organized materials. For example, you could label the module as "diversity" and have units labeled "ethnic," "religious," "socioeconomic standing," "gender," and so on, within the module (see Appendix A). Another option is to organize topics by folders and have modules within the topics.

Organization of the Modules

It is helpful to provide all required sections of a module within the module. For instance, although assignments can be located under the assignment tab, it is helpful for students to find assignments that are due at the end of a given module located within that module as well. Organizing each module in a similar manner provides students confidence in their ability to locate the needed information from module to module. An outline for module organization is provided in Appendix B.

Determine How to Manage the Topics and Discussion of the Course

It is necessary to determine how to move students through the course so that students who procrastinate do not arrive at the end of the semester and realize that neither learning nor completing assigned work for the semester has occurred. Therefore, using specific management tools to move students through weeks or modules may be beneficial. Predetermine which day at what time within a week is suitable to end and begin a module. It is appropriate and sometimes beneficial to include a weekend for each module so students may have the opportunity to work on the coursework during the weekend. My preference is to close the module at 5:00 pm on a weekday and open the next module at 8:00 am the following day. This provides the instructor the opportunity to close the module at a reasonable hour during the week and open the next module in a timely manner. It also provides the opportunity to summarize the discussion in the module that is ending prior to moving to the next module.

MANAGING AN ONLINE COURSE

Effective management of the online environment requires preplanning and careful time management. Although the instructor could take a traditional role and provide audiovisual taped lectures, teaching online is not meant to simply convert traditional coursework to the online medium. It may be more fruitful to understand the strengths and limitations of the online environment and to design and deliver a course using the strengths of the medium.

Making Initial Contact With Students

It is best to make contact with students prior to the beginning of the semester to orient them to the online class. This may be done through e-mail or snail mail, providing the students with adequate information to enter and navigate through the course. In this letter, I explain that I will make phone calls to those who do not enter the course by the deadline provided. If all students registered for a given course are from the local area, at times, I have offered a one-time non mandatory in person group orientation.

Getting Students Acquainted With the Content and Format of the Course

Once contact is made with the students, it is useful to orient students to the course so that they can find content and other requirements of the course. Although an instructor could expect master's-level counseling students to orient themselves on their own, my personal preference is to provide them with an online navigational activity to complete for a minimum number of points toward their final grade. Such an activity actually forces the student to begin the course and provides the instructor the opportunity to identify those students who may need assistance with technology and direct them to necessary services. In addition, it may be beneficial to have an open dialogue, through threaded discussion or other form of discussion on anxiety related to engaging in online coursework.

Establishing Communication and Participation Guidelines

Student Requirement

It is necessary that the instructor provide clear guidelines for expectations for communication and participation from students. Establishing some netiquette guidelines (Appendix C) may prevent future problems. Establishing requirements for utilizing certain methods of communication (i.e., e-mail, announcements, journals, blogging, help threads) will ensure smoother sailing during the course. Clarifying participation requirements and assigning points for quality-based participation also improves the quality and quantity of content discussion.

Instructor Responsibility

Expectations for communication from the instructor also need to be explained. It is reasonable to announce that students will receive a response within 24 hours with the exception of weekends and holidays to e-mail communications. It is also important to acknowledge receipt of documents even if they will not be evaluated or receive an immediate full response. Instructor presence in the online environment to facilitate learning must be communicated.

Determine How to Create and Manage a Learning Community Online

For active learning to take place, the students must complete the course as designed. It is prudent to determine a method to move students through the course content without expecting students to complete the work solely by themselves. Therefore, I suggest moving students from module to module or topic to topic by providing deadlines to complete modules. The best active learning in online courses occurs with smaller class sizes (i.e., about 15). However, in today's economic times, such small classes may not be a reality. It may be beneficial to create groups of learners. Too many members in a group can become overwhelming due to the volume of written interaction and is discouraged because students within groups must engage in useful ways of interacting (Smith & Dirkx, 2007) for learning to occur. In a class of 15 students, an instructor may choose to facilitate two discussion groups. Such small groups provide the opportunity to learn the subject matter through appropriate problem solving, critical thinking, and working collaboratively (Smith & Dirkx, 2007). A strong social presence of the instructor online is necessary to facilitate the direction, purpose, and scope of discussion (Smith & Dirkx, 2007). Instructors can show their presence by individual or group e-mails, announcements, and posts. Even with the best of intention and excellent facilitation, online group work can be frustrating at times.

Groups can also be formed for assignment purposes. A group of three to five students is preferable because the smaller size allows each student the opportunity to express his or her opinion and feel heard (Ball Foundation, 2002). Groups can be established for the entire semester or the instructor may change group membership as needed. The instructor may need to assist each group facilitator in keeping the group organized through timetables, helping clarify expectations for other group member work, and keeping groups on task through productive discussion (Smith & Dirkx, 2007). The group facilitator should rotate (Smith & Dirkx, 2007) so that all students have the opportunity to experience group facilitation and one student is not burdened with additional responsibilities.

Evaluation of Students and Course

Evaluation of the Students

Similar to that of the traditional class, student evaluation needs to take place in online courses. These assessments could occur either as content specific or as leaner centered. Content-specific evaluation involves providing students with tests and assignments appropriate for the online medium. Learner-centered assessment involves students identifying their progress in meeting objectives specified for either the modules or the course (Rocco, 2007).

Evaluation of Course

Evaluation of online courses can be problematic (Grosjean & Sork, 2007). The return rate of course evaluations is lower in the online setting than in the traditional setting. Summative evaluations may also include not only the content and the relationship with the instructor but also the student's experience with the medium (i.e., technology, user interface, and design issues). A strength of the online environment is that formative evaluations can be easily gathered for modules or topics if so designed into the course. For instance, an instructor can request students to provide a short critique of what was useful and not useful within a module for the learning.

CONCLUSION

I enjoy teaching online due to the flexibility and ability to provide individual feedback based on the individual learner's learning style and level of development. I also enjoy the active learning that occurs in well designed, developed, and delivered online coursework. The most important aspect of facilitating active online learning is regular presence of availability of, and feedback from the instructor. To provide such assistance, it is essential that the instructor is organized and able to manage time efficiently. For instance, I check on my online courses each morning and have allocated at least an hour daily Monday through Friday for course facilitation. I also mindfully protect my time, because online teaching can be boundless. Hopefully, this chapter has provided you a starting point for either converting a traditional course to online or for developing an online course.

APPENDIX A

Organizational Structure for an Online Course

- Orientation Letter—This is a must-read! This letter provides an explanation of the features available.
- Course Information—Contains useful information pertaining to the course including a traditional syllabus in pdf format.
  - Instructor Information
    - Instructor Contact Information
    - Audiovisual Clip of Instructor
  - Classroom Documents
    - Traditional Syllabus in pdf format
    - Checklist of Items Due Weekly
    - Technical Assistance
    - Goals and Objectives
  - Classroom Policies and Procedures
    - Academic Misconduct Policy
    - Communication Policy
    - Disability Statement
    - Netiquette Guidelines
    - Technology Requirement
- Learning Modules—Contains the weekly modules for this course. Best place to find everything needed for a week.
  - Module 1
  - Module 2—For Example: Diversity
    - Unit 1—Socioeconomic standing
    - Unit 2—Ethnic
    - Unit 3—Religious
    - Unit 4—Gender
- Assignments—Contains the main assignments for the course with links to the assignment.
- Web links—Contains web links that are included as part of the course.
- Student Lounge—This is a place for you to meet and mingle with your classmates to discuss assignments, class content, and other school counselor relevant information.

There are also two HELP! threads available:

- Student lounge thread
- Someone Please HELP! This is an idea I received from a colleague who also facilitates online courses. If students have a question, they post it

on this thread. By posting the question on this thread, a student or the instructor can respond, providing a faster response time.

- Technology HELP!

APPENDIX B

Organization Structure With a Module

- Module number
  - Introduction
    - Objectives for the module
    - Reading assignment (link library course reserve material to this heading)
    - Instructor's notes (if available)
  - Discussion
    - Use threaded discussion
  - Assignments
    - Use assignment tool
  - Web exploration
    - Use blog discussion
  - Module feedback
    - Use journal discussion

APPENDIX C

Netiquette Guidelines

Online communication is an integral part of an online course. In this course, we will be using e-mail, threaded discussions, chat, blogs, and journals. Below are some guidelines you must follow when communicating with your instructor and fellow students. Following these will ensure a healthy and productive learning community.

- Follow the same standards of behavior in online communications that you would follow in real life.
- Abusive or insulting comments will not be tolerated. This is referred to as *flaming*.
- Refrain from posting complete messages in all caps. This is considered shouting.

- Respect other people's time by keeping replies short and to the point and attachments small in file size (around 2 MB is a reasonable limit).
- Though you should fully express your thoughts, try to keep all paragraphs and messages short and to the point.
- Spell-check your messages and use appropriate punctuation and grammar to ensure that your message is clear.
- Use caution when using sarcasm and humor. It is difficult to convey human emotion online. Instead, use emoticons to express humor and other emotions.
- Remember that everyone has the right to participate. Though that includes you, do not dominate a discussion.
- Instead of criticizing a fellow classmate's opinion, question and analyze their points and form a response that is reasonable. Use evidence to support your own viewpoints.
- Do not assume that e-mail messages are private—they are easily forwarded. A good rule of thumb is to not say anything you would not say on the evening news.
- Though all students deserve feedback in a reasonable amount of time, do not expect instantaneous feedback from your instructor, students, or technical support.
- At the same time, fellow students may need feedback from you on group projects. Check your e-mail every day and try to get back to your group in a timely fashion.
- Consequences:
  - The first time, you will receive an e-mail from the instructor requesting explanation and modification of behavior.
  - If the behavior persists, you may be asked to drop the class. Other consequences may be determined depending on the nature of the behavior.

REFERENCES

Anderson, T., Rourke, L., Garrison, D. R., & Archer, W. (2001). Assessing teaching presence in a computer conference context. *Journal of Asynchronous Learning Networks, 5*, 1–17.

Ball Foundation. (2002). Education initiatives. Retrieved from http://www.ballfoundation.org/ei/tools/consensus.html

Bloom, B., Englehart, M., Furst, E., Hill, W., & Krathwohl, D. (1956). *Taxonomy of educational objectives: The classification of educational goals. Handbook I: Cognitive domain*. New York: Longmans, Green.

Conceiçáo, S. C. O. (2007). Understanding the environment for online teaching. *New Directions for Adult and Continuing Education, 113*, 5–11.

Coppola, N. W., Hiltz, S. R., & Rotter, N. (2001). Becoming a virtual professor: Pedagogical roles and asynchronous learning networks. *Journal of Management Information Systems, 18*, 169–190.

Graham, C., Cagiltay, K., Lim, B., Craner, J., & Duffy, T. M. (2001). Seven principles of effective teaching: A practical lens for evaluating online courses. Retrieved from http://technologysource.org/article/seven_principles_of_effective_teaching/

Grosjean, G., & Sork, T. J. (2007). Going online: Uploading learning to the virtual classroom. *New Directions for Adult and Continuing Education, 113*, 13–24.

Rocco, S. (2007). Online assessment and evaluation. *New Directions for Adult and Continuing Education, 113*, 75–86.

Simonson, M., Smaldino, S., Albright, M., & Zvacek, S. (2006). *Teaching and learning at a distance: Foundations of distance education* (3rd ed.). Upper Saddle River, NJ: Merrill Prentice Hall.

Smith, R. O., & Dirkx, J. M. (2007). Using consensus groups in online learning. *New Directions for Adult and Continuing Education, 113*, 25–35.

Wilczenski, F. L., & Coomey, S. M. (2006). Distance learning: Finding its place in school counseling practice, education and professional development. *Professional School Counseling, 9*, 327–331.

Appendix: 2009 CACREP Standards

SECTION I

The Learning Environment: Structure and Evaluation

A. The institutional media accurately describe the academic unit and each program offered, including admissions criteria, accreditation status, delivery systems used for instruction, minimum program requirements, matriculation requirements (e.g., examinations, academic-standing policies), and financial aid information.
B. The academic unit is clearly identified as part of the institution's graduate degree offerings and has primary responsibility for the preparation of students in the program. If more than one academic unit has responsibility for the preparation of students in the program, the respective areas of responsibility and the relationships among and between them must be clearly documented.
C. The institution is committed to providing the program with sufficient financial support to ensure continuity, quality, and effectiveness in all of the program's learning environments.
D. The institution provides encouragement and support for program faculty to participate in professional organizations and activities (e.g., professional travel, research, and leadership positions).
E. Access to learning resources is appropriate for scholarly inquiry, study, and research by program faculty and students.
F. The institution provides technical support to program faculty and students to ensure access to information systems for learning, teaching, and research.
G. The institution provides information to students in the program about personal counseling services provided by professionals other than program faculty and students.
H. A counseling instruction environment (on or off campus) is conducive to modeling, demonstration, supervision, and training and is available and used by the program. Administrative control of the counseling instruction environment ensures adequate and appropriate access by faculty and students. The counseling instruction environment includes all of the following:

1. Settings for individual counseling, with assured privacy and sufficient space for appropriate equipment.
2. Settings for small-group work, with assured privacy and sufficient space for appropriate equipment.
3. Necessary and appropriate technologies and other observational capabilities that assist learning.
4. Procedures that ensure that the client's confidentiality and legal rights are protected.

The Academic Unit

I. Entry-level degree programs in career counseling, school counseling, and student affairs and college counseling are comprised of approved graduate-level study with a minimum of 48 semester credit hours or 72 quarter credit hours required of all students. Entry-level degree programs in addiction counseling and in marriage, couple, and family counseling are comprised of approved graduate-level study with a minimum of 60 semester credit hours or 90 quarter credit hours required of all students.

Beginning July 1, 2009, all applicant programs in clinical mental health counseling must require a minimum of 54 semester credit hours or 81 quarter credit hours for all students. As of July 1, 2013, all applicant programs in clinical mental health counseling must require a minimum of 60 semester credit hours or 90 quarter credit hours for all students.

J. The counselor education academic unit has made systematic efforts to attract, enroll, and retain a diverse group of students and to create and support an inclusive learning community.

K. Admission decision recommendations are made by the academic unit's selection committee and include consideration of the following:
  1. Each applicant's potential success in forming effective and culturally relevant interpersonal relationships in individual and small-group contexts.
  2. Each applicant's aptitude for graduate-level study.
  3. Each applicant's career goals and their relevance to the program.

L. Before or at the beginning of the first term of enrollment in the academic unit, the following should occur for all new students:
  1. A new student orientation is conducted.
  2. A student handbook is disseminated that includes the following:
     a. mission statement of the academic unit and program objectives;
     b. information about appropriate professional organizations, opportunities for professional involvement, and activities potentially appropriate for students;
     c. written endorsement policy explaining the procedures for recommending students for credentialing and employment;
     d. student retention policy explaining procedures for student remediation and/or dismissal from the program;
     e. academic appeal policy.

SECTION II

Professional Identity

Foundation

A. A comprehensive mission statement has been developed that brings the counseling program into focus and concisely describes the program's intent and purpose. The mission statement is publicly available and systematically reviewed.

B. The program area objectives meet the following requirements:
   1. Reflect current knowledge and projected needs concerning counseling practice in a multicultural and pluralistic society.
   2. Reflect input from all persons involved in the conduct of the program, including program faculty, current and former students, and personnel in cooperating agencies.
   3. Are directly related to program activities.
   4. Are written so they can be evaluated.

C. Students actively identify with the counseling profession by participating in professional organizations and by participating in seminars, workshops, or other activities that contribute to personal and professional growth.

Knowledge

D. Syllabi are distributed at the beginning of each curricular experience, are available for review by all enrolled or prospective students, and include all of the following:
   1. Content areas.
   2. Knowledge and skill outcomes.
   3. Methods of instruction.
   4. Required text(s) and/or reading(s).
   5. Student performance evaluation criteria and procedures.

E. Evidence exists of the use and infusion of current counseling-related research in teaching practice among program faculty and students.

F. Evidence exists of the use and infusion of technology in program delivery and technology's impact on the counseling profession.

G. Common core curricular experiences and demonstrated knowledge in each of the eight common core curricular areas are required of all students in the program.
   1. Professional orientation and ethical practice—studies that provide an understanding of all of the following aspects of professional functioning:
      a. history and philosophy of the counseling profession;

b. professional roles, functions, and relationships with other human service providers, including strategies for interagency/interorganization collaboration and communications;
c. counselors' roles and responsibilities as members of an interdisciplinary emergency management response team during a local, regional, or national crisis; disaster; or other trauma-causing event;
d. self-care strategies appropriate to the counselor role;
e. counseling supervision models, practices, and processes;
f. professional organizations, including membership benefits, activities, services to members, and current issues;
g. professional credentialing, including certification, licensure, and accreditation practices and standards, and the effects of public policy on these issues;
h. the role and process of the professional counselor advocating on behalf of the profession;
i. advocacy processes needed to address institutional and social barriers that impede access, equity, and success for clients;
j. ethical standards of professional organizations and credentialing bodies and applications of ethical and legal considerations in professional counseling.

2. Social and cultural diversity—studies that provide an understanding of the cultural context of relationships, issues, and trends in a multicultural society, including all of the following:
   a. multicultural and pluralistic trends, including characteristics and concerns within and among diverse groups nationally and internationally;
   b. attitudes, beliefs, understandings, and acculturative experiences, including specific experiential learning activities designed to foster students' understanding of self and culturally diverse clients;
   c. theories of multicultural counseling, identity development, and social justice;
   d. individual, couple, family, group, and community strategies for working with and advocating for diverse populations, including multicultural competencies;
   e. counselors' roles in developing cultural self-awareness, promoting cultural social justice, advocacy and conflict resolution, and other culturally supported behaviors that promote optimal wellness and growth of the human spirit, mind, or body;
   f. counselors' roles in eliminating biases, prejudices, and processes of intentional and unintentional oppression and discrimination.
3. Human growth and development—studies that provide an understanding of the nature and needs of persons at all developmental levels and in multicultural contexts, including all of the following:
   a. theories of individual and family development and transitions across the life span;

  b. theories of learning and personality development, including current understandings about neurobiological behavior;
  c. effects of crises, disasters, and other trauma-causing events on persons of all ages;
  d. theories and models of individual, cultural, couple, family, and community resilience;
  e. a general framework for understanding exceptional abilities and strategies for differentiated interventions;
  f. human behavior, including an understanding of developmental crises, disability, psychopathology, and situational and environmental factors that affect both normal and abnormal behavior;
  g. theories and etiology of addictions and addictive behaviors, including strategies for prevention, intervention, and treatment;
  h. theories for facilitating optimal development and wellness over the life span.
4. Career development—studies that provide an understanding of career development and related life factors, including all of the following:
  a. career development theories and decision-making models;
  b. career, avocational, educational, occupational, and labor market information resources and career information systems;
  c. career development program planning, organization, implementation, administration, and evaluation;
  d. interrelationships among and between work, family, and other life roles and factors, including the role of multicultural issues in career development;
  e. career and educational planning, placement, follow-up, and evaluation;
  f. assessment instruments and techniques relevant to career planning and decision making;
  g. career counseling processes, techniques, and resources, including those applicable to specific populations in a global economy.
5. Helping relationships—studies that provide an understanding of the counseling process in a multicultural society, including all of the following:
  a. an orientation to wellness and prevention as desired counseling goals;
  b. counselor characteristics and behaviors that influence helping processes;
  c. essential interviewing and counseling skills;
  d. counseling theories that provide the student with models to conceptualize client presentation and that help the student select appropriate counseling interventions. Students will be exposed to models of counseling that are consistent with current professional research and practice in the field so they begin to develop a personal model of counseling;
  e. a systems perspective that provides an understanding of family and other systems theories and major models of family and related interventions;
  f. a general framework for understanding and practicing consultation;

g. crisis intervention and suicide prevention models, including the use of psychological first aid strategies.

6. Group work—studies that provide both theoretical and experiential understandings of group purpose, development, dynamics, theories, methods, skills, and other group approaches in a multicultural society, including all of the following:
   a. principles of group dynamics, including group process components, developmental stage theories, group members' roles and behaviors, and therapeutic factors of group work;
   b. group leadership or facilitation styles and approaches, including characteristics of various types of group leaders and leadership styles;
   c. theories of group counseling, including commonalities, distinguishing characteristics, and pertinent research and literature;
   d. group counseling methods, including group counselor orientations and behaviors, appropriate selection criteria and methods, and methods of evaluation of effectiveness;
   e. direct experiences in which students participate as group members in a small-group activity, approved by the program, for a minimum of 10 clock hours over the course of one academic term.
7. Assessment—studies that provide an understanding of individual and group approaches to assessment and evaluation in a multicultural society, including all of the following:
   a. historical perspectives concerning the nature and meaning of assessment;
   b. basic concepts of standardized and nonstandardized testing and other assessment techniques, including norm-referenced and criterion-referenced assessment, environmental assessment, performance assessment, individual and group test and inventory methods, psychological testing, and behavioral observations;
   c. statistical concepts, including scales of measurement, measures of central tendency, indices of variability, shapes and types of distributions, and correlations;
   d. reliability (i.e., theory of measurement error, models of reliability, and the use of reliability information);
   e. validity (i.e., evidence of validity, types of validity, and the relationship between reliability and validity);
   f. social and cultural factors related to the assessment and evaluation of individuals, groups, and specific populations;
   g. ethical strategies for selecting, administering, and interpreting assessment and evaluation instruments and techniques in counseling.
8. Research and program evaluation—studies that provide an understanding of research methods, statistical analysis, needs assessment, and program evaluation, including all of the following:
   a. the importance of research in advancing the counseling profession;

b. research methods such as qualitative, quantitative, single-case designs, action research, and outcome-based research;
c. statistical methods used in conducting research and program evaluation;
d. principles, models, and applications of needs assessment, program evaluation, and the use of findings to effect program modifications;
e. the use of research to inform evidence-based practice;
f. ethical and culturally relevant strategies for interpreting and reporting the results of research and/or program evaluation studies.

SECTION III

Professional Practice

Professional practice, which includes practicum and internship, provides for the application of theory and the development of counseling skills under supervision. These experiences will provide opportunities for students to counsel clients who represent the ethnic and demographic diversity of their community.

Supervisor Qualifications and Support

A. Program faculty members serving as individual or group practicum/internship supervisors must have the following:
   1. A doctoral degree and/or appropriate counseling preparation, preferably from a Council for the Accreditation of Counseling and Related Educational Programs (CACREP)-accredited counselor education program.
   2. Relevant experience and appropriate credentials/licensure and/or demonstrated competence in counseling.
   3. Relevant supervision training and experience.
B. Students serving as individual or group practicum student supervisors must meet the following requirements:
   1. Have completed a master's degree, as well as counseling practicum and internship experiences equivalent to those in a CACREP-accredited entry-level program.
   2. Have completed or are receiving preparation in counseling supervision.
3. Be supervised by program faculty, with a faculty–student ratio that does not exceed 1:6.
C. Site supervisors must have the following qualifications:
   1. A minimum of a master's degree in counseling or a related profession with equivalent qualifications, including appropriate certifications and/or licenses.

2. A minimum of 2 years of pertinent professional experience in the program area in which the student is enrolled.
3. Knowledge of the program's expectations, requirements, and evaluation procedures for students.
4. Relevant training in counseling supervision.

D. Orientation, assistance, consultation, and professional development opportunities are provided by counseling program faculty to site supervisors.

E. Supervision contracts for each student are developed to define the roles and responsibilities of the faculty supervisor, site supervisor, and student during practicum and internship.

Practicum

F. Students must complete supervised practicum experiences that total a minimum of 100 clock hours over a minimum 10-week academic term. Each student's practicum includes all of the following:

1. At least 40 clock hours of direct service with actual clients that contributes to the development of counseling skills.
2. Weekly interaction that averages one hour per week of individual and/or triadic supervision throughout the practicum by a program faculty member, a student supervisor, or a site supervisor who is working in biweekly consultation with a program faculty member in accordance with the supervision contract.
3. An average of 1½ hours per week of group supervision that is provided on a regular schedule throughout the practicum by a program faculty member or a student supervisor.
4. The development of program-appropriate audio/video recordings for use in supervision or live supervision of the student's interactions with clients.
5. Evaluation of the student's counseling performance throughout the practicum, including documentation of a formal evaluation after the student completes the practicum.

Internship

G. The program requires completion of a supervised internship in the student's designated program area of 600 clock hours, begun after successful completion of the practicum. The internship is intended to reflect the comprehensive work experience of a professional counselor appropriate to the designated program area. Each student's internship includes all of the following:

1. At least 240 clock hours of direct service, including experience leading groups.
2. Weekly interaction that averages one hour per week of individual and/or triadic supervision throughout the internship, usually performed by the onsite supervisor.

3. An average of 1½ hours per week of group supervision provided on a regular schedule throughout the internship and performed by a program faculty member.
4. The opportunity for the student to become familiar with a variety of professional activities and resources in addition to direct service (e.g., record keeping, assessment instruments, supervision, information and referral, in-service and staff meetings).
5. The opportunity for the student to develop program-appropriate audio/video recordings for use in supervision or to receive live supervision of his or her interactions with clients.
6. Evaluation of the student's counseling performance throughout the internship, including documentation of a formal evaluation after the student completes the internship by a program faculty member in consultation with the site supervisor.

Clinical Mental Health Counseling (CMHC)

Students who are preparing to work as clinical mental health counselors will demonstrate the professional knowledge, skills, and practices necessary to address a wide variety of circumstances within the clinical mental health counseling context. In addition to the common core curricular experiences outlined in Section II.G, programs must provide evidence that student learning has occurred in the following domains.

Foundation

A. Knowledge
1. Understands the history, philosophy, and trends in clinical mental health counseling.
2. Understands ethical and legal considerations specifically related to the practice of clinical mental health counseling.
3. Understands the roles and functions of clinical mental health counselors in various practice settings and the importance of relationships between counselors and other professionals, including interdisciplinary treatment teams.
4. Knows the professional organizations, preparation standards, and credentials relevant to the practice of clinical mental health counseling.
5. Understands a variety of models and theories related to clinical mental health counseling, including the methods, models, and principles of clinical supervision.
6. Recognizes the potential for substance use disorders to mimic and coexist with a variety of medical and psychological disorders.
7. Is aware of professional issues that affect clinical mental health counselors (e.g., core provider status, expert witness status, access to and practice privileges within managed care systems).

8. Understands the management of mental health services and programs, including areas such as administration, finance, and accountability.
9. Understands the impact of crises, disasters, and other trauma-causing events on people.
10. Understands the operation of an emergency management system within clinical mental health agencies and in the community.

B. Skills and Practices
1. Demonstrates the ability to apply and adhere to ethical and legal standards in clinical mental health counseling.
2. Applies knowledge of public mental health policy, financing, and regulatory processes to improve service delivery opportunities in clinical mental health counseling.

Counseling, Prevention, and Intervention

C. Knowledge
1. Describes the principles of mental health, including prevention, intervention, consultation, education, and advocacy, as well as the operation of programs and networks that promote mental health in a multicultural society.
2. Knows the etiology, diagnostic process and nomenclature, treatment, referral, and prevention of mental and emotional disorders.
3. Knows the models, methods, and principles of program development and service delivery (e.g., support groups, peer facilitation training, parent education, self-help).
4. Knows the disease concept and etiology of addiction and co-occurring disorders.
5. Understands the range of mental health service delivery—such as inpatient, outpatient, partial treatment, and aftercare—and the clinical mental health counseling services network.
6. Understands the principles of crisis intervention for people during crises, disasters, and other trauma-causing events.
7. Knows the principles, models, and documentation formats of biopsychosocial case conceptualization and treatment planning.
8. Recognizes the importance of family, social networks, and community systems in the treatment of mental and emotional disorders.
9. Understands professional issues relevant to the practice of clinical mental health counseling.

D. Skills and Practices
1. Uses the principles and practices of diagnosis, treatment, referral, and prevention of mental and emotional disorders to initiate, maintain, and terminate counseling.
2. Applies multicultural competencies to clinical mental health counseling involving case conceptualization, diagnosis, treatment, referral, and prevention of mental and emotional disorders.

3. Promotes optimal human development, wellness, and mental health through prevention, education, and advocacy activities.
4. Applies effective strategies to promote client understanding of and access to a variety of community resources.
5. Demonstrates appropriate use of culturally responsive individual, couple, family, group, and systems modalities for initiating, maintaining, and terminating counseling.
6. Demonstrates the ability to use procedures for assessing and managing suicide risk.
7. Applies current record-keeping standards related to clinical mental health counseling.
8. Provides appropriate counseling strategies when working with clients with addiction and co-occurring disorders.
9. Demonstrates the ability to recognize his or her own limitations as a clinical mental health counselor and to seek supervision or refer clients when appropriate.

Diversity and Advocacy

E. Knowledge
1. Understands how living in a multicultural society affects clients who are seeking clinical mental health counseling services.
2. Understands the effects of racism, discrimination, sexism, power, privilege, and oppression on one's own life and career and those of the client.
3. Understands current literature that outlines theories, approaches, strategies, and techniques shown to be effective when working with specific populations of clients with mental and emotional disorders.
4. Understands effective strategies to support client advocacy and influence public policy and government relations on local, state, and national levels to enhance equity, increase funding, and promote programs that affect the practice of clinical mental health counseling.
5. Understands the implications of concepts such as internalized oppression and institutional racism, as well as the historical and current political climate regarding immigration, poverty, and welfare.
6. Knows public policies on the local, state, and national levels that affect the quality and accessibility of mental health services.

F. Skills and Practices
1. Maintains information regarding community resources to make appropriate referrals.
2. Advocates for policies, programs, and services that are equitable and responsive to the unique needs of clients.
3. Demonstrates the ability to modify counseling systems, theories, techniques, and interventions to make them culturally appropriate for diverse populations.

Assessment

G. Knowledge

1. Knows the principles and models of assessment, case conceptualization, theories of human development, and concepts of normalcy and psychopathology leading to diagnoses and appropriate counseling treatment plans.
2. Understands various models and approaches to clinical evaluation and their appropriate uses, including diagnostic interviews, mental status examinations, symptom inventories, and psychoeducational and personality assessments.
3. Understands basic classifications, indications, and contraindications of commonly prescribed psychopharmacological medications so that appropriate referrals can be made for medication evaluations and so that the side effects of such medications can be identified.
4. Identifies standard screening and assessment instruments for substance use disorders and process addictions.

H. Skills and Practices

1. Selects appropriate comprehensive assessment interventions to assist in diagnosis and treatment planning, with an awareness of cultural bias in the implementation and interpretation of assessment protocols.
2. Demonstrates skill in conducting an intake interview, a mental status evaluation, a biopsychosocial history, a mental health history, and a psychological assessment for treatment planning and caseload management.
3. Screens for addiction, aggression, and danger to self and/or others, as well as co-occurring mental disorders.
4. Applies the assessment of a client's stage of dependence, change, or recovery to determine the appropriate treatment modality and placement criteria within the continuum of care.

Research and Evaluation

I. Knowledge

1. Understands how to critically evaluate research relevant to the practice of clinical mental health counseling.
2. Knows models of program evaluation for clinical mental health programs.
3. Knows evidence-based treatments and basic strategies for evaluating counseling outcomes in clinical mental health counseling.

J. Skills and Practices

1. Applies relevant research findings to inform the practice of clinical mental health counseling.
2. Develops measurable outcomes for clinical mental health counseling programs, interventions, and treatments.
3. Analyzes and uses data to increase the effectiveness of clinical mental health counseling interventions and programs.

Diagnosis

K. Knowledge
1. Knows the principles of the diagnostic process, including differential diagnosis, and the use of current diagnostic tools, such as the current edition of the *Diagnostic and Statistical Manual of Mental Disorders* (*DSM*).
2. Understands the established diagnostic criteria for mental and emotional disorders and describes treatment modalities and placement criteria within the continuum of care.
3. Knows the impact of co-occurring substance use disorders on medical and psychological disorders.
4. Understands the relevance and potential biases of commonly used diagnostic tools with multicultural populations.
5. Understands appropriate use of diagnosis during a crisis, disaster, or other trauma-causing event.

L. Skills and Practices
1. Demonstrates appropriate use of diagnostic tools, including the current edition of the *DSM*, to describe the symptoms and clinical presentation of clients with mental and emotional impairments.
2. Is able to conceptualize an accurate multi-axial diagnosis of disorders presented by a client and discuss the differential diagnosis with collaborating professionals.
3. Differentiates between diagnosis and developmentally appropriate reactions during crises, disasters, and other trauma-causing events.

School Counseling (SC)

Students who are preparing to work as school counselors will demonstrate the professional knowledge, skills, and practices necessary to promote the academic, career, and personal/social development of all K–12 students. In addition to the common core curricular experiences outlined in Section II.G, programs must provide evidence that student learning has occurred in the following domains.

Foundations

A. Knowledge
1. Knows history, philosophy, and trends in school counseling and educational systems.
2. Understands ethical and legal considerations specifically related to the practice of school counseling.
3. Knows roles, functions, settings, and professional identity of the school counselor in relation to the roles of other professional and support personnel in the school.

4. Knows professional organizations, preparation standards, and credentials that are relevant to the practice of school counseling.
5. Understands current models of school counseling programs (e.g., American School Counselor Association [ASCA] National Model) and their integral relationship to the total educational program.
6. Understands the effects of (a) atypical growth and development, (b) health and wellness, (c) language, (d) ability level, (e) multicultural issues, and (f) factors of resiliency on student learning and development.
7. Understands the operation of the school emergency management plan and the roles and responsibilities of the school counselor during crises, disasters, and other trauma-causing events.

B. Skills and Practices
1. Demonstrates the ability to apply and adhere to ethical and legal standards in school counseling.
2. Demonstrates the ability to articulate, model, and advocate for an appropriate school counselor identity and program.

Counseling, Prevention, and Intervention

C. Knowledge
1. Knows the theories and processes of effective counseling and wellness programs for individual students and groups of students.
2. Knows how to design, implement, manage, and evaluate programs to enhance the academic, career, and personal/social development of students.
3. Knows strategies for helping students identify strengths and cope with environmental and developmental problems.
4. Knows how to design, implement, manage, and evaluate transition programs, including school-to-work, postsecondary planning, and college admissions counseling.
5. Understands group dynamics—including counseling, psycho-educational, task, and peer helping groups—and the facilitation of teams to enable students to overcome barriers and impediments to learning.
6. Understands the potential impact of crises, emergencies, and disasters on students, educators, and schools and knows the skills needed for crisis intervention.

D. Skills and Practices
1. Demonstrates self-awareness, sensitivity to others, and the skills needed to relate to diverse individuals, groups, and classrooms.
2. Provides individual and group counseling and classroom guidance to promote the academic, career, and personal/social development of students.
3. Designs and implements prevention and intervention plans related to the effects of (a) atypical growth and development, (b) health and wellness, (c) language, (d) ability level, (e) multicultural issues, and (f) factors of resiliency on student learning and development.

4. Demonstrates the ability to use procedures for assessing and managing suicide risk.
5. Demonstrates the ability to recognize his or her limitations as a school counselor and to seek supervision or refer clients when appropriate.

Diversity and Advocacy

E. Knowledge
1. Understands the cultural, ethical, economic, legal, and political issues surrounding diversity, equity, and excellence in terms of student learning.
2. Identifies community, environmental, and institutional opportunities that enhance—as well as barriers that impede—the academic, career, and personal/social development of students.
3. Understands the ways in which educational policies, programs, and practices can be developed, adapted, and modified to be culturally congruent with the needs of students and their families.
4. Understands multicultural counseling issues, as well as the impact of ability levels, stereotyping, family, socioeconomic status, gender, and sexual identity, and their effects on student achievement.

F. Skills and Practices
1. Demonstrates multicultural competencies in relation to diversity, equity, and opportunity in student learning and development.
2. Advocates for the learning and academic experiences necessary to promote the academic, career, and personal/social development of students.
3. Advocates for school policies, programs, and services that enhance a positive school climate and are equitable and responsive to multicultural student populations.
4. Engages parents, guardians, and families to promote the academic, career, and personal/social development of students.

Assessment

G. Knowledge
1. Understands the influence of multiple factors (e.g., abuse, violence, eating disorders, attention deficit hyperactivity disorder, childhood depression) that may affect the personal, social, and academic functioning of students.
2. Knows the signs and symptoms of substance abuse in children and adolescents, as well as the signs and symptoms of living in a home where substance abuse occurs.
3. Identifies various forms of needs assessments for academic, career, and personal/social development.

H. Skills and Practices
1. Assesses and interprets students' strengths and needs, recognizing uniqueness in cultures, languages, values, backgrounds, and abilities.

2. Selects appropriate assessment strategies that can be used to evaluate a student's academic, career, and personal/social development.
3. Analyzes assessment information in a manner that produces valid inferences when evaluating the needs of individual students and assessing the effectiveness of educational programs.
4. Makes appropriate referrals to school and/or community resources.
5. Assesses barriers that impede students' academic, career, and personal/social development.

Research and Evaluation

I. Knowledge
   1. Understands how to critically evaluate research relevant to the practice of school counseling.
   2. Knows models of program evaluation for school counseling programs.
   3. Knows basic strategies for evaluating counseling outcomes in school counseling (e.g., behavioral observation, program evaluation).
   4. Knows current methods of using data to inform decision making and accountability (e.g., school improvement plan, school report card).
   5. Understands the outcome research data and best practices identified in the school counseling research literature.

J. Skills and Practices
   1. Applies relevant research findings to inform the practice of school counseling.
   2. Develops measurable outcomes for school counseling programs, activities, interventions, and experiences.
   3. Analyzes and uses data to enhance school counseling programs.

Academic Development

K. Knowledge
   1. Understands the relationship of the school counseling program to the academic mission of the school.
   2. Understands the concepts, principles, strategies, programs, and practices designed to close the achievement gap, promote student academic success, and prevent students from dropping out of school.
   3. Understands curriculum design, lesson plan development, classroom management strategies, and differentiated instructional strategies for teaching counseling- and guidance-related material.

L. Skills and Practices
   1. Conducts programs designed to enhance student academic development.
   2. Implements strategies and activities to prepare students for a full range of postsecondary options and opportunities.

3. Implements differentiated instructional strategies that draw on subject matter and pedagogical content knowledge and skills to promote student achievement.

Collaboration and Consultation

M. Knowledge
1. Understands the ways in which student development, well-being, and learning are enhanced by family–school–community collaboration.
2. Knows strategies to promote, develop, and enhance effective teamwork within the school and the larger community.
3. Knows how to build effective working teams of school staff, parents, and community members to promote the academic, career, and personal/social development of students.
4. Understands systems theories, models, and processes of consultation in school system settings.
5. Knows strategies and methods for working with parents, guardians, families, and communities to empower them to act on behalf of their children.
6. Understands the various peer programming interventions (e.g., peer mediation, peer mentoring, peer tutoring) and how to coordinate them.
7. Knows school and community collaboration models for crisis/disaster preparedness and response.

N. Skills and Practices
1. Works with parents, guardians, and families to act on behalf of their children to address problems that affect student success in school.
2. Locates resources in the community that can be used in the school to improve student achievement and success.
3. Consults with teachers, staff, and community-based organizations to promote student academic, career, and personal/social development.
4. Uses peer helping strategies in the school counseling program.
5. Uses referral procedures with helping agents in the community (e.g., mental health centers, businesses, service groups) to secure assistance for students and their families.

Leadership

O. Knowledge
1. Knows the qualities, principles, skills, and styles of effective leadership.
2. Knows strategies of leadership designed to enhance the learning environment of schools.
3. Knows how to design, implement, manage, and evaluate a comprehensive school counseling program.
4. Understands the important role of the school counselor as a system change agent.

5. Understands the school counselor's role in student assistance programs, school leadership, curriculum, and advisory meetings.

P. Skills and Practices

1. Participates in the design, implementation, management, and evaluation of a comprehensive developmental school counseling program.
2. Plans and presents school counseling–related educational programs for use with parents and teachers (e.g., parent education programs, materials used in classroom guidance, and advisor/advisee programs for teachers).

Index

I

L

M

N

O